Arthur Lillie

Buddhism in Christendom

Or, Jesus, the Essene

Arthur Lillie

Buddhism in Christendom
Or, Jesus, the Essene

ISBN/EAN: 9783337231590

Printed in Europe, USA, Canada, Australia, Japan

Cover: Foto ©Lupo / pixelio.de

More available books at **www.hansebooks.com**

BUDDHISM IN CHRISTENDOM

OR

JESUS, THE ESSENE

BY

ARTHUR LILLIE

AUTHOR OF "THE POPULAR LIFE OF BUDDHA"

"He shall be the last to obtain the great spiritual light; and he will become a Lord called the Buddha of Brotherly Love (Maitreya)."—*Buddha's prophecy of his successor in the "Saddharma Pundarika"*

WITH NUMEROUS ILLUSTRATIONS

LONDON

KEGAN PAUL, TRENCH & CO., 1, PATERNOSTER SQUARE

1887

PREFACE.

IT has been wisely said that, to understand any solitary religion, two, at least, must be studied. This seems essentially important when the religion is Eastern, and the student has been educated in the West. There is a tendency in the human mind to explain to itself that which is remote by that which is familiar. The Western mind is logical, matter-of-fact, impatient of symbolism. And yet Christianity is an Asiatic religion, and all Asiatics tell us that symbolism is the only language by which the facts of the spiritual world can be treated.

Thus it has been shown by the Orientalist, Professor Wilson, that the three Avesthâs of the Trinity (translated "hypostases" by the Gnostics) have come from India.[1] Colebrooke has pointed out that the hymns of the Rig Veda, though avowedly addressed to many deities, are, "according to the most ancient annotations of the Indian scripture," resolvable into a triad, and, ultimately, "one God."[2] It seems to result from this that the meaning of this triad may be more profitably sought in the ancient Indian books than in vaticinations of the blunt and literal monks that composed the Council of Nicœa.

We interpret the great drama that began our era by our local experience. Thus the author of "Ecce Homo" has pictured to himself the great sacramentum, or mystery of

[1] "Vishṇu Purâṇa," p. 7, note.   [2] "Essays," vol. i. p. 25.

a 3

Christianity, by his experience of "club dinners." And Archdeacon Paley has seen in the twelve apostles twelve British jurymen empannelled to investigate "miracles." I must confess that, until I studied the religions of the East, the great drama of Palestine appeared to me a drama with unintelligible antagonisms and a motiveless character.

The Old and New Testaments are studied very carefully in England, and the Indian religions are scarcely studied at all. And yet the latter throw quite invaluable light on the former. To this day the maidens of Krishṇa weep for the Indian Tammuz, the departed god of summer. To this day, as in the days of Aaron, the priest of Śiva throws ashes in the air to bring a malediction on his foemen. To this day the Indian prophet sits under the "tree of Deborah" and the "oak of enchantments."[1] He explains to us the mystery of yoga, or union between the seen and the unseen worlds. He explains to us what the Roman Catholic Prayer-book means by its prayer that, as Christ deigned to become a participator in our humanity, we may be allowed to partake of His Divinity.

If only for the sake of historical illustration, a civilization which is still so like the civilization of Palestine in the holy epoch deserves to be studied.

The position of her gracious Majesty Queen Victoria is a very peculiar one. In the sixteenth century, one Trithemius, a Benedictine, uttered a strange prophecy. He announced that, in November, 1879, a new universal kingdom would arise which would seize the gates of the East. Whatever may be thought of this prediction, it is plain that the gates of the East are now in English hands. Owing to free-trade, also, fifty-five out of every hundred sailors on the ocean are Englishmen; and the even balance of military force on the Continent, as well as in the opposing sections of the United States, has given to us a physical prominence that the

[1] See Dean Stanley's "Sinai and Palestine," p. 141.

victories of Marlborough and Wellington failed to gain us.
But if we leave the plane of matter, the position of the queen
is more remarkable still. She holds in her dominions the
most vital sections of all the great religions of the past. Her
subjects pray to Christ, and Buddha, and Brahma, and
Jehovah. They honour Zarathustra and Moses and Mahomet. Benares, the holy city of the greatest religious section
of her subjects, is in her domains. She guards the so-called
"Tooth of Buddha," whose possessor is always promised the
empire of the world. No wonder that thoughtful minds
begin to see in all this a possible mission for England,
namely, to fuse the old creeds in one great crucible, and
eliminate the superstitious parts. Ancient creeds had much
once in common, and it is chiefly this common portion, the
vital essence, that has been allowed to evaporate.

"Five hundred years, Ânanda," said Buddha, in the "Cul-
lavagga," "will the doctrine of the truth abide!"[1] He also
prophesied that a new Buddha would come—Maitreya (the
Buddha of Brotherly Love). Buddha died 470 B.C.; so
exactly five hundred years after his death, the Buddha of
Brotherly Love began to preach.

[1] Cited by Dr. Oldenberg, "Buddhism," p. 327 ; see also Beal,
"Romantic History," p. 16.

CONTENTS.

—·—

CHAPTER VII.

CHAPTER XXIV.

CHAPTER XXV.

CHAPTER XXVI.

CHAPTER XXVII.

ILLUSTRATIONS.

BUDDHISM IN CHRISTENDOM.

CHAPTER I.

Object of Ancient Scriptures—To reveal the Mysteries—The "Kabbalah"
—Origen—The Heavenly Man—The Conceivable and the Inconceivable God—Genealogies of Buddha and Christ—Miraculous Conception—The Elephant.

ANCIENT SCRIPTURES.

ORIGEN informs us that all Scriptures have two meanings
—the one spiritual, the other "historical" or "bodily," the last
for those that are not prepared to know the mysteries of the
kingdom of heaven.

These mysteries in all ancient religions were, in brief, that
man had matter for a mother, and spirit for a father; and that
the object of his earth-life was to conquer his material nature
and unite himself with the Great Spirit of the universe. The
Christian "mysteries" did not differ in essence from the other
mysteries. This fact was put forward as a virtue by the
early Fathers of the Church, although it has since been deemed
a blemish and denied.

The process by which man advanced in knowledge of
spirit was called the "contemplative life" in Palestine;
"magic" in Persia; the "Bodhi," or "Buddhism," in India;
"Gnosticism," the Greek equivalent of the Indian word in
Alexandria.

B

About two hundred years before the Christian era a remarkable mystical movement arose amongst the Jews. It came from Alexandria, but its head-quarters in Palestine nestled amongst the protecting malaria of the shores of the Lake Marea, for it was bitterly persecuted. In Egypt these mystics were called Therapeuts ; in Palestine, Essenes and Nazarites. In the view of Dean Mansel, this movement was due to Buddhist missionaries, who visited Egypt within two generations of the time of Alexander the Great [1]—a proposition which I shall show is confirmed by the stones of King Aśoka in the East, and by Philo in the West. I shall show, further, that the rites of this, the higher section of Judaism, were purely Buddhist, and that two remarkable works, which embody their teaching, minutely reproduce the theogony of Buddhism. These works are the " Sohar " of the " Kabbalah," and the " Codex Nasaraeus."

I purpose further to show that Christianity emerged from this, the higher Judaism, and that its Bible, containing the life of its Founder, its rites, dress, teachings, hierarchy, architectural buildings, Councils to put down heresy, theogony and cosmogony, bear so minute a resemblance to the rites, etc., of Buddhism, that it seems hard to doubt that some communication existed and long continued between the two. Does this mean that Christianity " was borrowed *en bloc* from Buddhism "? as the *Church Quarterly Review*, misquoting an early work of mine, reports me to have announced. It certainly does not mean that, for no mysticism can be borrowed from the outside world at all. It simply means that the movement of Jesus sought the aid of mystical, and not anti-mystical, Israel. In Palestine, as in India, the *gnosis*, or knowledge of the mysteries of the kingdom of heaven, was restricted to a priestly faction, and Christ's main design, like that of Buddha, was to break up this exclusiveness.

To get the meaning of an ancient Scripture eighteen hundred years after it was written, it is important to study less the words than the writers of the words. Christianity and its gospel emerged from the mystical section of Israel.

---

[1] " Gnostic Heresies," p. 31.

Have we any means of judging what canons of composition would guide such writers in framing a life of Jesus, or Samson, or David ? Fortunately we possess the " Kabbalah," the secret wisdom of these mystics. Listen to the " Sohar " on the Jewish Scriptures—

" If the Law simply consisted of ordinary expressions and narratives, *e.g.* the words of Esau, Hagar, Laban, the ass of Balaam, or of Balaam himself, why should it be called the Law of truth, the perfect Law, the true witness of God ? Each word contains a sublime source, each narrative points, not only to the single instance in question, but also to generals " (" Sohar," iii. 149 *b*).

" Woe be to the son of man who says that the *Tora* [Pentateuch] contains common sayings and ordinary narratives. For if this were the case, we might in the present day compose a code of doctrines from profane writings which should excite greater respect. If the Law contains ordinary matter, then there are nobler sentiments in profane odes. Let us go and make a selection from them, and we shall be able to compile a far superior code. But every word of the Law has a sublime sense and a heavenly mystery. . . . Now, the spiritual angels had to put on an earthly garment when they descended to earth ; and if they had not put on such a garment they could neither have remained nor have been understood on the earth. And just as it was with the angels, so it is with the Law. When it descended on earth the Law had to put on an earthly garment to be understood by us, and the narratives are its garment. There are some who think that this garment is the real Law, and not the spirit which it clothed ; but these have no portion in the world to come. And it is for this reason that David prayed, ' Open Thou mine eyes, that I may behold the wondrous things out of Thy Law' (Ps. cxix. 18). What is under the garment of the Law? There is the garment which every one can see ; and there are foolish people who, when they see a well-dressed man, think of nothing more worthy than his beautiful garment, and take it for the body, whilst the worth of the body itself consists in the soul. The Law, too, has a body.

This is the commandments which are called the body of
the Law. This body is clothed in garments which are the
ordinary narratives. The fools of this world look at nothing
else but this garment, which consists of the narratives of the
Law. They do not know any more, and do not understand
what is beneath this garment. But those who have more
understanding do not look at the garment, but at the body
beneath it (*i.e.* the moral); whilst the wisest, the servants of
the heavenly King who dwells at Mount Sinai, look at
nothing else but the soul (*i.e.* the secret doctrine), which is the
root of all the real Law; and these are destined in the world
to come to behold the *Soul of this soul* (*i.e.* the Deity), which
breathes in the Law" ("Sohar," iii. 152 *a*).[1]

Origen also affirms that the object of all Scriptures, the
Jewish and the Christian, is "to wrap up and conceal, under
the covering of some history and narrative of visible things,
the hidden mysteries."[2] He says, further, that the outside
story or historical narrative contains purposely interruptions,
improbabilities, impossibilities. All this is done by the Holy
Spirit, "in order that, seeing those events which lie on the
surface can be neither true nor useful, we may be led to the
investigation of that truth which is more deeply concealed,
and to the ascertaining of a meaning worthy of God in those
Scriptures which we believe to be inspired by Him."[3]

He says, further, that the Christian Scriptures, like the
Jewish, are to be subjected to the same canons of interpretation. In the case of Christ's temptation, for instance, on the
surface this cannot plainly be a literal narrative of a purely
historical event. "And many other instances similar to this
will be found in the Gospels by any one who will read them
with attention and will observe that in those narratives which
appear to be literally recorded there are inserted and inter-
woven things which cannot be admitted historically, but which
may be accepted in a spiritual signification."[4]

[1] Ginsburg, "The Kabbalah," p. 47.
[2] "De Principiis," lib. iv. cap. 1.
[3] "Anti-Nicene Christian Library: Origen," i. p. 311.
[4] Ibid., p. 317.

Turning to the life of Buddha, as contained in the "Lalita Vistara," we find that that work also explicitly states that it is written to reveal the mysteries of the Indian wise men (Buddhas), and show how a mortal can acquire the "divine vision," with its concomitant "magical powers." [1]

When we see thus that the lives of Jesus and of Buddha are framed upon the same lines, we should not be astonished to find considerable analogy between them. As a revelation of the mysteries, they must be almost identical, if there is great divergence historically. But if our somewhat material modern theology errs in one direction in attempting to eliminate the mystical element, certain mystical writers, like Mr. Melville and Mr. Frederick Tennyson, have erred as conspicuously in another. They have sought to eliminate the historical element with equal completeness, forgetting a prominent doctrine of all mysticism, that all things in the unseen world have their counterparts in the seen.

"The lower world," says the "Sohar" (ii. 20 *a*), "is made after the pattern of the upper world. Everything that exists in the upper world is to be found, as it were, in a copy upon earth. Still the whole is one." [2]

PURUSHA, THE HEAVENLY MAN.

"God, who at sundry times and in divers manners spake in time past unto the fathers by the prophets, hath in these last days spoken unto us by His Son, whom He hath appointed Heir of all things, by whom also He made the worlds; who being the Brightness of His glory, and the express Image of His Person, and upholding all things by the word of His power, when He had by Himself purged our sins, sat down on the right hand of the Majesty on high" (Heb. i.).

In the Pâli legendary life of Buddha, when the holy infant first sees the light, the immortal spirits thus greet him—

"O Purusha, the equal to thee exists not here. Where will a superior be found?"

Who was Purusha?

From very early days man seems to have known that

[1] Foucaux's translation, pp. 7, 401.
[2] See Ginsburg, p. 22.

he had a great destiny before him. This was to unite himself at length, without loss of individuality, with the Great Spirit of the universe. Thus a delicate problem arose, namely, how to find some analogy or symbolic connection between the two-legged creature, man, and the splendid mountains and seas and stars that clothed the Great Spirit. Two answers suggested themselves.

1. God was imaged as a transcendental man. In the "Kabbalah," or secret wisdom of the Jews, he was called "the Heavenly Man," and he represented the universe and its breathing inhabitants. This was the Indian Purusha.

2. The second solution took for symbol the dome of heaven, with the ecliptic for base, and the Dragon, "the Centre of the Macrocosm," as it is called in the "Kabbalah," for apex. This figured God, and it was feigned that man, in his passage from the animal to the deific, passed through the various mansions of the ecliptic like the sun. "The mysteries are written in the vault of heaven," says the "Kabbalah."

The great bible of Catholic mystics has always been the works of the so-called Dionysius the Areopagite. These may not be quite due to St. Denis of France, as Parisian abbés imagine; and A.D. 90 may be too early a date for them; but it is difficult to date them A.D. 600, as is now the fashion, for without doubt we get in them an able exposition of early Christian Gnosticism. The absence of anything like a controversial tone is very remarkable. The writer does not seem to be aware that there is any other Christianity besides his lofty mysticism. If he had had any knowledge of the shallow diatribes of Irenæus and Tertullian, he would certainly have met some of their anti-Gnostic arguments at least indirectly.

St. Dionysius affirms that, in the view of the Therapeut, or perfected mystic, God is a Being dwelling in the super-luminous obscurity which it is the special function of the mystic to try and pierce. This God can only be defined by negatives, and He is to be understood by Agnosticism rather than Gnosticism. He has no form, body, quantity, quality, action, passion. He cannot be called Soul, Knowledge, Wisdom, Father, Son. "He made darkness His secret place," says the writer, citing Ps. xviii. 12. "His pavilion round about Him was the dark waters."[1]

The descent of this inert, inconceivable God is the main teaching of Buddhism. The Indian Capricorn (I copy a bas-

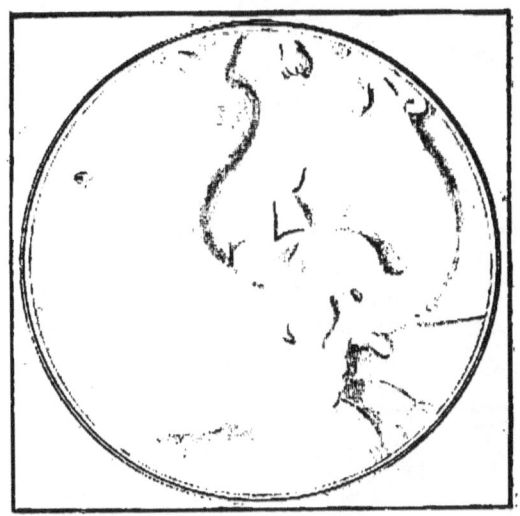

Fig. 1.

relief from Buddha Gàya) is an elephant emerging from a makara, or leviathan. This is the meaning of Buddha coming to earth as a white elephant. It is called in the "Lalita Vistara," Airàvana (born of the waters).[2] In the symbolism of the catacombs this sea-monster is equally prominent. "The sign of the kingdom of heaven

Fig. 2.

is the Prophet Jonah," said Christ. In consequence, we constantly see his figure emerging from a sea-monster. But

---

[1] St. Denys, "Œuvres," traduites par l'Abbé J. Deluc, pp. 306, 314.
[2] "Lalita Vistara," p. 196.

sometimes the "Jonah" is only a child (Fig. 3). This, of
course, means that Jonah is the Child Christ. Fig. 4, also

from the catacombs, is an
interesting one. Christ's
special symbol is Aries,
which in India is a horse.
Here we see the horse
emerging from the waters.

It is significative of the
great distance that we have
travelled from the epoch
of Christ that modern
thought pronounces all

Fig. 3.

this barren and fanciful, and modern theology actually condemns it. In point of fact, the Gnosticism that is taught in
the rude frescoes of Jonah in the catacombs is the sole idea
in this world of appearances that is not barren. We have

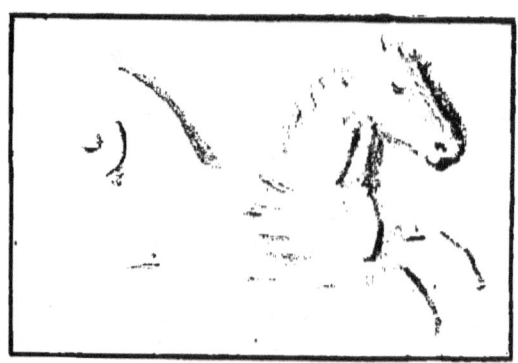

Fig. 4.

come here to learn by experience the distinction between
matter and spirit ; and St. Dionysius, whatever his date, gives
us the secret teaching of the early Church. In the Fathers
we get often the same teaching, less lucidly expressed.

Tertullian draws a distinction between the active Christ
and "the Father who is invisible and unapproachable and

placid." He cites the Saviour as saying that "no man knoweth the Father, save the Son." Of Christ he says that " He it was who at all times came down to hold converse with men from Adam on to the patriarchs and prophets in vision, in dream, in mirror, in dark saying ;" He is Creator and Judge.[1]

From this veiled God it is possible, of course, to derive atheism ; but it is patent that the basic idea is the very reverse of atheistic. "God is called Reason," says St. Dionysius.[2]

In Buddhism, both the veiled and the unveiled God are called Buddha (divine intelligence)—a curious name to select if God then meant unintelligent causation. Many Asiatics now hold that God is not a Being, but only a lofty state of the human soul. Such an idea could only have sprung from theism. We must conceive God before we can strive to be like Him. We must believe in Him before we can discard Him.

This Heavenly Man of the "Kabbalah" was plainly also St. Paul's idea of Christ: "For as the body is one, and hath many members, and all the members of that one body, being many, are one body : so also is Christ. For by one Spirit are we all baptized into one body, whether we be Jews or Gentiles, whether we be bond or free ; and have been all made to drink into one Spirit. But now hath God set the members every one of them in the body, as it hath pleased Him. And if they were all one member, where were the body ? But now are they many members, yet but one body. Now ye are the body of Christ, and members in particular " (1 Cor. xii.).

Let us turn now to the first chapter of Colossians : " Who hath delivered us from the power of darkness, and hath translated us into the kingdom of His dear Son : who is the Image of the invisible God, the Firstborn of every creature : for by Him were all things created, that are in heaven, and that are

---

[1] See Tert., "V. Marc.," bk. ii. cap. xxvii. ; also "Treatise against Praxeas," xvi.

[2] "On the Divine Name," cap. vii. par. 4.

in earth, visible and invisible, whether they be thrones, or dominions, or principalities, or powers : all things were created by Him, and for Him : and He is before all things, and by Him all things consist. And He is the Head of the body, the Church : who is the beginning, the Firstborn from the dead ; that in all things He might have the pre-eminence."

This gives us St. Paul's idea of Christ. He is humanity, like the Indian Purusha, the fashioned kosmos as distinguished from the unfashioned. Buddha is the "Lord of the three regions (heaven, earth, and hell)." The Pope's tiara is called Triregno.

GENEALOGIES.

"The book of the generation of Jesus Christ" (Matt. i. 1).

Seydel has a chapter on the genealogies of Buddha and Christ.[1] In the "Lalita Vistara" and other biographies of Buddha are long lists of the ancestors, both of Queen Mâyâ the mother, and King Śuddhodana, who, like Joseph, had nothing at all to do with the paternity of the holy child. It is announced that a Buddha must be of royal and illustrious race, and so must his mother and his putative father—points more appropriate, perhaps, to the son of a king than the son of a carpenter.

Seydel cites from Weber a portion of the long genealogy of King Śuddhodana, which has a considerable analogy with the Christian lists of Joseph's ancestors—

"King Mahâsammata had a son named Roja, whose son was Vararoja, whose son was Kalyâna, whose son was Varakalyâna, whose son was Mandhâtar, whose son was Varamandhâtar, whose son was Uposatha, whose son was Kara, whose son was Upakara, whose son was Maghâdeva."[2]

This list is from the "Dîpawanso," and it is also given by Mr. Turnour, in the *Journal of the Asiatic Society of Bengal,* vol. vii. p. 925. It is needless to say the list is a very long one indeed—Sihassero's descendants alone were eighty-two thousand, who all reigned supreme in Kapilavastu.

[1] "Evangelium von Jesu," p. 105.   [2] Seydel, p. 106.

"The last of these was Jayaséno. His son was Séhahanu, who was endowed with great personal splendour. Unto the said Séhahanu were born five sons—Śuddhodano, Dhótodano, Sukkodano, Ghutitodano, and Amitodano. Siddatho (Buddha), the Saviour of the World, was the son of Śuddhodano."

The history of the birth of Buddha is briefly this. When the legendary narratives open he is disclosed residing in the heaven Tuśita, and exercising the functions of Purusha, or God viewed as a transcendental man. He rules the Triloka. He is called in the Tibetan Scripture the "Heavenly Father," the "Light of the World," the "God of Gods," the "King of Kings," the "Omniscient." But certain atheistical teachers being abroad in the world deluding mankind, it is determined that these shall be nullified by the avatâra of a Buddha to earth—his incarnation, in point of fact.

Search is made for a suitable mother in whose womb the divine child may be born; and in the city of Kapilavastu (Nagar Khas, N. Oude) is found a queen named Mâyâ Devî, married to King Śuddhodana. This lady is beautiful as a heavenly spirit. Her hair is glossy as the body of a black bee. Her voice is as musical as the kokila, or Indian cuckoo. She is a personification of chastity and virtue.

Discussion takes place among the heavenly spirits as to the form to be assumed by a Buddha about to become incarnate, and the spirit of an ancient ṛishi, or holy man, announces that in the Rig Veda and the ancient books it is laid down that this form must be that of a white elephant. The reason of this will be patent to those who have read the previous section. Mârtaṇḍa, the solar god-man, the vice-gerent of the universe, was symbolized as an elephant.[1] It is also a symbol of the Holy Spirit.

CONCEPTION.

"A Virgin shall conceive."

Attempts have recently been made to prove that the mother of Buddha was not a virgin; but this goes completely counter both to the northern and southern Scriptures. It is

---

[1] "Satapatha Brâhmaṇa," iii. 1–33.

stated in the "Lalita Vistara" that the mother of a Buddha "must never have had a child."[1] In the southern Scriptures, as given by Mr. Turnour, it is announced that a womb in which a Buddha-elect has reposed is like the sanctuary of a chaitya (temple). On that account the mother of Buddha always dies in seven days, that no human being may again occupy it.[2] The name of the queen is borrowed from Brahminism. She is Mâyâ Devî, one of the names of Durgâ, who is also Kanyâ, the Virgin of the Zodiac. The conception was miraculous, and, of course, entirely independent of the good King Śuddhodana. "By the consent of the king," says the "Lalita Vistara," "the queen was permitted to lead the life of a maiden, and not of a wife, for the space of thirty-two months."

In the "Kabbalah" it is announced that the Heavenly Man comes to earth in the mercaba, or chariot. This chariot is, of course, the seven stars of the Great Bear, imaged in the old religions as the Seven Rishis, the Seven Amesha Spentas, the Seven Manushi or Mortal Buddhas, the Seven Angels of the Apocalypse. As each of these stars, as I shall show, represents a legion of beatified saints, the meaning of this is not far to seek. God, as the Heavenly Man, comes to earth through the mouthpiece of His saints and angels. These, in the Bible, are frequently convertible terms.

Buddha, too, when he came to earth under the symbol of the white elephant, travelled, as we learn from the "Lalita Vistara," in the chariot of the gods. Millions of heavenly spirits, headed by Indra, the King of Heaven, accompanied him—beautiful cloud-nymphs, and the four mahârâjas, the great kings who are believed to support the Kosmos at the four cardinal points. The chariot that brings down the little white elephant has four faces, as, of course, it images the Kosmos, and each corner is supported by one of the mahârâjas.

In the Armenian ritual this is the Collect for Good Friday : "Thou who, seated in majesty on the fiery chariot of four faces, ineffable Word of God, hast come down from

---

[1] Foucaux, p. 31.   [2] *Journ. Ben. As. Soc.*, vol. vii. p. 800.

heaven for Thy creatures, and deigned to-day to sit at table with Thy disciples. Surprised with admiration, the seraphim and cherubim and principalities of the celestial cohorts gathered round, crying in their astonishment, 'Holy, holy, holy, is the Lord of hosts.' "[1]

It is to be remarked that four stars of the Great Bear make a square, the chariot of the four faces.

In the southern versions Buddha also descends as a white elephant. The queen, in a vision, is transported to Himavat, the fabled mountain of the sky, by the side of which grows the mighty tree, which is fifty miles high. Four great queens carry her in her couch to the shores of a delicious lake that sparkles under a mountain of silver. On the eastern side of this mountain was a cavern, and into this Queen Mâyâ was carried. Whilst she was lying there, Buddha, in the form of a young white elephant, approached, carrying a pure white lotus in his trunk. He marched three times round the queen, and then entered her right side.

On this narrative the Rev. Spence Hardy makes the following comments : " The resemblance between this legend and the doctrine of the perpetual virginity of the mother of our Lord cannot but be remarked. The opinion that she had ever borne other children was called heresy by Epiphanius and Jerome long before she had been exalted to the station of supremacy she now occupies amongst the saints in the estimation of the Romish and Greek Churches. They suppose that it is to this circumstance that reference is made in the prophetical account of the eastern gate of the temple : 'Then said the Lord unto me, This gate shall be shut. It shall not be opened, and no man shall enter in by it, because the Lord the God of Israel hath entered in by it. Therefore it shall be shut' " (Ezek. xliv. 2).[2]

It is to be remarked in Buddhism that the mother of a Buddha always dies after giving birth to the divine child, as we have shown.

---

[1] Compare Migne, vol. viii. p. 1303, with Lapostilet, "Liturgie de la Messe Arménienne," p. 28.

[2] Spence Hardy, "Manual of Buddhism," p. 145 ; Bigandet, p. 35.

CHAPTER II.

The Double Annunciation—Birth of Buddha under a Bending Tree—
Similar Legends concerning Christ—The Star of Buddha and the
Star of Christ—The Buddhist Simeon—Name-giving not a Jewish
Rite—The Child Christ and the Sparrows—King Herod and King
Bimbisâra—" Thy Parents seek Thee."

THE DOUBLE ANNUNCIATION.

IT is recorded that when Queen Mâyâ received the supernal
Buddha in her womb, in the form of a beautiful white elephant,
she said to her husband, " Like snow and silver, outshining
the sun and the moon, a white elephant of six defences, with
unrivalled trunk and feet, has entered my womb. Listen ; I
saw the three regions (earth, heaven, and hell), with a great
light shining in the darkness, and myriads of spirits sang my
praises in the sky." [1]

A similar miraculous communication was made to King
Śuddhodana by the devas immediately after the miraculous
conception—

" The spirits of the Pure Abode, flying in the air, showed
half of their forms, and hymned King Śuddhodana thus—

> " ' Guerdoned with righteousness and gentle pity,
> Adored on earth and in the shining sky,
> The coming Buddha quits the glorious spheres,
> And hies to earth, to gentle Mâyâ's womb.' " [2]

Seydel has a chapter headed " Conception by the Holy
Ghost." He cites several passages of the Buddhist legends ;
amongst others the following from the " Lalita Vistara," describing the abnormal nature of the birth—

[1] Foucaux, " Lalita Vistara," p. 63.   [2] Foucaux, p. 62.

"Thus, O monks, Buddha was born, and the right side of his mother was not pierced, was not wounded ; it remained as before."[1]

I may mention here that an objection has been taken to the parallelism so often traced of late between the lives of Buddha and Christ. The Rev. R. Collins, a gentleman who has lived in India, and contributed papers to the *Indian Antiquary* in illustration of its archæology, has taken a recent writer to task. His position is that "the supposed miraculous conception, the bringing down of Buddha from the Tuśita heaven, the devas acknowledging his supremacy, the presentation in the temple when the images of Indra and other gods threw themselves at his feet, the temptation by Mâra"—which legends are embellished by the modern writer I have already quoted (Mons. Ernest de Bunsen), under such phrases as "Conceived by the Holy Ghost," "Born of the Virgin Mâyâ," "Song of the heavenly host," "Presentation in the Temple and Temptation in the Wilderness"—"none of these are found in the early Pâli texts ; "[2] and Mr. Collins lays down the further proposition that all these points were inserted in the northern Buddhist scriptures after the Malabar Christians had formed a sect in India, and made known the Christian Gospels. I shall examine these statements each in its proper place.

By early Pâli texts Mr. Collins means the two brief lives of Buddha given in Buddhaghosa's "Aṭṭhakathâ." The one has been translated in part by Mr. Turnour, and the other by Professor Rhys Davids.

Surely Mr. Collins cannot have read these lives. Mr. Turnour's biography distinctly tells us that Indra and the four mahârâjas and the heavenly host came and worshipped Buddha in the heaven Tuśita, on the occasion of his approaching "advent" to earth "for the purpose of redeeming the world."[3]

---

[1] Foucaux, p. 97.

[2] The Rev. R. Collins, "Buddhism in Relation to Christianity," p. 5.

[3] Turnour, "Pâli Buddhistical Annals," *Journ. Ben. As. Soc.*, vol. vii. pp. 798, 799.

This is surely an "acknowledgment of supremacy" on the part of the devas; and it is also as certainly stated that Buddha was "conceived in the womb of the great Máya,"[1] and that in a miraculous manner. "At the instant of this great personage being conceived in the womb of his mother, the whole of the ten thousand worlds (the kosmos) simultaneously quaked, and thirty-two miraculous indications were manifested. For the protection also of the Buddha-elect, as well as his mother, four spirits mounted guard with sword in hand."[1]

Whilst Buddha was in his mother's womb, it is stated also that the womb was transparent.[1] Dr. Rhys Davids has pointed out the interesting fact that certain mediæval frescoes represent Christ as visible when in His mother's womb.[2]

In southern scriptures, as well as the northern ones, the conception is described as immaculate.

"A Buddha-elect, with extended arms and erect in posture, comes forth from his mother's womb undefiled by the impurities of that womb, clean and unsoiled, refulgent as a gem deposited in a Kashmir shawl."[3]

Since I wrote the above, a book has appeared, entitled "The Light of Asia and the Light of the World." It takes up much the same line as Mr. Collins. The *Saturday Review,* in an able article condemning the narrowness of its author, Professor Kellogg, points out that in the Chinese books Buddha is said over and over again to have been incarnate of the "Holy Spirit." The critic says further that, since the publication of Seydel's book, it is impossible any longer to maintain that there has been no derivation from the Buddhist books.[4]

We have seen that the divine annunciation was to the father as well as the mother. It is a singular fact that, in the New Testament, there is also a double annunciation. In Luke (i. 28), the angel Gabriel is said to have appeared to the Virgin Mary before her conception, and foretold to her the miraculous

[1] Turnour, *Journ. Ben. As. Soc.,* vol. vii. p. 800.
[2] "Birth Stories," p. 65.   [3] Turnour, *Journ. Ben. As. Soc.,* vol. vii. p. 801.
[4] *Saturday Review,* February 6, 1886.

birth of Christ. In Matthew (i. 19), an angel comes to Joseph after his nuptials, and announces that what is conceived in his wife is of the Holy Ghost. Dr. Giles remarks that it is a singular fact that Mary seems never to have told her husband a word about the miracle of which she was a witness, and that "Joseph found out the fact (of his wife's pregnancy) for himself."[1]

This double annunciation in the case of both Buddha and Christ is most important. In the New Testament we get it from two distinct writers, whose accounts stultify one another. The Buddhist narrative, on the other hand, is harmonious. If there has been derivation, as Mr. Collins asserts, the original narrative in this case seems plainly to have been the Eastern one.

BIRTH OF BUDDHA.

Amongst the "thirty-two signs" that indicate the mother of a Buddha, the fifth is that, like Mary, the mother of Jesus, she should be "on a journey" at the time of her expected labour.[2] It so happened, as we learn by the narrative given to us by Mr. Turnour, that when Queen Mâyâ was ten months gone with child, a desire seized her to return to her father's city. King Suddhodana consented to this. The road from Kapilavastu to that city was made smooth and spread with foot-clothes. Arches of green plantains and the areca flower were set up, and the queen set out with much pomp in a "new gilt palanquin."

Between the two cities was a lovely forest, which rivalled the nandana grove in the soft luxury of its blossoms and boughs. A nandana grove is at once a forest in paradise, and its counterpart on earth the garden of a monastery. There, amid the soft songs of the Indian cuckoo, the queen alighted, and sought the shade of a fine śâla tree (*Shorea robusta*). Whilst there the pains of labour seized her, and the śâla tree bent down its branches to overshadow her. At this moment the queen was transfigured. Her countenance

---

[1] Giles, "Hebrew and Christian Records," vol. ii. p. 175.
[2] Beal, "Romantic History," p. 32.

C

shone like "glimmering lightning," and the halo of the Queen
of Nandana was round her head. Then the infant Buddha
came forth, and the great kings of the four cardinal points
received him in a cloth or net. Two miraculous jets of water
came from the sky to baptize him. Afar, from the lips of
immortal spirits, was heard the song before cited—

> " O Purusha,
> The equal to thee exists not here.
> Where will a superior be found ? " [1]

In a version of the "Gospel of the Infancy" in the library
of Berne, a palm tree bends down in the same way to Mary.[2]
That some such legend was current in Palestine is proved, I
think, from the account of Christ's birth in the Koran—

"So she conceived him, and she retired with him into a
remote place. And the labour-pains came upon her at the
trunk of a palm tree, and she said, 'Oh that I had died before
this, and been forgotten out of mind!' And He called to her
from beneath her, 'Grieve not, for thy Lord has placed a
stream beneath thy feet ; and shake towards thee the trunk
of the palm tree—it will drop upon thee fresh dates fit to
gather.'"[3]

In the "Protevangelion" Mary and Joseph are described as
journeying near a cave when the pains of labour seize her.
She alights from her ass and enters it, and Joseph hastens
to Bethlehem for a Jewish midwife. As he proceeds certain
marvels are visible. The clouds are astonished, and the birds
of the air stop in their flight. The dispersed sheep of some
shepherds near cease to gambol, and the shepherds to beat
them. The kids near a river are arrested with their mouths
close to the water. All nature seems to pause for a mighty
effort.[4] In the "Lalita Vistara" the birds of the air also
pause in their flight when Buddha comes to the womb of
Queen Máyá.[5] And fires go out and rivers are suddenly

[1] Turnour, *Journ. Ben. As. Soc.*, vol. vii. p. 801.
[2] Given with the other Apocryphal Gospels by Voltaire " Œuvres," vol. xl.
[3] E. H. Palmer, "The Qur'ân," xix. 22.
[4] Chap. xiii.   [5] Foucaux, p. 53.

arrested in their flow when his holy feet touch earth.[1] Joseph succeeds in finding a midwife. He brings her to Mary ; and a mighty light dazzles them. This supernatural light continues until the holy Child appears and begins to suck His mother's breast.

"Then the shepherds came and made a fire, and the heavenly host appeared, praising and adoring the supreme God. And as the shepherds were engaged in the same employment, the cave at that time seemed like a glorious temple, because at that time the tongues of angels and men united to adore and magnify God on account of the birth of the Lord Christ."

In the "Lalita Vistara," Queen Mâyâ is also attended by a midwife when she retires under her tree. This woman is said to be the mother of the previous Buddha.[2] In the "Abinish Kramana" Indra himself, disguised as an old woman, attempts to act as midwife.

THE STAR AND THE MAGI.

Buddha, like Christ, had a star presiding at his birth— Pushya,[3] the "King of Stars." Colebrooke, the best astronomer of Oriental philologists, identifies this as the δ of Cancer.[4]

The "Protevangelion" announces that the "extraordinary large star shining among the stars of heaven and outshining them all," stood just above the cave where Mary lay with the young Child.[5]

Much has been written about the star that is supposed to herald the Christ, the Buddha, the Zarathustra, the Mahomet—the seven great prophets of the Kalpa. One thing seems plain, and that is, that if there is such a star, it does not come at regular intervals.

The "Vishnu Purâna" gives a curious fact *apropos* of the avatâras of Vishnu. It says that the star that heralds

---

[1] Foucaux, p. 100.　　[2] Page 86.　　[3] Foucaux, p. 61.
[4] "Essays," vol. ii. p. 334.　　[5] "Prot.," xv. 9.

these is a star of the asterisms that makes itself visible inside
the square made by the four stars of the Great Bear. This
in India is the vimâṇa (chariot) of the gods, with its seven
fiery steeds.

Who were the "Wise Men" who came to greet the infant
Christ? Much has been written on this subject. They
were kings, according to some; adepts in occult lore, according to others, who have taken the description in its literal
sense. Seydel identifies them with the heavenly kings—
Brahma, Indra, etc., who figure in the "Lalita Vistara."[1]   I
think here he has overlooked the importance of the southern
legend. When the infant Buddha is born, four Brahmins,
the wise men of India, receive him in a golden net. Then the
Mahârâjas, the four great kings of the kosmos, bear him; for
is he not Purusha, the kosmos imaged as a heavenly man?
"Fragrant flowers" and other offerings were made to him,
says the narrative.

THE INDIAN SIMEON.

The close parallelism between the incident of Simeon in
the second chapter of Matthew, and the story of Asita in the
Buddhist legendary life, has been often pointed out. Asita
is called Kaladevala in the Pâli version, both words having
for root the adjective "black."

Asita dwells on Himavat, the holy mount of the Hindoos,
as Simeon dwells on Mount Zion. The "Holy Ghost is
upon" Simeon. That means that he has obtained the faculties of the prophet by mystical training. He "comes by the
Spirit" into the temple.

Now let us turn to Asita. We will take the Pâli version
of his story. It is quite a mistake on the part of Mr. Collins
to suppose that he is only to be met with in the "Lalita
Vistara," or northern scripture.

Asita is an ascetic, who has acquired the eight magical
faculties, one of which is the faculty of visiting the Tawa-
tinsa heavens. Happening to soar up into those pure regions

---

[1] "Evangelium von Jesu," p. 135.

one day, he is told by the host of devatas, or heavenly spirits, that a mighty Buddha is born in the world, "who will establish the supremacy of the Buddhist Dharma." The "Lalita Vistara" announces that, "looking abroad with his divine eye, and considering the kingdoms of India, he saw in the great city of Kapilavastu, in the palace of King Suddhodana, the child shining with the glitter of pure deeds, and adored by all the worlds." Afar through the skies the spirits of heaven in crowds recited the "hymn of Buddha."[1]

This is the description of Simeon in the "Gospel of the First Infancy," ii. 6—"At that time old Simeon saw Him (Christ) shining as a pillar of light when St. Mary the Virgin, His mother, carried Him in her arms, and was filled with the greatest pleasure at the sight. And the angels stood around Him adoring Him as a King; guards stood around Him."

Asita was, as we have seen, a Brahmin adept, with the eight magical faculties of Patanjali's "Yogi Śâstra." One of these, according to Colebrooke, is the power of levitation, or "rising like a sunbeam to the solar orb."[2] Taking advantage of this power, the old Brahmin, says the "Lalita Vistara," "after the manner of the King of the Swans, rose aloft in the sky, and proceeded to the great city of Kapilavastu."[3] When he reached the palace of the king a throne was given to him, and a very gracious reception.

"Râja," he said, "to thee a son has been born. Him I will see."

"The Raja," says the Pâli version,[4] "caused the infant, richly clad, to be brought, in order that he (the infant) might do homage to the Brahmin. The feet of the Buddha-elect, at that instant, performing an evolution, planted themselves on the top-knot of the Brahmin. There being no one greater to whom reverence is due than a Buddha-elect, the Brahmin, instantly rising from the throne on which he was seated, bowed down, with his clasped hands raised over his head, to

---

[1] Foucaux, "Lalita Vistara," p. 103.
[2] "Essays," vol. i. p. 250.   [3] Foucaux, p. 104.
[4] Turnour, *Journ. Ben. As. Soc.*, vol. vii. p. 802.

the Buddha elect. The râja also, witnessing this miraculous result, bowed down to his own son." [1]

But the courtiers of the good King Śuddhodana were plunged into the greatest consternation, for the ascetic burst suddenly into a flood of tears.

" Is there any misfortune impending over the infant of our ruler ? " they said, anxiously.

" Unto him there is no misfortune impending," said the Brahmin. " Without doubt he is destined to become the Buddha."

" Why, then, dost thou weep ? "

" Because I am old and stricken in years, and shall not live to see the glory of his Buddhahood. Therefore do I weep."

The points of contact between Simeon and Asita are singularly close. Both are men of God, "full of the Holy Ghost." Both are brought "by the Spirit" into the presence of the holy Child, for the express purpose of foretelling his destiny as the anointed one.

NAME-GIVING.

Five days after the birth of Buddha an important ceremony occurred. The Brahmins of the city met together, and the young boy received a name. This name was Siddhârtha (He who succeeds in all things),[1] and it was chosen by means of occult knowledge. Eight days after the birth of Jesus the holy Child underwent the ceremony of name-giving and circumcision. This occurred in the temple at Jerusalem, according to the canonical Gospels ; but the "Gospel of the First Infancy" announces that the rite took place in the cave where He was born. He was called Jesus (Saviour), by command of the angel Gabriel. It also foreshadowed the fact that he would be the Saviour of the world.

I think this narrative of the highest importance, because this ceremony of name-giving and casting the horoscope was not a Jewish rite. There is no mention of any such ceremony

---

[1] Turnour, *Journ. Ben. As. Soc.*, vol. vii. p. 802.

until we read of it in the narrative of St. Luke. This would indicate that the rite of name-giving came through the Therapeuts from India. The dominant party were rigid sticklers for the letter of the Law. Even in the early Church, name-giving at baptism was not for a long time universal.

PROPHECY.

"That it might be fulfilled which was spoken by the prophet."

Christianity, like Buddhism, was a radical revolution, which it was sought afterwards to disguise in some of the vestments of the priestly tyranny that it had superseded. In both cases the bibliolatry of the common people had to be dealt with. Christianity took over the Bible of the Jews, but reversed its meaning. Buddhism discarded the vedas as holy books, but appealed to their higher spiritual teaching. Seydel points out likewise, from Lefmann and from Foucaux (" Lalita Vistara," p. 13, *et seq.*), an attempt on the part of the Buddhist writers to find the career of Buddha foreshadowed in the Rig Veda and in the Brâhmaṇas. He is Purusha, the heavenly man of the old Hindoo religion. His symbol is the elephantlike Martaṇḍa, the mystic egg. In consequence, certain heavenly spirits disguise themselves as Brahmins, and fly off to earth to discover in the holy books when an avatâra of the god-man is due. After due research, it is pronounced that in twelve years the Buddha must enter the womb of a mother. The Brahmin books are consulted on other occasions. Buddhism tolerated Brahminism, and made use of its superstitions for the common people. Christianity also sought to conciliate the lower Judaism. I shall show by-and-by that each creed suffered much in consequence.

HYMNS.

Seydel has pointed out that the Buddhist scriptures, like the Christian ones, are written in prose, with hymns and lyrical passages inserted from time to time.[1] In the case of the

[1] "Evangelium von Jesu," p. 140.

Buddhist writings this was a necessity. They were composed before the letters of the alphabet had been introduced into India, and metre helped the monks to preserve them in memory. By-and-by prose writings were introduced. Hence the mixture.

THE CHILD CHRIST AND THE SPARROWS.

When Buddha was twelve years old, he wandered into the royal gardens with a bow and arrows. His young companions were in other gardens near, enjoying themselves in the same way. Suddenly a flock of wild geese flew over, and Deva-datta, a cousin of Buddha's, let fly an arrow, which brought one of them to the ground. The young Buddha rested the wounded bird on his lap, and anointed the wound with oil and honey.

Devadatta claimed the bird, on the ground that he had shot it. Buddha answered thus : " If the bird were dead it would belong to Devadatta. It lives, and therefore it is mine."

This answer failed to satisfy the cousin, who again claimed the bird, alive or dead.

But a shining deva from the heaven of Brahma came down to earth, and adjudicated between the cousins.

" The bird belongs to Buddha," he said, " for his mission is to give life to the world. He who shoots and destroys is by his own act the loser and disperser." [1]

Devadatta is the Judas of Buddhism, and in the " Gospel of the Infancy" the youthful Judas also shares Christ's sports. He strikes Christ on one occasion, and, in return, the young boy casts out a devil from his assailant. On another occasion Jesus makes some sparrows of clay, and gives life to them—a parable very like that of Buddha and the wounded bird. [2]

KING HEROD AND KING BIMBISÂRA.

It is recorded that King Bimbisâra, the King of Magadha, was fearful that some enemy would subvert his kingdom. In

[1] " Romantic History," p. 73.   [2] " First Infancy," i. 8.

consequence he summoned his chief councillors, and said to them, " Make search and discover if there be any one capable of compassing my downfall, and if there be, take care that he be hindered in such an attempt." The councillors of the king sent forth two trusty messengers, who searched east and west in the râja's dominions. They then passed over the borders, and there met a man, who said to them—

"Away to the north there is a precipitous mountain of the Himâlayan range. Underneath the wooded belt of that mountain is a tribe called the Śâkyas. In that tribe is a youth newly born, the first begotten of his mother. On the day of his birth the Brahmins calculated his horoscope, and they fixed that he will either be a Chakravartin and rule the great empire of Jambudwîpa, or else he will become a hermit and win the ten names of Tathâgata, the Buddha."

At once the two messengers returned to the king, and narrated what they had heard. They counselled him to raise a large army and to march and destroy the child.

King Bimbisâra, unlike King Herod, here replied, " Speak not thus. If the youth become a Chakravarti Râja, he will wield a righteous sceptre, and we are bound to obey him. If he become the mighty Buddha, his love and compassion leading him to deliver and save all flesh, then we must become his disciples."[1]

"Thy Parents seek Thee."

Seydel has a chapter with the above heading, drawing attention to another point of resemblance between the lives of the young Buddha and the young Christ. On one occasion, each in early youth wandered away from his parents, and a search had to be instituted to recover him. Some of these points of contact are less striking than others, but I think all worthy of notice, because probably in every case there is a meaning of some importance not now always traceable.

At the spring festival, like the modern râjahs in India, the king went with his court to take part in the ploughing.

[1] "Romantic History of Buddha," p. 104.

The king ploughed with a plough ornamented with gold ; his nobles ploughed with a plough ornamented with silver ; but the little prince, who was taken to the show, wandered away and sat under a jambu tree (the rose-apple). Whilst there he was accosted by five rishis, or wise men. They, by the force of their magical vision, were able to detect his mighty destiny.

The rishis began to repeat the following gâthâs :—
The first rishi said—

> " In a world devoured by the fire of sin
> This lake hath appeared ;
> In him is the Law
> Which brings happiness to all flesh ! "

The second rishi said—

> " In the darkness of the world
> A light has appeared,
> To lighten all who are in ignorance ! "

The third rishi said—

> " Upon the tossing ocean
> A bark has approached,
> To save us from the perils of the deep ! "

The fourth rishi said—

> " To all who are bound in the chains of corruption
> This great Saviour has come ;
> In him is the Law
> That will deliver all ! "

The fifth rishi said—

> " In a world vexed by sickness and old age
> A great Physician has appeared,
> To provide a Law
> To put an end to both."

Soon the king appeared searching for his son, when lo ! this marvel was visible. The shadows of all the other trees had turned, but the jambu tree still screened the young boy with its shade.

The rishis having saluted the feet of Buddha, flew off through the air.

The five rishis mystically are the Dhyâni Buddhas, the first officers in the celestial hierarchy of the transcendental Buddha. They are present to bear witness to his mighty mission, and to the fact that it is distinct from that of his earthly father.

"Wist ye not that I must be about My Father's business." These words of Christ have a similar import. The miracle of the light coming from the young boy, and not from the material sun, is the same lesson objectivized.

CHAPTER III.

The Homage of the Idols—"Gold, and Frankincense, and Myrrh"—The
Disputation with the Doctors.

THE HOMAGE OF THE IDOLS.

IT is recorded in the "Lalita Vistara" that certain elders
came and gave counsel to the king, saying, "It is meet,
O king, that the infant should be now presented at the temple
of the Gods."

"It is proper that this should be done," said Śuddhodana.
"Let the streets and bazaars be splendidly adorned. Beat
the drums, ring the bells. Let the lame, the deaf, the blind,
the unsightly be removed from the line of procession, and
everything else of evil augury. Assemble the neighbouring
kings, the nobles, the merchants, the householders in gala
dress. Let the Brahmins decorate the temples of the gods."

The king's orders were promptly obeyed. In due time,
accompanied by the loud blare of Indian instruments—the
conch shell, the flute, the tambourine, the "drum of joy,"—the
young infant went in "great and pompous royal ceremony"
to the temple. Elephants in crowds, and horses and chariots,
citizens and soldiers, joined in the procession. Parasols were
reared aloft, streamers waved, banners were unfurled. Villagers and nobles, the poor and the rich, pressed forward to
the show. The streets and the squares were carpeted with
flowers, and vases of sweet scent were lavishly flung about.
Also, in harmony with the crude ideas of early art that a
perfectly smooth plain was the highest ideal of beauty, rough

places were made smooth and tortuous paths straightened. Rude designs of these flags and drums, and " long horns and flagcolets," [1] are given in the earliest sculptures. The men have kummerbunds, and bare legs and chests ; the women are clothed chiefly in heavy arm and leg bangles. We can see the procession of good King Śuddhodana in modern India.

The car of the young Buddha was borne respectfully along by a procession of gods. Beautiul apsarases sounded seraphic notes ; flowers fell from heaven.

When the procession reached the temple, the images of the gods—Indra, Brahmâ, Nârâyana, Kouvera the God of wealth, Skanda, and the Four Mahârâjas—stood up in their places and saluted the feet of the young infant, and worshipped him as the transcendental Deity revealed on earth. A hymn which they sang on the occasion plainly shows this :—

> " Tall Meru, King of Mountains, bows not down
> To puny grain of mustard seed. The sea,
> The yeasty palace of the Serpent King,
> Ne'er stoops to greet the footprints of a cow :
> Shall Sun or Moon salute a glistening worm ?
> Or shall our Prince bend knee to gods of stone?
> Who worships pride, the man or God debased,
> Is like the worm, the seed, the cow-foot puddle ;
> But like the sun, the sea, and Meru Mount,
> Is Swayaṁbhû, the self-existent God ;
> And all who do him homage shall obtain
> Heaven and Nirvritti."

When the gods had finished this hymn, their statues became animate, and the temple shone with all the glory of the heavenly host.

A passage from the "First Gospel of the Infancy " may be cited here. When Mary and Joseph fled to Egypt, they reached a city where a mighty idol was worshipped. This idol made the following revelation to its priests : " In this city has arrived an unknown God, who is the true God, and none other but he is worthy of worship, because He is the Son of

---

[1] See Cunningham, " Bhilsa Topes," p. 30, also plate xiii.

God."[1] The idol then tumbled off its pedestal, and was broken to fragments.

It is difficult to conceive that these two narratives could have been written quite independently. Plainly they both convey the same meaning, namely, that the idols of a dead religion were greeting its successor.

The Presentation of Gifts.

A short time after this, a Brahmin, named Purohita, respectfully suggested to the king that the young Buddha should receive the customary "gifts." So at sunrise he was carried in the arms of his aunt, Mahâ Prajâpatî Gautamî, to the beautiful Vimalaviyûha, the Stainless Garden. There, for seven days and nights, he was decked with rings and bracelets and diadems, with strings of pearls, with rich silks and golden tissues ; and young girls in thousands gazed at him in rapture. In China, God depicted as an Infant is as popular as Bala Krishna in India, or the Virgin and Child in Italy. But on this occasion, in the Stainless Garden, those who believed in the efficacy of trinkets and tawdry finery received a rebuke. Suddenly a majestic spirit made half of its divine form visible and sang in the clouds—

> "Cast off this tawdry show !
> The streams of earth wash down their shining gold ;
> Men gather it for their bedizenments,
> But in that far-off river, on whose banks
> The sweet rose-apple[2] clusters o'er the pool,
> There is an ore that mocks all earthly sheen—
> The gold of blameless deeds."

Seydel, in a chapter headed " Gold, and Frankincense, and Myrrh,"[3] draws attention to the similarity of the gift presentations in the Indian and Christian narratives.

In the Dulvâ it is more than once announced that " myrrh, garlands, incense, etc.," were sacrificed to Buddha.[4] Gold pieces are placed on the Buddhist altar by the Chinese, and

---

[1] Ch. x.   [2] Jambu.   [3] " Evangelium von Jesu," p. 139.
[4] " Asiatic Researches," vol. xx. p. 312.

the consecrated elements remain on the altar by a lacquered tabernacle.[1]

THE DISPUTATION WITH THE DOCTORS.

A little Brahmin was "initiated," girt with the holy thread, etc., at eight, and put under the tuition of a holy man. Buddha's like Râma's guru was named Viśvâmitra. But the youthful Buddha soon showed that his lore was far greater than that of his teacher. When Viśvâmitra proposed to teach him the alphabet, the young prince went off—

" In sounding '*a*,' pronounce it as in the sound of the word '*anitya*.'

" In sounding '*i*,' pronounce it as in the word '*indriya*.'

" In sounding '*u*,' pronounce it as in the word '*upagupta*.' "

And so on through the whole Sanskrit alphabet.[2]

At his writing-lesson he displayed the same miraculous proficiency; and no possible sum that his teachers or young companions could set him in arithmetic[3] could baffle him. In poetry, grammar, in music, in singing, he also proved without a rival. In "joining his hands in prayer," in the knowledge of the Rig Veda and the holy books, in rites, in magic, and in the mysteries of the yogi or adept his proficiency was proclaimed.

In the "Gospel of the First Infancy," it is recorded that, when taken to his schoolmaster, Zacchæus—

" The Lord Jesus explained to him the meaning of the letters Aleph and Beth.

" 8. Also which were the straight figures of the letters, which were the oblique, and what letters had double figures; which had points and which had none; why one letter went before another; and many other things He began to tell him and explain, of which the master himself had never heard nor read in any book.

" 9. The Lord Jesus further said to the master, 'Take notice how I say to thee.' Then He began clearly and dis-

---

[1] Langlés, "Rituel des Tartares Mantchous."
[2] "Rom. Hist.," p. 70.   [3] "Lalita Vistara," pp. 121 and 149.

tinctly to say, 'Aleph, Beth, Gimel, Daleth ;' and so on to the end of the alphabet.

"10. At this the master was so surprised that he said, 'I believe this boy was born before Noah.'"

We read, also, in the twenty-first chapter of the "First Gospel of the Infancy," the following amplification of the disputation with the doctors :—

"5. Then a certain principal Rabbi asked Him, 'Hast Thou read books ?'

"6. Jesus answered that He had both read books and the things which were contained in books.

"7. And He explained to them the books of the Law, and precepts, and statutes, and the mysteries which are contained in the books of the prophets, things which the mind of no creature could reach.

"8. Then said that Rabbi, 'I never yet have seen or heard of such knowledge. What do you think that boy will be ?'

"9. Then a certain astronomer who was present asked the Lord Jesus whether He had studied astronomy ?

"10. The Lord Jesus replied, and told him the number of the spheres and heavenly bodies, as also their triangular, square, and sextile aspects ; their progressive and retrograde motions, their size, and several prognostications, and other things which the reason of man had never discovered.

"11. There was also among them a philosopher, well-skilled in physic and natural philosophy, who asked the Lord Jesus whether He had studied physic.

"12. He replied, and explained to him physics and metaphysics.

"13. Also those things which were above and below the power of nature.

"14. The powers, also, of the body ; its humours and their effects.

"15. Also the number of the bones, veins, arteries, and nerves.

"16. The several constitutions of body, hot and dry, cold and moist, and the tendencies of them.

"17. How the soul operated on the body.

"18. What its various sensations and faculties were.

"19. The faculty of speaking, anger, desire.

"20. And, lastly, the manner of its composition and dissolution, and other things which the understanding of no creature had ever reached.

"21. Then that philosopher worshipped the Lord Jesus, and said, 'O Lord Jesus, from henceforth I will be Thy disciple and servant.'"

Visvâmitra in like manner worshipped Buddha by falling at his feet.

I have now shown, I think, that Mr. Collins's assertions that the points of contact between the lives of Buddha and Christ are found only in the northern scriptures, is based on error.

I must cite from his lecture another passage—

"There is no thought in the early Buddhism of which we read in the Pâlis texts, of a deliverance at the hand of a god ; but the *man* Gautama Buddha stands alone in his striving after the true emancipation from sorrow and ignorance. The accounts of his descending from heaven, and being conceived in the world of men when a preternatural light shone over the worlds, the blind received sight, the dumb sang, the lame danced, the sick were cured, together with all such embellishments, are certainly added by later hands."[1]

Again I must ask, Has Mr. Collins read the Pâli texts ? or their translations by Professor Rhys Davids or Mr. Turnour ? I will cite a passage from the "Birth Stories"—

"Now, at the moment when the future Buddha made himself incarnate in his mother's womb, the constituent elements of the ten thousand world-systems quaked and trembled, and were shaken violently. The Thirty-two Good Omens, also, were made manifest. In the ten thousand world-systems an immeasurable light appeared. The blind received their sight as if from very longing to behold his glory ; the deaf heard the noise ; the dumb spake one with another ; the crooked became straight ; the lame walked ; all prisoners

---

[1] "Buddhism in relation to Christianity," p. 6.

D

were freed from their bonds and chains.   In each hell the fire
was extinguished." [1]

Surely this is a " deliverance."   Buddha rules the Triloka
(heaven, earth, and hell), and his avatâra clears out the latter
region of torment.   Have there not been efforts in the English
Church to prove that the dominions of Christ are far less
extensive ?

This brings us to the close of the earlier history, both
of Christ and Buddha, and it is not astonishing that these
histories should be similar, for they symbolize the same
crucial phenomenon.   The higher mystics, like St. Dionysius,
St. John of the Cross, and Fenelon, have not, on the surface,
been as frank as Origen upon the subject of the relative value
of the historical and the mystical elements of Scripture ; but
practically they have allowed the mystical portion to overshadow the historical.   To assert, as some grave divines have
done, that Origen's interpretation is exceptional and heretical
is to ignore the Jewish genius at the epoch of Philo and
Christ.   The latter distinctly asserted that a parabolic teaching of the mysteries of the kingdom of Heaven was alone
permissible to the outside public ; and St. Paul tells us that
the narrative of Agar and Sarah is purely an allegorical
exposition of the " bondage " of the lower life and the freedom
of those " born after the spirit " (Gal. iv. 22–29).   " My little
children of whom I travail in birth again until Christ be
found in you " (Gal. iv. 19).

The child Christ is in every human being.   It is of royal
line, for its father is the universal spirit.   It comes to earth,
and the branches of the tree of knowledge bend down to it,
for the tree of knowledge in the " Kabbalah " represents the
kosmos from the material side.   Its life is sought by the
kings and high priests of Beelzebub, and the thrones and
kings of ghost-land greet it with spiritual incense and gold.
It is by-and-by reborn of water and the Spirit, and sits under,
or is nailed upon the tree of life, which, in the " Kabbalah,"
images the life of the Spirit.

[1] Rhys Davids, " Birth Stories," p. 64.

CHAPTER IV.

"Out of Egypt have I called My Son"—"The Great City which spiritually is called Sodom and Egypt"—Two Mothers of the Perfected Mystic—Two Births—Why Mary and her Son are always together in the "Gospel of the Infancy."

"OUT OF EGYPT HAVE I CALLED MY SON."

MODERN exegesis gives to the "Gospel of the Infancy" a much later date than our four Gospels. The chief reason for this is that the work is full of impossible and apparently aimless marvels. This would be a sufficient reason if it could be proved that these gospels were indigenous to Palestine ; but if the tales of wonder in them are probably derived from a foreign source, then such an argument has a modified force. It must be noticed, too, that when the "Gospel of the Infancy" was written, its author did not seem to be aware of the existence of our canonical gospels, at least, in their present form. The only other gospel that he takes cognizance of is the "Gospel of Perfection" ("First Infancy," ch. viii. v. 13). That such a Gospel was once in the Church is proved by Epiphanius ("Hær." 26, para. 2).

But a careful study of the "First Gospel of the Infancy" has brought to my mind another curious fact. It is a revelation of the Christian mysteries, rounded and concise. The time has now come to state what the ancient mysteries really were. They shadowed forth the earth-life of the ideal man, under the symbolism of the sun's yearly journey. For the first six months he is in the "great city which spiritually is called Sodom and Egypt" (Rev. xi. 8). Then comes the turning-point of his career. At the date of the Indian festival of the Tree, the Jewish Feast of Tabernacles, he forsakes the lower life for the life of what the "Kabbalah" calls the "chosen one." He enters a second time into his mother's womb, and is born again, this time of the celestial virgin now dominating the sky. Hence, in the "Litany of the Blessed Virgin," she is still hymned as "Janua Cœli."

Man is born of matter and spirit. The life of the Jina, the Jesus, the Buddha, begins at the last octave of the old year, the festival in India of the Black Durgâ, called also the Mâyâ Devî, whose name, in consequence, the Buddhists adopted for the mother of Buddha. She dies in a week, because in a week the festival closes with her death. Her image is thrown into the Ganges yearly in India. The burning of the yule-log, according to Wilson, is another presentation of this death. When Buddha abandons his palace for the life of the Bhiksu, or Beggar, his mother comes down from heaven to him once more ; but it is in reality a new mother—Dharma the Holy Spirit. The Buddhist ascetics are called the sons of Dharma.

In the great Bible of Christian mystics, the works of St. Dionysius, this great change is called the "God Birth ;" and the "Mother of Adoption," as he calls it, is symbolized by the baptismal font, which in his day must have been something like the tanks in Buddhist temples in China, for a triple immersion was part of the ceremony. In the benediction of fonts in the Catholic Church occurs this passage, "ad recreandos novos populos quos tibi fons baptismatis parturit, Spiritum adoptionis emitte." St. Dionysius tells us that the Perfected Mystic in the early Church was called the "Therapeut." There were three stages of spiritual progress—

1. Purification.
2. Illumination.
3. Perfection.

In the Middle Ages mysticism was profoundly studied. I give from Didron (Plate I.) an illumination from a missal. It is the planisphere of the Apocalypse. I add a little design to make its meaning more clear.

PLATE I.

THE FOUR HORSES OF THE APOCALYPSE.
From Didron.   [*Page* 36.

The special symbol of Christ was Aries, in India a horse; and here we see it passing along the ecliptic.

The stages in the Apocalypse are—

1. The white horse with a sword (Gemini).

2. The black horse with the scales (Virgo, strictly, but the balance was very important in Kabbalistic mysticism).

3. The white horse with the bow (Sagittarius).

4. The pale horse of death (Pisces, in India, as I shall show, Dharma Chakra, the Quoit of Death, see Fig. 5). The ancient mystics divided the planisphere into two halves. I shall go more deeply into this subject by-and-by. The first, or lower life, is spiritually called Egypt in the Apocalypse. The second is the New Jerusalem. These in India figure as women, the black and the white Durgâ.

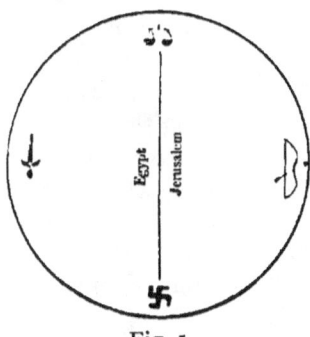

Fig. 5.

In the "Kabbalah" these are Sophia and "the Whore." The husband of the latter is Samaël, the Prince of Darkness. The pair in union were known as "the Beast."[1]   "There are two cities," says St. Augustine, "one of angels and good men, the other the city of the wicked."[2]

The four grades of spiritual progress with Essenes and Buddhists were represented by the four cardinal points. These are the four sphinxes of Ezekiel, formulated when the Bull dominated. The sphinx with the face of a man is Aquarius. The lion-faced sphinx is Leo. The ox-faced sphinx is Taurus. And I shall be able to show later on that the eagle Garuda in India was the early sign for the Balances of the Zodiac."

It is the Jewish Sun of Righteousness with healing in its wings.

[1] Ginsburg, "The Kabbalah," p. 28.
[2] "City of God," bk. xii. c. i.

The ingenious symbolic turns and twists that have been given to these four cardinal points by the mystics of all nations would fill volumes. They represent the four spiritual grades of Buddhists, Essenes and Pythagoreans. The Adept in the "Golden Verses" is called "the Quaternary." They explain the mystical figure of Durgâ in India, with the four arms bearing the club, the shell, the sword or lingam, and the noose of death. They were represented by the four great officers of the Eleusinian Mysteries—the Hierophant, who was in reality En Soph, Brahma, God viewed a pure spirit; the Torch-Bearer and Altar Minister, who had for symbols the sun and moon, and meant, of course, the fatherly and motherly principles; and the Herald, whose symbol was Mercury. These four characters, it is urged, have come down to us by route of the mysteries and miracle-plays in the modern pantomime. Harlequin, with his jod or wand, and Columbine from *Columba*, the dove or eagle, the old man, and the clown. In the cards, too, it has been contended we get them likewise. Cards were originally the tarot used for divination, and in them we have the ace or monod, the father and mother, and the herald or messenger. And each little army of thirteen months is again marshalled under one of the four mystic signs—the red heart, the club or "tree" (Virgo); the black spade, which is like the thunderbolt of Indra.

In the apparatus of the old magician, the four points run riot. His four great instruments—his wand, his crescent, his lamp, and his sword—are nothing more than these four points. The Essene was bound by a terrible oath to keep the secrets of the "Cosmogony" and the "Tetragrammaton"—two secrets, in fact, rolled into one.

The Kabbalists said they could class mankind by gazing on their faces. The animal nature of those who were in the first or ox stage needs no interpreter. This animal stage terminates in India with the sign of the Twins, called in India by a homely word which signifies sexual love.

"Out of Egypt have I called My Son!"

The meaning of this passage will now be more plain, and

the "Gospel of the Infancy" appear less extravagant. The mother and the Child Jesus pass into the mystic "Egypt," and then the mother and the Christ-child pass into "Jerusalem." The gnostics drew a wide distinction between "Jesus" and "Christ."

This is the story told every Sunday in the Christian ritual. The "Lesser Entrance" of the priest signifies Christ's descent into the flesh, "Egypt;" the "Greater Entrance" typifies "Jerusalem," the new and higher life of the Therapeut.

It is to be observed that in the "Gospel of the Infancy" the mother and the child are inseparable, and Christ always a child. There is a deep meaning in this. They heal the sick, they give sight to the blind, cure deafness, restore the impotent.

This is always done, likewise, through the instrumentality of the water that has washed the Child Christ. This is very Buddhistic. Mary herself is the water of life, and it is only by the birth of the Child Christ in each of us that we can hope to gain it. I give from Didron a design, which manifestly signifies much more than a mere mother and child on the material plane. Whether this means to represent or not the Child Christ in the transparent womb of the mother,[1] I cannot say.

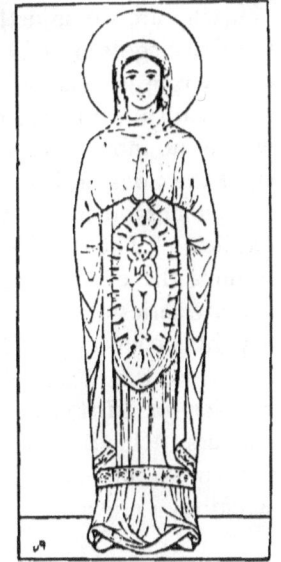

Fig. 6.

Neither Christ nor the early Christian writers held the modern jealousy of the "mysteries" of other nations.

Christ: "I will utter things which have been kept secret from the foundation of the world." [2]

St. Paul: "Even the mystery which hath been hid from ages and from generations, but now is made manifest to his saints." [3]

[1] See *ante*, p. 16. [2] Matt. xiii. 35. [3] Col. i. 26.

" The gospel which ye have heard, and which was prea hed to every creature under heaven, whereof I Paul am made a minister." [1]

Clement of Alexandria : "And those who lived according to the Logos were really Christians, though they have been thought to be atheists, as Socrates and Heraclitus were among the Greeks, and such as resembled them." [2]

St. Augustine : " For the thing itself which is now called the Christian religion really was known to the ancients, nor was wanting at any time from the beginning of the human race until the time that Christ came in the flesh, from whence the true religion which had previously existed began to be called 'Christian ;' and this in our day is the Christian religion, not as having been wanting in former times, but as having in later times received this name." [3]

Justin Martyr : "If, then, we hold some opinions near of kin to the poets and philosophers in greatest repute amongst you, why are we unjustly hated ? . . . By declaring the Logos the first-begotten of God, our Master, Jesus Christ, to be born of a virgin without any human mixture, and to be crucified and dead, and to have risen again and ascended into heaven, we say no more in this than what you say of those whom you style the Sons of Jove."

Violent polemical writers like Tertullian are still more explicit : " The devil, whose business it is to pervert the truth, mimics the exact circumstances of the divine sacraments in the mysteries of idols. He himself baptizes some—that is to say, his believers and followers. He promises forgiveness of sins from the sacred fount, and thus initiates them into the religion of Mithras. He marks on the forehead his own soldiers. He then celebrates the Oblation of Bread, and introduces an image of the resurrection, and before a sword wreathes a crown." [4]

[1] Col. i. 23.
[2] Clemen. Alex., " Strom."
[3] " Opera," vol. i. p. 12.
[4] " Hær.," cap. xl.

CHAPTER V.

CHRIST has frequently been judged a non-existent person, and so has Buddha. The main reason for this is, that the lives of each have for symbolism the course of the sun during its yearly journey. For this, however, there were two reasons quite distinct from vulgar sun-worship.

The first was, that all the mysteries consisted in the revealing of the infinite transcendental God, through the medium of the heavenly Man, whose symbol was the great dome of heaven. This was not God Himself, as Dupuis asserted, but what the "Kabbalah" calls the "Garment of God." Indian Upanishads draw the same distinction. And along the zodiacal hem of this garment, it was figured that the "Chosen One" had to travel to become one with the heavenly Man. Hence the importance of the word Chakravartin in the Buddhist scriptures. The stages of spiritual, or in mystic parlance *interior* progress, were marked by the signs of the zodiac. A second sufficient reason was, that the grosser anthropomorphic forms of worship for the least spiritual of the community had, of course, to be regulated by the kalendar.

Proof that both Christ and Buddha were historical personages comes most completely from examining their lives together. Much is like and much is unlike. At this point their histories diverge for some time, and I will turn to Buddha, condensing my "Popular Life of Buddha," to which all who wish for more ample details are referred.

The soothsayers had pronounced that the infant would be

one of two things—a mighty earthly conqueror or a hermit.
This prophecy plainly gave the king much concern. An
earthly emperor, surrounded by elephants and horsemen, and
spearmen and bowmen was a tangible object—tangible as his
rich palaces and towers and shining emeralds ; but the advan-
tages of the pious hermit were very unsubstantial indeed—

> "Gaining, who knows what good, when all is lost
> Worth keeping."[1]

So by-and-by it came into the mind of the king that he would
consult more soothsayers, to see if more definite knowledge
about the young man's future could be obtained. A number
of pious hermits, gifted with the divine wisdom, were in consequence got together. They pronounced the following :—

"The young boy will, without doubt, be either a king of
kings or a great Buddha. If he is destined to be a great
Buddha, 'four presaging tokens' will make his mission plain.
He will see—

"1. An old man.
"2. A sick man.
"3. A corpse.
"4. A holy recluse.

"If he fails to see these four presaging tokens of an
avatâra, he will be simply a Chakravartin."

King Śuddhodana was very much comforted by the last
prediction of the soothsayers. He thought in his heart, It
will be an easy thing to keep these four presaging tokens
from the young prince. So he gave orders that three magni-
ficent palaces should at once be built—the Palace of Spring,
the Palace of Summer, the Palace of Winter. These palaces,
as we learn from the "Lalita Vistara," were the most beautiful
palaces ever conceived on earth. Indeed, they were quite
able to cope in splendour with Vaijayanta, the immortal
palace of Indra himself. Costly pavilions were built out in
all directions, with ornamented porticoes and furbished doors.
Turrets and pinnacles soared into the sky. Dainty little oval
windows gave light to the rich apartments. Galleries, balus-

---

[1] "Light of Asia," p. 25.

trades, and delicate trellis-work were abundant everywhere. A thousand bells tinkled on each roof. We seem to have the lacquered Chinese edifices of the pattern which architects believe to have flourished in early India. The gardens of these fine palaces rivalled the chess-board in the rectangular exactitude of their parterres and trellis-work bowers. Cool lakes nursed on their calm bosoms storks and cranes, wild geese and tame swans ; ducks, also, as parti-coloured as the white, red, and blue lotuses amongst which they swam. Bending to these lakes were bowery trees—the champak, the acacia serisha, and the beautiful asoka-tree with its orange-scarlet flowers. Above rustled the mimosa, the fan-palm, and the feathery pippala, Buddha's tree. The air was heavy with the strong scent of the tuberose and the Arabian jasmine.

It must be mentioned that strong ramparts were prepared round the palaces of Kapilavastu, to keep out all old men, sick men, and recluses, and, I must add, to keep in the prince.

And a more potent safeguard still was designed. When the prince was old enough to marry, all the young girls of the kingdom were marshalled before him. To each he gave a rich bangle, or a brooch set in diamonds, or some expensive gewgaw. But the spies who had been set to watch him remarked that he gazed upon them all with listless eye. When the rich collection of jewels was quite exhausted, a maiden of exquisite beauty entered the apartment. Buddha gazed at her spell-bound, and felt confused because he had no gift to offer to her. The young girl, without any false modesty, went to him, and said abruptly—

"Young man, what offence have I given thee, that thou shouldst contemn me thus ?"

"I do not contemn thee, young girl," said the prince, "but in truth thou hast come in rather late !" And he sent for some other jewels of great value, which he presented to the young girl.

"Is it proper, young man," she said, with a slight blush, "that I should receive such costly gifts from thee ?"

"The ornaments are mine," he said, "therefore take them away !"

The young girl answered simply, "Not having any trinkets I could not deck myself, but now I will bear me bravely." The spies, cunning in furtive glances and blushes, reported everything to the king.

The name of the young girl was Gopâ. M. Foucaux conceives that the name is identical with the "milkmaid," beloved by Krishna.

The king was delighted that his son had fallen in love. He at once sent the Brahmin Purohita to Śâkya Daṇḍapâṇi, the young girl's father, to demand her hand in marriage for his son. Daṇḍapâṇi's reply to the king was this :—

"The noble young man has lived all his life in the sloth and luxury of a palace, and my family never gives a daughter excepting to a man of courage and strength, one who can ply the bow and wield the two-handed sword."

This answer made the king sad. Several other haughty Śâkya families had previously said, "Our daughters refuse to come near a young milksop."

When the king confided the source of his sadness to his son, the latter said, with a smile—

"If this is the cause of thy grief, O father, let me try conclusions with these valiant young Śâkyas."

"Canst thou wrestle? Canst thou shoot with the bow?"

"Summon these young heroes, and we will see."

Immense importance was attached by the Âryas to the festival of the Summer Solstice. The Greeks had their Olympia, when the whole population met together to witness the wrestling, the bow shooting, the chariot races. The victor in these was carried home in a pompous procession. In ancient India, a woman, famous for her beauty, was made the chief prize, and the marriage was called Swayaṁvara (marriage by athletic competition). By this institution the manhood and courage of the State were powerfully stimulated. It must be borne in mind that a skilful use of the bow, the club, and the war-chariot meant independence to the community. On the other hand, an unskilful use subjected the whole tribe to be captured and detained as prisoners of war. They might be sacrificed to Rudra at the autumn festival. Or if they were lucky enough to escape this, they were slaves for the rest of their lives. As details of the memorable Swayamvara where the beautiful Gopâ was the prize are rather meagre, perhaps I may be permitted to supply some from the epics.

A vast plain was selected on these occasions, and levelled and swept. Round this pavilions and lacquered palaces of the Chinese pattern were hastily erected. Their dainty spires and columns and roofs stood out against the blue sky, "like the snowy pinnacles of the mountain range Kailaśa," says the Mahâbhârata. Carpets and sofas and thrones were spread in these for the kings and competing heroes. In front of each pavilion were heavy awnings on glittering poles. The powerful perfumes of India, the aloes, and the balm, could be scented from afar. The priests poured clarified butter into the holy fire. Mummers and dancers and singers performed miracle-plays, not differing much from the modern pantomime; religious disputants chopped logic. Each guest was expected to be lavish of his gifts. This made the poor man as merry as the rich one.

Devadatta, a rival of Buddha, slaughters an elephant, and places it in the pathway of Buddha when he was proceeding to the tournament. Buddha, with unexpected strength hurls it to a distance to prevent it from infecting the neighbourhood. "The elephantine cloud," says M. Senart, "and the lightning were much to Indian myth-makers."

A competition for a high-born princess includes learning, as well as the athleticism. Buddha, as I have already mentioned, first eclipses his neighbours in the former. Then come swimming, jumping, running, and none have a chance against him. Then comes the important issue of wrestling. This in India has been cultivated and honoured from time immemorial. Buddha first vanquishes Nanda and Ânanda. Ânanda is the brother of the unfriendly Devadatta, who next comes forward to avenge him :—

" Then the young Śâkya Devadatta, puffed with the pride of race and the insolence of strength, came forth to the contest. He circled round with much rapidity and skill, and, watching his opportunity, he sprang upon the prince."

But Buddha is merciful as well as strong. He causes the conceited young man to execute a somersault in the air, and then catches him before he can be hurt. Afterwards, all the young heroes in a body attack the prince, but with the same ill-fortune.

But the Âryas, like their descendants, the Anglo-Saxons of Crecy, were unrivalled bowmen. Archery was the real test of a hero in the old epics. Preparations now take place for that crucial issue.

Ânanda sets up a drum of iron. Devadatta sets up another at double the distance. Sundarananda sets up a third drum at a distance of six krosas. Daṇḍapâṇi sets up a drum at a greater distance still. By Daṇḍapâṇi's drum are seven tall palm-trees, and beyond this a figure of a wild beast in iron.

Ânanda lets fly a shaft. It pierces the drum which he had set up. Beyond that distance he cannot shoot. Devadatta pierces his drum. Sundarananda pierces the drum set up at six krosas. Daṇḍapâṇi smites his drum. But beyond his selected distance each archer is powerless.

And now it is the turn of Buddha to shoot, but no bow is strong enough to bear the strength of his arm. One after another they break in the stringing. At last it is recollected that, in one of the shrines, there is the bow of his grandfather, Simhahanu (Lion Jaw), a weapon so mighty that no warrior can even lift it. Attendants are sent off to fetch it. The strongest Śâkyas attempt to string it, but all in vain.

Then the prince himself takes up the bow of the mighty Lion Jaw. With ease he strings it, and the sound of its stringing re-echoes through the wide city of Kapilavastu. Amid immense excitement he adjusts an arrow and prepares to shoot. His shaft transfixes the first drum, the second drum, the third drum, the fourth drum, and then tearing swiftly through the seven trees and the wild beast of iron, buries itself like the lightning in the ground.

Other competitions take place. The prince shows his superiority in riding the horse, riding the elephant with an iron goad; in poetry, painting, music, dancing, and even jocularity, in the "art of the fist" and in "kicking." He also shines in his knowledge of occult mysteries, in "prophecy," in the explanation of dreams, in "magic," in "joining his hands in prayer."

After this manner Buddha won the beautiful Gopâ. She is called Yaśodhara in the Southern narrative.

Perhaps, at this time, the good King Śuddhodana was more happy than even the prince in the ecstasy of his honeymoon. He had found for that prince the most beautiful wife in the world. He had built him palaces that were the talk of the whole of Hindostan. No Indian mahârâja before had had such beautiful palaces, such lovely wives and handmaidens, such dancing girls, singers, jewels, luxuries. In his bowers of camphor cinnamon, amid the enchanting perfumes of the tuberose and the santal-tree, his life must surely be one long bliss, a dream that has no awakening.

But suddenly this exultation was dashed with a note of woe. The king dreamt that he saw his son in the russet cowl of the beggar-hermit. Awaking in a fright, he called an eunuch—

"Is my son in the palace?" he asked abruptly.

"He is, O king."

The dream frightened the king very much, and he ordered five hundred guards to be placed at every corner of the walls of the Palace of Summer. And the soothsayers having announced that a Buddha, if he escapes at all, always escapes by the Gate of Benediction, folding doors of immense size were here erected. The sound of their swing on their hinges resounded to a distance of half a yogana (three and a half miles). Five hundred men were required to stir either gate. These precautions completely quieted the king's mind, until one day he received a terrible piece of news. His son had seen the first of the four presaging tokens. He had seen an Old Man.

This is how the matter came about. The king had prepared a garden even more beautiful than the garden of the Palace of Summer. A soothsayer had told him that if he could succeed in showing the prince this garden, the prince would be content to remain in it with his wives for ever. No task seemed easier than this, so it was arranged that on a certain day the prince should be driven thither in his chariot. But, of course, immense precautions had to be taken to keep all old men, and sick men, and corpses from his sight. Quite an army of soldiers was told off for this duty, and the city was decked with flags. The path of the prince was strewn with flowers and scents, and adorned with vases of the rich kadali plant. Above were costly hangings and garlands, and pagodas of bells.

But, lo and behold! as the prince was driving along, plump under the wheels of his chariot, and before the very noses of the silken nobles and the warriors with javelins and shields, he saw an unusual sight. This was an old man, very decrepit and very broken. The veins and nerves of his body were swollen and prominent; his teeth chattered; he was wrinkled, bald, and his few remaining hairs were of dazzling whiteness; he was bent very nearly double, and tottered feebly along, supported by a stick.

"What is this, O coachman?" said the prince. "A man with his blood all dried up, and his muscles glued to his body! His head is white; his teeth knock together; he is scarcely able to move along, even with the aid of that stick!"

"Prince," said the coachman, "this is Old Age. This man's senses are dulled; suffering has destroyed his spirit; he is contemned by his neighbours. Unable to help himself, he has been abandoned in this forest."

"Is this a peculiarity of his family?" demanded the prince, "or is it the law of the world? Tell me quickly."

"Prince," said the coachman, "it is neither a law of his family, nor a law of the kingdom. In every being youth is conquered by age. Your own father and mother and all your relations will end in old age. There is no other issue to humanity."

"Then youth is blind and ignorant," said the prince, "and sees not the future. If this body is to be the abode of old age, what have I to do with pleasure and its intoxications? Turn round the chariot, and drive me back to the palace!"

Consternation was in the minds of all the courtiers at this untoward occurrence; but the odd circumstance of all was that no one was ever able to bring to condign punishment the miserable author of the mischief. The old man could never be found.

King Śuddhodana was at first quite beside himself with tribulation. Soldiers were summoned from the distant provinces, and a cordon of detachments thrown out to a distance of four miles in each direction, to keep the other presaging tokens from the prince.[1] By-and-by the king became a little more quieted. A ridiculous accident had interfered with his plans: "If my son could see the Garden of Happiness he never would become a hermit." The king determined that another attempt should be made. But this time the precautions were doubled.

On the first occasion the prince left the Palace of Summer by the eastern gate. The second expedition was through the southern gate.

But another untoward event occurred. As the prince was driving along in his chariot, suddenly he saw close to him a man emaciated, ill, loathsome, burning with fever. Companionless, uncared for, he tottered along, breathing with extreme difficulty.

"Coachman," said the prince, "what is this man, livid and loathsome in body, whose senses are dulled, and whose limbs are withered? His stomach is oppressing him; he is covered with filth. Scarcely can he draw the breath of life!"

"Prince," said the coachman, "this is Sickness. This poor man is attacked with a grievous malady. Strength and comfort have shunned him. He is friendless, hopeless, without a country, without an asylum. The fear of death is before his eyes."

"If the health of man," said Buddha, "is but the sport of a dream, and the fear of coming evils can put on so loathsome

---

[1] Spence Hardy, "Manual of Buddhism," p. 155, *et seq.*

E

a shape, how can the wise man, who has seen what life really means, indulge in its vain delights? Turn back, coachman, and drive me to the palace!"

The angry king, when he heard what had occurred, gave orders that the sick man should be seized and punished, but although a price was placed on his head, and he was searched for far and wide, he could never be caught. A clue to this is furnished by a passage in the "Lalita Vistara." The sick man was in reality one of the Spirits of the Pure Abode, masquerading in sores and spasms. These Spirits of the Pure Abode are also called the Buddhas of the past, in many passages.

And it would almost seem as if some influence, malefic or otherwise, was stirring the good King Śuddhodana. Unmoved by failure, he urged the prince to a third effort. The chariot this time was to set out by the western gate. Greater precautions than ever were adopted. The chain of guards was posted at least twelve miles off from the Palace of Summer. But the Buddhas of the Ten Horizons again arrested the prince. His chariot was suddenly crossed by a phantom funeral procession. A phantom corpse, smeared with the orthodox mud, and spread with a sheet, was carried on a bier. Phantom women wailed, and phantom musicians played on the drum and the Indian flute. No doubt also, phantom Brahmins chanted hymns to Jâtavedas, to bear away the immortal part of the dead man to the home of the Pitris.

"What is this?" said the prince. "Why do these women beat their breasts and tear their hair? Why do these good folks cover their heads with the dust of the ground. And that strange form upon its litter, wherefore is it so rigid?"

"Prince," said the charioteer, "this is Death! Yon form, pale and stiffened, can never again walk and move. Its owner has gone to the unknown caverns of Yama. His father, his mother, his child, his wife cry out to him, but he cannot hear."

Buddha was sad.

"Woe be to youth, which is the sport of age! Woe be to

health, which is the sport of many maladies! Woe be to life, which is as a breath! Woe be to the idle pleasures which debauch humanity! But for the 'five aggregations' there would be no age, sickness, nor death. Go back to the city. I must compass the deliverance."

A fourth time the prince was urged by his father to visit the Garden of Happiness. The chain of guards this time was sixteen miles away. The exit was by the northern gate. But suddenly a calm man of gentle mien, wearing an ochre-red cowl, was seen in the roadway.

" Who is this?" said the prince, "rapt, gentle, peaceful in mien? He looks as if his mind were far away elsewhere. He carries a bowl in his hand."

" Prince, this is the New Life," said the charioteer. " That man is of those whose thoughts are fixed on the eternal Brahma [Brahmacharin]. He seeks the divine voice. He seeks the divine vision. He carries the alms-bowl of the holy beggar [bhikshu]. His mind is calm, because the gross lures of the lower life can vex it no more."

" Such a life I covet," said the prince. " The lusts of man are like the sea-water—they mock man's thirst instead of quenching it. I will seek the divine vision, and give immortality to man!"

King Śuddhodana was beside himself. He placed five hundred corseleted Śâkyas at every gate of the Palace of Summer. Chains of sentries were round the walls, which were raised and strengthened. A phalanx of loving wives, armed with javelins, was posted round the prince's bed to "narrowly watch" him. The king ordered all the allurements of sense to be constantly presented to the prince.

" Let the women of the zenana cease not for an instant their concerts and mirth and sports. Let them shine in silks and sparkle in diamonds and emeralds."

Mahâ Prajâpati, the aunt who since Queen Mâyâ's death has acted as foster-mother, has charge of these pretty young women, and she incites them to encircle the prince in a " cage of gold."

The allegory is in reality a great battle between two camps

—the denizens of the Kâmaloka, or the Domains of Appetite, and the denizens of the Brahmaloka, the Domains of Pure Spirit. The latter are unseen, but not unfelt.

For one day, when the prince reclined on a silken couch, listening to the sweet crooning of four or five brown-skinned, large-eyed Indian girls, his eyes suddenly assumed a dazed and absorbed look, and the rich hangings and garlands and intricate trellis-work of the golden apartment were still present, but dim to his mind. And music and voices, more sweet than he had ever listened to, seemed faintly to reach him. I will write down some of the verses he heard, as they contain the mystic inner teaching of Buddhism.

" Mighty prop of humanity
　March in the pathway of the Rishis of old,
　Go forth from this city !
　Upon this desolate earth,
　When thou hast acquired the priceless knowledge of the Jinas,
　When thou hast become a perfect Buddha,
　Give to all flesh the baptism (river) of the Kingdom of Righteousness.
　Thou who once didst sacrifice thy feet, thy hands, thy precious body,
　　　and all thy riches for the world,
　Thou whose life is pure, save flesh from its miseries !
　In the presence of reviling be patient, O conqueror of self !
　Lord of those who possess two feet, go forth on thy mission !
　Conquer the evil one and his army."

Thus run some more of these gâthâs :—

" Light of the world ! [lamp du monde—Foucaux],
　In former kalpas this vow was made by thee :
　'For the worlds that are a prey to death and sickness I will be a
　　　refuge !'
　Lion of men, master of those that walk on two feet, the time for thy
　　　mission has come !
　Under the sacred Bo-tree acquire immortal dignity, and give Amrita
　　　(immortality) to all !
　When thou wert a king (in a former existence), and a subject inso-
　　　lently said to thee : ' These lands and cities, give them to me !'
　Thou wert rejoiced and not troubled.
　Once when thou wert a virtuous Rishi, and a cruel king in anger hacked
　　　off thy limbs, in thy death agony milk flowed from thy feet and thy
　　　hands.
　When thou didst dwell on a mountain as the Rishi Syama, a king
　　　having transfixed thee with poisoned arrows, didst thou not forgive
　　　this king ?

When thou wert the king of antelopes, didst thou not save thine enemy the hunter from a torrent?

When thou wert an elephant and a hunter pierced thee, thou forgavest him, and didst reward him with thy beautiful tusks!

Once when thou wert a she-bear thou didst save a man from a torrent swollen with snow. Thou didst feed him on roots and fruit until he grew strong;

And when he went away and brought back men to kill thee, thou forgavest him!

Once when thou wert a white horse,[1]

In pity for the suffering of man,

Thou didst fly across heaven to the region of the evil demons,

To secure the happiness of mankind.

Persecutions without end,

Revilings and many prisons,

Death and murder,

These hast thou suffered with love and patience,

Forgiving thine executioners.

Kingless, men seek thee for a king!

'Stablish them in the way of Brahma and of the ten virtues,

That when they pass away from amongst their fellow-men, they may all go to the abode of Brahma.

In times past, having seen men fallen into evil ways, and vexed by age, sickness, and many griefs, thou didst make them understand which was the straight way from this world of destruction!

Conqueror of the darkness, thou hast done priceless service to the worlds!

To creatures of all sorts thou madest many offerings.

Thou gavest thy wife, thy son, thy daughter, thy body, thy kingdom, thy life!

Strong king! thou didst prefer the glory of blameless deeds.

Thou who art Krishna, Nimindara, Nimi, Brahmadatta, Dharmachinti, etc., having pondered upon the aim of life, thou hast abandoned to mortals things difficult to abandon.

Rishi of kings, of body like the moon-god (Chandra), thy march is over the horizon and the dust.

King of Kaśi (Benares), thou proclaimest the peace of heaven.

Long hast thou seen that the life of man is like the sands of the Ganges.

In pursuit of the spiritual knowledge (Bodhi), O first of the pure! thou hast made innumerable offerings to the Buddhas:

To Amoghadarsi, the flowers of the Sâla-tree;

To Vairochana, a gentle thought;

To Chandana, a torch of kuśa-grass;

---

[1] Yearly the sun-god as the zodiacal horse (Aries) was supposed by the Vedic Âryans to die to save all flesh. Hence the horse-sacrifice.

To Remi thou didst fling a handful of gold-dust!

Didst thou not encourage Dharmeśvara, when he was teaching the law, by saying, 'Well!'

Upon beholding Sarmantadarsi thou didst cry, 'Adoration! Adoration!'

Thou gavest the garb of the Muni to Nâgadatta!

To Sâkya Muni [1] thou gavest a handful of suvarṇas [pieces of gold]."

" By these gâthâs the prince is exhorted," says the narrative. And whilst the Jinas sing, beautiful women, with flowers and perfumes, and jewels and rich dresses, try to incite him to mortal love. Again the music of the immortals breaks through their songs :—

" Guide of the world! think quickly of thy resolve to appear in it ;
Make no delay!

In the old times a precious treasure, gold, silver, and ornaments, were abandoned by thee.

To Bhaichadyarâja thou didst offer a precious parasol ;

Thou gavest thy kingdom to Tâgaraśikhin ;

To Mahâpradîpa thou didst offer thine own self ;

To Dipañkara a blue lotus ;

Remember the Buddhas of the past, their teachings and thy sacrifices.

Contemn not poor mortals without a guide.

When thou didst see Dipankara thou didst acquire the Great Patience and the five transcendental sacrifices!

Then, after innumerable kalpas, in all parts of the world, having taken delight in making offerings inconceivably precious to all these Buddhas,

The kalpas have rolled away,

The Buddhas have gone to Nirvâna,

And all their bodies, that once belonged to thee, and even their names —Where are they?

It is the work of the Law of Righteousness to put an end to the aggregations of matter.

That which has been created is not durable.

Earthly empire, earthly desire, earthly riches are as a dream.

In the terminable kalpas of the world, like a fire that burns with a fearful light, sickness, age, and death draw near with their tremors.

The Law of Righteousness alone can put an end to substance. What is composite is not durable.

Look at the unhappy creatures of earth ;

Go forth into the world!"

---

[1] Much of this is plainly esoteric Buddhism. The inspirer of prophets, and not the prophet himself, is addressed.

But the king was on the other side.

It is recorded that he offered to resign his royal umbrella in favour of his son. His urgent entreaty that the prince should abandon all thoughts of a religious life was answered thus :—

"Sire, I desire four gifts. Grant me these, and I will remain in the Palace of Summer."

'What are they?" said King Śuddodhana.

"Grant that age may never seize me. Grant that I may retain the bright hues of youth. Grant that sickness may have no power over me. Grant that my life may be without end." [1]

This gives us the very essence of the apologue. Mâra, the tempter, describes the story in a sentence :—

"This is a son of King Śuddodhana, who has left his kingdom to obtain deathless life [amṛita]." [2]

About this time Gopâ had a strange dream. She beheld the visible world with its mountains upheaved and its forests overturned. The sun was darkened, the moon fell from heaven. Her own diadem had fallen off her head, and all her beautiful pearl necklaces and gold chains were broken. Her poor hands and feet were cut off ; and the diadem and ornaments of her husband were also scattered in confusion upon the bed where they were both lying. In the darkness of night lurid flames came forth from the city, and the gilded bars that had been recently put up to detain the prince were snapped. Afar the great ocean was boiling with a huge turmoil, and Mount Meru shook to its very foundations.

She consulted her husband about this dream, and he gave her the rather obvious interpretation that this dismemberment of her mortal body, and this passing away of the visible universe and its splendours, was of good, and not bad augury. She was becoming detached from the seen, the organic ; her inner vision was opening. She had seen the splendid handle of Buddha's parasol broken. This meant that in a short time he was to become the "unique parasol of the world."

But to bring about this result more quickly, the Spirits of

1 "Lalita Vistara," p. 192.   2 Ibid., p. 287.

the Pure Abode have conceived a new project. The beautiful women of the zenana are the main seductions of Mâra, the tempter, whom philologists prove to be closely connected with Kâma, the god of love. The Spirits of the Pure Abode determine that the prince shall see these women in a new light. By a subtle influence they induce him to visit the apartments of the women at the moment that they, the Jinas, have put all these women into a sound sleep.

Everything is in disorder—the clothes of the women, their hair, their trinkets. Some are lolling ungracefully on couches, some have hideous faces, some cough, some laugh sillily in their dreams, some rave. Also deformities and blemishes that female art had been careful to conceal are now made prominent by the superior magic of the spirits. This one has a discoloured neck, this one an ill-formed leg, this one a clumsy fat arm. Smiles have become grins, and fascinations a naked hideousness. Sprawling on couches in ungainly attitudes, all lie amidst their tawdry finery, their silent tambourines and lutes.

"Of a verity I am in a graveyard!" said the prince, in great disgust.

And now comes an incident in his life which is of the highest importance. He has determined to leave the palace altogether. "Then Buddha uncrossed his legs, and turning his eyes towards the eastern horizon, he put aside the precious trellis-work, and repaired to the roof of the palace. Then joining the ten fingers of his hands, he thought of all the Buddhas and rendered homage to all the Buddhas, and, looking across the skies, he saw the Master of all the gods, he of the ten hundred eyes" (Daśaśata Nayana). Plainly he prayed to Indra. The Romantic Life also retains this incident, but it omits Indra, and makes Buddha pray only to all the Buddhas.

At the moment that Buddha joined his hands in homage towards the eastern horizon, the star Pushya, which had presided at his birth, was rising. The prince on seeing it said to Chandaka—

"The benediction that is on me has attained its perfection

this very night. Give me at once the king of horses covered with jewels!"

"Guide of men!" said the poor charioteer, "thou knowest the hour and the commands of the king. The great gates are shut."

Buddha persisted, and mounted his good horse Kaṇtaka, The gates were opened by the heavenly spirits. And through them he passed out of the debasing palace with the seven moats. It was the change to the higher life. He became a yogi.

The Buddhist movement was the revolt of the higher Brahminism against the lower. It was led by one of the most searching reformers that ever appeared upon the page of history. He conceived that the only remedy lay in awakening the spiritual life of the individual. The bloody sacrifice, caste, the costly tank pilgrimages, must be swept completely away.

This is proved by a very valuable Sûtra, the "Sutta Nipâta," one of the most ancient books of Ceylon.

It records that when the great Muni was at Śrâvasti (Sahet Mahet), certain old Brahmins came to listen to his teaching. They asked him if the Brahmin religion (Brahmaṇa Dharma) was the same as in ancient days. Buddha replied that, in olden time, the Brâhmaṇa Dharma was completely different. It was this Dharma that he proposed to restore in its original purity. The points of difference that he detailed were these—

1. The ancient Brâhmaṇas were simple ascetics (isayo), who had abandoned the "objects of the five senses."

2. They ate contentedly the food that was placed at their door. They had no cattle, or gold, or corn. The gold and corn of holy dreaming alone was theirs.

3. They never married a woman of another caste, or bought wives. The most rigid continence was theirs.[1]

4. They made sacrifices of rice, butter, etc., and never

---

[1] Fausböll "Sutta Nipâta," p. 49, ver. 10. It was not clear whether Buddha means that marriage was quite unknown to them. The verses are contradictory.

killed the cows, the best friends of man, the givers of medicines.

5. But the kings of the earth by-and-by grew powerful, and had palaces and chariots and jewelled women.

6. Then the Brâhmaṇas grew covetous of these beautiful women and this vast wealth, and schemed to gain both. They instituted costly sacrifices, the horse sacrifice (assa-medha), the man sacrifice (purisa-medha), and other rites. Through these they obtained costly offerings—gold, cows, beds, garments, jewelled women, bright carpets, palaces, grain, chariots drawn by fine steeds.

7. "Hundreds of thousands of cows" were slaughtered at these sacrifices—"cows that like goats do not hurt any one with their feet or with either of their horns—tender cows, yielding vessels of milk.

" Seizing them by the horns, the king caused them to be slain with a weapon."

The true Dharma being lost, the world plunged into sensuality, caste disputes, blood. That lost Dharma it is the mission of Buddha to hold up once more " as an oil lamp in the dark, that those who have eyes may see." [1]

I now come to another piece of evidence. The " Tevigga Sutta," or " Sûtra," plainly belongs to the " Little Vehicle," and shows that in the view of its disciples Buddha proclaimed the existence of an intelligent eternal God.

When the great Tathâgata was dwelling at Manasâkata in the mango grove, some Brahmins, learned in the three Vedas, come to consult him on the question of union with the eternal Brahma. They ask if they are in the right pathway towards that union. Buddha replies at great length. He suggests an ideal case. He supposes that a man has fallen in love with the " most beautiful woman in the land." Day and night he dreams of her, but has never seen her. He does not know whether she is tall or short, of Brahmin or Sûdra caste, of dark or fair complexion ; he does not even know her name. The Brahmins are asked if the talk of that man about that woman be wise or foolish. They confess that it is " foolish

---

[1] " Sutta Nipâta," p. 52.

talk." Buddha then applies the same train of reasoning to them. The Brahmins versed in the three Vedas are made to confess that they have never seen Brahma, that they do not know whether he is tall or short, or anything about him, and that all their talk about union with him is also foolish talk. They are mounting a crooked staircase, and do not know whether it leads to a mansion or a precipice. They are standing on the bank of a river and calling to the other bank to come to them.

Now it seems to me that if Buddha were the uncompromising teacher of atheism that Dr. Rhys Davids pictures him, he has at this point an admirable opportunity of urging his views. The Brahmins, he would of course contend, knew nothing about Brahma, for the simple reason that no such being as Brahma exists.

But this is exactly the line that Buddha does not take. His argument is that the Brahmins knew nothing of Brahma, because Brahma is purely spiritual, and they are purely materialistic.

Five "Veils," he shows, hide Brahma from mortal ken. These are—

1. The Veil of Lustful Desire.
2. The Veil of Malice.
3. The Veil of Sloth and Idleness.
4. The Veil of Pride and Self-rightcousness.
5. The Veil of Doubt.

Buddha then goes on with his questionings:

" Is Brahma in possession of wives and wealth ? "

" He is not, Gautama," answers Vâsettha the Brahmin.

" Is his mind full of anger, or free from anger ? "

" Free from anger, Gautama."

" Is his mind full of malice, or free from malice ? "

" Free from malice, Gautama."

" Is his mind depraved or pure ? "

" It is pure, Gautama."

" Has he self-mastery, or has he not ? "

" He has, Gautama."

The Brahmins are then questioned about themselves.

" Are the Brahmins versed in the three Vedas, in possession of wives and wealth, or are they not ? "

" They are, Gautama."

" Have they anger in their hearts, or have they not ? "

" They have, Gautama."

" Do they bear malice, or do they not ? "

" They do, Gautama."

" Are they pure in heart, or are they not ? "

" They are not, Gautama."

" Have they self-mastery, or have they not ? "

" They have not, Gautama."

These replies provoke, of course, the very obvious retort that no point of union can be found between such dissimilar entities. Brahma is free from malice, sinless, self-contained, so, of course, it is only the sinless that can hope to be in harmony with him.

Vâsettha then puts this question : " It has been told me, Gautama, that Śramaṇa Gautama knows the way to the state of union with Brahma ? "

" Brahma I know, Vâsettha," says Buddha in reply, " and the world of Brahma, and the path leading to it."

The humbled Brahmins learned in the three Vedas then ask Buddha to " show them the way to a state of union with Brahma."

Buddha replies at considerable length, drawing a sharp contrast between the lower Brahminism and the higher Brahminism, the " householder " and the " houseless one." The householder Brahmins are gross, sensual, avaricious, insincere. They practice for lucre black magic, fortune-telling, cozenage. They gain the ear of kings, breed wars, predict victories, sacrifice life, spoil the poor. As a foil to this he paints the recluse, who has renounced all worldly things, and is pure, self-possessed, happy.

To teach this " higher life," a Tathâgata " from time to time is born into the world, blessed and worthy, abounding in wisdom, a guide to erring mortals." He sees the universe face to face, the spirit world of Brahma and that of Mâra the tempter. He makes his knowledge known to others. The houseless one, instructed by him, "lets his mind pervade one quarter of the world with thoughts of pity, sympathy, and equanimity ; and so the second, and so the third, and so the fourth. And thus the whole wide world, above, below, around, and everywhere, does he continue to pervade with heart of pity, sympathy and equanimity, far-reaching, grown great, and beyond measure." [1]

"Verily this, Vâsettha, is the way to a state of union with Brahma," and he proceeds to announce that the Bhikshu, or Buddhist beggar, "who is free from anger, free from malice, pure in mind, master of himself, will, after death, when the body is dissolved, become united with Brahma." The Brahmins at once see the full force of this teaching. It is as a conservative in their eyes that Buddha figures, and not an innovator. He takes the side of the ancient spiritual religion of the country against rapacious innovators.

"Thou hast set up what was thrown down," they say to him. In the Burmese Life he is described more than once as one who has set the overturned chalice once more upon its base.

An extract from the Muṇḍaka Upanishad of the Atharva Veda may here throw a light on Brahma and union with him : "He is great and incomprehensible by the senses, and consequently his nature is beyond human conception. He, though more subtle than vacuum itself, shines in various ways. From those who do not know him he is at a greater distance than the limits of space, and to those who acquire a knowledge of him he is near ; and whilst residing in animate creatures is perceived, although obscurely, by those who apply their thoughts to him. He is not perceptible by vision, nor is he describable by means of speech, neither can he be the object of any of the organs of sense, nor can he be conceived by the help of austerities or religious rites ; but a person whose mind is purified by the light of true knowledge through incessant contemplation perceives him the most pure God. Such is the invisible Supreme Being. He should be seen in the heart wherein breath consisting of five species rests. The

[1] "Buddhist Suttas," p. 201.

mind being perfectly freed from impurity, God, who spreads over the mind and all the senses, imparts a knowledge of himself to the heart."[1]

In point of fact the language of the Buddhist mystic is very like that of all other mystics. Thomas à Kempis, in his "Soliloquy of the Soul," has a chapter headed, "On the Union of the Soul with God."[2] Indeed, all the Christian mystics sought this "union" quite as earnestly as Buddha. St. Theresa had her *oraison d'union*.[3] St. Augustine based all his mysticism on the text (John xiv. 23), "Jesus answered and said unto him, If a man love Me, he will keep My words: and My Father will love him, and We will come unto him, and make Our abode with him."[4]

Clement of 'Alexandria sketches the end to be kept in view by the "Christian Gnostic:" "Dwelling with the Lord He will continue His familiar friend, sharing the same hearth according to the Spirit."[5]

Madame Guyon renewed her mystical "Marriage with the Child Jesus" every year.

The mystics of all religions sought this union with God by means of extasia. The method is described in the Persian Sharistan and the Zerdusht Afshâr; and the processes are completely similar to those of the Indian yogi. He whom the ancient Persian called Izad, and the modern Persian Allah, is thus described by Maulâvi Jami—

"Thou but an atom art, He, the Great Whole. But if for a few days thou meditate with care on the Whole thou becomest one with it."[6]

Mr. Vaughan, in his "Hours with the Mystics," shows that the motto of the Neo-Platonist was, "Withdraw into thyself; and the Adytum of thine own soul will reveal to thee profounder secrets than the cave of Mithras." He asserts that a mystic, according to Dionysius the Areopagite, is not merely a sacred personage acquainted with the doctrines,

[1] Rajah Rammohun Roy, "Translation of the Veds," p. 36.
[2] Ch. xiii.   [3] Madame Guyon, "Discours Chrétiens," vol. ii. p. 344.
[4] Cited by Madame Guyon.   [5] "Misc.," p. 60.
[6] Olcott, "Yoga Philosophy," p. 271.

and participator in the rites called mysteries, but one also
who, exactly after the Neo-Platonist pattern, by mortifying
the body attains the " divine union." [1] Cornelius Agrippa
and Behmen held the same views.

I may mention, as an interesting fact, that catholic
mysticism has very nearly the same terminology as Buddhism.
Madame Guyon and the mystics have their " states " likewise,
the " mystic indifference," [2] " l'anéantissement," [3] the mystical
" death." [4] When Buddha was performing his " Dhyâna," it
is said that the " Chakravâla " (visible universe) became
invisible, and the azure domains of the Buddhas (the spirit
world) " luminous." [5] Madame Guyon, in her " Moyen Court,"
cites Revelations iii. 7, 8, to show that the mystic " key of
David " consists in " shutting the eyes of the body and
opening the eyes of the soul." [6] Of course this " annihilation,"
this " death," this " indifference " only refers to the lower life
with St. Francois de Sales and Madame Guyon. And I think
we must say the same of early Buddhism.

---

[1] Vaughan, vol. i. p. 22.   [2] L. Guerrier, " Madame Guyon," p. 342.
 [3] Ibid., p. 112.   [4] Ibid., p. 116.
 [5] " Lalita Vistara," p. 267.   [6] " Moyen Court," p. 10.

CHAPTER VI.

The Nazarite—Mystical and Anti-mystical Israel—Christ usually supposed to have belonged to the latter—Position combated—Early Persecution of Disciples.

THE NAZARITE.

THE theory about Christ at present the most in vogue is based upon the idea that He accepted the religion of Israel as interpreted by its recognized interpreters. It is held that when He declared that not a jot or tittle of the Law should be relaxed until the heavens and earth shall pass away, He alluded to the Law of Moses as interpreted by the dominant party. His life in consequence, in respect to customs, conduct, and rites, was strictly in accordance with the Mosaic edicts.

Dr. Lightfoot, as well as Baur, and Strauss, and Gibbon, holds this view. The latter writers lay emphasis on the fact that He announced that His mission was to be confined to the house of Israel, and that He called the rest of the world "dogs." Dr. Lightfoot expresses practically the same idea ; for he says that, "after Christ's death the Church was still confined to one nation," and that "the Master Himself had left no express instructions" for a wider propagandism. "Emancipation," he says, from the "swathing-bands" of the Mosaic ritual, came from the Apostles "under the guidance of the Holy Spirit,"[1] the doctor failing to explain why in the matter of institutions that God Almighty had just come on earth in bodily form expressly to perpetuate any "emancipation," was required.

[1] "Commentary on Galatians," pp. 286, 287.

But will this theory bear scrutiny? In an early chapter of St. Matthew's Gospel, we read the following :—

" And, behold, there was a man which had his hand withered. And they asked Him, saying, Is it lawful to heal on the sabbath days? that they might accuse Him. And He said unto them, What man shall there be among you, that shall have one sheep, and if it fall into a pit on the sabbath day, will he not lay hold on it, and lift it out? How much then is a man better than a sheep? Wherefore it is lawful to do well on the sabbath days. Then saith He to the man, Stretch forth thine hand. And he stretched it forth; and it was restored whole, like as the other. Then the Pharisees went out, and held a council against Him, how they might destroy Him. But when Jesus knew it, He withdrew Himself from thence : and great multitudes followed Him, and he healed them all ; And charged them that they should not make Him known " (Matt. xii. 10–16).

This is from Matt. ix. 32–35—

" As they went out, behold, they brought to Him a dumb man possessed with a devil. And when the devil was cast out, the dumb spake : and the multitudes marvelled, saying, It was never so seen in Israel. But the Pharisees said, He casteth out devils through the prince of the devils. And Jesus went about all the cities and villages, teaching in their synagogues, and preaching the gospel of the kingdom, and healing every sickness and every disease among the people."

This is another passage—

" They answered Him, We be Abraham's seed, and were never in bondage to any man : how sayest Thou, Ye shall be made free? Jesus answered them, Verily, verily, I say unto you, Whosoever committeth sin is the servant of sin. And the servant abideth not in the house for ever : but the Son abideth ever. If the Son therefore shall make you free, ye shall be free indeed. I know that ye are Abraham's seed ; but ye seek to kill Me, because My word hath no place in you. I speak that which I have seen with My Father : and ye do that which ye have seen with your father. They answered and said unto Him, Abraham is our father. Jesus

F

saith unto them, If ye were Abraham's children, ye would do
the works of Abraham. But now ye seek to kill Me, a man
that hath told you the truth, which I have heard of God : this
did not Abraham " (John viii. 33–40).

It will be seen from these passages that the Jews sought
the life of Jesus on the following charges :—

1. Sabbath breaking.

2. Demonology.

3. "Speaking the truth," or assailing the views of the
dominant party.

If one of these narratives is an authentic narrative, it is
plain that the theory that Jesus was a strict observer of the
Law of Moses, as interpreted by the dominant party, falls to
the ground.

I come to a still more striking passage. It seems to me
to traverse the position of Bishop Lightfoot, who, in his
"Commentary on the Colossians," maintains that Christ
attended the three bloody festivals of the sacrificial or anti-
mystical Israel.

"And the Pharisees also, who were covetous, heard all
these things : and they derided Him. And He said unto
them, Ye are they which justify yourselves before men ; but
God knoweth your hearts : for that which is highly esteemed
among men is abomination in the sight of God. The Law
and the prophets were until John : since that time the kingdom of God is preached, and every man presseth into it.
And it is easier for heaven and earth to pass, than one tittle
of the law to fail " (Luke xvi. 14–17).

This passage is of great importance. If Christ actually
uttered the speech contained in it, it unmistakably shows
that, far from considering the Mosaic edicts as interpreted by
their recognized interpreters binding until the day of judgment, he believed them to have been annulled by John the
Baptist, who, according to Josephus, was put to death to
satisfy the priestly party.

Here is another pregnant passage—

"And He came to Nazareth, where He had been brought
up : and, as His custom was, He went into the synagogue on

the sabbath day, and stood up for to read. And there was delivered unto Him the book of the prophet Esaias. And when He had opened the book, He found the place where it was written, The Spirit of the Lord is upon Me, because He hath anointed Me to preach the gospel to the poor; He hath sent Me to heal the broken-hearted, to preach deliverance to the captives, and recovering of sight to the blind, to set at liberty them that are bruised, to preach the acceptable year of the Lord. And He closed the book, and He gave it again to the minister, and sat down. And the eyes of all them that were in the synagogue were fastened on Him. And He began to say unto them, This day is this scripture fulfilled in your ears. And all bare Him witness, and wondered at the gracious words which proceeded out of His mouth. And they said, Is not this Joseph's son? And He said unto them, Ye will surely say unto Me this proverb, Physician, heal Thyself: whatsover we have heard done in Capernaum, do also here in Thy country. And He said, Verily I say unto you, No prophet is accepted in his own country. But I tell you of a truth, many widows were in Israel in the days of Elias, when the heaven was shut up three years and six months, when great famine was throughout all the land; But unto none of them was Elias sent, save unto Sarepta, a city of Sidon, unto a woman that was a widow. And many lepers were in Israel in the time of Eliseus the prophet; and none of them was cleansed, saving Naaman the Syrian. And all they in the synagogue, when they heard these things, were filled with wrath, and rose up, and thrust Him out of the city, and led Him unto the brow of the hill whereon their city was built, that they might cast him down headlong. But He, passing through the midst of them, went His way, and came down to Capernaum, a city of Galilee, and taught them on the sabbath days. And they were astonished at His doctrine: for His word was with power" (Luke iv. 16–32).

This seems of the greatest importance. Instead of beholding soldiers strike down their most prominent champion by reason of a mistaken password—a necessary inference if

Christ belonged to anti-mystical Israel,—we see here the word
" Messiah " interpreted by two sets of disputants with the
utmost precision.   Christ says that he is " Messiah," or
" Anointed," in the sense that Isaiah announces that he also
is " Anointed."   He is the "prophet," like Elijah.   The Spirit
of God is upon Him in order that He may preach the gospel
to the poor.   In 1 Kings xix. 16, we find also that Elisha
was anointed as Messiah.   The word, with the Jews, meant a
prophet as well as a king.

The action of anti-mystical Israel is equally intelligible.
They remember, of course, that it is laid down in the Tora
(Lev. xviii. 20), that "the prophet who shall presume to
speak a word " in God's name, which the Almighty has not
commanded him to speak must die.   They remember, also,
that divination (the occultism of rivals) is also (Lev. xviii.
10) a capital offence.   And if Christ had really pronounced
that the Law of Moses was annulled, the scribes and doctors
would quickly have jumped to the conclusion that a prophet
so speaking was not the mouthpiece of Jehovah, who had
positively pronounced that the law and covenant was an everlasting covenant (1 Chron. xvi. 17 ; Isa. xxiv. 5) ; and that
" the statutes, and ordinances, and the law, and the commandment which He wrote, was to be observed for evermore "
(2 Kings xvii. 37).

Another instructive group of facts may here be adduced—
the circumstances attending the death of Stephen.

We there see that within three short years of Christ's
death, there was a vast apparatus of persecution actively at
work.   St. Paul tells us that he himself persecuted to the
"death ; " that "entering every house and haling men and
women, he committed them to prison."   He shows also that
this vast apparatus of "havock," and "threatenings and
slaughter," had already branches in Damascus and in the
provinces, as well as in Jerusalem.   What is the explanation
of this ?   Certainly Caiaphas, who denied any after-life, could
at this time have had no view of Christ's Kingship in heavenly
abodes definite enough to stir up all this activity.   The explanation given by Dean Howson and Mr. Conybeare appears

the true one. These Christians were persecuted not because they were Christians, but because they were Jews, who set the Laws of Moses at defiance. Was not this the charge against Paul as late as his last visit to Jerusalem.

"And when the seven days were almost ended, the Jews which were of Asia, when they saw him in the temple, stirred up all the people, and laid hands on him, crying out, Men of Israel, help: this is the man, that teacheth all men everywhere against the people, and the law, and this place" (Acts xxi. 27).

As I go on I shall make it plain that from the very earliest institution of the disciples the Laws of Moses, as interpreted by the dominant party, were systematically violated. From the same early period I shall make it also plain that the recognized interpreters of those laws sought the lives of Christ and His followers for capital offences against Jerusalem and the Mosaic edicts. And the answer of the Christians from first to last may be summed up in the words of Paul—

"Neither against the law of the Jews, neither against the temple, nor yet against Cæsar, have I offended anything at all" (Acts xxv. 8).

What is the meaning of this paradox? Here we have two sets of disputants, both of a nation not behind, but rather ahead of the rest of the world in acuteness, reasoning apparently with the inconsequence of a nightmare. The position of the first set is something after this fashion. Jehovah, they say, through his Prophet Moses, has categorically given forth certain edicts for the avowed object of making the Hebrew nation an ensample to the other nations of the earth for ever and ever. Thus it has been ordained that every male shall come up to Jerusalem, the capital city, for the three great yearly festivals. Certain rites and sacrifices must then be gone through to honour God and enrich the priesthood. It is ordained also that the sabbath day shall be strictly kept holy. It is ordained that the phenomena of supernaturalism, prophecy, healing by exorcism, etc., shall not be practised except under the supervision of the recognized priesthood. And yet the rival party violate these plain edicts, not inad-

vertently, upon occasion ; but perpetually, on system. Plainly
the punishments of the Laws of Moses, whatever their rigour,
must everywhere be put in force to protect the religion of
Jehovah.

To all this the second party make one plain answer:
" Not one tittle of the law have we violated, or will we violate
till doomsday."

Is it not plain, that by the word "law," each party mean
something different.

This will, I think, come out more clearly if we consider
the curious way in which another section of the Jews, the
Essenes and Therapeuts, like the early Christians, professed
to be extra strict followers of the edicts of Moses, and yet
violated those laws at every turn.

" Our law-giver," says Philo, " trained into fellowship great
numbers of pupils who bear the name of Essenes, being, I
imagine, honoured with the appellation by virtue of their
holiness."   This is from his work, " Every Virtuous Man is
Free."   A passage from another work of his leaves us in no
doubt as to who this legislator was to taken to be—

" I will set in contrast the entertainments of those that
have consecrated their private life and themselves to gnosis
and the contemplation of the affairs of Nature, in accordance
with the most sacred guidance of the Prophet Moses " (" Vit.
Contempl."). And Josephus does not hesitate to describe these
mystics as refusing to take part altogether in the yearly festivals and the sacrifices of the Mosaic ritual as interpreted by
those who sat in Moses's seat.

" They perform no sacrifices on account of the different
rules of purity which they observe. Hence, being excluded
from the common sanctuary, they perform sacred rites of their
own " (" Antiq.," 1, 2, and 5). That the Essenes were also persecuted, I think is quite plain. Philo talks of their " hiding-
places," and of the terrible oaths that each took to preserve
the secrets of the order " in the presence of force and at the
hazard of his life."   Josephus alludes to the terrible tortures
that they cheerfully submitted to, rather than eat of things
forbidden.   It is true that this second assertion refers to them

at a later date than the description of Philo ; but Christ tells
us that from the date of Zacharius, and even of Abel, mystical
Israel was persecuted from city to city at the blood-stained
hands of the Pharisees and Scribes (Matt. xxiii. 35).

My citations from Origen and the " Kabbalah," in my first
chapter, explain in part the crucial issues between mystical
and anti-mystical Israel.

The latter party said practically : We have a book of
sacred law, and that law must be interpreted like any other
legal document, or immense confusion will arise.

The mystics replied that all scriptures are written by
mystics to teach mysticism, and a book must be judged by
the canons of its writers. The secret wisdom handed down
in the " Kabbalah " taught them that the Tora was intended
to conceal more than it was intended to reveal. There was
a knowledge that was made known to the " Chosen of God "
after painful initiations. It was called the " Luminous Mirror,"
in contrast with the " Non-luminous Mirror," the vision of
ordinary mortals. It was called the " Tree of Life," as contra-
distinguished from the " Tree of Knowledge." [1]

" Come and see when the soul reaches that place which
is called the Treasury of Life—she enjoys a bright and luminous
mirror which receives its light from the highest heaven. The
soul could not bear this light but for the luminous mantle
which she puts on. For just as the soul when sent to this
earth puts on an earthly garment to preserve herself here, so
she receives above a shining garment in order to be able to
look without injury into the mirror whose light proceeds
from the Lord of Light. Moses, too, could not approach to
look into that higher light which he saw without putting
on such an ethereal garment as it is written—' And Moses
went into the midst of the cloud,' which is translated by
means of the cloud wherewith he wrapped himself as if dressed
in a garment. At that time Moses almost discarded the
whole of his earthly nature, as it is written—' And Moses was
on the mountain forty days and forty nights.' And he thus
approached that dark cloud where God is enthroned. In this

---

[1] Ginsburg, " The Kabbalah," p. 37.

wise the departed spirits of the righteous dress themselves in the upper regions in luminous garments, to be able to endure that light which streams from the Lord of Light."[1]

Origen calls this luminous mirror the "soul" of the scriptures, whereas the historical part is "body," is intended only for minds yet in darkness.

Clement of Alexandria also held that there was a twofold knowledge, and that the higher knowledge was imparted by Christ to James, Peter, John, and Paul. "It was not designed for the multitude, but communicated to those only who were capable of receiving it orally, not by writing."[2]

The same system was prominent amongst the Essenes, who expounded their "hereditary laws" every seventh day. "Then one takes the books and reads," says Philo; "and another of the most experienced comes forward and expounds such things as are not well known, for most things are philosophically treated among them through symbols, according to the old-fashioned mode of pursuit."[3]

Of the Therapeuts he writes also: "For they read the sacred scriptures, and seek after wisdom by allegorical exposition of the hereditary philosophy, inasmuch as they regard what constitutes the letter of each utterance as the symbol of a nature that is withheld from sight but revealed in the hidden meanings. They possess, besides, compositions of ancient men who were the founders of the school, and bequeathed many a memorial of the allegorical manner of which they avail themselves by way of archetypes, and so closely follow the method of the original school."[4]

Let us now study mystical Israel a little more closely, beginning with the Essenes and Therapeuts.

[1] Ginsburg, "The Kabbalah," p. 38.
[2] See "Clement of Alexandria," by Dr. Kaye, Bishop of Lincoln, p. 241.
[3] "Every Virtuous Man is Free."   [4] Philo, "Vit. Contempl."

CHAPTER VII.

MYSTICAL ISRAEL.

Neander divides Israel at the date of Christ into three
sections—

1. Phariseeism, the " dead theology of the letter."

2. Sadduceeism, "debasing of the spiritual life into worldliness."

3. Essenism, Israel mystical—a "commingling of Judaism
with the old Oriental theosophy."[1]

Concerning this latter section, Philo wrote a letter to a
man named Hephæstion, of which the following is a portion :—

" I am sorry to find you saying that you are not likely to
visit Alexandria again. This restless, wicked city can present
but few attractions, I grant, to a lover of philosophic quiet.
But I cannot commend the extreme to which I see so many
hastening. A passion for ascetic seclusion is becoming daily
more prevalent among the devout and the thoughtful, whether
Jew or Gentile. Yet surely the attempt to combine contemplation and action should not be so soon abandoned. A man
ought at least to have evinced some competency for the discharge of the social duties before he abandons them for the
divine. First the less, then the greater.

" I have tried the life of the recluse. Solitude brings no

---

[1] Neander, "Life of Christ," vol. i. pp. 36–40 ; also " History of
the Christian Religion," vol. i. p. 60.

escape from spiritual danger. If it closes some avenues of
temptation, there are few in whose case it does not open more.
Yet the Therapeutæ, a sect similar to the Essenes, with whom
you are acquainted, number many among them whose lives
are truly exemplary. Their cells are scattered about the
region bordering on the farther shore of the Lake Mareotis.
The members of either sex live a single and ascetic life,
spending their time in fasting and contemplation, in prayer
or reading. They believe themselves favoured with divine
illumination—an inner light. They assemble on the Sabbath
for worship, and listen to mystical discourses on the traditionary lore which they say has been handed down in secret
among themselves. They also celebrate solemn dances and
processions of a mystic significance by moonlight on the
shore of the great mere. Sometimes, on an occasion of
public rejoicing, the margin of the lake on our side will be
lit with a fiery chain of illuminations, and galleys, hung with
lights, row to and fro with strains of music sounding over the
broad water. Then the Therapeutæ are all hidden in their
little hermitages, and these sights and sounds of the world
they have abandoned make them withdraw into themselves
and pray.

"Their principle at least is true. The soul which is occupied with things above, and is initiated into the mysteries of
the Lord, cannot but account the body evil, and even hostile.
The soul of man is divine, and his highest wisdom is to
become as much as possible a stranger to the body with its
embarrassing appetites. God has breathed into man from
heaven a portion of His own divinity. That which is divine
is invisible. It may be extended, but it is incapable of separation. Consider how vast is the range of our thought over
the past and the future, the heavens and the earth. This
alliance with an upper world, of which we are conscious,
would be impossible, were not the soul of man an indivisible
portion of that divine and blessed spirit. Contemplation of the
divine essence is the noblest exercise of man ; it is the only
means of attaining to the highest truth and virtue, and therein
to behold God is the consummation of our happiness here.

PLATE II.

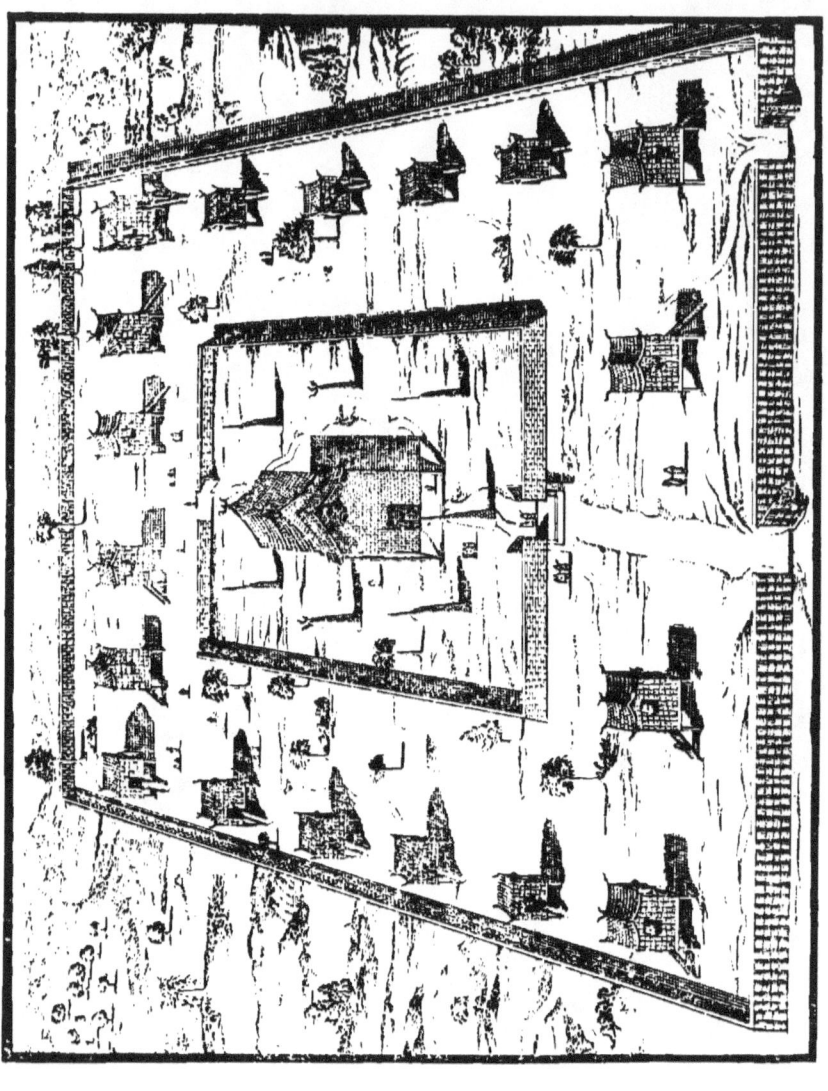

NUDE MONASTERY, SIAM.

(Page 75.)

"The confusion of tongues at the building of the tower of Babel should teach us this lesson. The heaven those vain builders sought to reach, signifies symbolically the mind, where dwell divine powers. Their futile attempt represents the presumption of those who place sense above intelligence—who think that they can storm the Intelligible by the Sensible. The structure which such impiety would raise is overthrown by spiritual tranquility. In calm retirement and contemplation we are taught that we know like only by like, and that the foreign and lower world of the sensuous and the practical may not intrude into the lofty region of divine illumination."

"An alliance with the upper world" was, we see here, the object of these dreaming Essenes. This in India is called yoga (union). Was there any connection between the Indian and Jewish mystics?

The most subtle thinker of the modern English Church, the late Dean Mansel, boldly maintained that the philosophy and rites of the Therapeuts of Alexandria were due to Buddhist missionaries who visited Egypt within two generations of the time of Alexander the Great. In this he has been supported by philosophers of the calibre of Schelling and Schopenhauer, and the great Sanskrit authority, Lassen. Renan, in his work "Les Langues Sémitiques," also sees traces of this Buddhist propagandism in Palestine before the Christian era. Hilgenfeld, Mutter, Bohlen, King, all admit the Buddhist influence. Colebrooke saw a striking similarity between the Buddhist philosophy and that of the Pythagoreans. Dean Milman was convinced that the Therapeuts sprung from the "contemplative and indolent fraternities" of India.

Until I came across this bird's-eye view of a rude monastery in Siam (see Plate II.), I had no very clear idea of a monastery of the Therapeuts in the jungle near Alexandria. It is a drawing by an old traveller, given to us by Picart. We see the house of assembly in the centre, where the Therapeuts, according to Philo, assembled every Sabbath for religious services. We see the cells of the monks sprinkled round in a rude city "four-square." Modern India gives us a far more accurate picture than we can get elsewhere of ancient Palestine, for it is an ancient Asiatic civilization that has not yet passed away. When I campaigned against a rude tribe called Sonthals, in 1855, I saw everywhere the "booths of leaves" of the Bible, the pansil of early Buddhist books. Since the days of Job, thieves "dig into" the rude mud walls of the East. Visitors to the Indian and Colonial Exhibition may have seen several straw-thatched houses where this would have been feasible. Of such a pattern with mud or matted walls were the huts, perhaps, of the Therapeuts.

Father La Loubére, in his "Description du Royaume de Siam,"[1] gives us some very interesting details of Buddhist convent life. In a central quadrangle is the chief building surrounded by mortuary pyramidal columns, each covering the ashes of some rich man or saint, but dedicated to one of the Buddhas, and suggesting the columns in a Christian grave-yard. In a second enclosure are the little mat-built pansils of the monks, surrounding the central building. Each holds a sramana and his servant-pupils, to the number sometimes of three. Each, too, has two little chambers in which a wandering beggar can obtain food and shelter, as amongst the Essenes. "I was an hungred, and ye gave me no meat: I was thirsty, and ye gave me no drink: I was a stranger, and ye took me not in; naked, and ye clothed me not: sick and in prison, and ye visited me not" (Matt. xxv.).

Each monastery is presided over by a sancrat or bishop, whose insignia is an accurate mitre, carved on a stone pedestal, which fact satisfied the good father that the Buddhists had stolen many ideas from the Christians. Matins began when a monk could see the veins of his hand, or see clearly enough to prevent him destroying reptile life in walking to the temple. The chanting went on for two hours, and then the begging friars, two and two, as in the Catholic Church, went round the neighbourhood and collected their scanty food. The meal seems to have been something after the pattern of the Thera-peut bloodless oblation, for a portion of the food is always solemnly offered to Buddha. Then comes teaching, reading,

---

[1] Picart, vol. vii.

meditation ; and then what the father calls " La Méridiane," noon-day prayers. His description of a sermon with a text taken from the sayings of Buddha is most interesting. The monks are ranged on one side of the temple, and the nuns on the other. At the close, they say solemnly, " This is the Word of God !" The Catholic father cites some of their texts : " Judge not thy neighbour. Say not this man is good. This man is wicked ! " This seems specially to have struck him.

Assisted by Philo, let us draw up some more points of contact between the Therapeut and Buddhist monks :—

1. Enforced vegetarianism, community of goods, rigid abstinence from sexual indulgence, also a high standard of purity, were common to both the Buddhists and the Therapeuts.

2. Neither community allowed the use of wine.

3. Both were strongly opposed to the blood sacrifice of the old priesthoods.

4. The monks of both communities devoted their lives exclusively to the acquirement of a knowledge of God.

5. Long fastings were common to both.

6. With both silence was a special spiritual discipline.

7. The Therapeut left " for ever," says Philo, " brothers, children, wives, father, and mother," for the contemplative life. This is Buddhism.

8. Like the Buddhists, the Therapeuts had nuns vowed to chastity. These were quite distinct, as Philo points out, from the vestals of the Greek temples. With the latter the chastity was enforced, with the former voluntary.

9. The preacher and the missionary, two original ideas of Buddhism, were conspicuous amongst the Therapeuts. This was in direct antagonism to the spirit of Mosaism.

10. The Therapeut, as his name implies, was a healer (or " curate " as Eusebius calls him) of body and soul. The Buddhist monks are the only physicians in most Buddhist countries. They cure by simples, and by casting out devils.

11. The Therapeut squatted on a " mat of papyrus " in his sanctuary. The monks " took their seats on mats covered

with white calico," says Mr. Dickson, describing a general confession in a Buddhist temple.[1]

12. The Therapeuts were classed as, first, presbyters (elders), an exact equivalent for the word Arhat, used in Buddha's day for his fully initiated monks. Under the presbyter was the deacon (διάκονος, covered with dust or dirt). These novices were servant-pupils, the servitor friars (Sâmanêros) of Buddhism. An ephemereut, or temporary head, presided at the Therapeut service as in Buddhism. That the Christians should have taken over this ephemereut and these presbyters, or priests, and deacons, as their three chief officers, is perhaps the greatest stumbling-block in the way of those writers, chiefly English and clerical, who maintain that there was no connection between Christianity and mystic Judaism.

We have seen from Philo's letter to Hephæstion that he considered the Therapeuts the same as the Essenes. Indeed in another work, he calls the Essenes, "Therapeuts of God. From Josephus we get some additional facts relative to these mystics.

1. Enforced vegetarianism was one of the main principles of the Essenes as well as of the Buddhists. They refused to go to Jerusalem to the temple sacrifices at the risk of being stoned.

2. The Essenes had a "Sanhedrim of Justice" like the Buddhist Sangha. Excommunication in both was the chief punishment. This was altogether foreign to the lower Mosaism, which allowed no Jew to escape the obligations of the Jewish law.

3. The Essenes, like the Buddhists, forbade slavery, war, revenge, avarice, hatred, worldly longings, etc.

4. Although to "face towards the east" and "worship the sun towards the east" is one of the "abominations" of Ezekiel, the Essenes were not allowed to speak of a morning until they had bowed down to the rising sun. The sun is Buddha's special emblem. In Wung Puh's Life, he is called the "sublime sun, Buddha, whose widespread rays brighten and

---

[1] "Pâtimokkha," p. 2.

illumine all things." In the same volume Buddha is reported to have said that "bowing to the east was the *páramitá* of charity."

5. The Essenes, like the Buddhist monks, had ridiculous laws relating to spitting and other natural acts, those of the Essenes being regulated by a superstitious veneration for the Sabbath day, those of the Buddhists, by a superstitious respect for a pagoda.[1]

6. In Buddhist monasteries a rigid obedience, together with a quite superstitious respect for the person of a superior, is enacted. In Buddhagosa's Parables is a puerile story of a malicious Muni, who, when an inferior monk had gone out of a hut where the two were sleeping, lay across the doorway in order to make the novice inadvertently commit the great sin of placing his foot above his superior's head. The penalty of such an act is that the offender's head ought to be split into seven pieces. With the Essenes similar superstitions were rife. If an Approacher accidently touched the hem of the garment of an Associate, all sorts of purifications had to be gone through.

7. The principle of thrift and unsavouriness in dress was carried to extremes by both Essenes and Buddhists. The sramana (ascetic) was required to stitch together for his *kowat* the refuse rags acquired by begging. The Essenes were expected to wear the old clothes of their co-religionists until they tumbled to pieces.

In the Tibetan "Life of Buddha," by Rockhill, it is announced that when the great teacher first cast off his kingly silks he donned a foul dress that had been previously worn by ten other saints.[2] This throws light on the story of Elisha.

Dr. Ginsburg ("The Essenes," p. 13) shows that the Essenes had eight stages of progress in inner or spiritual knowledge.

1. Outward or bodily purity by baptism.

2. The state of purity that has conquered the sexual desire.

---

[1] Beal, "Catena," pp. 236, 237.   [2] Rockhill, p. 26.

3. Inward and spiritual purity.

4. A meek and gentle spirit which has subdued all anger and malice.

5. The culminating point of holiness.

6. The body becomes the temple of the Holy Ghost, and the mystic acquires the gift of prophecy.

7. Miraculous powers of healing, and of raising the dead.

8. The mystic state of Elias.

The Buddhists have likewise eight stages of inner progress, the Eightfold Holy Path. The first step, "Those who have entered the stream," the Nairañjana, the mystic river of Buddha, is precisely the same as the first Essene step. Then follow advances in purity, holiness, and mastery of passion. In the last two stages, the Buddhists, like the Essenes, gained supernatural powers, to be used in miraculous cures, prophecies, and other occult marvels. It must be mentioned that the Essenes were circumcised as well as the other Jews.[1]

The word "Essenes," according to some learned philologists, means the "Bathers" or "Baptisers," baptism having been their initiatory rite. Josephus tells us that this baptism was not administered until the aspirant had remained a whole year outside the community, but "subjected to their rule of life."[2]

I will here give the rite of Buddhist baptism (abhisheka) when a novice is about to become a monk. It consists of many washings, borrowed plainly by the early Buddhists from the Brahmins, and brings to mind the frequent use of water attributed to the Hemero Baptists or disciples of John. It may be mentioned that in some Buddhist countries, Nepál for instance, the various monkish vows are now taken only for form sake. This makes the letter, retained after the spirit has departed, all the more valuable.

The neophyte having made an offer of scents and unguents (betel-nut, paun, etc.) to his spiritual guide (guru), the latter, after certain formalities, draws four circles in the form of a cross in honour of the Tri Ratna (trinity) on the ground, and

---

[1] See Origen's version of Josephus's narrative.
[2] Josephus, De B. J. II. 8, 2–13.

the neophyte, seated in a prescribed position, recites the
following text: " I salute Buddha-nâth, Dharma, and Saṅgha,
and entreat them to bestow upon me the Parivrajyâ Vrata."
It is plain here that the prayer is addressed to the transcendental triad. The first and second day of the ceremonial are
consumed in prayers and formalities carried on by the guide
and his pupil alone ; on the second day, another mystic cross
is drawn upon the ground, called the " Swastika âsan."
A pot containing water and other mystic ingredients, a gold
lotus, and certain confections and charms, figures conspicuously
in these early rites, and is at last poured on the neophyte's
head. This is the baptism.

The abbot, or head of the vihâra, now appears upon the
scene, and sprinkles four seers of rice and milk upon the head
of the aspirant. This ceremony is repeated three times.
The next day, a barber makes a clean shave of the neophyte's
head, leaving only the forelock. Previous to this, the latter
has pledged himself to forsake intoxicating liquors, women,
evil thoughts, pride ; and promised not to injure any living
creature. More washings take place, including a fresh
baptism by four ecclesiastics of rank. It must be mentioned
that a Buddhist baptism is preceded by a confession of sins
and much catechising. The catechumen's name is changed
after the baptism. He promises to devote his future life to
the Divine triad. The monks of rank then invoke a blessing
on his head: " May you be as happy as he who dwells in
the hearts of all, who is the Universal Soul, the Lord of
all, the Buddha called Ratna Saṁbhava ! "

The change is called the " whole birth ; " and at one
moment a light is kindled. The early Christians after
initiation were called the " illuminati." A solemn address
is made to the triad individually—Buddha, whom "gods and
men alike worship," who is apart from the world, " the
quintessence of all good ; " Dharma, who is the Prajñâ Pâramitâ, the mother, the guide to perfect wisdom and peace ;
and Saṅgha, the son. A mitre like the Mithraic cap is put
on at one portion of the ceremonial. The ceremonies for
Buddha's new birth of water and the spirit must sound hollow

G

indeed, now that nothing but form remains ; but this form to an inquirer into early Buddhism has a special value.

In Tibet this baptism also exists. In Japan that excellent authority, Mr. Pfoundes, tells me that he has frequently seen neophytes being baptized, or sprinkled with water mixed with aromatic simples. Mr. Oung Gyee tells me that baptism is unknown in Southern Buddhism, although in Burmah they sometimes initiate the novice at the bank of a river, without sprinkling. This last seems a trace of it as having once existed, and so do the mighty tanks excavated in Ceylon. Wung Puh informs us that at " Vaiśâlî, Buddha resided under a tree (the music-tree), and there delivered a sûtra entitled ' The baptism that rescues from life and death, and confers salvation.' " [1]

The other great rite of the Essenes was what the mystical societies of the era of Christ called the " Bloodless Oblation." This is the name that was given to the Christian sacrament in the early rituals. According to Josephus, this rite, like the early Christian rite, was practically the daily dinner. To it, "as if to the most holy precincts," the monks, bathed and " purified," assembled. Its hour was the fifth hour after sunrise. White garments were donned, and strangers and catechumens rigidly excluded. Philo, speaking of the Therapeuts, calls it "that portion of the mysteries which is most transcendent." He compares, also, the bread used to the shew-bread of the temple, thus explicitly showing that these mysteries were the Jewish mysteries filched from an exclusive priesthood and given to the people. The shew-bread, literally the " Bread of the Faces," or " of the Presence," consisted of twelve loaves, which denoted the "presence " of Jehovah himself, under his twelve mystical faces at the altar.[2]

In the " Lalita Vistara," it is announced that those who have faith will become sons of Buddha, and partake of " the food of the kingdom." [3] Four things draw disciples to the Great Banquet of Buddha—gifts, soft words, production of

[1] *Journ. As. Soc.* vol. xx. p. 172.
[2] Smith's " Dictionary of the Bible," *sub voce* " Shew-bread."
[3] Foucaux, p. 94.

PLATE III.

WORSHIP OF BUDDHA AS THE PLEIADES.
From Anradapura.

benefits, conformity of benefits.[1] In Buddhism, the chief food
of the ascetic, the rice and milk, is, by an intelligible trope,
called the amrita, the food of immortal life ; and Buddha's
era the epoch when the rice and milk came into the world.
This use of food, and especially rice and milk, as a symbol of
God, existed in India at a very early date. The main rite
of the Brahmins, when they worshipped in a temple of unhewn upright stones, was an exhibition of the birth of the
Śiśur Jâtah, or new-born child. "The clarified butter is
the milk of the woman," says the earliest ritual, the "Aitareya
Brâhmana," "the husked rice grains belong to the male."[2]
This symbol of food was perhaps the earliest symbol of God.
In India, at certain seasons, it is made up into little idols ;
and also in Tibet.

In many of the early Buddhist sculptures, groups are to
be seen worshipping a large wheaten or rice cake, as big and
as round as a footstool. Mr. Pfoundes tells me that at the
time of the new year, in Japan, he has seen cakes as large as
this on the Buddhist altars. I copy one of these sculptures
from the marbles of the Amarâvatî tope at the British Museum
(see Plate III.). I am certain that this object is food. I saw
in the South Kensington Museum, on a miniature chaitya
from Sanchi, a similar object, ranged by a vase and covered
with a cloth.

The details of this mystic Therapeut dinner, as given by
Philo, have caused Eusebius and a long line of Catholic
writers to maintain that we have simply a description of the
Christian *sacramentum*, a Latin form of the Greek word,
μυστήριον, or "mystery."

In the main building of the convent the monks and nuns
assembled, being separated the one from the other by a partition. After the chief monk had read some passages of the
sacred writings and delivered an exhortation, "stretching forth
one finger of his right hand" the while, the presbyters began
to sing hymns in the choir and also at various "stations" of
the building (as the Rev. Dom Bernard de Montfauçon translates the passage) and "altars." Whilst the ephemereut sang,

Foucaux, p. 51.   [2] Vol. ii. p. 5.

the rest of the community chanted responses in a solemn manner. Then a "table" was brought in by the deacons, and a solemn prayer was offered up to God, "that the feast shall be agreeable to Him." On the table was bread, salt, and hyssop and water, "the most sacred of all elements in holiness."

After the "mysteries" of this holy feast had been gone through, and all the community had satisfied hunger, the monks and nuns danced together under some strange ecstatic influence until sunrise the next morning. This dance has puzzled the Roman Catholic commentators before alluded to, but some of them find records of religious dances in the early Church.

This description of the assembly in the hall of the monastery, the sermons, the reading of the holy books, etc., is purely Buddhist. The processions round the shrines of the temple is a marked feature of the Buddhist ritual, which the litany in praise of the seven Buddhas and similar rituals were designed specially to meet. In all Buddhist temples the priest intones and the lower monks chant responses — the Gregorian chant, according to Balfour's "Indian Cyclopædia," being a Buddhist originality.[1]

Fig. 7.—Tabernacle for the Real Presence of Buddha.

Mr. Pfoundes tells me that in Japan and China the hours of feeding and the customs vary amongst different sects.

---

[1] *Sub voce* "Buddha."

Noonday is the chief meal, and each monk takes his portion from the common mess, and usually retires to his own hut, or cell, except when there is a feast, when they eat together in some portion of the temple, not the sanctuary. But wherever they eat, a portion of the food is always offered to Buddha at a little miniature altar. The Buddhists have a little tabernacle, like the Catholics, for the Real Presence of Buddha on the high altar. I copy one from the French Orientalist, Langlés.[1] He affirms that the sacred elements are placed inside, but this must be an exception. The rice and the scented water are placed in front usually. In the early Christian Church, the *sacramentum* was called the " giving," and the Greek Church still calls the sacred bread " Corban." [2] " Leave there thy gift before the altar," said Christ (Matt. v. 24), alluding, no doubt, to the "giving" of the Essenes. The "Corban" of the Greek Church has twelve impressions of the cross, thus further connecting it with the twelve mystical "faces" of the Jewish shew-bread.

[1] " Rituel des Tartares Mantchous."　　　[2] Picart, iii. 189.

CHAPTER VIII.

BUDDHISM AND THE "KABBALAH."

IN Philo's letter to Hephæstion we have seen that the Therapeuts listened every sabbath to discourses on the traditionary lore which was handed down in secret amongst themselves. Has this secret lore passed away from the earth? Scholars of the calibre of Reuchlin, Joel, and M. Franck, of the Institute of France, affirm that we have it still in the "Kabbalah." This word implies secret tradition.

The legend runs that this secret wisdom was first taught by Jehovah to the seven angels that stand round his throne. It was then handed down orally through the seven earthly messengers (Adam, Moses, David, etc.).

Finally, the Rabbi Simon Ben Jochai, in a cavern amid earth rocking and supernatural coruscations, delivered it to the world in a "Book of Splendour," the "Sohar."

It must be confessed, however, that the genuineness of the work, the "Sohar," is disputed. Dr. Ginsburg affirms that it is the original composition of a Spanish Jew, named Moses de Leon, who lived as recently as the fourteenth century, A.D. This question shall be discussed later on. If the work is a forgery, it is a very clever forgery; for on its appearance in modern times it wrought quite a revolution in the Jewish religion. Philosophical Jews, who had been unable to accept the traditional Christianity, became Christian converts in large numbers; and Christians felt that without the "Kabbalah" it was impossible to fully understand Christianity. It is asserted by Dr. Ginsburg, that Reuchlin's treatise upon the "Kabbalah"

powerfully influenced the early reformers.[1] It produced also
an illustrious school of mystics. Cornelius Henry Agrippa,
John Baptist von Helmont, Robert Fludd, and Raymond
Lully, developed under its teaching.

Assisted by Dr. Ginsburg, let us briefly consider its
theosophy.

Being boundless in his nature, which necessarily implies
that he is an absolute unity and inscrutable, and there is
nothing without him, or that the τὸ πᾶν is in him, God is
EN SOPH—Endless, Boundless. In this boundlessness, or as
the En Soph, he cannot be comprehended by the intellect or
described in words, for there is nothing which can grasp and
depict him to us ; and as such he is, in a certain sense, non-
existent, because, as far as our minds are concerned, that
which is perfectly incomprehensible does not exist. To make
his existence perceptible, and to render himself compre-
hensible, the En Soph, or the Boundless, had to become
active and creative. But the En Soph cannot be the direct
creator, for he has neither will, intention, desire, thought,
language, nor action, as these properties imply limit and
belong to finite beings, whereas En Soph is boundless.
Besides, the imperfect and circumscribed nature of the creation
precludes the idea that the world was created or even designed
by him, who can have no will nor produce anything but what
is like himself, boundless and perfect. On the other hand,
again, the beautiful design displayed in the mechanism, the
regular order manifested in the preservation, distinction, and
renewal of things, forbid us to regard this world as the offspring of chance, and constrain us to recognize therein an
intelligent design. We are therefore compelled to view the
En Soph as the creator of the world in an *indirect manner.*

Now, the *medium* by which the En Soph made his existence known in the creation of the world, are ten sephiroth
or *intelligences,*[2] which emanated from the Boundless One in
the following manner : At first, the En Soph, or Aged of the
Aged, or the Holy Aged, as he is alternately called, sent forth

---

[1] "The Kabbalah," p. 131.

[2] Translated also "attributes," "powers" (ὑποστάσεις).

from the spiritual light one spiritual substance or intelligence. This first *sephira*, which existed in the *En Soph* from all eternity, and became a reality by a mere act, has no less than seven appellations.

I. *The Crown*, because it occupies the highest position.

II. *The Aged*, because it is the oldest, or the first emanation.

III. *The Primordial Point*, or *the Smooth Point*, because, as the " Sohar" tells us, "When the Concealed of the Concealed wished to reveal himself, he first made a single point. The infinite was entirely unknown, and diffused no light before this luminous point violently broke through into vision " ("Sohar" I., 15 *a*).

IV. *The White Head.*

V. *The Long Face, Macro prosopon*, because the whole ten *sephiroth* represent the primordial or heavenly man, of which the first *sephira* is the head.

VI. *The Inscrutable Height*, because it is the highest of all the sephiroth, proceeding immediately from the En Soph.

VII. *Absolute Being*, expressed in the Bible by *Ehejeh*, or *I am*, representing the infinite as distinguished from the finite, and in the angelic order by the celestial beasts of Ezekiel, called *chajoth.* The first sephira contains the other nine sephira. Plainly it is En Soph reproduced.

These nine sephiroth are as follows :—

1. *Wisdom*, called also *the Father*, an active male potency.

2. *Intelligence*, called also *the Mother*, a passive or female potency.

It is from the union of these two, the Ophanim and Arelim, that the other seven sephiroth were produced.

3. Love, greatness.

4. Judgment, justice, strength.

5. Beauty.

6. Firmness.

7. Splendour.

8. Foundation.

9. Kingdom.

Summed up, these ten sephiroth, or perfections, were the

perfections of the heavenly man, God imaged as the seen universe, and as a man, the active, the conceivable God.

Now, it is certainly singular that this complete system of theogony, which is supposed by Dr. Ginsburg to be the original composition of Moses de Leon, a Jew who died in Spain, A.D. 1305, should be a literal, I might almost say a servile, reproduction in terminology as well as idea of the theogony of the Buddhists. And the portion that Dr. Ginsburg considers the most modern and spurious part of the " Kabbalah," namely, that of En Soph and the ten sephiroth,[1] happens to be the part that is most conspicuously Buddhist in every detail.

Buddha, called also the Swayambhu (the Self-Existent), Bhagavan (God), Âdi Buddha (the First Intelligence), etc., is the formless, passionless, inactive, indefinable, illimitable, being that the " Kabbalah " describes under the title En Soph.

" Know that when in the beginning all was perfect void and the five elements were not, then Âdi Buddha, the stainless, was revealed in the form of flame and light.

" He is without parts, shapeless, self-sustained, void of pain and care (Kâranda Vyûha)." " He is the essence of all essences. He is the Vajra âtmâ (Being of Adamant). He is the instantly produced lord of the Universe (Nâma Sangîti)."

Let us see if there are any other points of contact between En Soph and the transcendental Buddha.

"The Aged of the Aged," says the "Sohar," "the Unknown of the Unknown has a form, yet has no form. He has a form whereby the universe is preserved, and yet has no form, because he cannot be comprehended. When he first assumed the form (of the first sephira) he caused nine splendid lights to emanate from it, which, shining through it, diffused a bright light in all directions. Imagine an elevated light sending forth its rays in all directions. Now, if we approach it to examine the rays, we understand no more than that they emanate from the said light. So is the Holy Aged an absolute light, but in himself concealed and incomprehensible. We can only comprehend him through those luminous

---

[1] " The Kabbalah," p. 89.

emanations which again are partly visible and partly concealed.   These constitute the sacred name of God." [1]

This is asserting what we have seen written down of the
Primordial Buddha, that he is "the form of all things yet
formless," and that he was "first revealed in the form of
light."

A favourite Kabbalistic simile for En Soph is a point
or dot.

" The indivisible point who has no limit, and who cannot
be comprehended because of his purity and brightness, expanded from without and formed a brightness which served
as a covering to the indivisible point.   Yet it, too, could not
be viewed in consequence of its immeasurable light.   It, too,
expanded from without, and this expansion was its garment.
Thus everything originated through a constant upheaving
agitation, and thus finally the world originated" ("Sohar," 1.
20 *a*).

Now listen to the Buddhists : " He whose image is Śun-
yata (no image), who is like a cypher, or point, infinite,
unsustained in Nirvritti, and sustained in Pravritti, whose
essence is Nirvritti, of whom all things are forms, and who is
yet formless, who is the Iśvara (God), the first intellectual
essence, the first Buddha was revealed by his own will." [2]
I will proceed to show that the Buddhists have ten pâramitâs
or perfections of Buddha, very like the sephiroth of the " Kabbalah."

The conventional image of Buddha is that of an ascetic
seated, with his eyes closed in the rapturous trance called
Dhyâni.   'Twas thus that a man was supposed to gain
miraculous powers.   The rationale of this, according to
modern psychology, is that it is possible, by a species of self-
mesmerism, to temporarily detach spirit from its mortal
envelope, and to allow it to put forth its full powers.   With
such ideas current, it would be natural to image God by the
figure of a man in Dhyâni.   This shows us the full force of
the first Buddhist sephira or pâramitâ.   The first Jewish
sephira represents, as we have seen, " absolute being," " the

[1] Ginsburg, p. 15.   [2] Cited by Hodgson, p. 77.

infinite as distinguished from the finite." By a fiction, it is represented as the one sephira that had been in existence from all eternity, the meaning, of course, being that the heavenly man must be En Soph as well as the anthropomorphic God. This first Buddhist pâramitâ is Dhyâni, and this seems to symbolize this truth better than the Jewish sephira.

We then get two pâramitâs, Upâya and Prajnâ, which represent the fatherly and motherly principles, as in the " Kabbalah."

"From the union of Upâya and Prajnâ," says an old Buddhist book cited by Mr. Hodgson, " proceeded the world."[1]

Prajnâ is the exact equivalent of the Alexandrine word Sophia—wisdom imaged as a woman. Upâya is variously translated. Its literal meaning is "approach." Burnouf renders it "wish" or "prayer."

Upâya-Prajnâ, with the Buddhists, is a conception similar to the Ardha Nârî (literally, half woman) of the Brahmins— the kosmos imaged as a bi-sexual God.[2]

"The Anointed they call male-female," says Cyril of Jerusalem.[3]

The Karmikas hold that Upâya and Prajnâ parented Manas, the lord of the senses, and that he produced the tangible virtues and vices.[4]

There are three major and seven minor sephiroth in the " Kabbalah," as Franck shows. The seven minor pâramitâs are—

1. Charity (Dâna).
2. Morality (Sila).
3. Patience (Santi).
4. Industry (Virya).
5. Fortitude (Bala).
6. Foreknowledge (Pranidhi).
7. Gnosis (Jnana).

But if we are to accept the dictum of Dean Mansel, that Buddhist missionaries visited Alexandria within two genera-

---

[1] "Essays," p. 88. [2] See Hodgson, pp. 80, 81.
[3] Bk. vi. 11. [4] Hodgson, p. 78.

tions of the time of Alexander the Great, we can conceive
that such missionaries would meet with one crucial difficulty.
Prominent amongst Buddhist teaching would be the doctrine
of Purusha, the heavenly man, and prominent amongst the
Buddhist apparatus of worship brought from India would be
marble and bronze statues of Purusha, with the celebrated
thirty-two signs. But how would a graven image be received
by a Jew? Did he not interpret the second commandment
as forbidding statues, pictures, all art?

The answer given to this question quite proves, I think,
the genuineness of the "Kabbalah." It is quite impossible
that Moses de Leon, A.D. 1300, could have hit upon so ingenious
a device, because it is quite certain that in his day the question to be solved could not have been appreciated in its full
force. The solution was twofold.

1. A compromise was adopted in the matter of the second
commandment. Flat representations, pictures, bas-reliefs
were permitted. This is proved from the many Alexandrian
talismans and incised stones. We have also the evidence of
the catacombs, modelled as Dean Stanley has shown, on the
sepulchral crypts and rock chapels of Palestine. The Greek
Church still only permits "flat icons."

2. As many of the "signs" of Purusha—fingers like
copper, feet flat, and figured with lotuses and swastikas, head
shaped like a temple, with a toran at the top, and so on—
could only be made intelligible by sculpture, it was resolved
to mix up the signs and the pâramitâs. Thus, the sephiroths
give physical qualities as well as moral, in that they differ
from the pâramitâs. The heavenly man has a dazzling
"crown," "splendour," "beauty," "white hair," a "long face,"
"firmness," "kingdom"—all these are symbols of Purusha.

Sign 1. His head has for crown a raised knob. It is confessed in many Buddhist writings that the conventional
Buddha's head represents a chaitya; so this raised knob is the
most lofty of symbols. It is the toran, the heaven of the
transcendental Buddha.

Sign 4. Wool (ûrna) appears between his eyebrows, white
as snow and sparkling like silver.

Sign 17. His skin glitters like burnished gold.

Sign 20. His trunk is firm as the banyan tree.

Sign 31. On the sole of each foot is the impress of the wheel of a thousand spokes. This is the symbol of "kingdom," of universal dominion. No. 38 of the Minor Signs announces that from him issues a pure light which dispels the darkness.

I will cite here a passage from the first chapter of the Apocalypse, when St. John, apparently in a Christian temple on "the Lord's day," hears a voice—

"And I turned to see the voice that spake with me. And being turned, I saw seven golden candlesticks; And in the midst of the seven candlesticks one like unto the Son of man, clothed with a garment down to the foot, and girt about the paps with a golden girdle. His head and his hairs were white like wool, as white as snow; and his eyes were as a flame of fire; And his feet like unto fine brass, as if they burned in a furnace; and his voice as the sound of many waters. And he had in his right hand seven stars: and out of his mouth went a sharp two-edged sword: and his countenance was as the sun shineth in his strength."

The hands of Buddha are said to be "like copper," and the feet of the mystic Alpha and Omega are "like brass." Do both descriptions refer to the conventional effigies of each? Both, too, have a lambent coruscation, and hair like white wool. The coincidence is remarkable. The Buddhist initiate is called Arahat, the "Aged," the "Venerable."

Let us now consider the arguments brought forward to impugn the antiquity of the "Sohar."

1. The wife and daughter of one Moses de Leon, who died at Arevelo, in Spain, A.D. 1305, positively declared that the said Moses had "confessed to them that he had composed the 'Sohar' from his own head, and that he wrote it with his own hand." They were promised by a rich man, named Joseph de Avila, a large sum of money if they could produce an ancient manuscript of which Moses de Leon had boasted. This was their reply.[1]

[1] Ginsburg, p. 91.

2. The "Sohar" contains whole passages translated by Moses de Leon from his other works.

3. The doctrine of En Soph and the ten Sephiroth is asserted by Dr. Ginsburg to have been unknown before the thirteenth century. To this he adds, oddly enough, the "doctrine of metempsychosean retribution."

4. The "Sohar" alludes to very modern events—a "comet that appeared in Rome, July 25, 1264;" the "Crusades and Crusaders;" the "descendants of Ishmael, or the Mohammedans." It mystically explains the Hebrew vowel-points, which were unknown before A.D. 570. It steals two verses from a writer who was not born until A.D. 1021.[1]

5. A fifth objection might be here stated. It is affirmed by Franck that the "Sohar" is written in a Hebrew that is not the archaic Hebrew that Rabbi Ben Jochai would have used. It is a form of Hebrew known to scholars as the "dialect of Jerusalem." It disappeared about the sixth century A.D. This form of Hebrew is, however, utterly unlike the Hebrew of the thirteenth century.

Now, I appeal to Dr. Ginsburg. Is it not plain, on the very surface, that these objections are internecine? A scholar has wit enough to compose a work that contains the sublimated essence of the three greatest creeds that the world has seen—the religions of Moses, Buddha, and Christ. With unrivalled sympathy and insight, he can put forth the postulates of the higher Christianity in such a manner that numbers of Jews, on reading the work, became converts. And yet the same man is represented as being dense enough to clumsily allude to "Crusaders," "Roman comets," "Mohammedans," etc. Are not these rather the sort of accretions that come to a genuine manuscript after a long voyage, like barnacles to a ship? Then, too, if this unrivalled scholar is capable of the unparalleled feat of writing reams upon reams of manuscript in the accurate Hebrew of the sixth century A.D., the question arises, why did he select the sixth century Hebrew, and not the Hebrew of some ten, or at least five, centuries before? To such a scholar one feat would have been as easy as the

---

[1] Ginsburg, "The Kabbalah," p. 85, *et seq.*

other; and his cheat required, perforce, the most archaic Hebrew possible.

I think, too, that his alleged citations from his own works are capable of a different construction. A genius of the pattern that we have described would certainly have avoided so clumsy a blunder; but a poor cheat, who had access to a secret manuscript, might have stolen some of its ideas and found himself unable to conceal his theft. Dr. Ginsburg's theory is that Moses de Leon, for the hope of a few doubloons, worked out his colossal forgery in many rambling books. But are not means and end entirely incommensurate? At the end of his colossal labour, what certainty would he have of any doubloons at all? Franck accentuates this difficulty.

He points out, moreover, that the Rabbi Guedelia affirmed that Moses ben Nachman found the manuscript in Palestine, and sent it to Spain, where Moses de Leon saw it.

Franck points out other difficulties in the way of the theory that the "Sohar" is the original composition of Moses de Leon.

1. There is no trace in it of the philosophy of Aristotle, so rampant in the thirteenth century.[1]

2. There is no trace of Christ and Christianity.[2]

3. An examination of its style, want of unity, etc., makes it impossible to set it down as the work of one man.[3]

4. More than a century after its publication in Spain, certain Jews still handed down the bulk of the ideas contained in it by oral tradition.[4]

5. The discovery of the "Codex Nasaræus" sets at rest the question whether the ideas and philosophy of the "Sohar" were in existence in ancient Palestine.[5]

"But why," says Franck, "should we glean laboriously, a few scattered hints in the Acts of the Apostles and in the hymns of St. Ephrem, when we can fill our hands from a monument of great price recently published in a Syriac text, and translated by a learned Orientalist. We speak of the 'Codex Nasaræus,' that Bible of purely oriental gnosticism.

---

[1] See Franck, " La Kabbale," p. 93.   [2] Ibid., p. 106.
[3] Ibid., p. 107.   [4] Ibid., p. 123.   [5] Ibid., p. 133.

It is well known that St. Jerome and St. Epiphanius trace up the sect of the Nazarenes to the birth of Christianity. Well, such is the similarity of a great number of its dogmas, and the most essential points of the system of the 'Kabbalah,' that in reading them in the work cited, we fancy that we have come across a stray variorum manuscript of the 'Sohar.' God always figures as the 'King' and the 'Master' of 'Light.' He is Himself 'Pure Splendour,' the 'Eternal and Infinite Light.' He is 'Beauty,' 'Life,' 'Justice,' and 'Pity.' From Him emanate all forms that we see in the world. He is the Creator and Artisan. But His proper wisdom is His own essence. None know them. All creatures ask each other what is His name, and are compelled to reply that He has none. The King of Light, of that infinite light that has no name that can be evoked, no nature that can be known. Only with a pure heart can one attain to that light, a just soul and a faith abounding in love."[1]

"The gradation by which the Nazarene teaching descends from the Supreme Being to the extreme limits of creation is exactly the same as in a passage of the 'Sohar' already quoted more than once in this work. The djins, the kings and the creatures, with prayer and hymn celebrate the supreme king of the light from whom issue five miraculous rays. The first is the light which lights every being. The second is the soft breath of life. The third is the gentle voice with which they breathe forth their gladness. The fourth is the word which instructs them and trains them to bear witness to the faith. The fifth is the type of all the forms under which they develop, as fruits grow ripe when warmed by the sun."[2]

"It is impossible," pursues the French scholar, "not to recognize in these lines, to which we had restricted ourselves in our translation, the different degrees of existence set forth by the Kabbalists by thought, breath, or soul, voice or the word. Here are other familiar images that express the same idea—

"Before all creatures was the Life. It was hidden within

---

[1] "Codex Nas.," i. p. 11.　　　　[2] Ibid., p. 9.

itself; Life eternal and incomprehensible, without light, without form. From its bosom was born the luminous atmosphere (Ajar zivo), called also the Word, the Garment, or the symbolical river which represents Wisdom. From this river issue the living waters which the Nazarines and Kabbalists represent as the third manifestation of God. It is intelligence or spirit which in its turn produces the second life, a conception far removed from the first. This second life is called Juschamin, the region of forms, of ideas, in the bosom of which was conceived first of all the idea of the creation of which it is the loftiest and purest type. The second life by-and-by parented the third life, also called the Good Father, the Unknown Old Man, the Ancient of the World. The Good Father having inspected the abyss, the darkness, and the black waters, left there his image which, under the name of Fetahil, became the demiurge or architect of the universe. Then begins an interminable series of æons, a hierarchy both infernal and celestial which has no further interest for us. Sufficient that these three lives, these three grades in the Pleroma hold the same position as the three Kabbalistic "faces," whose very name (farsufo) is found in the language of this sect; and we can be the more confident of this interpretation since we meet with them also the ten sephiroth divided as in the " Sohar" into three superior and seven inferior attributes. As the singular accident that caused the birth of the demiurge and the generation more or less imperfect of the subaltern spirits they are the mythological expression of this idea, also very clearly laid down in the ' Codex Nasaræus' that darkness and evil are nothing more than the gradual weakening of the divine light." [1]

Franck holds that the "Sohar" is neither borrowed from Plato nor the Alexandrian school of Philo, but is anterior to both.[2] The question of the profound and accurate Buddhism of the work has not been touched on. In the almost total paralysis of Oriental studies in the thirteenth century how could a Spaniard know all about the ten pâramitâs, and the thirty-two lakshanas? The Portuguese Ribeyro as late as

[1] "Codex Nas.," p. 211.   [2] Page 388.

H

1701 announces in his "History of Ceylon" that Buddha is St. Thomas.

In our next chapter we have to treat of a very important character, whose advent, according to the Christ of St. Luke, put an end to the law and the prophets.

CHAPTER IX.

THE BAPTIST.

I WILL write down a few texts about John—

" But the angel said unto him, Fear not, Zacharias : for thy prayer is heard ; and thy wife Elisabeth shall bear thee a son, and thou shalt call his name John. And thou shalt have joy and gladness ; and many shall rejoice at his birth. For he shall be great in the sight of the Lord, and shall drink neither wine nor strong drink ; and he shall be filled with the Holy Ghost, even from his mother's womb. And many of the children of Israel shall he turn to the Lord their God. And he shall go before Him in the spirit and power of Elias, to turn the hearts of the fathers to the children, and the disobedient to the wisdom of the just ; to make ready a people prepared for the Lord " (Luke i. 13–17).

" The Word of God came unto John the son of Zacharias in the wilderness. And he came into all the country about Jordan, preaching the baptism of repentance for the remission of sins ; As it is written in the book of the words of Esaias the prophet, saying, The voice of one crying in the wilderness, Prepare ye the way of the Lord, make His paths straight. Every valley shall be filled, and every mountain and hill shall be brought low ; and the crooked shall be made straight, and the rough ways shall be made smooth ; and all flesh shall see the salvation of God. Then he said to the multitude ['Pharisees and Sadducees,' according to Matthew] that came forth to be baptized of him, O generation of vipers, who hath

warned you to flee from the wrath to come? Bring forth
therefore fruits worthy of repentance, and begin not to say
within yourselves, We have Abraham to our father : for I say
unto you, That God is able of these stones to raise up children
unto Abraham. And now also the axe is laid unto the root
of the trees : every tree therefore which bringeth not forth
good fruit is hewn down, and cast into the fire. And the
people asked him, saying, What shall we do then? He
answereth and saith unto them, He that hath two coats, let
him impart to him that hath none ; and he that hath meat,
let him do likewise. Then came also publicans to be baptized, and said unto him, Master, what shall we do? And he
said unto them, Exact no more than that which is appointed
you. And the soldiers likewise demanded of him, saying,
And what shall we do? And he said unto them, Do violence
to no man, neither accuse any falsely ; and be content with
your wages " (Luke iii. 2–14).

"And all the people that heard him, and the publicans
justified God, being baptized with the baptism of John. But
the Pharisees and lawyers rejected the counsel of God against
themselves, being not baptized of him."

"For I say unto you, Among those that are born of
women there is not a greater prophet than John the Baptist."

"For John the Baptist came neither eating bread nor
drinking wine ; and ye say, He hath a devil."

Now, if in this we do not get the portrait of an Essene, it
is difficult to imagine to what section of the Jews the Baptist
belonged. He used the rite of baptism which was peculiar to
the Essenes. He ordered a partition of clothes and neces-
saries. He abstained from wine and "soft raiment." He
strongly assailed the Pharisees and Sadducees, that is, all
Israel except the Essenes. They rejected his baptism, and
accused him of demonology, the favourite indictment of
anti-mystical versus mystical Israel. Moreover, the Baptist
is stated to have reached the eighth or crowning Essene state
of spiritual advancement, the "spirit and power of Elias."

Another point is of the highest importance. The scene
of his ministry was the stony "wilderness," the arid moun-

tain region that stretches from Jerusalem to the Quarantania
mountain, and from the Quarantania to En-Gedi. Now this,
according to Pliny the elder, was the very spot where the bulk
of the Essenes was to be found. Their numbers in his day
were enormous. Josephus fixes these numbers at four thousand souls. We learn of John, too, that his followers were
multitudes, in fact a whole "people prepared for the Lord."

Thus, on the hypothesis that John was not an Essene,
there must have been two large groups of Israelites independently dwelling in a mountainous waste which was of all
spots in Palestine the least fitted for the sustenance of a
crowd. Both were using, moreover, the same rites. How is
it that the second vast group has been completely ignored by
the writers who have chronicled the deeds of John and his
disciples the Nazarenes?

But, before we go further, we must consider the term
Nazarene or Nazarite. Christ, in the inscription on the cross,
was called "The Nazarite" (ὁ Ναξωραῖος, Luke iv. 31). The
Church of Jerusalem was called the Church of the Nazarenes,
or Nazarites. It is the only name for Christians mentioned
in the Acts.[1] The followers of John the Baptist were called
Nazarites or Nazarenes, and they still exist and are called
Nazarenes to this day. The Essenes, according to Epiphanius, were called Nazarines or Nazoræans.[2]

Calmet's Dictionary makes the words "Nazarene" and
"Nazarite" identical, and so does Tertullian. Speaking of
the Christians he says, "For we are they of whom it is
written, Their Nazarites were whiter than snow."[3]

The Nazarite in old Israel was the prophet, the mystic.
The root word is nâzîr, and it signifies "separation." The
true Nazarite, like the prophet Samuel, was separated to the
Lord from his mother's womb. He made a vow to let his
hair grow like the Indian yogi. He made a vow to abstain
from wine. This vow, in the case of the real Nazarite, was
for life. Jeremiah (Lam. iv. 7) uses the word as synonymous
with the prophets of Israel. "Her Nazarites were purer than

[1] Acts xxiv. 5.　　　[2] "Adv. Hær.," xi. 29.
[3] V. Marcion, cap. viii. p. 196.

snow." Amos does the same: "I raised up of your sons for prophets, and of your young men for Nazarites" (Amos ii. 11).

There is a popular theory amongst English divines that Christ was called ὁ Ναξωραῖος, the Nazarite, or as we translate it, "Jesus of Nazareth," because, according to Matthew (ii. 23), he stayed for a short time at Nazareth with his parents on his return from Egypt; but Pilate, in writing up Christ's offence upon the cross, would scarcely have taken this small event of His life into consideration. He intended most probably to write up that Jesus was the anointed leader of the Nazarites. So fearful was the importance of the great mystical movement in Palestine in the view of the dominant party, that all devout Jews were required to utter the following curse three times a day—

"Send thy curse, O God, upon the Nazarenes." [1]

But when Israel began to slaughter prophets instead of listening to them, the Nazarite from a reality became a sham. The form remained, and it was customary on certain occasions for a pious Jew to let his hair grow and to abstain from wine for a week. He was not, of course, a real prophet. The Tree of Deborah with its mystical dreams had been cut down by the priest.

Let us examine a little more carefully the picture of the Nazarenes given to us in the recently recovered "Book of Adam," which Franck considers so invaluable. They are also called Sabeans and Mandaites. I make use of the version by Norberg, translated by F. Tempestini. [2]

The Nazarenes, or Disciples of John, believed in an "inert God," who remained quiescent and concealed in the "black waters." He is also called the Self-existent (p. 71).

They divided space into Fira (ethereal spirit substance, the Buthos of the Gnostics) and Ayar (the Pleroma). From the inert God dwelling in Fira emanated Mana, the "Lord of Glory," the "King of Light," and Youra, the "Lord of Light." The word Mana has puzzled Hebrew scholars. It signifies a "vase." Is it an accidental circumstance that the first

---

[1] Jerome, cited by Riddle, "Christian Antiquities," p. 135.
[2] Migne, "Dict. des Apocryphes," vol. i. p. 2.

emanation of Âdi Buddha is called Manas in India? The
Sanskrit word Manas is equivalent to the Greek word Nous.
The divine beings Manas, Mana, and Nous, are identical.
They represent the inert God in his active form.

The Nazarenes held that Mana produced millions of
Manas, peopling space with many starry systems, and Fira
millions of Firas and Schekintas. Schekinta is a form of
the word Shechinah, and signifies "divine majesty rendered
present and living with men" (p. 69).

"All these stand up and praise Mana, the Lord of Glory,
dwelling in Ayar."

Important amongst the creations of Mana, the Lord of
Glory, was a heavenly Jordan planted with immortal trees
(p. 68). This Jordan produced millions of other Jordans.
For the benefit of the "Nazarenes of the world" was also
instituted the great "Baptism of Light," (pp. 39, 121), called
also the "Baptism of the First Life" (p. 59), the various presentments of God being likewise called the "First Life," the
"Second Life," and so on.

It is recorded in the "Book of Adam" that Fetahil, a
subordinate spirit of light, formed a project to bridge earth
and heaven with a mighty bridge. In this he was opposed
by the Touros, the giant spirits of darkness (p. 82). The
institution of the Nazarenes was plainly this bridge. They
proposed to bring a "Kingdom of Light" (p. 64) down to the
dull dark earth. The denizens of this Kingdom of Light
were clothed in white, like the Essenes (p. 39). They were
"Apostles of Righteousness."

They had the "seal of the Father." They warred with
"arms not made of steel." They were "the Elect," the
Illuminati. To the humble Nazarenes it was given to know
the mysteries of the kingdom of heaven.

"Revealer, who makest known the inmost secrets, have
mercy on us," says one of their invocations (p. 63).

I will write down a few texts from this bible of pre-
Christian Christianity—

"Blessed are the peaceful" (p. 24).

"Blessed are the just, the peacemakers, and the faithful."

" Blessed are the peacemakers that abstain from evil "
(p. 64).

" Desire not gold nor silver, nor the riches of the world.
For this world will perish, and all its riches."

" Bow not down to Satan, nor to idols and graven images ",
(p. 31).

" When thou makest a gift, O chosen one, seek no witness
thereof to mar thy bounty. He who collects witnesses of his
almsgiving loses his merit. Let thy right hand be ignorant
of the gifts of thy left " (p. 32).

" Feed the hungry, give drink to the thirsty, clothe the
naked ; for he who gives will receive abundantly " (p. 32).

" Submit yourselves to the powers " (p. 66).

Here is a description of the city of light in the clouds—

" The mercy and goodness and majesty of the King of
Light cannot be fathomed. None can know these things
save the life that is within thee, and the spirits and messengers
that gird thee around.

" Thy creatures they know not even thy name.

" The kings of light ask one another, What is the name of
the Great Light ?   They answer, He has no name.

" His throne is stable, like the throne of the Most High.
It is stablished from generation to generation.

" No poor sculptor of earth has fashioned this throne.
The palace of the king was not built up by earthly masons.
Immovable he dwells in a city of diamonds, a city without
discord and broils.

" In that city are no butchers, nor gluttons surcharged
with meat. It knows not the wine of wantonness nor the
songs of riot.

" Its vesture is spotless, and its crown eternal. The tears
of weeping women disturb it not.

" No corpses are seen in its streets, nor war, nor warriors.
The King of Light gives of his own pure joy to all his
children.

" Monarch of angels and kings, wearing upon his brow
a mighty crown, he rules every being by his sweetness and
power " (p. 26).

This is how the Nazarenes attacked orthodox Mosaism—

"Then will appear that ignoble nation which will slaughter fat offerings and make God's sanctuary swim in blood. It will commit wicked acts and call itself the People of the House of Israel. It will circumcise with a bloody sword, and smear its face and lips with gore. Its sons will burn with infamous lust, perverting the faith. I say to the chosen ones, My disciples, peacemakers, and faithful, who live in these days, follow not their example. Shun their feasts and avoid their drinks; marry not their daughters. A generation of slaves and adulterers, instead of honouring the Most High, they will discard Moses, the prophet of the Holy Ghost, who gave them the Law, and dishonour Abraham, that other prophet of God. . . .

"I, the first of Apostles, tell all the sons of Adam who have been, or will be, born into the world, shun the speech of these angels of apostasy. They are able to render apostate the sons of men, creating the pride of gold and silver, of treasure and possessions, the lust of false appearances, and illusive shows.

"Their sons will take up arms and engage in the agonies of strife. They will say, fear us, adore us, set up altars in our midst. They will wear the cloak of hypocrisy, and make a pretence of fasting and of deeds of bounty. . . .

"Put on your stoles and white garments, O peacemakers, symbols of the water of life. Put on your heads white crowns, like the crowns of glory of heaven's angels. . . .

"You who are peacemakers say not, This is hidden, and this is unknown. Say not that to the Most High alone is known the mysteries. He has revealed them to you. Take up arms not of steel, but of more worthy metal, the weapons of faith and justice, the weapons of the Nazarene" (pp. 54, 55).

The following passages throw some light on the rites of the peacemakers :—

"Listen to my words, O chosen ones. Observe the great fast, that fast which contemns the food and drink of this mortal world.

"When thou eatest, or drinkest, or sleepest, or restest, in

all things strive to exalt the Name of the great King of Light,
and hasten to the Jordan to receive His baptism."

"Give bread, water, and a home, to him who is tormented
by the tyranny of persecution" (p. 35).

"Assemble the faithful. Read to them the scriptures.
Pray to the Lord for His mercy, that His splendour may go
before and his light follow after. Say to the chosen ones the
soft words that I have spoken to thee, and give them the
hymn that I have inspired" (p. 35).

CHAPTER X

Jesus and the Baptist—Great importance of the Baptism of Jesus—Initiation of Early Christians—Buddha's Baptism, Fasting, and Temptation.

JESUS AND THE BAPTIST.

WE now come to the adult Jesus. The first prominent fact of His life is His baptism by John. If John was an Essene the full meaning of this may be learnt from Josephus—

"To one that aims at entering their sect, admission is not immediate ; but he remains a whole year outside it, and is subjected to their rule of life, being invested with an axe, the girdle aforesaid, and a white garment. Provided that over this space of time he has given proof of his perseverance, he approaches nearer to this course of life, and partakes of the holier waters of cleansing ; but he is not admitted to their community of life. Following the proof of his strength of control, his moral conduct is tested for two years more ; and when he has made clear his worthiness, he is thus adjudged to be of their number. But before he touches the common meal, he pledges to them, in oaths to make one shudder, first that he will reverence the Divine Being, and, secondly, that he will abide in justice unto men, and will injure no one, either of his own accord or by command, but will always detest the iniquitous, and strive on the side of the righteous ; that he will ever show fidelity to all, and most of all to those who are in power, for to no one comes rule without God ; and that, if he become a ruler himself, he will never carry insolence into his authority, or outshine those placed under him by dress or any superior adornment ; that he will always love truth, and press forward to convict those that tell lies ; that he will keep his hands from peculation, and his soul pure from unholy gain ; that he will neither conceal anything from the brethren of his order, nor babble to others any of their secrets, even though in the presence of force, and at the hazard of his life.   In addition to all this, they take oath not to communicate the doctrines to any one in any other way than as imparted to themselves ; to abstain from robbery, and to keep close, with equal care, the books of their sect and the names of the angels.   Such are the oaths by which they receive those that join them " (Josephus, De B. J., II. 8, 2, 13).

As a pendant to this, I will give the early Christian initiation from the Clementine " Homilies."

" If any one having been tested is found worthy, then hand over to him according to the initiation of Moses, by which he delivered his books to the Seventy who succeeded to his chair."

These books are only to be delivered to " one who is good and religious, and who wishes to teach, and who is circumcised and faithful."

" Wherefore let him be proved not less than six years, and then, according to the initiation of Moses, he (the initiator) should bring him to a river or fountain, which is living water, where the regeneration of the righteous takes place."   The novice then calls to witness heaven, earth, water, and air, that he will keep secret the teachings of these holy books, and guard them from falling into profane hands, under the penalty of becoming " accursed, living and dying, and being punished with everlasting punishment."

" After this let him partake of bread and salt with him who commits them to him." [1]

Now if, as is so widely believed in England, the chief object of Christ's mission was to stablish for ever the Mosaism of the bloody altar, and combat the main teaching of the ἀσκητής, or mystic, which " postulates the false principle of the malignity of matter," why did He go to an ἀσκητής to be baptized ? Whether or not Christ belonged to mystical Israel, there can be no discussion about the Baptist.   He was

[1] Clem., " Homilies," ch. 3, 4, 5.

a Nazarite "separated from his mother's womb," who had induced a whole "people" to come out to the desert and adopt
the Essene rites and their community of goods. And we see,
from a comparison of the Essene and early Christian initiations, what such baptism carried with it. It implied preliminary instruction and vows of implicit obedience to the
instructor.

Continuing our parallelism between the lives of Christ
and Buddha, we will now show that he, too, had his baptism,
fasting, and temptation. We will turn to the Buddhist
narrative, which may here throw light on the Christian
account.

The first temptation of Buddha was at the great gate of
the Palace of Summer. Suddenly Mâra, the very wicked
one, appeared in the air and called out to the prince—

"Prince Siddhârta, do not lead the life of a yogi. In seven
days' time you shall be a universal monarch, ruling the four
great continents. Return to the palace."

Buddha refused nobly ; but, by the magic influence of the
wicked one, he harboured a strong inclination to look once
more on the city of his father. He combated this fancy ; when
lo, and behold, by a mighty miracle, Mâra the tempter caused
the earth to pivot round "like the wheel of a potter." Suddenly the sad eyes of Buddha fell on the tall towers and
brilliant lamps of the great city sleeping in the moonlight.
The young man hesitated, and then rode on [1] in the direction
of Vaiśâlî.

In the morning he reached the Anoma (modern Aumi)
River below Sangrâmpura. At this point the god Indra,
disguised as a hunter, induced him to take off his emeralds
and silks and put on a hermit's dress. The prince cut off
his flowing locks with his own sword. He sent back the
charioteer and the good horse Kaṇṭaka. Each of these incidents was afterwards commemorated by a chaitya at the
spot. They meant, of course, that Buddha's guru, personify-
ing Indra, had made Buddha go through the customary
initiation, the tonsure, vows of poverty, etc.

[1] Bigandet, "Burmese Life," p. 65.

Leaving the Anoma, which is a branch of the modern Raptee, the prince made his first real halt at Vaiśâli (the modern Besârh), a spot about twenty miles north of Patna. Here he found a number of yogis undergoing their initiation in yoga-vidya, or white magic, in a forest.

In this wood, Buddha commenced what the "Lalita Vistara" calls the "ecstatic meditation on Brahma and his world." But to obtain yoga, or the mystic union with Brahma, the novice must become a servant-pupil of some eminent adept (Brahmajnâni). At Vaiśâli was a holy man, Arâṭa Kalama, and Buddha said to him, "By thee, O Arâṭa Kalama, must I be initiated into the condition of a seeker of Brahma (Brahmacharin)."

For six years Buddha sat cross-legged, seeking to obtain the visions of the higher Buddhism and the magical faculties which by all old mystics were considered a guarantee that the visions were genuine. He stopped his respiration, says the narrative, and got to eat only one grain of the jujube-tree per diem.

These practices began by-and-by to reduce the prince to a mere mass of dried skin and bone. The villagers thought he was dying. In the Chinese version it is recorded that he fasted forty-seven days and nights without taking an atom of food. When he was in these straits, Mâra appeared before him with a second temptation. He urged him to save his life by breaking his long fast and eating food—

"Sweet creature," said the tempter, in dulcet tones, "you are at the hour of death. Sacrifice food, and eat a portion of it to save your life."

The reply of Buddha is a fine one—

"Death, demon, is the inevitable end of life. Why should I dream of avoiding death? Who falls in battle is noble. Who is conquered is as good as dead. Demon, soon I shall triumph over thee. Lust is thy first army, ennui thy second, hunger and thirst are thy third army. Passions and idleness and fear and rage and hypocrisy are amongst thy soldiers, backbitings, flatteries, false renown,—these are thy inky allies, soldiers of a chief whose doom is near."

It is to be observed how close all this is to the two temptations of Christ—the appeal to hunger and the magical view of the glorious material Jerusalem.

A third temptation is with the daughters of Mâra, disguised as beautiful women. Then Mâra again accosts Buddha—

"I am the lord of desire; I am the master of this entire world. Gods and men and beasts have all fallen into my power. Thou art in my domain. I charge thee, leave that tree and speak to me!"

"If thou art the lord of appetite," replies Buddha, "thou art not the prince of light. I am the lord of the kingdom of righteousness. Forsake the way of evil."

"Ascetic," said the wicked one, "what you seek is not easy to attain. Bhrigu and Angiras by many austerities sought emancipation and failed to find it."

Bhrigu and Angiras were two of the seven Rishis of the Vedas.

The wicked one draws a sword from its scabbard, and thunders out in a menacing voice, "Rise up as I order. Obey me, or like a green reed thou shalt be cut in pieces."

At the same time the spirits of darkness hurl mountains and flames and mighty trees at Buddha. Globes of fire dart through the air, and huge masses of iron, and terrible javelins tipped with a deadly poison. From the four corners of heaven the turmoil rages, and huge monsters are summoned from the vast abyss beneath the earth.

With majestic calmness, Buddha views all these demon hostilities as a sickly dream, as illusion. By the aid of his guardians of the unseen world, the bolts launched against him are turned into beautiful flowers.

In the most solemn manner, Buddha then calls to Brahma Prajâpati, lord of creatures, and to his heavenly host, and to "all the Buddhas that live at the ten horizons." He smites the ground, and earth reverberates like a huge vessel of brass. His prayer is, "Disperse this inky crew!"

Immediately the horses and chariots and elephants of the demon army are tumbled into the mud and the mighty warriors dispersed. They fly like birds before a blazing forest. The Wicked One himself becomes haggard, immensely aged, depressed, overcome. A spirit of the immortal tree takes compassion upon him, and restores him with consecrated water.

"Because I refused to listen to the wise words of my sons, and opposed this pure being, misery has been my lot, and fear and humiliation. Cursings and contempt have come upon me by mine own seeking."

When Buddha was emaciated and almost dead with his terrible fastings, a mystic woman, named Sujâtâ, appeared upon the scene. She took the milk of a thousand cows; and skimming the cream seven times, she boiled it with rice. It was placed in a golden pot, and lo and behold, prodigies—the outline of the Indian cross (swastika) and Krishṇa's St. Andrew's cross (śrivatsa) appeared on the surface. Sujâtâ with her slave appeared before the failing devotee, and the latter, ashamed of his nakedness in the presence of the young girls, dug up the shroud of a slave recently buried. Then Buddha accepted the offering. When he had eaten the rice milk his body assumed a beauty never known before. From that time he was called "the comely śramaṇa (ascetic)." The gold pot was thrown into the river; it floated up the stream against the current. A serpent king got possession of it.

The name of Sujâtâ ("of happy birth") is a very thin disguise for the happy birth of the new Adam. She is, of course, Dharma or Prajñâ, divine wisdom personified as a woman. That there may be no mistake about this, a second episode in the "Lalita Vistara" brings down Queen Mâyâ from heaven to persuade her son to eat food.

It is said that Buddha after his long fast had his skin loose as a camel, that his ribs pierced through his poor skin and gave him the aspect of a crab. How could this poor emaciated fainting being be called the handsome śramana?

In the "Aitareya Brâhmaṇa" it is announced that the mystic marriage of the rice and milk each day in the temple rites was designed to produce a "sacrificial man," a spiritual double of the officiating priest, who was able to visit the heaven of Indra, and obtain cattle, propitious rain, and so on, for the worshippers. This was the exoteric explanation ; but the esoteric one is, I think, revealed in a Cingalese book, the "Sâmañña Phala Sutta." Buddha details at considerable length the practices of the ascetic, and then enlarges upon their exact object. Man has a body composed of the four elements. It is the fruit of the union of his father and mother. It is nourished on rice and gruel, and may be truncated, crushed, destroyed. In this transitory body his intelligence is enchained. The ascetic finding himself thus confined, directs his mind to the creation of a freer integument. He represents to himself in thought another body created from this material body—a body with a form, members, and organs. This body, in relation to the material body, is like the sword and the scabbard ; or a serpent issuing from a basket in which it is confined. The ascetic, then, purified and perfected, commences to practise supernatural faculties. He finds himself able to pass through material obstacles, walls, ramparts, etc. ; he is able to throw his phantasmal appearance into many places at once ; he is able to walk upon the surface of water without immersing himself ; he can fly through the air like a falcon furnished with large wings ; he can leave this world and reach even the heaven of Brahma himself.

Another faculty is now conquered by his force of will, as the fashioner of ivory shapes the tusk of the elephant according to his fancy. He acquires the power of hearing the sounds of the unseen world as distinctly as those of the phenomenal world—more distinctly, in point of fact. Also by the power of Manas he is able to read the most secret thoughts of others, and to tell their characters. He is able to say, "There is a mind that is governed by passion. There is a man that is enfranchised. This man has noble ends in view. This man has no ends in view." As a child sees his earrings reflected in the water, and says, "Those are my earrings," so the purified ascetic recognizes the truth. Then comes to him the faculty of "divine vision, and he sees all that men do on earth and after they die, and when they are again reborn. Then he detects the secrets of the universe,

I

and why men are unhappy, and how they may cease to
be so.

The "Lotus" tells us that "at the moment of death thousands of Buddhas show their faces to the virtuous man."[1]
This clairvoyance of Buddhism seems very like the "discerning of spirits" recorded by St. Paul. Professor Beal
shows that the aureole, adopted afterwards for saints in the
Christian religion, proceeded from an idea of the Buddhists
that the ascetic after practising *tapas* was supposed to be
furnished with an actual coruscation on his head. In all
Buddhist writings the double of Buddha, the "glorified body,"
to use St. Paul's words, is described as being exquisitely
beautiful. I think the words, " the handsome śramaṇa," must
allude to this phantasmal appearance, and not to the visible
body shrivelled and marred by long fastings.

To reach the abode of Yama the Indian had to cross the
Vaitaranî, the River of Death. This river became with
Buddhists the Nairañjana, which ran past Buddha's tree. To
cross this river and reach the "other bank," the heaven of the
mind, was the object of the Buddhist baptism. Buddha
plunges into the water. Before plunging in, he exclaims—

"I vow from this moment to deliver the world from the
thraldom of death and the wicked one! I will procure salvation for all men, and conduct them to the 'other shore.'"
But his strength has been so reduced by the penance of six
years that he cannot reach it. When lo! a spirit of the tree
stretches forth a hand and assists him. In the Burmese
version, the tree itself bends down its branches as at the birth
of the prince.

In the "Lalita Vistara," Mâra opposes in person, and
makes the bank grow higher as the prince tries to get out.
There is a certain significance in an incident of the Burmese
version. On emerging, Buddha dons for the first time the
holy yellow dress of the Muni.

The advantage of the "Lalita Vistara," in my view, is
that it is a jumble of many schools of Buddhism piled the one
on the top of the other. Each school has added its quantum

[1] " Lotus," p. 279.

and left the earlier matter still on its pages. In it Buddha
bathes in the mystic Jordan of India, the Nairañjana. But a
second narrative describes the gods and cherubs and nymphs
of the sky coming down with vases and garlands and fans
and umbrellas to perform the mystic abhisheka (baptism).[1]
The great dome of heaven, glittering with many stars, is
described as having become one vast chaitya,[2] or Buddhist
temple. Vases of water of exquisite perfume are poured
over the body of Buddha, and all that trickles down is seized
eagerly by some of the spirits, for has it not touched his
diamond body? In the "Gospel of the Infancy" many
miracles are done with water that has bathed the infant
Jesus. The time has come to go a little more deeply into the
ancient mysteries, especially the Buddhist ones.

[1] Page 351.   [2] Page 349.

CHAPTER XI.

Growth in Spirit symbolized by the Growth of the Food of the People—
Buddhist Festivals regulated by Rice Culture—The Zodiac as a
Symbol of Stages of Spiritual Progress—In Buddhism—In Chris-
tianity—The "Monastery of our Lord"—Description by Josephus.

" KEEP the mysteries for Me and the sons of My house"
(Jesus).[1]

I must begin by pointing out a prominent feature in
ancient mystic symbolism. The food of the people, its growth
and culture, was made use of as an image to veil the growth
and culture of man's spiritual nature. This was a marked
point in the Mysteries of Osiris in Egypt, and Ceres at
Eleusis. The grain, the Bread of Life, was buried in a
"cave" at the spring or Sowing Festival, like Christ and
Buddha, or in a coffin like Iacchus and Osiris. The cave was
the earth-life. Then at the great Feast of the Pentecost, the
Varshâ or Feast of the Waters in Buddhism, the Bread of
Life was baptized with heaven's own water. This was the
period of "Purification," the first of the three great steps
made by the mystic in spiritual knowledge according to
Dionysius the Areopagite. This was the Festival of the Lesser
Mysteries in Greece. It was called sometimes the "Feast of
Weeks" in Palestine, as it occurred exactly seven weeks after
the second day of the Feast of the Passover, and symbolized
the gift of the Law on Sinai and the descent of the Holy
Ghost in the Christian Church. The Lesser Mysteries with
early Christians are described by Clement of Alexandria as

---

[1] Cited in the Clementine "Homilies," xix. 20; apparently from the
"Gospel of the Hebrews."

taking the form of "catechetical instruction," "preparation" etc. They were, according to him, the "milk for babes" in contradistinction to the "Gnostic communication," the goal and focus of the Greater Mysteries. Then came the great festival of the year, the Festival of the Virgin, the Festival of Mary, the Festival of the Tree, the Festival of Tabernacles. The Bread of Life has come forth from the ground and the dark clouds of an Indian rainy season have been followed by the bright sun of an Indian September. This is the period of the "Illumination" of Dionysius the Areopagite, the Feast of Lanterns in Buddhist countries. Finally, at the spring festival, whose rites celebrate the dying as well as the new year, a mighty rice cake about the size of a footstool is placed on the altar. The worship of this is sculptured in all the old topes. The *pain bénit*, cross-buns, etc., symbolize the same fancy, the perfection of the mystic at the end of the year. Easter was, of course, the end of the old year and the beginning of the new year in the early Church.

A comparison of these rites with the times and seasons of various lands shows that they fit in admirably with the times and seasons of India, and fit in most imperfectly with those of Egypt, Greece, and the West, thus suggesting derivation.

India is a vast triangle, flat and torrid. It is admirably adapted to the cultivation of rice. From about the middle of June to the middle of September there falls an almost incessant deluge. On the volume of this hinges the question whether the poor, dark-skinned, cotton-clad vegetarians will have abundance in their thatch-roofed mud houses or famine. This suggests three great festivals in honour of the great Giver of Rice.

1. The Sowing Festival, the Feast of Flowers. It began formerly seven days before the commencement of the new year, which latter event took place on the 1st of March. In rice cultivation the rice fields have to be flattened and surrounded with mud banks to confine the water that falls during the rains. This may be the origin of the smoothing of rough places at the birth of Buddha.

2 The Feast of the Waters. In Siam and the South the image of Buddha is washed with great pomp, and every holy talapoin, or monk, is soused with jars of water by his inferiors. The poor folks then scramble for this sacred fluid. If they can lap up a drop or two that has touched a holy man or an idol they are happy for life. All classes souse and wash one another, sometimes with scented water, as in the Indian Holi. The two large tanks in Chinese temples, reproduced in the large fons or baptisterium of old Christian churches, which was ample enough to baptize a crowd at a time, seem to point to this rite. The Greek Christians still rush into the Jordan on a certain day and splash one another, and sousings were known to the Church of the Middle Ages. This is the Buddhist Varshâ, or Lent ; and the monks preach twice a day instead of once a week. During this period the temples are thronged, and the offerings very large. But, according to the acute Father La Loubére, the cultivation of the material rice has more to do with this lenten piety and generosity than the cultivation of the rice-milk of immortality. " The rice harvest depends upon plentiful rain, and plentiful rain upon piety," say the Siamese.[1]

3. The Feast of the Subsidence of the Waters, the Feast of the Tree, the Feast of Lanterns. To this day in India the Hindoos, headed by their Râjah, go out into the jungle and live like the Israelites, in tabernacles and booths of leaves. The Râjah goes solemnly to a rice field and plucks a stalk. His court scramble for the remainder. It is the season for the great illuminations in Buddhist countries, and the tala-poins of Siam, as Father La Loubére tells us, go out at this season for three weeks, and pass the nights in vigils in little huts built of leaves and boughs. Each day they return to the temple for a daily service.[2] In Pegu, the night is passed in illuminations by all the people, and the great gate of the city is thrown open. Thanks are everywhere given to Buddha for an abundant harvest.

[1] La Loubére, cited in Picart, vol. vii. pp. 64, 66. See also Purchas on the Pegu Festival, p. 37.

[2] Cited by Picart, " Cérémonies, etc.," p. 65.

PLATE IV.

OLD BUDDHIST ZODIAC.

This gives us the scaffolding of the story of Buddha, and of the other Avatâras.

1. For the due cultivation of the food of the people God was imaged as that food, and the festivals and the incidents during the mystical year that his life was supposed to last, arranged to promote that culture. Indeed, those who are familiar with the superstitions of the rice culture still existing in modern Ceylon, and the elaborate incantations performed for an auspicious day to turn the first sod, to soak the rice, to sow it, to charm away the rice grubs, to slaughter the rice flies, to obtain fruitful rain, and at last to reap it, would think that religion was at first the chief branch of agriculture.[1]

2. A man becoming at last one with God imaged as the kosmos is painted for the mystics, and the zodiac used to mark the stages of his spiritual progress.

This I learnt first from the life of Buddha. It is recorded in the "Lalita Vistara,"[2] that the star Pushya (δ of Cancer) was shining when he entered his mother's womb. This means, of course, that when Pushya rises in the sky the Celestial Elephant (Capricorn) enters the womb of Earth, the mighty mother. The spring festival, with its ploughing and sowing, is selected for the time of his birth ; his horse, Kaṇṭaka, is born at the same moment, because the symbol for Aries is the horse. The first three months lumped together may be classed under the sign of the Indian twins, who are represented as a naked young man and woman, and docketed with a coarse name. Buddha is in the earth-life, in the palace with the seven moats, in the kâma loka, or domain of appetite, pure and simple. We have the carnal marriage of the mystic as distinguished from the marriage of the lamb.

The period terminates with the Indian Olympia, when Krishṇa, Buddha, and Râma win each a bride at a great archery or wrestling competition.

When the Twins dominate the sky the Bow (Sagittarius) is shining at midnight.

But when we view the year as symbolizing the life of

[1] See Mr. Le Mesurier's paper in vol. xvii. p. 3, *Journ. As. Soc.*
[2] Page 61.

a mystic, this festival is of immense importance, for it was the festival of what the ancients called the " Lesser Mysteries."

See how the signs of the zodiac now prepare us for the " Greater Mysteries," at the crucial festival of the Tree (Virgo). With Cancer commences the gnawing away of animalism.

The Buddhist Virgo is often represented by a tree ; which explains the " lion throne" (Leo), round the " tree of know-ledge " that Buddha sat under, a tree on which the pearl Mani (the Balance) glistened. Here commences the great fight of the dreaming mystic with Mâra (Scorpio) conquered at length with the bow of Indra the conqueror (Sagittarius). In the Indian religion, this was called the state of Indra the Jina (the conqueror). " To him that overcometh will I give a crown of life," says the Apocalypse.

Buddha then attains the " elephant called Bodhi " (gnosis), as the " Lalita Vistara," calls it, the elephant being the symbol of occult wisdom. A mystic maiden then gives him a vase of amrita, or immortal food (Aquarius). Finally, the mystic reaches the sign called Dharma Chakra. This, with Brahmin heroes, was the " Quoit of Death," that never failed in its terrible flight. With Buddhists, it became the " Wheel of the Law," the Zodiac of Dharma, our mystic mother. Without any disguise, the spiritual adept was called Chakra-vartin (he who has turned through the zodiac).

Here we have the key of what St. Paul calls the "hidden wisdom." It was based on the text, " And God made man after His own image." To work this out, man had to become one with God's starry tabernacle. The Essenes, at the highest initiation, had to become "Temples of the Holy Ghost," and Christians were long called " Temples of God."

The mystic gate through which the soul passes from darkness to light is the " Porte Noire " of the Chinese Buddhist, Hwen Thsang. In the Mahâbhârata are passages describing a gate of a city of cloudland, over which the bird Garuda broods. With the masons it is the royal arch, with the two mystic columns, Jachin and Boaz. Madame Guyon and the Christian mystics saw at once that it was the " open door " of Rev. iii. 8, only to be unlocked by the " Key of

David" (probably the looped cross carried by all Egyptian initiates into the realms of Osiris).

I will write down, from the Catholic Prayer-book, a few sentences of the "Litany of the Blessed Virgin."

"Holy Mother of God!" "Mother of Christ!" "Gate of Heaven!" "Chalice of the Spirit!" "Mystical Rose!" "Tower of Ivory!" "Mirror of Justice!" "Seat of Wisdom!"

To these I will add a part of the hymn of incense from an older Christian ritual, that of the Armenian Church.

"Triumph and rejoice, O Sion, daughter of Light, Universal Mother with thy children. Don thy raiment and jewels, August Bride, Shining Tabernacle of Light, an image of Heaven; because the Anointed God, the Being of Beings, sacrifices himself for thee without being consumed. To reconcile us to the father, and to expiate our sins, he distributes his flesh and blood. By virtue of this sacrifice, pardon him who built this temple.

"The Holy Church recognizes and confesses the pure Virgin Mary as Mother of God, by whom has been given to us the bread of life and the consoling cup. Bless her in a spiritual song." ("Hymn of Incense," p. 17.)

This is another hymn from the same ritual—

> "Mother of faith, holy assembly of thousands,
> Sublime nuptial bed,
> Of the house of the immortal Spouse,
> Who decks thee from eternity.
> Thou art a second wondrous heaven,
> Springing from glory to glory.
> Like rays of light thou bearest us in thy great womb
> In the birth of baptism.
> Thou givest us the purifying bread ;
> Thou givest us the blood revered ;
> Rank over rank, thou raisest those aloft
> Who little understand these things.
> The ancient tabernacle is thy type.
> Thy new tabernacle is far above the old ;
> It has broken the gates of diamond,
> And thou hast broken the gates of hell.

We see here the Universal Mother, as the Armenian

ritual calls her, play the same part as she does in Buddhist mysticism. She is the "Gate of Heaven," separating the Golden Jerusalem from Babylon, the Tabernacle of Light from the Tabernacle of Darkness. She is "Wisdom," the palm tree, by En Gaddi, that gives forth "a sweet smell like cinnamon and aspalathus" (Eccl. xxiv.). "To him that overcometh will I give to eat of the Tree of Life which is in the midst of the Paradise of God,"[1] said the mystic Alpha and Omega.

Here she is as the corn-sheaf (Virgo), surmounted by the

dove (Libra), separating the two halves of the zodiac, symbolized by Leo and the old serpent. This is from Smith's "Christian Antiquities." From Martigny's "Antiquités Chrétiennes" (Fig. 9), we get her between the green tree and the dry, the words of Christ used to denote the two trees

Fig. 8.

of the Kabbalah, the Tree of Knowledge and the Tree of Life.

These also symbolize the black and white halves of the zodiac. Zodiacal amulets (Fig. 10) were known to the early Christians.[2] The scales, the Lion of Judah, the cup (Aquarius), the horse and lamb (Aries), are on all the monuments, and Christ is sometimes drawn as the archer. The Apocalypse has the "Woman" with the crescent under her feet, and the crown of

Fig. 9.

twelve stars. Like Aditi, of the Rig Veda, she is the mother of the twelve Adityas or months. Also, she has "the wings of an eagle," the significance of this symbol has already been

[1] Rev. ii. 7.

[2] See Martigny, article "Zodiaque."

noticed. She brings forth a "man child," and the mystic "dragon," with "seven heads," assails both mother and son. "My little children, of whom I travail in birth till Christ be · formed in you,"[1] said St. Paul. In mysticism the mystic must become the Son of God,[2] must be "born again" of the woman with the twelve stars, must be vexed of "scorpions five months," or the five months dominated by Scorpio, before he can reach the crown, the cross, the "mystical death."

Fig. 10.

The Gnostics, in their great controversy with Irenæus and the Romish Church, asserted that the twelve disciples signified the twelve æons, the twelve months of Christ's mystical life. They asserted that the woman with the issue of blood twelve years typified the same piece of mysticism, and her cure was, of course, the higher life. There were two Achamoths or mystical women, the higher residing beyond the Pleroma. The mystical "grace" of the Kabbalah was able to make us sit together "in heavenly places," even in this life, according to St. Paul (Eph. ii. 6).

"But Sophia is justified of all her children." Christ meant here, according to the Gnostics, the twelve stages of spiritual progress, the mystic woman with the twelve stars, the twelve æons that stand round the throne of God.[3]

In the Gnostic initiation, according to this same authority, was a nuptial couch. Do not bishops, nuns, and freemasons, in their initiations, lie down and personate death to this day? And does not Tertullian talk of a Christian rite that imitated the resurrection?

"Into the name of the Unknown Father of the Universe, into Truth the mother of all things, into Him who descended on Jesus, into union and redemption and communion with the powers." This is the form of Gnostic baptism given by Irenæus,[4] and is condemned by that very literal monk; and

[1] Gal. iv. 19.
[2] Rev. xxi. 7.
[3] See Irenæus, "Hær.," bk. i. c. 21, 23.
[4] Ibid., bk. i. c. 3.

so is another assertion of the Gnostics, that the real baptism was different from the mere outward rite. They cited, he tells us, these words of Christ : "And I have another baptism to be baptized with, and I hasten towards it."[1]   There is a text like it in Luke (xii. 50).

This brings us to the catacombs, which are immensely valuable as giving the veiled Christian and also veiled Essene symbolism.   The Abbé Martigny says very justly, "The monuments and writings of the earliest Christian ages are quite clothed in mystery.   Allegory and symbolism reign everywhere.   The language of the Fathers and teachers is full of reticences.   Christian art is a jumble of hieroglyphics and enigmas of which the initiates alone have the key."[2]   He cites St. Paul (1 Cor. iii. 1), who tells the Corinthians that he cannot tell the same truths to the "carnal" and the "spiritual."   He cites Christ as forbidding that which is holy (the secret doctrine) to be given to the "dogs" (Matt. vii. 6), a far more plausible interpretation than that of Baur.   It means, of course, the unspiritual in all regions, and not the material Gentiles.

The catacombs are sepulchral crypts modelled, as Dean Stanley thinks, on the crypts of Palestine.   Their symbolism is chiefly from the Old Testament.   On the tombs of bishops and martyrs figure rude frescoes of Moses striking the rock, Jonah and the whale, the "three children," Jonah naked, sitting under a trellis of gourds.   All this puzzled modern Christians when they were first opened.   No bleeding Christs were to be seen.   What connection was there between these designs and the dead saint whose poor little chapel sepulchre they illustrated ?

In point of fact, each design represented a stage of the spiritual progress of the entombed saint.   From Bosio ("Sculture et Pittore," etc., 1737) I copy four favourite frescoes for illustration.

[1] Irenæus, " Hær." bk. i. c. 81.
[2] "Antiquités Chrétiennes," art. " Secret."

1. The Child in the swaddling clothes of flesh introduced to the "manger" of animal life (Fig. 11).

Fig. 11.

Fig. 12.

2. Moses striking the rock. Purification, the first stage of spirituality in the life of the Chosen One. The water baptism (Fig. 12).

3. The fire baptism (illumination), almost invariably depicted in the catacombs by the three children of Daniel (Fig. 13).

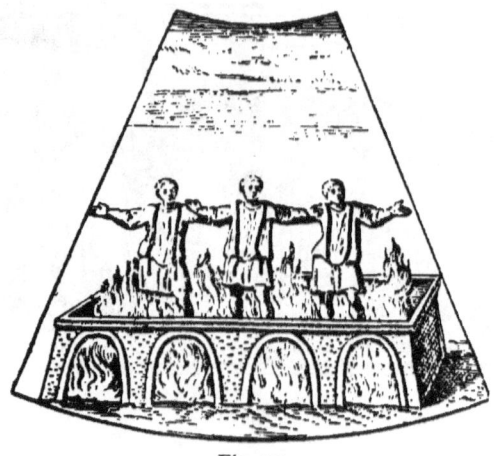

Fig. 13.

4. The Lazarus released from the swathings of the flesh by the jod of the Christus, after the four mystical days passed in the "tomb" or earth life (Fig. 14).

Fig. 14.

The young Christ in the frontispiece also represents the four stages of spiritual progress depicted by the beasts of Daniel. And so do the four horses, sword, or Gemini, scales, bow, and Indian quoit of death (p. 37). Observe that after His progress through the four stages the Christ has the cross on his nimbus. This was the mystical meaning of the cross.

THE MONASTERY OF OUR LORD.

Whilst Protestant polemics are ever seeking to show that Christ opposed mysticism and the ascetic life, the Roman Catholics are equally active in the other direction. Monseigneur Mislin calls the Essenes, Rechabites, and Therapeuts, the "Monks of the Old Law." [1] Catholic writers also call a monastery on the Quarantania mountain the "Monastery of Our Lord." "Monseigneur Mislin tells us that the number of cells pierced in this mountain is so considerable that the rocks of the Quarantania resemble a beehive." [2] Travellers in Burmah and other Buddhist countries record the same always of a hillside where the Buddhist monks have resided.

"The holy grotto," says the Franciscan, Liévin de Hamme, "which our Lord dwelt in during His forty days' fast has not yet lost the paintings that once covered it. Amongst other scenes of His ministry, Jesus is to be still seen here tempted by the devil."

The Carmelite monks maintain that their order has come down direct from Elijah through the sons of the prophets, the Essenes, etc. A book was published by the Carmelite Father Daniel in the seventeenth century with the following title, "The Mirror of Carmel, or the History of the Order of Elias, or the Brothers of Our Lady of Mount Carmel, in which its origin is traced to the Prophet Elias, its propagation to the Children of the Prophets, and its succession shown without interruption through the Essenes, Hermits, and Monks, in answer to attacks, etc. Antwerp, 1680."

It is asserted there that the Monastery of Our Lord dates from the Prophet Elisha. Finding the cells of Mount Carmel and the caverns of the prophets insufficient, he came over and established a new school of the prophets on the Quarantania.

Josephus gives us a description of this region in his day. It is the longest and most elaborate description that he indulges in of any part of Palestine. On this topic he is generally brief. We may argue from this that he knew the

[1] Cited by the author of "Jesus Bouddha," p. 195.
[2] "Jesus Bouddha," p. 194.

region well. Wishing to study the different opinions of the three main sects of the Jews of his day—the Pharisees, the Sadducees, and the Essenes—he tested all three with much labour.

"But all this did not satisfy me, and learning that one Banus was living in austerity in the wilderness, that he had no other raiment than the bark of trees, that his sole food was the fruits of the earth, and that to dominate the flesh he bathed many times day and night and summer and winter in cold water, I resolved to imitate him. Having passed three years with him, I returned to Jerusalem at the age of nineteen. I then commenced the duties of civil life, and embraced the sect of the Pharisees."

Banus was an Essene, and Josephus's ostentatious profession that he was a Pharisee was plainly a blind to escape the persecution of the Jews, and afterwards of the Romans. In describing the three sects, he dismisses the Pharisees and Sadducees in a few lines, but enlarges with abundant detail on the sect of the Essenes, which he calls the *most perfect of all.* Also he practised divination, which would have been viewed as an abomination by the Pharisees.

I cannot do better than here transcribe Josephus's account of the region where the " Monastery of Our Lord " is situate.

" Jericho sits on a plain dominated by a lofty mountain, sterile and naked, and so extensive that it stretches northwards to Scythopolis and southwards to Sodom. Owing to this sterility no one dwells upon it.

"Near Jericho is a large fountain, whose abundant waters fertilize the fields around. Its spring is nigh that ancient city which Jesus, the son of Nave, that brave Hebrew chief, gained by victory. Folks say that the waters of this fountain were of old so dangerous that they rotted earth's fruits, and made pregnant women bring forth before their time. Moreover, the waters spread their poison wherever it could harm. But since that time, the prophet Elisha, that worthy successor of Elias, has made the waters good to drink, and as pure, healthy, and as fecundating as they were formerly nocuous. All this came about thus. That illustrious man having been humanely received by the dwellers in Jericho, wished to mark his sense of gratitude by conferring a favour whose effects should never be seen to cease either by them or by the neighbourhood. Sinking to the bottom of the fountain a jug filled with salt, he lifted his eyes and his hands to heaven, and made oblations on the bank. He then prayed God to sweeten the many streams that, proceeding from this spring, watered the surrounding country ; to temper the air to make it more genial ; to give plenty to the earth, and abundant children to those who cultivated it, the waters never ceasing to be propitious as long as man was just. This earnest prayer had power to change the nature of the fountain, and to make it as fecundating as it was once sterile. The virtue of these waters is so great that a few drops thrown on the soil will render it fertile ; and spots where the waters have long remained bring forth no more than the spots where it rapidly passes, as if they wished to punish those who arrest them in mistrust of their miraculous effects. In all this region is no spring with so long a course.

"The ground it waters is seventy stadia in length and twenty in breadth. Many gardens abound there with palm-trees of many names and natures. Some, if you press them, give forth a honey like ordinary honey, which is here very abundant. Here, too, flourish the cypress and the Indian plum, and that tree which gives forth a balm that the juice of no other fruit can rival. Thus it may be said, as it seems to me, that a country where so many rare products so richly flourish has something divine in it ; and I doubt whether in any other part of the globe is to be found its equal, so rapid is the growth of all that is sown and planted. This is to be attributed to the balmy air and the fecundating attributes of the water. The one opens the flowers and leaves, the other strengthens the roots by forming plentiful sap in the heats of summer, which are so great that without the cooling moisture nothing could grow. But however great the heat may be, each morning there comes a light breeze, which cools the water which folks draw before sunrise. During the winter the climate is warm, and a single garment of cloth is enough

K

when snow is falling in other parts of Judea. This region is one hundred and fifty stadia (about fourteen miles) from Jerusalem, and sixty (about seven miles) from the Jordan. The country between it and Jerusalem is a stony wilderness; and although that which stretches from the Jordan to the Dead Sea is not so mountainous, it is not less sterile and uncultivated. I think I have detailed all the favours granted by nature to the environs of Jericho."

This passage lets us into some of the secrets of the great spiritual movement that changed the world.

The Essene mystics had selected the only spot in Palestine that was warm enough for the Indian yoga or mystic dreaming under trees.

One might almost say that this region had been prepared by nature for its work. It was protected by ranges of arid honey-combed hills, and by the mephitic air of the shores of the Dead Sea. To the dominant party in Jerusalem nature thus opposed Death, Famine, and Fever, three vigilant sentries. It is to be observed, too, that the want of water in the caverns and mountains was another prominent safeguard. It was impossible to remain long in the wilderness without knowing the whereabouts of the "cisterns," the rude reservoirs of rain-water. Hazazon Tamar, or the "City of Palms" (Engedi), was, according to Pliny, the head-quarters of the Essenes. He flourished A.D. 23-79.

This is what he says of the Essenes: "On the western shore (of the Dead Sea), but distant from the sea far enough to escape its noxious breezes, dwelt the Essenes. They are an eremite clan, one marvellous beyond all others in the whole world, without any women, with sexual intercourse entirely given up, without money; and the associates of palm trees. Daily is the throng of those that crowd about them renewed, men resorting to them in numbers, driven through weariness of existence and the surges of ill fortune in their manner of life. Thus it is that through thousands of ages, incredible to relate, their society, in which no one is born, lives on perennial" ("Hist. Nat." v. 17).

"Jésus Bouddha" is a powerful little work tracing out the

connection between Christianity and Buddhism, but from a point of view very hostile to both. The author urges with plausibility that John the Baptist was the head of this school of prophets on the Quarantania. There he was close to the Jordan, which was of so much importance in the religion of the Nazarites. The author argues that it would have been quite impossible for Christ to be baptized of John without the preliminary instruction prescribed to the novice. In point of fact, the "Gospel of the First Infancy" states positively that " He gave himself to the study of the law until he arrived at the end of his thirtieth year." [1]

[1] " First Infancy," chap. xxii. 2.

CHAPTER XII.

The "Signs of an Apostle"—Conflicting views of Catholics and Protestants about Miraculous Gifts—Magic Rites of the Kabbalah—The
"Twelve great Disciples" of Buddhism—"Go ye into all the world."

THE "SIGNS OF AN APOSTLE."

IT is recorded in the "Lalita Vistara," that when Buddha
had completely overcome the wicked one, the bright spirits
came round him as he sat under the tree of knowledge, and
proposed to offer him flowers, in the character of Purusha
(the God-Man). But an objection was raised that he had
not yet attested his great mission by miraculous "signs."[1]
In consequence, Buddha rose aloft into the air, and miraculously checked the flow of the river near him, and broke up
the roadway. "'Tis thus," he said, "that I will now check
the flow of grief in the world." As Buddha's life is an ensample and text book, all this meant that the monk, before
he came to be a perfect Arahat, had to pass an examination
in miraculous gifts at the hands of his brother-monks ; and
in Buddhist histories these examinations are not uncommon.

Dr. Ginsburg, in his work "The Essenes," maintains that
similar tests were required of the early Christians.

"Truly the signs of an apostle were wrought among you
in all patience, in signs, and wonders, and mighty deeds"
(2 Cor. xii. 12).

"And these signs shall follow them that believe: In My
name shall they cast out devils ; they shall speak with new
tongues ; they shall take up serpents ; and if they drink any

[1] Foucaux, p. 336.

deadly thing it shall not hurt them ; they shall lay hands on the sick and they shall recover " (Mark xvi. 17, 18).

" And many that believed came, and confessed, and shewed their deeds " (Acts xix. 18).

" How is it that every one of you hath a psalm, hath a doctrine, hath a tongue, hath a revelation ? If there come in those that are unlearned, or unbelievers, will they not say that you are mad ? " (1 Cor. xiv. 23).

We here get a great point of debate between Catholics and Protestants. All sects have Bibles distinct from their avowed testaments and articles of religion ; and the modern gospel of Protestants is, I think, Smith's " Dictionary of the Bible." In that, under the heading " Magic," it is laid down authoritatively, that man cannot gain what are called super-natural powers by any known natural processes. It is held that the wonders recorded in Gentile schools of magic were all illusory. A miracle is an experience that goes counter to a general law ; and such have been confined to the Hebrew race to " prove the truth " of Mosaism and Christianity, the writer failing to trace, with Dr. Edersheim, a wholesale antago-nism between the two. It is held, that a vague thing called " miraculous gifts," was given to the first Christians, not earned by them. It was not the reward of fastings and ascetic practices, but was gained at once by the touch of an " Apostle," plainly with the providential design of showing, that with the death of these, such " gifts " were to cease. All signs and won-ders since that have been unnecessary as well as unauthentic.

As opposed to this, the Catholics maintain that the visions and so-called miraculous powers of the mystic, or as he was called everywhere at the date of Christ, the ascetic, are due to certain processes which are still available. They appeal to the history and experience of the Jews. They also appeal to the history and experience of the Gentiles, who " had their schools of mysticism which found its highest expressions amongst the Brahmins and Buddhists." [1] If the miracles of the Old Testament were due to a special gift, and all training was considered illusory, the question arises—Why did Elijah

[1] Migne, " Dictionnaire d'Ascéticisme," vol. ii. p. 1514.

establish a school of the prophets at Mount Carmel, and Elisha another near Jericho?

In 1 Kings xviii. we read of a hundred prophets living in a cave. In the next chapter, we see Elias, with his long hair and leathern girdle, sitting under a juniper tree. In the fourth chapter of Judges, we see Deborah judging Israel from under a palm tree. Another prophet (1 Kings xx.) appears "disguised with ashes." St. Paul tells us that the old prophets in sheepskins and goatskins took refuge in mountains, and deserts, and caves. They were destitute, afflicted, tormented. They had trial of cruel mockings and scourgings and bonds. They were stoned, sawn asunder, or slain with a sword. The Indian missionaries get often a truer idea of an Asiatic people like the Jews, than those whose experience is confined to the West. Mr. Ward has recorded, that in India, Elias can still be seen sitting under his tree, and the prophet disguised with ashes.

Another difficulty is in the way of the Protestant theory that miraculous gifts were confined to the Hebrews, and that all training in the schools of the prophets was considered illusory. Many of the most conspicuous performers of miracles in the Old Testament were educated in Gentile schools of the prophets. Moses was trained in the schools of Magic, in Egypt. Joseph presided over those schools. Daniel was *Rab Mag*, or head of the Magicians of Babylon. The Witch of Endor, who recalled Samuel from the grave, was a Gentile, and so was Balaam.

The processes of the ascetic in Catholic mysticism are the same as in all other mysticisms. They have—

1. The "Contemplation Chérubique."
2. The Mystical Union.
3. The "Oraison passive."

The word "union" is the same word as the Indian word yoga. Contemplation is defined to be "the elevation of the soul to God by a simple intuition full of admiration and love."[1] The "oraison" is half prayer half mystic dreaminess, its effect being to dull the animal activity.

[1] Migne, "Dictionnaire de Mysticisme."

Here are some of the spiritual gifts that result from these processes—

1. Mystical seeing.
2. Mystical hearing.
3. Mystical smelling.
4. Discerning of spirits, the clairvoyance of St. Paul.
5. Flight through the air.
6. Mystical preaching.
7. Mystical healing by the laying on of hands, a power conspicuously developed by the celebrated Curé d'Ars.
8. Communication with the spirits of the dead, as when St. Martin was enabled to carry on long conversations with "Thiele and Agnes and Mary." All these topics are treated under their various heads in Migne's "Dictionnaire de Mysticisme."
9. Resurrection of the dead.

These "gifts" are very like those claimed by the Essenes, as already detailed.

What that sect meant by raising the dead it is not easy to settle. It could scarcely have been conceived that the dead man could permanently revive after decomposition has actually set in. A profound student of mysticism, Francis Barrett, who lived at the beginning of the century, wrote a work entitled "The Cabala," which may help us here. He says that the Kabbalists held that there were "two kinds of necromancy." The first consisted in "raising the carcasses." This, it was conceived, could only be effected by the effusion of blood, a fact that lets in some light on the bloody rites of the old creeds. The second process was called Sciomancy, "in which the calling up of the shadow only suffices."[1] The learned gentleman gives the Kabbalistic rites by which "the seven governors of the whole world according to the seven planets" are to be invoked, and other beings "which Origen called the invisible powers."[2] As in Buddhism, these rites seem nearly identical with the sacramental rites or mysteries.

"It is necessary that the invocant religiously dispose

[1] "The Cabala, or Ceremonial Magic." p. 69.
[2] Ibid., p. 43.

himself for the space of many days to such a mystery, and to conceive himself during the time chaste, abstinent, and to abstract himself as much as he can from all manner of foreign and secular business. Likewise he shall observe fasting, as much as shall seem convenient to him." [1] The "Kabbalah" enjoins a fast of forty days. "Now, concerning the place, it must be chosen, clean, pure, close, quiet, free from all manner of noise, and not subject to any stranger's sight. This place must first of all be exorcised and consecrated ; and let there be a table or altar placed therein, covered with a clean white linen cloth, and set towards the east ; and on each side thereof place two consecrated wax lights burning, the flame thereof ought not to go out all these days. In the middle of the altar let there be placed lamens [slips of paper with the ten great names of God] covered with fine linen, which is not to be opened until the end of the days of consecration. You shall also have in readiness a precious perfume, and a pure anointing oil, and let them both be kept consecrated. Then set a censer on the head of the altar, wherein you shall kindle the holy fire, and make a precious perfume every day that you pray.

"Now for your habit, you shall have a long garment of white linen, close before and behind, which may come down quite over the feet, and gird yourself about the loins with a girdle. You shall likewise have a veil made of pure white linen, on which must be wrote in a gilt lamen the name *Tetragrammaton ;* all which things are to be consecrated and sanctified in order. But you must not go into this holy place till it be first washed and covered with a cloth new and clean, and then you may enter, but with your feet naked and bare : and when you enter therein you shall sprinkle with holy water, then make a perfume upon the altar ; and then on thy knees pray before the altar as we have directed.

"Now when the time is expired, on the last day, you shall fast more strictly ; and fasting on the day following, at the rising of the sun, enter the holy place, using the ceremonies before spoken of, first by sprinkling thyself, then,

[1] "Ceremonial Magic." p. 92

making a perfume, you shall sign the cross with holy oil in the forehead, and anoint your eyes, using prayer in all these consecrations. Then, open the lamen [1] and pray before the altar upon your knees ; and then an invocation may be made as follows :—

"AN INVOCATION OF THE GOOD SPIRITS.

"In the name of the blessed and Holy Trinity, I do desire thee, strong and mighty angels (here name the spirits you would have appear), that if it be the divine will of him who is called Tetragrammaton, etc., the holy God, the Father, that thou take upon thee some shape as best becometh thy celestial nature, and appear to us visibly here in this place, and answer our demands, in as far as we shall not transgress the bounds of the divine mercy and goodness, by requesting unlawful knowledge ; but thou wilt graciously shew us what things are most profitable for us to know and do to the glory and honour of his divine Majesty, who liveth and reigneth, world without end. Amen.

"Lord, Thy will be done on earth as it is in heaven; make clean our hearts within us, and take not Thy holy spirit from us. O Lord, by Thy name we have called them, suffer them to administer unto us.

"And that all things may work together for Thy honour and glory, to whom with Thee, the Son and Blessed Spirit, be ascribed all might, majesty, and dominion, world without end Amen."

This is how a Buddhist acquires magical powers.

The novice must select an able teacher. He must be shaved, washed, cleaned. Of particular importance is the choice of the place of initiation. It must be without distinctions, free from the terrors of wild beasts, and haunted by the spirits of the past Buddhas.

The place must be well swept and otherwise cleaned; and fresh earth must be thrown upon it in order to make its surface even and smooth. A magical circle of the five sacred

---

[1] The lamen is the "book" of the Apocalypse.

colours must be drawn in order to overcome evil spirits, who will do all they can to mar the efforts of the devotee. Within the circle an altar is erected, upon which various vessels are ranged, filled with grain and perfumed water. The ceremonies consist in the reciting of incantations and the presentation of food offerings to the good spirits. The incantations must be recited slowly, without raising or lowering the voice. They must be repeated something like a hundred thousand times a day. A rosary with 108 beads helps the counting. A vajra (toy thunderbolt) all this time must be held tightly in the hand. The spirits prayed to are Vajrapâṇi, the holder of Indra's thunderbolt. Sweet dreams and sweet supernatural scents prelude the advent of the supernatural powers. In the rite called Dubed the novice has to fix his gaze on water in a vessel tricked out with knots of the five sacred colours. The modern mesmerist gains power over a sensitive in a somewhat similar manner. Vajra means "diamond" as well as "thunderbolt," and this second idea has been worked into the first. The head of the thunderbolt is shaped like a diamond. It is stated in one passage of the "Lalita Vistara," that Buddha indulged "in that ecstatic meditation whose essence is the diamond."[1] The Buddhists call the spirit body the "diamond body."[2]

The Twelve Disciples.

Buddha, like Christ, had twelve "great disciples."

"Only in my religion," he said solemnly a little before he died, "can be found the twelve great disciples who practise the highest virtues and excite the world to free itself from its torments."[3] These twelve great disciples are the Buddhas who figure round the great statue of Buddha on Buddhist altars. He had sixty minor disciples, and Christ seventy. In the view of Mosheim "Christ appointed seventy, just equal in number to the senators composing the Sanhedrim, to show

---

[1] See p. 206.

[2] For details of initiation, see Subâhu Pariprichcha, Schlagintweit, "Buddhism in Tibet," p. 242.

[3] Bigandet, p. 301.

that the authority of the regular Sanhedrim was at an end, and that He was Supreme Lord and Pontiff of the whole Hebrew race." [1]

The word "apostle" designated the shoeless wandering missionary of Christianity; but it was also used to describe the stationary councillors round the head of the Church. The twelve apostles, according to Renan, were not missionaries, but remained at Jerusalem. After the taking of that city, even the orthodox Jews used the word "apostle" to designate the council round their patriarch.[2] The Essene Sanhedrim abrogated to itself the power of inflicting death (to the blasphemer) and excommunication, a punishment which, according to Josephus, was almost its equivalent. That Christ had His Sanhedrim at an early date is manifest from more than one passage in the New Testament—

"And if he neglect to hear them, tell it unto the Church [assembly]: but if he neglect to hear the Church, let him be as a heathen man and a publican" (Matt. xviii. 17).

"Dare any of you, having a matter against another, go to law before the unjust, and not before the saints?" (1 Cor. vi. 1).

If Christ thus took over the Essene Sanhedrim and set up a government with the avowed purpose of superseding that of the dominant Jews, it is difficult to see how He can be held, when speaking of "every jot and tittle of the law," to have alluded to the law as interpreted by the historical Sanhedrim.

"Go Ye into all the World."

Professor Rhys Davids has pointed out the fact that Buddha's great object was to found a "kingdom of righteousness"[3] (dharma chakra) on earth. From Benares, in the first year of his ministry, he sent forth his sixty disciples on the work of propagandism—

"Depart each man in a different direction, no two on the

---

[1] Mosheim, vol. i. p. 33.

[2] Lightfoot, "Epistle to the Galatians," p. 93.

[3] "Birth Stories," p. 69.

same road. Let each preach dharma to all men without exception "[1] (see Plate V.).

.Let us note what commands Christ gave to His disciples—

"Go not into the way of the Gentiles, and into any city of the Samaritans enter ye not : but go rather to the lost sheep of the house of Israel. And as ye go, preach, saying, The kingdom of heaven is at hand. Heal the sick, cleanse the lepers, raise the dead, cast out devils : freely ye have received, freely give. Provide neither gold, nor silver, nor brass in your purses, nor scrip for your journey, neither two coats, neither shoes, nor yet staves : for the workman is worthy of his meat. And into whatsoever city or town ye shall enter, enquire who in it is worthy ; and there abide till ye go thence. And when ye come into an house, salute it. And if the house be worthy, let your peace come upon it : but if it be not worthy, let your peace return to you. And whosoever shall not receive you, nor hear your words, when ye depart out of that house or city, shake off the dust of your feet. Verily I say unto you, It shall be more tolerable for the land of Sodom and Gomorrha in the day of judgment, than for that city. Behold, I send you forth as sheep in the midst of wolves : be ye therefore wise as serpents, and harmless as doves. But beware of men : for they will deliver you up to the councils, and they will scourge you in their synagogues ; and ye shall be brought before governors and kings for my sake, for a testimony against them and the Gentiles, But when they deliver you up, take no thought how or what ye shall speak : for it shall be given you in that same hour what ye shall speak. But it is not ye that speak, but the Spirit of your Father which speaketh in you. And the brother shall deliver up the brother to death, and the father the child : and the children shall rise up against their parents, and cause them to be put to death. And ye shall be hated of all men for My name's sake : but he that endureth to the end shall be saved. But when they persecute you in this city, flee ye into another : for verily I say unto you, Ye shall not have gone over the cities of Israel, till the Son of man be

[1] Bigandet, p. 126.

PLATE V.

BUDDHA PREACHING.
From Amarávatí.

[*Page* 140.

come. The disciple is not above his master, nor the servant above his lord. It is enough for the disciple that he be as his master, and the servant as his lord. If they have called the master of the house Beelzebub, how much more shall they call them of his household? Fear them not therefore: for there is nothing covered, that shall not be revealed; and hid, that shall not be known. What I tell you in darkness, that speak ye in light: and what ye hear in the ear, that preach ye upon the housetops. And fear not them which kill the body, but are not able to kill the soul: but rather fear him which is able to destroy both soul and body in hell. Are not two sparrows sold for a farthing? and one of them shall not fall on the ground without your Father. But the very hairs of your head are all numbered. Fear ye not therefore, ye are of more value than many sparrows. Whosoever therefore shall confess Me before men, him will I confess also before My Father which is in heaven. But whosoever shall deny Me before men, him will I also deny before My Father which is in heaven. Think not that I am come to send peace on earth: I came not to send peace, but a sword. For I am come to set a man at variance against his father, and the daughter against her mother, and the daughter-in-law against her mother-in-law" (Matt. x. 5-35).

The Essenism of this passage is very remarkable, Jesus using at times the very words of John. His disciples are to be without money or two coats or shoes, like the barefooted Essenes. Also He says not a word about His divinity as in the Gospel of St. John, but tells His disciples to deliver the same gospel as John and the Book of Adam, the gospel of the kingdom of light.

Another point is remarkable. No Christian disciple had yet begun to preach, and yet what do we find? A vast secret organization in every city. It is composed of those who "are worthy" (the word used by Josephus for Essene initiates, see *ante*, p. 107), and they are plainly bound to succour the brethren at the risk of their lives. "Peace be with you!" was the password, says the author of "Jésus Bouddha." It is remarkable that this mystic greeting is also in the "Book of Adam." [1] And we find likewise that a vast organization of persecution is already afoot, with its councils, and scourgings, and stonings, and martyrdom. I think this is as strong a fact as we can have. The brethren were infringing the Jewish law as interpreted by the dominant party. Thaumaturgic healing and exorcisms were called witchcraft, raising the dead necromancy, speaking with the afflatus of the spirit possession.

An orthodox Jew, instead of succouring such, was bound by his law to help the recognized authorities to bring them to justice. And yet it is announced that the crime of Sodom and Gomorrha was as nothing to such an act. Plainly those that were "worthy" were not purblind Jews, but initiated children of light, who had taken fearful vows to obey the Grand Master.

And here I must point out that, until I had made a study of Buddhism, I was quite unable to piece together the somewhat contradictory accounts that have come down to us of the Essenes and their monasteries. Josephus describes them as congregated herdsmen and diggers. Philo paints them as communities of ascetics engaged in what he calls the "contemplation of the Divine Essence." Pliny shows them to us as a large section of the Jews, recruited entirely by propagandism. Then, too, although Josephus tells us they "shunned cities," it is plain, from the numbers that could be ferreted out by the secret police at Jerusalem in the early days of St. Paul, that many after their initiation went back to civil life, like Philo and Josephus. This probably was the class that, according to the latter, might have wives and children.

But my study of Buddhism threw light upon this subject. When that religion was chased from India, the âchârya of the great Buddhist convent at Nalanda, the "high priest of all the world," as he is called in the Mahawanso, took refuge in Tibet. As the Grand Lâma he is still acknowledged to be the head of the Buddhist Church by the Chinese, the Japanese, and the Tartars. This gives to the Buddhism of Tibet an exceptional value.

[1] Page 126.

According to the Abbé Huc,[1] the Buddhist lâmas in those regions may be divided into four classes—

1. Those dwelling in the Lâma Serais, and serving the temples.

2. Inferior lâmas told off to attend to the herds, etc., belonging to the Lâma Serais.

3. Lâmas who have undergone the initiation, but have found that they have no vocation, and have returned to civil life.

4. The wandering lâmas, whose tent, as they prettily term it, is the starry tent of Buddha.

These men, each with no luggage besides a stout staff, wander all over Tartary, Mongolia, Turkestan. They plunge into deserts, "sleep under a rock, or on the icy peak of a mountain," obeying no impulse except a fervid passion for a fresh start each morning. Sometimes a Tartar gives them a cup of tea, stirred up with a few pinches of flour. Sometimes they sleep for one night in a corner of a Tartar tent. These men are of the pattern of the formidable Parivrâjakas, that first preached dharma to humanity; and they account for the marvellous spread of Buddhism. Also, I think, they throw a side-light on the shoeless "apostles" sent forth by Christ.

[1] " Voyage dans la Tartarie, le Thibet, et la Chine," vol. i. p. 189.

CHAPTER XIII.

I WILL write down a few more texts that show Essenism in
the New Testament.

A RELIGIOUS COMMUNITY ESTABLISHED OF THOSE WHO HAVE OBTAINED THE GNOSIS, OR KNOWLEDGE OF THE MYSTERIES OF THE KINGDOM OF HEAVEN.

"It is given to you to know the mysteries of the kingdom
of heaven" (Matt. xiii. 11).

"The kingdom of God is come unto you" (Matt. xii. 28).

"The kingdom of God is within you" (Luke xvii. 21).

BAPTISM PRECEDED BY CONFESSION OF SINS, THE INITIATION INTO THIS SOCIETY.

"And were baptised of him [John] in Jordan, confessing
their sins" (Matt. iii. 6).

"And Jesus, when He was baptized, went up straightway
out of the water; and lo! the heavens were opened to Him,
and He saw the Spirit of God descending like a dove and
lighting upon Him" (Matt. iii. 16).

"When they heard this, they were baptized in the name
of the Lord Jesus; and when Paul had laid his hands upon
them, the Holy Ghost came on them, and they spake with
tongues and prophesied" (Acts xix. 5, 6).

New Name on Conversion.

"Thou shalt be called Cephas, which is by interpretation a stone" (John i. 42).

"Lebæus, whose surname was Thaddeus" (Matt. x. 3).

Fasting a Necessary Initiation.

"Howbeit this kind goeth not out but by prayer and fasting" (Matt. xvii. 21).

"But thou, when thou fastest, anoint thy head and wash thy face" (Matt. vi. 17).

Community of Goods.

"And all that believed were together, and had all things common" (Acts ii. 44).

"If thou wilt be perfect, go and sell that thou hast, and give to the poor, and thou shalt have treasure in heaven: and come and follow Me" (Matt. xix. 21).

"For some of them thought that, because Judas had the bag, that Jesus had said to him, Buy those things we have need of against the feast" (John xiii. 29).

Oaths prohibited as in Essenism.

"Swear not at all" (Matt. v. 34).

A Rigid Continence exacted.

"All men cannot receive this saying, save they to whom it is given. . . . There be eunuchs which have made themselves eunuchs for the kingdom of heaven's sake. He that is able to receive it, let him receive it" (Matt. xix. 11, 12).

"And I looked, and lo! a Lamb stood on the Mount Sion, and with Him an hundred forty and four thousand, having His Father's name written on their foreheads. . . . These are they which were not defiled with women, for they are virgins" (Rev. xiv. 1, 4).

Wine and Flesh-meat forbidden.

On the subject of flesh-meat and wine, I will now cite some verses of a remarkable chapter (Rom. xiv.). St. Paul

L

had not yet visited the eternal city, but some earlier Christian missionaries had. Thus two parties had sprung up amongst the converts, a party opposed to the consumption of flesh-meat and wine, and a second party, St. Paul's own converts. The second party was plainly the smaller party, as it is alluded to as a "remnant according to the election of grace." [1]

"The Church of Rome," says Renan, alluding to the earlier missionaries, "was a Jewish Christian foundation, in direct connection with the Church of Jerusalem." [2] In a word, it was the chief stronghold outside the Jewish capital of the Petrine party, and the usual controversy on the subject of "works" and "grace" had apparently arisen in the Roman capital between the Pauline and the Petrine party. The former had plainly appealed to their leader upon the points under discussion.

" I say then, Hath God cast away His people? God forbid. For I also am an Israelite, of the seed of Abraham, of the tribe of Benjamin. God hath not cast away His people which He foreknew. Wot ye not what the Scripture saith of Elias? how he maketh intercession to God against Israel, saying, Lord, they have killed Thy prophets, and digged down Thine altars; and I am left alone, and they seek my life. But what saith the answer of God unto him? I have reserved to Myself seven thousand men, who have not bowed the knee to the image of Baal. Even so then at this present time also there is a remnant according to the election of grace. And if by grace, then is it no more of works : otherwise grace is no more grace. But if it be of works, then is it no more grace : otherwise work is no more work."

This passage shows that by deeds of the Law St. Paul meant the Law as interpreted by Peter ; for the whole con-troversy in Rome, as we shall see, rolled upon the question whether meat or herbs only should be consumed, and water drunk or wine.

Now I am willing to stake the whole case of the Essenism of early Christianity on St. Paul's answer. That is the crucial

---

[1] Rom. xi. 5.   [2] "Conférences d'Angleterre," p. 65.

point. In the view of Bishop Lightfoot, Christianity was a
great anti-mystical and anti-ascetic movement, which had
substituted wine for water in the daily sacramental dinner
of the Nazarenes. Is it not perfectly plain that if St. Paul
had been aware of this fact, his reply would have been quite
triumphant? He would have pointed to the solemn injunctions of the Master, and condemned the innovating party in
no measured terms. Instead of this, what do we find? He
orders his disciples at Rome to drink nothing but water.
Furthermore, he orders them to eat nothing but "herbs," no
animal food. He ought, of course, to have been aware, as
pointed out by Bishop Lightfoot, that Christ at His model
supper ate lamb. But it seems that St. Paul was not aware
of this fact.

"Him that is weak in the faith receive ye, but not to
doubtful disputations. For one believeth that he may eat all
things: another, who is weak, eateth herbs. Let not him that
eateth despise him that eateth not; and let not him which
eateth not judge him that eateth: for God hath received him.
One man esteemeth one day above another: another esteemeth
every day alike. Let every man be fully persuaded in his own
mind. He that regardeth the day, regardeth it unto the Lord;
and he that regardeth not the day, to the Lord he doth not
regard it. He that eateth, eateth to the Lord, for he giveth
God thanks; and he that eateth not, to the Lord he eateth
not, and giveth God thanks. Let us not therefore judge one
another any more: but judge this rather, that no man put
a stumbling-block or an occasion to fall in his brother's way.
I know, and am persuaded by the Lord Jesus, that there is
nothing unclean of itself: but to him that esteemeth anything
to be unclean, to him it is unclean. But if thy brother be
grieved with thy meat, now walkest thou not charitably.
Destroy not him with thy meat, for whom Christ died. Let
not then your good be evil spoken of: For the kingdom of
God is not meat and drink; but righteousness, and peace, and
joy in the Holy Ghost. For he that in these things serveth
Christ is acceptable to God, and approved of men. Let us
therefore follow after the things which make for peace, and

things wherewith one may edify another. For meat destroy
not the work of God. All things indeed are pure ; but it is
evil for that man who eateth with offence. It is good neither
to eat flesh, nor to drink wine, nor any thing whereby thy
brother stumbleth, or is offended, or is made weak. Hast
thou faith ? have it to thyself before God. Happy is he that
condemneth not himself in that thing which he alloweth.
And he that doubteth is damned if he eat, because he eateth
not of faith : for whatsoever is not of faith is sin."

It is to be observed, too, that St. Paul advises Bishop
Timothy to "use a little wine for his stomach's sake"
(1 Tim. v.).

This is most important. A recently recovered work, the
" Teaching of the Twelve Apostles," has put beyond question
the fact that the sacramentum or mysterion of the early
Church was identical with the daily dinner of the brethren as
with the Essenes and Therapeuts. But Bishop Timothy was
plainly accustomed to celebrate it with water. Is not this a
complete proof that he knew nothing of Christ's command, to
use the " fruit of the vine " in the sacramentum ? Consider
also the reason that St. Paul gives for the change. Had he
been aware of what is now reported to have occurred at the
last supper, would he have merely urged a change to wine
on the utilitarian grounds here urged ? " For thy stomach's
sake, and thine often infirmities ! "

This puts us in a better position to consider the controversy
which raged in the second century, when Tatian protested
against the introduction of wine at the altar as being part and
parcel of a great scheme to destroy the spirituality of the
Christian movement.

" Ye gave the Nazarite wine to drink, and commanded the
prophets saying, Prophesy not ! "

St. Jerome for this has branded him as an innovator, and
attributed the Encratites and other water-drinking communities then confessedly existing in the Church to his teaching.
But this charge will not bear a moment's scrutiny. The fourteenth chapter of Romans shows that as early as the visit of
Paul to Rome water was used in the Roman Church.

This brings us to the passages describing the institution of the sacrament. St. Paul, who is first in the field, confesses that he received the account he gives of it " of the Lord," that is, in visions, and not historically. He says not a single word of the cup containing wine. On the contrary, in the previous chapter, in attempting to derive the Christian rites from Moses, he says distinctly that the followers of Moses and Christ had the "same spiritual drink," namely, the "Rock," which is Christ,[1] that is, of course, water.

This account, confessedly derived from the visions of St. Paul, is copied in the synoptic gospels, with this additional verse—

"Verily I say unto you, I will drink no more of the fruit of the vine until that day that I drink it new in the kingdom of God."

It is to be remarked, however, that the passage is so clumsily put in in St. Luke, that a second account of Christ's words when delivering the cup has been left, in which there is not a word about the " fruit of the vine." It is announced also that the disciples were heralded into the guest chamber by a man bearing a pitcher of *water*.

Another strong fact may be mentioned. Tatian composed a harmony of the four Gospels ; and Tatian maintained that the use of wine was an innovation. It is evident, therefore, that in the four gospels, as known to him, the passages about the "wine-bibber" and the "fruit of the vine" were not to be found ; or he would not have gone to the trouble of harmonizing gospels which disproved his main thesis, but would have taken his stand on the gospels of the gnostics. Tatian's "Harmony" was afterwards pronounced to contain added heretical matter, and was destroyed. This is silly ; for the composition of a diatessaron or harmony is the one literary feat where the addition of spurious matter is impossible. A "harmony" implies a scrupulous respect for the text. The charge confesses change, but proves that that change must have been subsequent.

One more piece of important evidence, and then I have

[1] 1 Cor. x. 4.

done. The Liturgy of St. Chrysostom, as given by Dr. Neale and Dr. Littledale,[1] shows that warm water was the ingredient of the cup when it was composed.

"Sir, fill the holy cup," says the deacon, plainly showing that at this moment it was empty. A piece of bread is then placed in it, and warm water. I will write down the passage—

"After the priest has broken the holy bread into four portions, he exclaims,

"'The Lamb of God is broken and distributed. He that is broken and not divided in sunder, ever eaten and never consumed, but sanctifying the communicants.'

"And the deacon, pointing with his orarion to the holy cup, saith,

"'Sir, fill the holy cup.'

"And the priest, taking the upper portion (that is the I.H.C.), makes with it a cross above the holy cup, saying,

"'The fulness of the cup of faith, of the Holy Ghost,' and thus puts it into the holy cup.

"Deacon, 'Amen.'

"And taking the WARM WATER he saith to the priest,

"'Sir, bless the warm water.'"[2]

After this the warm water is poured into the cup; and nowhere is any mention of wine. Had wine been used, it would have also been blessed.

Then *a priori* what conceivable reason could have made Jesus change the main Essene rite? He and His followers were so pursued and persecuted, that he envied the secure crannies of the fox (jackal) and the birds of the air. Why order a daily consumption of wine under such circumstances, when even cisterns of water in the craggy wastes must have been hard enough to find?

The Nazarites, or Nazarenes, were characterized from the outside by a special mark—a vow to drink nothing but water. Why suddenly introduce a change which would place before each disciple the cruel dilemma of disobedience or perjury? On the other hand, the motives of Pope Victor and his succes-

---

[1] Neale and Littledale, "Liturgies of the Greek Church," p. 120.
[2] Ibid.

sors are patent enough. They were going to restore Pontifex Maximus and the Roman worship of Bacchus, calling Bacchus "Christ." They were going to give to the victorious Christians the victory of terminology alone, but to the pagans the victory of ideas. "The Pope is the ghost of the deceased Roman empire," said Hobbes, "sitting crowned upon the grave thereof."

"FOLLOW ME!"

Buddha called his disciples with precisely the same words as Jesus. Almost his earliest converts were thirty profligate nobleman in the Kappâsya jangal. He said to them, "Follow me!" and they abandoned their lemans. He then converted three Hindu ascetics and all their followers. "He received them," says Dr. Rhys Davids, in his translation, "into the order with the formula, Follow me!"[1]

These words have received an extended meaning since those days. Nuns have their "vocation" and the disciples of Wesley their mystic "call." Zacchæus under his fig tree, like the Catholic saint, St. John of the Cross, before his crucifix, calls aloud, "Seigneur, faites que je vois!" and, lo, the Christ appears.

"THE SAME CAME TO JESUS BY NIGHT."

Professor Rhys Davids points out that Yásas, a rich young man, came to Buddha by night, for fear of his rich relations. Buddha spoke to him of love, of virtue, of heaven (swarga), and of the way to salvation, and made him a convert.[2]

"THE KING OF REMEDIES."

Buddha, like Christ, is the Great Physician who heals all sicknesses, bodily and mental. In China, he is called the "Unsurpassable Doctor;" in the "Lalita Vistara," the "King of Remedies."[3] He visits the sick man Su-ta, and heals his soul as well as his body.[4] At Vaiśali, likewise, he performs a

---

[1] "Birth Stories," p. 114.
[2] See "Tibetan Life," by Rockhill, p. 38.
[3] "Lalita Vistara," p. 99.   [4] "Chinese Dhammapada," p. 47.

very miraculous act. This city was afflicted with a pestilence something like modern cholera. It was due to a number of corpses festering on the river's bank. An appeal is made to Buddha, and he comes and dispels the pestilence with a strong wind.[1] A disciple has his feet hacked off by an unjust king, and Buddha cures even him.[2] King Śuddhodana is on the point of death. Buddha forms a sort of mesmeric chain round him, with the co-operation of four disciples, and arrests his malady.[3]

To all who have been in the East the gospel recitals of healings and the casting out of devils are very lifelike, the twanging of rude instruments, "the minstrels and the people making a noise." And sober travellers in Buddhist countries record many genuine cures. The Abbé Huc describes an old woman sick of a 'grievous fever in the Valley of the Black Waters. The only doctors known in those regions, he tells us, were in the Buddhist lamaseries ; and if the case is pronounced a grave one, or, in the language of the country, if a tchutgour, or devil, is in possession of the sick person, a strong array of Buddhist monks, with rude Tartar music, and scents and psalms, is despatched, with bell and book and candle. Eight lámas arrived, and thoroughly and instantaneously cured the old woman, says the Abbé.[4] In the old volumes of travels of Ribeyro and Knox in Ceylon are many wonderful narratives. Grievous choleraic pains were removed whilst the patient, lying on his back, was touched by the Buddhist śramaṇa, before a short hymn to Buddha had finished its echoes. The bites of venomous snakes were rendered harmless, not once but many times. A demoniacal possession called Lycanthropy, very prevalent in the island, was always cured.[5]

This brings me to a passage in the "Travels" of Abbé Huc, which seems to me to throw much light on the disputation with the doctors as recorded in the lives of both Christ

---

[1] Bigandet, p. 186. [2] Burnouf, Introduction, etc., p. 156.

[3] Bigandet, p. 192.

[4] "Voyage dans la Tartarie," tom. i. chap. ii.

[5] See "Cérémonies Religieuses," by Picart, vol. vii. pp. 143, *et seq.*

and Buddha. In Tibet, the novice, to strengthen his dialectics, is set up before a conclave of doctors learned in the four great branches of knowledge—namely, mysticism, medicine, liturgy, and prayers,—and is pelted with questions. He, on his side, is allowed to start all sorts of fantastic inquiries. "There is nothing so monstrous as these disquisitions," says the Abbé, " which suggest the discussions of the Middle Ages." [1] But a friend of mine tells me that young Jesuits have precisely the same method of training—logomachies, where such topics as the immaculate conception are very freely handled.

All this seems of great importance in settling the question whether or not Christ was an Essene. Such training would be quite out of place in the Mosaism of the Bloody Altar. Its main idea was that without the shedding of the blood of certain animals on certain fixed days there was no remission of sins. It expressly forbid the casting out of devils, and unorthodox dialectics.

THE SERMON ON THE MOUNT.

Buddha, like Christ, delivered a sermon on a mountain, which is held by the Buddhists to condense his teaching. [2] The heart of man, he said, was a burning fire, and so were all the objects in the three worlds, the objects that could be seen, felt, heard, or touched. This fire was the fire of lust, of anger, of ignorance. It was due to the shortcomings of a life exposed to rebirth, sickness, old age, mortal anxieties. Only the disciples of Buddha could escape the torments of this fiery furnace. Freed from lust and human passion, they had acquired the wisdom that leads to the Perfect Man. They were no longer bound by the sixteen laws, for they had passed into higher regions. This sermon was delivered on the Elephant's Head, a mountain near Buddha Gayâ.

This seems to throw much light on Christ's "æonial fire." Our version translates it "eternal fire," and turns its meaning topsy-turvy. The Jews in Christ's day believed in the metempsychosis, and the word "æon" was the Greek word for

---

[1] "Voyage," vol. ii. p. 118.   [2] Bigandet, p. 141, note.

one rebirth.   The sorrows and experiences of mortal life constitute the fire that purifies and gives us wisdom.

THE BEATITUDES.

The Buddhists, like the Christians, have got their Beatitudes. They are plainly arranged for chant and response in the temples.   It is to be noted that the Christian Beatitudes were a portion of the early Christian ritual.

"An Angel.

" 1 Many angels and men
  Have held various things blessings.
  When they were yearning for the inner wisdom.
  Do thou declare to us the chief good.

"Buddha.

" 2 Not to serve the foolish,
  But to serve the spiritual ;
  To honour those worthy of honour,—
      This is the greatest blessing.

" 3 To dwell in a spot that befits one's condition,
  To think of the effect of one's deeds,
  To guide the behaviour aright,—
      This is the greatest blessing.

" 4 Much insight and education,
  Self-control and pleasant speech,
  And whatever word be well spoken,—
      This is the greatest blessing.

" 5 To support father and mother,
  To cherish wife and child,
  To *follow a peaceful calling*,—
      This is the greatest blessing.

" 6 To *bestow alms* and *live righteously*,
  To give help to kindred,
  Deeds which cannot be blamed,
      These are the greatest blessing.

" 7 To *abhor and cease from sin*,
  Abstinence from strong drink,
  Not to be weary in well-doing,
      These are the greatest blessing.

"8 *Reverence* and *lowliness*,
   Contentment and gratitude,
   The hearing of the Law at due seasons,—
   This is the greatest blessing.

"9 To be *long suffering* and *meek*,
   To associate with the tranquil,
   Religious talk at due seasons,—
   This is the greatest blessing.

" 10 *Self-restraint* and *purity*,
   The knowledge of the noble truths,
   The attainment of Nirvâṇa,
   This is the greatest blessing.

" 11 In the midst of the eight world miseries,
   Like the man of pure life,
   Be calm and unconcerned,—
   This is the greatest blessing.

" 12 Listener, if you keep this law,
   The law of the spiritual world,
   You will know its ineffable joy,—
   This is the greatest blessing." [1]

"A NEW COMMANDMENT GIVE I UNTO YOU, THAT YE SHOULD LOVE ONE ANOTHER."

"By love alone can we conquer wrath. By good alone can we conquer evil. The whole world dreads violence. All men tremble in the presence of death. Do to others that which ye would have them do to you. Kill not. Cause no death." [2]

"Say no harsh words to thy neighbour. He will reply to thee in the same tone."

"I am injured. I am provoked. I have been beaten and plundered. They who speak thus will never cease to hate."

"Religion is nothing but the faculty of love." [3]

---

[1] "Khuddaka Pâṭha." See Rhys Davids, "Buddhism," p. 127, and Bigandet's translation, p. 118, note.

[2] Sutra of Forty-two Sections, v. 129. M. Léon Feer, in his translation, gives the very words of Luke vi. 31.

[3] Bigandet, p. 223.

" Let goodwill without measure impartial, unmixed, without enmity, prevail throughout the world, above, beneath around." [1]

" WHOSOEVER SHALL SMITE THEE ON THY RIGHT CHEEK, TURN TO HIM THE OTHER ALSO."

A merchant from Sûnaparanta having joined Buddha's society, was desirous of preaching to his relations, and is said to have asked the permission of the master so to do.

" The people of Sûnaparanta," said Buddha, " are exceedingly violent, if they revile you, what will you do ? "

" I will make no reply," said the mendicant.

" And if they strike you ? "

" I will not strike in return," said the mendicant.

" And if they try to kill you ? "

" Death," said the missionary, " is no evil in itself. Many even desire it, to escape from the vanities of life." [2]

"AND IF THINE EYE OFFEND THEE, PLUCK IT OUT, AND CAST IT FROM THEE."

De Carne (p. 113) relates that the Buddhists of Laos are accustomed to offer up parts of their bodies to Buddha. Whilst he was in their parts, a man cut off his forefinger and offered it up.

[1] " Khuddaka Pâtha," p. 16.   [2] Bigandet, p. 216.

CHAPTER XIV.

"Glad Tidings"—Faith—The Sower—The Armour of Light—"How hardly shall they that have riches instruct themselves in the way"—Names of Buddha—The Metempsychosis in Judaism and Christianity.

"GLAD TIDINGS OF GREAT JOY."

ODDLY enough the Buddhist gospel is also called "glad tidings," (subhâ shita). A worthy king named Subhâshita-gaveshî, desiring to learn this gospel, interrogated the god Indra in the guise of a demon.

"Leap, O king, into a fiery lake, heated day and night for seven days, and then I will tell thee."

The good king abdicated in favour of his son, and flung himself into the fiery lake. Forthwith it became pure cold water. Then Indra, appearing in his full majesty, recited the following stanza—

> "Walk in the path of duty.
> Do good to thy neighbour;
> Work no evil unto him.
> He who confers a benefit on a man
> Is lodged comfortably both here and in the next world."[1]

FAITH.

"Ânanda, have faith. Tathâgata enjoins it. All that thou hast to do Tathâgata has already accomplished."[2]

"Friends, faith is the first gate of the Law."[3]

"All who have faith in me obtain a mighty joy."[4]

"Ânanda, turn thy soul to faith. This is my command."[5]

[1] R. L. Mitra, "Northern Buddhist Literature," p. 29.
[2] "Lalita Vistara," p. 95.   [3] Ibid., p. 39.
[4] Ibid., p. 188.   [5] Ibid., p. 96.

"Ânanda, have faith, and I will conduct thee to the saints, and say, 'These are my friends!' Thus, if a man with a beloved son should die, the friends of the father would succour the son. In this way, Ânanda, those who have faith in me I love and cherish; for they are my friends, and come to seek in me a refuge." [1]

In point of fact, as Colebrooke shows, discussions on the "efficacy" of faith and works, on "grace" and free-will are especially Indian.[2] They would be much out of place in a religion of State ceremonial like the Lower Judaism.

The Sower.

It is recorded that Buddha once stood beside the ploughman Kasibhâradvâja, who reproved him for his idleness. Buddha answered thus—

"I, too, plough and sow, and from my ploughing and sowing I reap immortal fruit. My field is religion. The weeds I pluck up are the passions of cleaving to existence. My plough is wisdom, my seed purity." [3]

On another occasion he described almsgiving as being like "good seed sown on a good soil that yields an abundance of fruits. But alms given to those who are yet under the tyrannical yoke of passions are like a seed deposited in a bad soil. The passions of the receiver of the alms choke, as it were, the growth of merits." [4]

"Not that which goeth into the Mouth defileth a Man."

In the "Sutta Nipâta," chap. ii. is a discourse on the food that defiles a man (Âmagandha). Therein it is explained at some length that the food that is eaten cannot defile a man, but, "destroying living beings, killing, cutting, binding, stealing, falsehood, adultery, evil thoughts, murder,—this defiles a man, not the eating of flesh."

[1] "Lalita Vistara," p. 96.   [2] "Essays," vol. i. p. 376.
[3] Hardy, "Manual," p. 215.   [4] Bigandet, p. 211.

"Where your Treasure is."

"A man," says Buddha, "buries a treasure in a deep pit, which, lying concealed therein day after day, profits him nothing; but there is a treasure of charity, piety, temperance, soberness, a treasure, secure, impregnable, that cannot pass away, a treasure that no thief can steal. Let the wise man practise virtue; this is a treasure that follows him after death."[1]

Buddha's Third Commandment.

"Commit no adultery." Commentary by Buddha: "This law is broken by even looking at the wife of another with a lustful mind."[2]

The House on the Sand.

"It [the seen world] is like a city of sand. Its foundations cannot endure."[3]

The Armour of Light.

Buddha called the Bodhi, or Gnosis, "the great armour that makes perfect the saint."[4]

"Thou canst not Tell Whence it cometh nor Whither it goeth."

"The men of wisdom have seen that speech is like an echo. It is like a note on the lute. The wise man asks, Whence has it come? Whither has it gone?"[5]

Blind Guides.

"Who is not freed, cannot free others. The blind cannot guide in the way."[6]

The Way.

The "Way" that touches not earth.

The "Way" of the one great conqueror of the three thousand great worlds.[7]

---

[1] "Khuddaka Pâtha," p. 13.
[2] See "Buddhaghosa's Parables," by Max Müller and Rogers, p. 153.
[3] "Lalita Vistara," p. 172. [4] Ibid., p. 264.
[5] Ibid., p. 175. [6] Ibid., p. 179. [7] Ibid., p. 262.

" The way of freedom."

" The way of God " (Swayambhu).

" The way which leads to the Gnosis." [1]

" AND NOW ALSO THE AXE IS LAID TO THE ROOT OF THE TREES." [2]

" Having collected together a large multitude of trees, dowered with virtue, austerity, patience, and brave hearts, and sheafed with divine meditation. Mounted in the ship whose essence is the adamant, I will pass myself and transport countless beings across the flood." [2]

" HEAVEN AND EARTH SHALL PASS AWAY, BUT MY WORD WILL NOT PASS AWAY."

"Though the heavens were to fall to the earth,
And the great world be swallowed up and pass away ;
Though Mount Sumeru were to crack to pieces,
And the great ocean be dried up :
Yet, Ánanda, be assured,
The words of the Buddha are true." [3]

" FOR THEY SAY AND DO NOT " (Matt. xxiii. 3).

" As a bright but scentless flower, is the talk of the man that speaks but does not act " (" Dhammapada ").

" NEITHER DOTH A CORRUPT TREE BRING FORTH GOOD FRUIT " (Luke vi. 43).

" The fool is his own enemy, doing the deed that produces bitter fruit " (" Dhammapada ").

" PROVIDE YOURSELVES BAGS THAT WAX NOT OLD, A TREASURE IN THE HEAVENS THAT FADETH NOT " (Luke xii. 33).

" The unchaste, that seek not the divine treasure in youth, lament the past, and lie like broken bows " (" Dhammapada ").

---

[1] " Lalita Vistara," p. 262.   [2] Ibid., p. 206.
[3] Beal, " Romantic History," p. 11.

"I SAY UNTO ALL, WATCH" (Mark xii. 37).

"Watch thine own self. Of the three watches of the night, the wise man watches at least through one" ("Dhammapada").

"YE MAKE CLEAN THE OUTSIDE OF THE CUP AND THE PLATTER, BUT WITHIN THEY ARE FULL OF EXTORTION AND EXCESS" (Matt. xxxiii. 25).

"Why this goat-skin (O Brahmin) and thy matted hair. Without is varnish, but within is filth" ("Dhammapada").

"Not matted hair, nor birth, nor gold, make the Brahmin, but truth and justice. He who has burst the cord and the strap, who is awakened, . . . who, being innocent, patiently endures abuse, blows, and chains,—the awakened man, the divine singer, he who overcometh, him I call the Brahmin" ("Dhammapada").

"AND HE STRETCHED FORTH HIS HAND TOWARDS HIS DISCIPLES, AND SAID, BEHOLD MY MOTHER AND MY BRETHREN."

"Root up the love of self like a lotus in autumn. A father, children, kinsmen avail not in the domains of Death. As a sleeping village swept off by the torrent is the fate of him who trusts in his flocks and family" ("Dhammapada").

"The cares and fears that come from children, and wives, and riches, and houses are like the chains and terrors of prison. From one is escape, not from the former" (Sutra, in Forty-two Sections).

"HOW HARDLY SHALL THEY THAT HAVE RICHES," ETC.

"How hardly shall the rich man instruct himself in the Way. Who shall have riches and power, and not become their slave?"

"Beauty and riches are like a sharp blade smeared with honey. The child sucks, and is wounded" (Sutra, in Forty-two Sections).

M

"ALL LIARS HAVE THEIR PART IN THE LAKE THAT
BURNETH WITH FIRE."

"Who says what is not true goes to hell" ("Dhammapada").

"FOR NOW WE SEE THROUGH A GLASS DARKLY"
(1 Cor. xiii. 12).

Buddha was once asked, "What are the signs of the
divine Gnosis (Bodhi)?" He answered that it was like a
glass cleaned and polished. When the disciple has entered
the Way and conquered self, the mirror begins to manifest
itself in all its clearness" (Sutra, in Forty-two Sections).

NAMES OF BUDDHA.

"The Lord," "The Lord Buddha (Buddhanâth)," "The
Lord of the Universe (Jagannâtha),"[1] "Saviour,"[2] "The
Adored of Men and Gods," "The Omniscient," "The God
above Gods," "The King of Remedies,"[3] "The Artificer of
Happiness,"[4] "The God-man (Purusha),"[5] "The Father of
Heaven (Lokabandhu),"[6] "The Father."[7]

In the "Lalita Vistara" the Buddhas of the past come
down in glorious forms, and thus address him : "Light of the
world, this vow was made by thee : 'To the worlds subject
to old age and death I will be a refuge!'"[8]

Here is another passage : "Good shepherd, full of wisdom,
deign to guide those who have fallen over the great precipice."[9]

THE ONE THING NEEDFUL.

Certain subtle questions were proposed to Buddha, such
as : What will best conquer the evil passions of man? What
is the most savoury gift for the alms-bowl of the mendicant?
Where is true happiness to be found? Budhha replied to
them all with one word, *Dharma*[10] (the heavenly life).

[1] "Lalita Vistara," p. 126.   [2] Ibid., p. 128.
[3] Ibid., p. 6.   [4] Ibid., p. 97.   [5] Ibid., p. 335.
[6] Ibid., 367.   [7] Ibid., p. 351.   [8] Ibid., p. 163.
[9] Ibid., p. 372.   [10] Bigandet, p. 225.

"Who did Sin, this Man or his Parents, that he was born Blind?" (John ix. 3).

Professor Kellogg in his work entitled " The Light of Asia and the Light of the World," condemns Buddhism in almost all its tenets. But he is especially emphatic in the matter of the metempsychosis. The poor and hopeless Buddhist has to begin again and again "the weary round of birth and death,"[1] whilst the righteous Christians go at once into life eternal.[2]

Now it seems to me that this is an example of the danger of contrasting two historical characters when we have a strong sympathy for the one and a strong prejudice against the other. Professor Kellogg has conjured up a Jesus with nineteenth century ideas, and a Buddha who is made responsible for all the fancies that were in the world 500 B.C. Professor Kellogg is a professor of an American University, and as such must know that the doctrine of the *gilgal* (the Jewish name for the metempsychosis) was as universal in Palestine A.D. 30 as it was in Râjagriha 500 B.C. An able writer in the *Church Quarterly Review* of October, 1885, maintains that the Jews brought it from Babylon.[3] Dr. Ginsburg, in his work on the " Kabbalah," shows that the doctrine continued to be held by Jews as late as the ninth century of our era. He shows, too, that St. Jerome has recorded that it was "propounded amongst the early Christians as an esoteric and traditional doctrine."[4]

The author of the article in the *Church Quarterly Review*, in proof of its existence, adduces the question put by the disciples of Christ in reference to the man that was born blind. And if it was considered that a man could be born blind as a punishment for sin, that sin must have been plainly committed before his birth. Oddly enough, in the "White Lotus of Dharma" there is an account of the healing of a blind man, "Because of the sinful conduct of the man [in a former birth] this malady has arisen."[5]

[1] Page 250.   [2] Page 248.
[3] Article, "Esoteric Buddhism."   [4] The "Kabbalah," p. 43.
[5] Chap. v.

But a still more striking instance is given in the case of the man sick with the palsy (Luke v. 18). The Jews believed, with modern Orientals, that grave diseases like paralysis were due, not to physical causes in this life, but to moral causes in previous lives. And if the account of the cure of the paralytic is to be considered historical, it is quite clear that this was Christ's idea when He cured the man, for He distinctly announced that the cure was effected not by any physical processes, but by annulling the "sins" which were the cause of his malady.

Traces of the metempsychosis idea still exist in Catholic Christianity. The doctrine of original sin is said by some writers to be a modification of it. Certainly the fancy that the works of supererogation of their saints can be transferred to others is the Buddhist idea of good karma, which is transferable in a similar manner.[1]

"IF THE BLIND LEAD THE BLIND, BOTH SHALL FALL INTO THE DITCH" (MATT. XV. 14).

"As when a string of blind men are clinging one to the other, neither can the foremost see, nor the middle one see, nor the hindmost see. Just so, methinks, Vâsittha is the talk of the Brahmins versed in the Three Vedas" (Buddha in the "Tevigga Sutta," i. 15).

"THIS IS A HARD SAYING."

I have recently come across two passages in two widely different works which read rather curiously together.

The first is from a work recently quoted, "The Light of Asia and the Light of the World." In it Professor Kellogg condemns Buddha's teaching as "one of the most uncompromising and unmitigated systems of pessimism that human intellect, in the deep gloom of its ignorance of Him who is the Light and Life of men, has ever elaborated."[2] In proof of this he cites certain passages from Buddhist books. These are the most noteworthy—

---

[1] See Stone, "Christianity before Christ," p. 209.
[2] Page 266.

"All created things are grief and pain. He who knows this becomes passive in pain."

"So long as the love of man towards woman, even the smallest, is not destroyed, so long is his mind in bondage."[1]

Turning to the author of "Jésus Bouddha," we find that he brings precisely the same accusations against the "abominable theories" of Christ. He cites Luke xiv. 26.

"If any man come to Me, and hate not his father, and mother, and *wife*, and children, and brethren, and sisters, yea, and his own life also, he cannot be My disciple."

He adduces also—

"Let the dead bury their dead."

"Think not that I have come to send peace on earth: I come not to send peace, but a sword. For I am come to set a man at variance against his father, and the daughter against her mother, and the daughter-in-law against her mother-in-law. And a man's foes shall be they of his own household" (Matt. x. 34–36).

"And the brother shall deliver up the brother to death, and the father the child: and the children shall rise up against their parents, and cause them to be put to death" (ver. 21).

"So likewise, whosoever he be of you that forsaketh not all that he hath, he cannot be my disciple" (Luke xiv. 33).

The author says that all this is pure nihilism and Essene communism. "The most sacred family ties are to be renounced, and man to lose his individuality and become a unit in a vast scheme to overturn the institutions of his country.

"Qu' importe au fanatisme la ruine de la société humaine."[2]

Now I believe that these two writers would judge that they were as far apart as Calvinist and Positivist can possibly be, but they have one prominent feature in common, a total paralysis of the sympathetic insight which allows a mind to wander to a remote past. Whether Christ or Buddha, if they were alive now, would seek to make use of modern monastic institutions to spiritualize the world is a question that most of us would probably answer in the negative. When Christ

---

[1] Page 227. [2] "Jésus Bouddha," pp. 244, *et seq.*

came, Cæsar had recently constructed fine roads all over Europe, and along these marched well-drilled armies of soldiers and priests, bringing slavery to the nations. Atheism was high priest, and mockery the thurifer. Religion consisted of puerile ceremonial, and orgies whose records have to be concealed in the crypts of modern museums. The greed of priests pandered to lasciviousness, drunkenness, gluttony. This religion, as Gibbon says, was tolerant, but only as long as it was no religion at all. As long as a man sacrificed to the statue of Antinous or Commodus he might hold in secret loftier views. But if he expressed them he ran the risk of meeting the fate of Socrates or St. Paul.

Now it seems to me that, judged by the canons of the lowest expediency, the work of Christ was almost worthy of divinity. It was, in a word, to use the great weapon of materialism against itself. Materialism had woven a huge network of roads to bind tightly together the thrall of the civilized world ; and along these roads was to march a new army, shoeless, penniless, wifeless, homeless, like the "wanderers" of Buddha. It was not until I had made a study of Buddhism that I understood the full force of the early Christian movement. Even from the materialistic point of view, it was necessary that the hungry, hunted "apostle" who overturned Cæsar should be wifeless, childless, without ties, or he could not have done his work. Neither could he have done it without some new and potent inner force. Thus with Christ, as with Buddha, the first step towards emancipating society was to spiritualize the individual. With the Nazarites were no half measures. There were two cities. In the first city might be found ease and comfort, and material schemes and dreams. Its denizens married and were given in marriage. They lived in rich houses, and aspired to robes of dignity. The other city was tenanted by beggars. Its robes of dignity were rags ; its guerdon was hunger and thirst ; stripes and death were its day-dreams. But until a man could thoroughly understand that there was no possible connection between these two cities, he could not be a son of the mystic Sophia.

CHAPTER XV.

Feeding the Multitudes—Similarity to Buddhist Festivals—Feet-washing
—Walking on the Water—Parables—Dress.

THE GREAT BANQUET OF BUDDHA.

IN the "Lalita Vistara," it is announced that those who
have faith will become sons of Buddha, and partake of the
"food of the kingdom." [1] Four things draw disciples to his
banquet—gifts, soft words, production of benefits, conformity
of benefits.[2] The banquet of Buddha is the great festival of
contrition (Nyungue).

This festival throws much light on the accounts that we
have of the multitudes collected by Christ and John the
Baptist. The yearly festivals of the Buddhists, even as late
as the date of Hwen Thsang, the Chinese pilgrim, were taken
advantage of for the purpose of proselytizing. Religious
debates were encouraged ; as also at the old festivals of the
India of the Brahmins. At the great feast of Nyungue, in
Tibet, the first day is passed in prayers and in the reading
of passages of scripture, to which the laity as well as the
lâmas are invited. They must wear clean garments well
washed, and each bring his rosary and his cup. The second
day is called Chorva (the Preparation), and all prostrate themselves to the supreme "Lotus Holder" at sunrise, as the
healers fell down before the Sun of Righteousness. Then
the chief Lâma solemnly urges all to confess their sins and
amend their vicious lives. The day is also chiefly passed in
prayer ; tea, and a rude vegetable dinner being served out at

---

[1] "Lalita Vistara," p. 97.   [2] Ibid., p. 51.

two o'clock. The third day is called "the Reality," and is a complete fast-day of twenty-four hours. These Buddhist festivals, with their lamps and night service and mighty crowds, enable us to picture to ourselves the prayers and preachings and illuminated boats on the Lake Mareotis. They explain how it was that such vast multitudes crop up so suddenly in starved-out, desolate regions.

"Jesus called his disciples unto Him, and saith unto them, I have compassion on the multitude, because they have now been with Me three days, and have nothing to eat : And if I send them away fasting to their own houses, they will faint by the way : for divers of them came from far. And His disciples answered Him, From whence can a man satisfy these men with bread here in the wilderness? And He asked them, How many loaves have ye? And they said, Seven. And He commanded the people to sit down on the ground : and He took the seven loaves, and gave thanks, and brake, and gave to His disciples to set before them ; and they did set them before the people. And they had a few small fishes : and He blessed, and commanded to set them also before them. So they did eat, and were filled : and they took up of the broken meat that was left seven baskets. And they that had eaten were about four thousand : and He sent them away" (Mark viii. 1–9).

The fourth gospel, in recording the same transaction, adds an important detail—

"After these things Jesus went over the sea of Galilee, which is the sea of Tiberias. And a great multitude followed Him, because they saw His miracles which He did on them that were diseased. And Jesus went up into a mountain, and there He sat with His disciples. And the passover, a feast of the Jews, was nigh " (John vi. 1–4).

Plainly the two passages record the Essene feast of the Passover. We saw from Philo's letter to Hephæstion that the Therapeuts celebrated their own great festivals instead of repairing to Jerusalem. We see, from the account in St. John's Gospel, that the Passover was close at hand just before the great multitude came to Christ,—four thousand souls, the exact number of the Essenes, according to Josephus. We see that the fast lasted three days.

" Listen to my words, O chosen ones. Observe the great Fast—that Fast that contemns the food and drink of this mortal world." [1]

A friend of mine, Major Keith, the designer of the fine stone gateway so much admired in the recent Indian and Colonial Exhibition, having done a kindness to the Jains in India, was allowed to witness one of their great feasts. The Jains are a sect of schismatic Buddhists, who were on that account spared when the rest of the Buddhists were turned out of India. The privilege of seeing their great festival was never before granted to an Englishman. After their fast they were fed, when they had sat down upon the grass by hundreds and by fifties. The passage of scripture (Mark vi. 40) came forcibly into Major Keith's mind.

A Buddha multiplying Food.

King Sudarsana was a model king. In his dominions was no killing or whipping as punishment ; no soldiers' weapons to torture or destroy. His city, Jambunada, was built of crystal and cornelian, and silver and yellow gold. A Buddha [2] visited it one day.

Now in that city was a man who was the next day to be married, and he much wished the Buddha to come to the feast. Buddha passing by, read his silent wish, and consented to come. The bridegroom was overjoyed, and scattered many flowers over his house and sprinkled it with perfumes.

The next day, Buddha, with his alms-bowl in his hand and with a retinue of many followers, arrived ; and when they had taken their seats in due order, the host distributed every kind of exquisite food, saying, " Eat, my lord, and all the congregation, according to your desire ! "

But now a marvel presented itself to the astonished mind of the host. Although all these holy men ate very heartily, the meats and the drinks remained positively quite undiminished ; whereupon he argued in his mind, " If I could

---

[1] " Book of Adam," p. 35.   [2] Not Sâkya Muni.

only invite all my kinsmen to come, the banquet would be sufficient for them likewise."

And now another marvel was presented. Buddha read the good man's thought, and all the relatives, without invitation, streamed in at the door. They, also, fed heartily on the miraculous food. It is almost needless to add that the Chinese book " Fu-pen-hing-tsi-king" (as translated by the invaluable Mr. Beal) announces that all these guests, having heard a few apposite remarks on Dharma from the lips of the Tathâgata, to the satisfaction of everybody (excepting, perhaps, the poor bride), donned the yellow robes.

"IF I THEN, YOUR LORD AND MASTER, HAVE WASHED YOUR FEET."

Christ gave an example of the great truth, that to perform menial acts, is more godlike than to receive them. Just before the last supper (John xiii. 5), He took a towel and washed the feet of all His disciples.

It is recorded in the "Chinese Dhammapada," that in a monastery near Peshawur, there was an old monk with a disease so loathsome that none of his brother-monks could come near him. Everything was poisoned with the smell and virus of his disorder. Buddha came to the monastery, and hearing how matters stood, went in and carefully washed the body of this poor old monk, and attended to his disorders. "The purpose of Tathâgata, in coming to the world," he said, "is to befriend the poor, the helpless, the unprotected ; to nourish those in bodily affliction, to help the orphan and the aged." [1]

PETER WALKING ON THE WATER.

The incident of Peter walking on the water (Matt. xiv. 28) has its counterpart in the "Chinese Dhammapada."

" O thou of little faith, wherefore didst thou doubt ?" said Christ, when His apostle, for want of faith, was sinking.

Buddha was once preaching on the banks of a broad and

[1] Beal, "Chinese Dhammapada," p. 94.

deep river near Śravastî. The people there were unbelievers.
Suddenly, to their astonishment, a man was seen crossing the
river by walking on the surface of the water. "What means
this portent?" they said to the man. He gave answer, that
being unable to procure a boat, and wishing to hear the
preaching of Buddha, he had boldly walked over "because he
believed."

Buddha took advantage of the miracle : "Faith can cross
the flood. Wisdom lands us on the other shore." The unbelievers were promptly converted.[1]

There is another Buddhist legend that may be of interest
here. Pûrna, a disciple of Buddha, had a brother once in
imminent danger of shipwreck in a "black storm." "The
spirits that were faithful to Pûrna, the Ârya," apprised him of
this. At once he performed the miracle of transporting himself to the deck of the ship. "Immediately the black tempest
ceased, as if Sumern had arrested it."[2]

The penitent thief, too, is to be heard of in Buddhism.
Buddha confronts a cruel bandit in his mountain retreat and
converts him. All great movements, said St. Simon, must
begin by working on the emotion of the masses. In the
"Chinese Dhammapada," there is a pretty story of a very
beautiful Magdalen who had heard of Buddha, and who
started off to hear him preach. On the way, however, she
saw her beautiful face in a fountain near which she stopped
to drink, and she was unable to carry out her good resolution.
As she was returning, she was overtaken by a courtesan still
more beautiful than herself, and they journeyed together.
Resting for a while at another fountain, the beautiful stranger
was overcome with sleep, and placed her head on her fellow-
traveller's lap. Suddenly the beautiful face became livid as
a corpse, loathsome, a prey to hateful insects. The stranger
was the great Buddha himself, who had put on this appearance to redeem poor Pûndari.[3] "There is a loveliness that is
like a beautiful jar full of filth, a beauty that belongs to eyes,

---

[1] Beal, "Chinese Dhammapada," p. 50.
[2] Burnouf, Introduction, etc., p. 229.
[3] Beal, "Chinese Dhammapada," p. 35.

nose, mouth, body. It is this womanly beauty that causes
sorrow, divides families, kills children." These words, uttered
by the great teacher on another occasion, were perhaps re-
tailed a second time for the Buddhist Magna Civitatis Peccatrix.[1]

PARABLES.

Buddha, like Christ, taught in parables. I give three or
four which have been considered more or less like certain
parables in the New Testament. For a collection of very
beautiful ones, I beg to refer the reader to the " Popular Life
of Buddha."

"THOU FOOL, THIS NIGHT WILL THY SOUL BE REQUIRED OF THEE!"

Angati, a king in Miyala (Tirhût), had a daughter, Ruchâ.
At first he lived piously, but one day he heard some false
teachers who declared that there is no future world, and that
man, after death, is resolved into water and the other elements. After this he thought it was better to enjoy the
present moment, and he became cruel.

One day Ruchâ went to the king and requested him to
give her one thousand masûrans, as the next day was a
festival and she wished to make an offering. The king replied that there was no future world, no reward for merit ;
religious rites were useless, and it was better to enjoy herself
in the present world.

Now Ruchâ possessed the inner vision, and was able to
trace back her life through fourteen previous existences. She
told the king that she had once been a nobleman, but an
adulterer, and as a punishment she was now only a woman.
As a further punishment, she had been a monkey, a bullock,
a goat, and had been once born into the Rowra hell. The
king, unwilling to be taught by a woman, continued to be
a sceptic. Ruchâ then, by the power of the Satcha Kirya
(incantation), summoned a spirit to her aid, and Buddha himself, in the form of an ascetic, arrived at the city. The king

asked him from whence he came. The ascetic replied that
he came from the other world. The king in answer, laugh-
ingly said—

"If you have come from the other world, lend me one
hundred masûrans, and when I go to that world I will give
you a thousand."

Buddha answered gravely—

"When any one lends money, it must be to the rich. If
he bestow money on the poor, it is a gift, for the poor cannot
repay. I cannot lend you, therefore, one hundred masûrans
for you are poor and destitute."

"You utter an untruth," said the king, angrily. "Does
not this rich city belong to me?"

The Buddha replied—

"In a short time, O king, you will die. Can you take
your wealth with you to hell? There you will be in un-
speakable misery, without raiment, without food. How, then,
can you pay me my debt?"

At this moment, on the face of Buddha was a strange
light which dazzled the king.

The Prodigal Son.[1]

A certain man had a son who went away into a far
country. There he became miserably poor. The father,
however, grew rich, and accumulated much gold and treasure,
and many storehouses and elephants. But he tenderly loved
his lost son, and secretly lamented that he had no one to
whom to leave his palaces and suvernas at his death.

After many years, the poor man, in search of food and
clothing, happened to come to the country where his father
had great possessions. And when he was afar off his father
saw him, and reflected thus in his mind: "If I at once acknowledge my son and give to him my gold and my treasures,
I shall do him a great injury. He is ignorant and undis-
ciplined; he is poor and brutalized. With one of such
miserable inclinations 'twere better to educate the mind little
by little. I will make him one of my hired servants."

[1] This is the title adopted in the translation of M. Foucaux.

Then the son, famished and in rags, arrived at the door of his father's house, and seeing a great throne upraised and many followers doing homage to him who sat upon it, was awed by the pomp and the wealth around. Instantly he fled once more to the highway. "This," he thought, "is the house of the poor man. If I stay at the palace of the king perhaps I shall be thrown into prison."

Then the father sent messengers after his son; who was caught and brought back in spite of his cries and lamentations. When he reached his father's house, he fell down fainting with fear, not recognizing his father, and believing that he was about to suffer some cruel punishment. The father ordered his servants to deal tenderly with the poor man, and sent two labourers of his own rank of life to engage him as a servant on the estate. They gave him a broom and a basket, and engaged him to clean up the dung-heap at a double wage.

From the window of his palace the rich man watched his son at his work; and disguising himself one day as a poor man, and covering his limbs with dust and dirt, he approached his son, and said, "Stay here, good man, and I will provide you with food and clothing. You are honest, you are industrious. Look upon me as your father."

After many years, the father felt his end approaching, and he summoned his son and the officers of the king, and announced to them the secret that he had so long kept. The poor man was really his son, who in early days had wandered away from him; and now that he was conscious of his former debased condition, and was able to appreciate and retain vast wealth, he was determined to hand over to him his entire treasure. The poor man was astonished at this sudden change of fortune, and overjoyed at meeting his father once more.

The parables of Buddha are reported in the " Lotus of the Perfect Law " to be veiled from the ignorant by means of an enigmatic form of language.[1] The rich man of this parable, with his throne adorned by flowers and garlands of jewels, is announced to be Tathâgata, who dearly loves all his children, and has prepared for them vast spiritual treasures. But each

---

[1] " Lotus," p. 45.

son of Tathâgata has miserable inclinations. He prefers the dung-heap to the pearl mani. To teach such a man Tathâgata is obliged to employ inferior agents, the monk and the ascetic, and to wean him by degrees from the lower objects of desire. When he speaks himself, he is forced to veil much of his thought, as it would not be understood. His sons feel no joy on hearing spiritual things. Little by little must their minds be trained and disciplined for higher truths.

THE MAN WHO WAS BORN BLIND.

Once upon a time there was a man born blind, and he said, "I cannot believe in a world of appearances. Colours bright or sombre exist not. There is no sun, no moon, no stars. None have witnessed such things!" His friends remonstrated with him, but all in vain. He still repeated the same words.

In those days there was a holy man cunning in roots and herbs, one who had acquired supernatural gifts by a life of purity and abstinence. This man perceived by his spiritual insight that away amongst the clouds on the steeps of the lofty Himalayas were four simples that had power to cure the man who was born blind. He fetched these simples, and, mashing them together with his teeth, he applied them. Immediately the man who was born blind was cured of his infirmity. He saw colours and appearances. He saw the bright sun in the heavens. He was overjoyed, and pronounced that no one now had any advantage over him in the matter of eyesight.

Then certain holy men came to the man who had been born blind, and said to him, "You are vain and arrogant, and nearly as blind as you were before. You see the outside of things but not the inside. One whose supernatural senses are quickened sees the lapis-lazuli fields of the Buddhas and hears conch-shells sounded at a distance of five yoganas. Go off to a desert, a forest, a cavern in the mountains, and conquer this thirst for earthly things." The man who was born blind did as these holy men enjoined, and by-and-by acquired the supernatural gifts.

The interpretation of this parable is, that the man who is born blind is one afflicted with the blindness of spiritual ignorance. Tathâgata is the great physician who loves him as a father loves a son. The four simples are the four holy truths. The holy men who accosted him are the great rishis, who teach the spiritual life in caves and in deserts, and wean mankind from the love of lower things.

THE WOMAN AT THE WELL.

Ânanda, the loved disciple of Buddha, was once thirsty, having travelled far. At a well he encountered a girl named Matanga, and asked her to give him some water to drink. But she, being a woman of low caste, was afraid of contaminating a holy Brahmin, and refused humbly.

"I ask not for caste, but for water," said Ânanda. His condescension won the heart of the girl Matanga. It happened that she had a mother cunning in love philtres and weird arts, and when this woman heard how much her daughter was in love, she threw her magic spells round the disciple, and brought him to her cave. Helpless, he prayed to Buddha, who forthwith appeared and cast out the wicked demons.

But the girl Matanga was still in wretched plight. At last she determined to appeal to Buddha himself.

The great physician, reading the poor girl's thought, questioned her gently—

"Supposing that you marry my disciple, can you follow him everywhere?"

"Everywhere!" said the girl.

"Could you wear his clothes, sleep under the same roof?" said Buddha, alluding to the nakedness and beggary of the "houseless one."

By slow degrees the girl began to take in his meaning and at last took refuge in the Divine Triad.[1]

I give three new parables of great beauty.

---

[1] Burnouf, Introduction, etc., p. 183.

"THE KING AND THE PIG.

" There was a king renowned in Indian story ;
　　　With bow and brand
He spread abroad the record of his glory
　　　In every land.

" Grey warriors said, ' O ne'er was such a leader,
　　　Wary and bold ! '
He had a palace built of scented cedar
　　　Fretted with gold.

" One hundred courts with trees and plashing fountains
　　　And marble screens,
Rare flowers, like those of the Kailaśa mountains,
　　　A thousand queens.

" He died, and from this world of adulations
　　　Was borne alone,
What time court poets sang their base laudations
　　　To Buddha's throne.

" Said Buddha, ' What of this man is recorded ? '
　　　An angel read ;
It was a tale of woe, blood-stained and sordid,
　　　A wail of the dead.

" ' O'er many a city once the home of freeman
　　　The ivy twines ;
Each daughter and each wife was made a leman;
　　　Men slaved in mines

" ' To spread the royal dress with many a jewel,
　　　So thick they stood ;
Each diamond was a tear, congealed and cruel,
　　　Each ruby blood.

" ' A million slaves reared up a pompous building—
　　　Ten thousand died—
Of marble lace-work, flecked with gems and gilding—
　　　The Fane of Pride.

" ' Vast crowds were butchered for his entertainment
　　　In war and shows ;
They march in legions to his huge arraignment,
　　　Vassals and foes.

" ' Fetch him the Mirror ! ' On its surface speckless
　　　He gazed with dread,
And saw a false old man, malformed and feckless,
　　　With brainless head.

N

" O, who shall gaze upon that vision awful,
         The naked truth
 Limned by himself, limned by his deeds unlawful
         In age and youth !

" Said Buddha, ' Is there nothing true nor loyal
         In any page ? '
 ' Once,' said the angel, ' in a province royal
         A plague did rage,

" ' And in the sun a dying pig was craning
         To reach the shade.
 The king said, " Watch those eyes of mute complaining,
         And give it aid ! "

" ' But o'er the courtiers was a deep dejection ;
         'Twas Death's grim feast.
 The king sprang down, and, heedless of infection,
         Moved the poor beast.' "

" Said Buddha then majestic in his kindness,
         ' He is forgiven !
 That deed wipes out the record of his blindness,
         And wins him heaven ! ' "

Victor Hugo has made the king a Mussulman, but if one
of the faithful had touched an unclean pig, such an act would
have counterbalanced, not a life of evil deeds, but a life of
good deeds.

FORGIVENESS.

" Once to a mighty king in ancient Ind
 Were born two sons ; Kshemaṇkara, the first,
 Was brave and just and truthful, dear to all.
 One day the daughter of a king, concealed
 Behind the purdah, chanced to hear his voice ;
 She said, ' He is my husband— he or none.'
 Pâpaṇkara, his brother, hated him,
 Pâpaṇkara, whom jackals, kites, and swine
 Greeted with evil noises at his birth.
 The king one day spake to his elder boy :
 ' A sweet princess would wed thee, and her sire
 Has urged this union.   Marry her my son ! '
 Kshemaṇkara replied, ' An idle prince
 Brings little luck or joy to any one ;
 Give me a ship, and let me sail abroad
 And see far countries, bringing back their wealth,

Rare stones and silks and produce to my bride.'
The king consented ; and a goodly prow,
With bamboo masts and sails of shining stuffs,
Crept through lethargic seas and anchored now
By islands of rich gums and cinnamon,
And now near purple mountains velvety
What time the sun behind a screen of mist
Steeps sea and sky in floods of liquid gold.
There did Kshemankara collect his gems,
Moving his brother's gall.   He too had come.
But lo ! a mighty change is o'er the sea :
A dread tuffàn is whistling through the shrouds,
The waves are giant, and the bellowing cloud
Chases the blood from the young brother's cheek.
They neared not safety, but an island grim.
The elder brother said : ' Cling to my waist ! '
And with wet bales and spars of sandal wood
The pair were promptly tossing in the foam.
At length they landed ; and the vast fatigue
Of swimming made the elder brother sleep.
The younger chose two thorns, and drove them through
His brother's eyes ; and taking from his waist
A girdle filled with pearls, announced his death.
    Ten months have passed.   To-day a fair princess
Must choose a husband—'tis her sire's decree—
And in bright tents are many sons of kings,
The king Pâpankara, whose sire is dead,
To win a smile from her who smiles no more.
Drums sound, the trumpets blare, and once or twice
Was heard a low voice singing to a lute.
Up sprang the princess : ''Tis my husband's voice.'
The angry king said, ' Fetch that singer here ! '
He was a beggar grimed and blind.   Again
The princess said, ' That is my husband there ! '
The suitors loudly laughed, but in their midst
The princess stood and raised her hands to heaven :
' Spirits invisible that watch our acts,
That I have loved the Prince Kshemankara,
And clung to him through love and through despair,
Give evidence by a portentous act,
Restore the vision to one wounded eye ! '
And lo, the beggar saw, and fear seized all.
Then said Pâpankara, ' A kingly bride
Requires a kingly spouse.   The Shasters rule
That such must have two eyes, in limbs be perfect ;
This cannot be the prince.   I saw him die.'
The beggar then raised up his hands to heaven :

'A kingly ruler first must rule himself,
If in the presence of a mighty wrong
I nourish hate to none ; if schooled by care
And thirst and hunger, trusty councillors,
I have been trained to rule the sad and hungry ;
Spirits invisible complete your task,
Restore my other eye !'   At once he saw.
Thus was Pâpaṇkara hurled from his throne,
And at the jousts the princess chose her spouse."

ALCHEMY.

"A vain young Brahmin once was told
Of holy spells that made red gold ;
This fancy vexed him day and night,
His life was gross, his heart was light.
Said one, ' In Uravilva's wood
There dwells the Buddha, calm and good.
He knows all secrets.   Ask his aid !'
The Brahmin sought the holy shade
Said Buddha, ' What you wish, my son,
May most undoubtedly be done.
But gold is crime !   It whets the knife ;
Designs the drops that poison life.
It parents lust, and hate, and ire ;
For gold the son will kill the sire,
For gold the maiden sell her shame,
Kings spread wide lands with sword and flame ;
The sons of Dharma never tell
Their mantras and their potent spell
Except to those whose lives are pure,
To those who've conquered earthly lure,
Who know in fact the gold's true worth,
The tawdriest tinsel upon earth.'
The Brahmin said, ' My life is pure,
I've conquered every earthly lure ;
Who, like a Brahmin, knows the right !'
His life was gross, his heart was light.
One night the couple when the moon
Hides for two weeks her light in June
(The only fortnight in the year
When man can make red gold appear),
Sought out a cavern, where a rill
Dashed down a chasm in the hill ;
The mantras now were promptly told,
And Buddha spread the ground with gold,
Six thousand pieces the amount,
A robber saw the Brahmin count.

Then Buddha hurled it in the foam,
Repeating as he journeyed home
His solemn caution : 'Son, beware !
Use not this knowledge, have a care !'
But as they trudged, at break of day,
Five hundred robbers barred the way !
' O holy masters, we are told,'
They said, ' that you have countless gold.'
Said Buddha, ' Gold sheds human blood,
And so we flung it in the flood.'
The chieftain said, ' Such words are vain
And one as hostage must remain—
The younger one. So promptly hie
And fetch the gold, or he must die,
Within a week he will be slain !'
'Within a week I come again,'
Said Buddha, ' Fear not, Brahmin youth,
A Buddha's tongue is simple truth.'
Grim terror pales the young man's brow,
Will the great Buddha keep his vow ?
Five days have passed away too soon,
To-night will end the weeks in June
When spells can work ; and if he wait,
To-morrow will be all too late.
' O take me to the rocky dell,
To-night I'll work a mystic spell.'
The gold was made. Quick spread its fame,
A rival band of robbers came ;
' Divide or fight !' they loudly cried,
When the broad pieces they espied.
' He made this gold,' the first clan said,
' We give him up to you instead.'
O pity now the Brahmin's fate,
He thinks of Buddha's word too late.
Though all unfit the time of year,
The greedy robbers will not hear,
They cut his throat ; and then assail
Their rivals for their lying tale.
Swords flash and fall on sounding crest,
On cloven targe, and stricken breast,
Sharp cries of anguish over all
Outroar the angry waterfall,
Whose snowy stream is soon a flood
Of dying men and human blood,
Borne off to Yama's realm of death ;
Two robbers soon alone draw breath.
Exhausted with three days of fast,

They watch the gold. Says one at last,
"You guard the cave ; but we must eat.
I'll to the town for drink and meat."
One hied him to a leech's stock,
One nursed a dagger by a rock ;
Each muttered, "Soon 'tis all mine own ! "
One perished, stabbed without a groan ;
The other seized his drink and meat
And soon was writhing at his feet.

Dress.

Of the close resemblance between the dress of Buddhist monks and Romish priests we have the best possible evidence, that of the Roman Catholic priests in many lands from the earliest times.

Father Grueber, who visited Tibet in 1661, has recorded that the dress of the lâmas corresponded with that handed down to us in ancient paintings as the dress of the apostles.[1]

Now let us listen to the Abbé Huc—

"If the person of the grand lâma struck us little, I cannot say the same of his dress, which in every detail was that of our own bishops. He wore on his head a yellow mitre. In his right hand was a staff in the form of the crosier. His shoulders were covered with a cloak of violet silk, fastened across the chest with a hook, and resembling our cope. Later on we will point out many similarities between Catholic and Lamanesque rites."[2]

This lâma was not the Delai lâma.

In the "Life of Gabriel Durand" occurs an extract of a letter from Father Ephrem, written in 1883—

"There (in the Bell Pagoda, Pekin) we saw a Chinese priest dressed almost pin for pin like a Benedictine monk."[3]

I copy two Japanese monks from Siebold's "Nippon." (See Plate VI.)

"Much of the costume of the Buddhist priests," says Balfour's "Indian Cyclopædia," "and of the ritual, has a similarity to those of Christians of the Romish and Greek forms ;

[1] Cited by Prinsep, "Tibet, Tartary," etc. p. 14.
[2] "Voyage dans la Tartarie," etc. vol. ii.
[3] "Gabriel Durand," vol. i. p. 493.

PLATE VI.

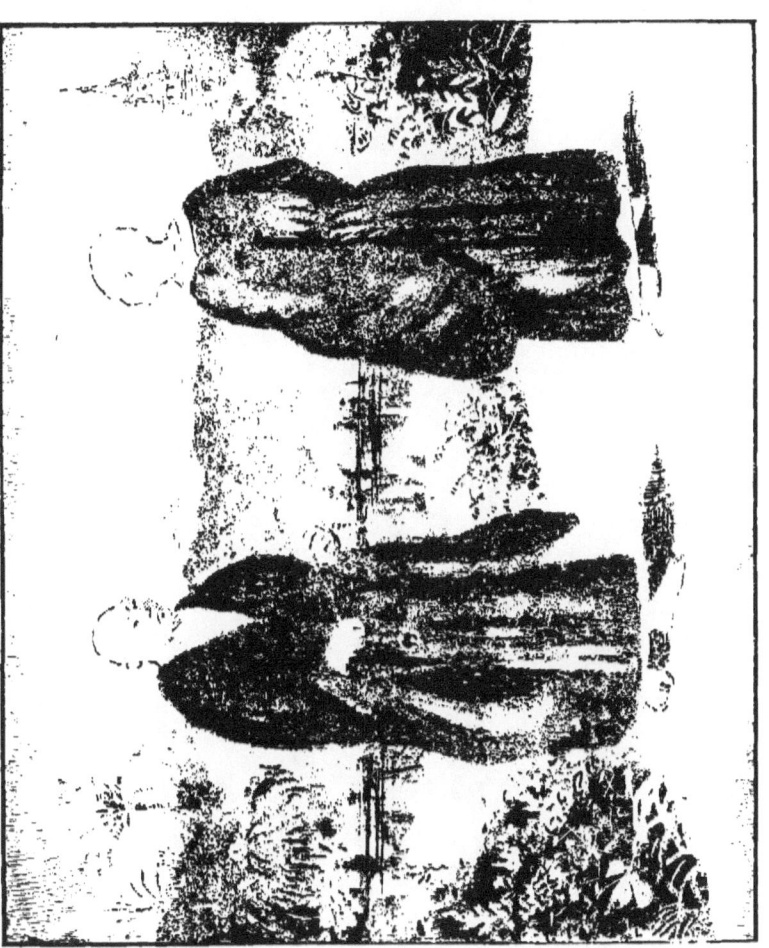

BUDDHIST MONKS.
From Siebold's Nippon.

[*Page* 132.

and De Guignes, De Gama, Clavijo, Anthony Jenkinson, all notice statements regarding the Greek Church, the Chinese, and the Burmans, indicative of the belief in the identity of the form of worship." Sir Rutherford Alcock bears similar testimony to this identity of costume "amongst the priests, acolytes, and choristers." The missionaries of St. Francis Xavier were struck with it.

"Two systems and ceremonials of worship presenting such marvellous identity in small particulars, and in larger characteristics, could not possibly have been born of chance and wholly independent the one of the other." [1]

In point of fact, the Abbé Huc tells us that the Buddhist priests of Tibet have the dalmatic and the cope exactly like the Roman Catholics.

These two garments have played a conspicuous part in all the mystic societies of the West. The dalmatic is the close-fitting white garment which envelopes the person from the neck to the heels. The cope, called also *pluvial*, in French ; *peviale*, in Italian, is the rain cloak. Both were worn by Buddha. (See Plate V. p. 140.) .

According to Philo, the Therapeuts of Alexandria had two garments, "a thick cloak of some shaggy felt for winter, and a sleeveless vest, or fine linen garment, for summer."

"Put on your stoles and white garments, O peacemakers, symbols of the Water of Life."

This is from the "Book of Adam," and was addressed to the disciples of John the Baptist. Do we not learn also that their leader had a raiment of camel's hair.

"If any man sue thee at the law, and take away thy coat, let him have thy cloke also" (Matt. v. 40). This cloke may also be the garment "without seam" of Jesus that the four executioners cast lots for (John xix. 23).

We know from history that the early dress of the Christians, like that of the Essenes, was white. Many passages in the gospels support this statement. I quote one (Rev. iii. 17.) whose Essenism is very pronounced.

"Because thou sayest, I am rich, and increased with goods,

---

[1] "Capital of the Tycoon," vol. ii. p. 310.

and have need of nothing; and knowest not that thou art wretched, and miserable, and poor, and blind, and naked. I counsel thee to buy of me gold tried in the fire, that thou mayest be rich; and white raiment, that thou mayest be clothed, and that the shame of thy nakedness do not appear; and anoint thine eyes with eyesalve, that thou mayest see."

Here is another passage (Matt. x. 10)—

" Provide neither gold, nor silver, nor brass in your purses, nor scrip for your journey, neither two coats, neither shoes."

This seems to show that Christ's disciples went barefooted like early Christian and early Buddhist monks, and had only one " coat " (dalmatic) like the Essenes.

In the *Daily News* of May 30th, 1885, appeared an account of a ceremony that takes place every Whit Monday, at Argenteuil, in France. A portion of the Saviour's robe is carried in procession in a golden casket in the presence of many of the most high-born Catholics of France and England. This fragment is made of camel's hair, is dark brown in colour, and of stuff very like that of a garment worn by modern Arabs. Pius IX. begged a little fragment of it, which shows that it is thought authentic. I mention this to show an early tradition of the Church. In the days of St. Antony, Christian monks still wore a garment of camel's hair.

The Buddhist nuns have the black and the white veil, but these, as in Spain, are for protection against heat in summer, and cold in winter. They do not denote spiritual grades. The nun with the white veil I copied from Siebold's " Nippon;" [1] the nun with the black veil from a photograph. In the Greek Church the nuns have similar long sleeves to hide their hands. (See Plate VII.)

[1] Siebold, "Archiv zur Beschreibung von Japan."

PLATE VII.

BUDDHIST NUNS, THE BLACK AND WHITE VEIL.

[Page 12a

CHAPTER XVI.

"SEE THAT THOU TELL NO MAN"

How was Buddhism spread by Buddha?

A vivacious critic, in a print called the *Indian Antiquary*, has charged me with "crass" ignorance and other unkind things, because I assert that Buddhism, in the first instance, made its progress as a secret society. The critic points triumphantly to the abundant chronicles of the Southern Buddhists, where every step of the reformer and his movement is set down.

I wish I could agree with my critic, and accept these chronicles without critical sifting. According to them, Buddha first preached the law in a deer forest, about four miles to the north of the holy city of Benares. The spot is called Sârnâth (Sârugganâtha, the "Lord of Deer") to this day. Aśoka built a splendid temple in this wilderness. The dome is ninety-three feet in diameter, and its imposing mass still dominates the plain. Pilgrims from China have visited it; and pilgrims from all countries in the world go to it still. It is called Dhamek, a corruption for the Temple of Dharma. Now, the Cingalese historian, evidently writing long after this temple of Dharma had become famous, makes Buddha put up in a fine temple and vihâra in a "suburb of Benares"[1] during the first rainy season after his conversion.

Benares was already the most holy city of the Hindoos, and yet it is recorded that Buddha preached openly against the Brahmin religion, and made sixty-one converts.

He then proceeded to the powerful Brahmin kingdom of Magadha, and arrived at the capital, Râjâgriha, attended by over a thousand followers. The king at once became a convert, with a large proportion of his subjects ; and handed over to Buddha the grove in which the celebrated Veṇuvana Monastery was afterwards situated. The Cingalese writer does not take the trouble to say a word about the building of it, being evidently under an impression that it was already there. Five months after Buddha had attained the Bodhi he started off to Kapilavastu, a distance of sixty leagues, to see his father. He was accompanied by twenty thousand yellow-robed shaven bhikshus ; and he marched along the high-roads of the various Brahmin kingdoms that were on his road without any molestation. At Kapilavastu, he found another fine vihâra ready for him ; and the bulk of the nation and the king became converts to his religion. He returned shortly to Râjâgriha to find a convenient merchant ready at once to hand over to him the rich vihâra, or monastery, of Jetavana at Śrâvastî (Sahet Mahet). Buddha went at once to the spot ; and this time the chronicler allows a vihâra to be built, a *new* one, he again fancying apparently that one was there. There was "a pleasant room for the sage," separate apartments for "eighty elders," and "other residences with single and double walls, and long halls and open roofs ornamented with ducks and quails ; and ponds also he made, and terraces to walk on by day and by night."[2]

When Buddha arrived at Śrâvastî, this convent was dedicated to him by the merchant, who went through a formula well known in the ancient inscriptions of Ceylon. He poured water out of a bowl, and made over the land to the monks. Then a gorgeous festival took place, which lasted nine months. Exactly five hundred and forty millions of

---

[1] "Buddhist Birth Stories," p. 91.   [2] Ibid., p. 130.

gold pieces were expended on this feast and on the convent; so that we may presume, I suppose, that most of the inhabitants of the powerful Brahmin kingdom of Śrâvastî had become converts. Thus, in less than a year, Buddha had practically converted the Brahmin kingdoms that stretch from Śrâvastî (Sahet Mahet) to Gayâ.

In a word, his creed had already won what is called the Holy Land of the Buddhists.

Is all this true? Even by lopping off Eastern exaggerations and accretions, can we reduce it in any way to a plausible story?

I say that the task is impossible. If in the holiest city of the Hindoos Buddha had proclaimed that there was no God, and in a complete and categorical manner had announced that man had no soul nor anything of any sort that existed after death, the cruel laws of the Brahmins against heresy would have been put in force against him. Dr. Rhys Davids contends that it is proved by the Upanishads that "absolute freedom of thought" existed in ancient India.[1] But the Upanishads were secret—he forgets that. They were whispered to pupils who had passed through a severe probation. Magasthenes, the Greek ambassador to Patna, bears witness to this.[2]

Bishop Bigandet accounts for the rise of Buddhism, by supposing that it was at once adopted as the official religion in Magadha. Then there are theories abroad that some of the kingdoms of India were Turanian, and their creeds were Jinism, or some non-Brahminic religion. And it is affirmed that some of these monarchs befriended Buddha. In the way of all these theories stand the Aśoka stones. They distinctly record that the Brahminism of the animal sacrifice was the official creed all over India until Aśoka superseded it. It is to be remembered that Patna was his capital, which is in the very heart of the Holy Land of the Buddhists; so the king could no more make a mistake about the official creed of the neighbouring Magadha than the Archbishop of Canterbury

[1] "Hibbert Lectures," p. 26.
[2] Cory, "Ancient Fragments," p. 225.

be wrong about the official creed of Sussex.   The Aṭṭhakathâ
in tracing his history also confesses that the official religion
was Brahmin up to the king's conversion.[1]

The question of the great missionary success of early
Buddhism is no doubt a difficult one.   The enormous area
conquered by it at the date when Aśoka made it an official
creed seems to indicate a victory already won.   Aśoka was a
politician.   He had swum to the throne in the blood of many
slaughtered brothers.   He seems scarcely the man to have
offended the powerful Brahmin priesthoods of every kingdom
in India, except under the pressure of a more potent force.
If the formidable " Sons of Dharma " had silently undermined
these kingdoms, and a vast organization able to make and
unmake kings, united, secret, terribly in earnest, had revealed
themselves to him, his proceedings are intelligible, not
otherwise.   The vast empires of the palmy days of
Indian Buddhism were found unattainable by the most gory
Mogul.

In this matter we are not quite without historical data.
China was officially converted A.D. 61, by the apparition of a
" golden man," " a spirit named Foe."   The Emperor Mingti
on perceiving this " golden man " at once made his religion
the official creed.   But in the notes of Klaproth and De
Rémusat to their translation of the " Pilgrimage of Fa Hian," [2]
it is made quite clear that Buddhism came to China nearly
two hundred years earlier.   Lassen believes that it reached
Babylon 250 B.C.   Buddha's name is mentioned with praise
in the " Zend Avesta," " Go ye into all the world and preach
Dharma ! " said Buddha.

It seems to me that the biographies of Jesus and Buddha
throw constant light the one on the other.   We know the
fearful oaths of secrecy enjoined on Christians in the Clementine " Homilies ; " and we remember the many earnest injunctions of Christ in the direction of a similar caution.   When
I was a little boy I could never understand this excess of
caution as applied to the parables.   Why was it so necessary
to keep secret the fact that the seed in the parable of the

---

[1] *Journ. Ben. As. Soc.*, vol. vi. p. 731.   [1] Page 40, *et seq.*

sower signified the Word of God ? But if by " Word of God,"
Christ meant that Word as interpreted by the Jewish mystics,
such caution was of course necessary, for hearer and utterer
ran great danger of being stoned. Christianity for many
years after its founder's death was a secret society, and the
catechumens were rigidly excluded from its mystic rites.
The author of " Jésus Bouddha " holds that Christ's speech
about the kingdom of heaven coming "not with observation "
(*sans éclat*), and the Son of man appearing in the lifetime of
the living generation, was an allusion to the speedy success of
his secret propagandism.[1] The " Son of man " was a movement rather than an individual. This interpretation has the
advantage that the prophecy then would not have been
falsified by the event. The higher modern mystics, like
Swedenborg, have maintained that the avatâra of God is the
truth uttered and not the utterer.

"HE DESCENDED INTO HELL."

Buddha, like Christ, preached to the spirits in prison.

It is recorded that on one occasion when visiting Sravastî
he remembered that the Buddhas of the past had gone to the
heavens of the Devas, each to preach to his mother. In
consequence he repaired to Mount Meru, which is the nearest
point on earth to the heavens of the Devas, and then soared
away to the heaven Tawadeintha.

There he preached to his mother and to millions of spirits
for three months.[2] The heavens of the Devas are six in
number and are tenanted by mortals still subject to rebirths,
but who are receiving rewards (temporary) for past good deeds.
Those whose deeds require punishment (also temporary) are
conducted into the bowels of the earth to the hell Avîchi (the
Rayless Place).

It is needless to say that Buddha converted his mother,
and that she represents the physical universe with the whole
of its breathing inhabitants. The avatâra of the Buddha
makes happy every suffering mortal. The Chinese hold that
every thousand years Buddha, in the form of a beautiful

[1] Page 252. [1] Bigandet, p. 203.

young man, goes down to the hell Avichi and clears that region of suffering.

Turning to the Gospel of Nicodemus, chap. xiii., we read that at the time of Christ's crucifixion, in "the depth of hell," in "the blackness of darkness, on a sudden there appeared the colour of the sun like gold, and a purple-coloured light enlightening the place." At this all the Jewish patriarchs and prophets rejoiced, and Isaiah announced that this was the light of the Son of God.

"The land of Zabulon and the land of Nephthalem beyond Jordan, a people who walked in darkness saw a great light, and to them who dwelt in the region of the shadow of death light is arisen. And now," added the old Hebrew prophet, "He is come and hath enlightened us who sate in death."

"Then all the saints who were in the depth of hell rejoiced the more."

These occurrences alarmed Satan ; when suddenly there was a voice as of thunder pronouncing these words—

"Lift up your gates, O ye princes, and be ye lift up ye everlasting doors, and the King of Glory shall come in !"

Then the Prince of Hell, a distinct being from Satan, called out, "Shut the brass gates of cruelty !" But the patriarchs remonstrated, and David called to mind his prophecy—

"He hath broken the gates of brass, and cut the bars of iron in sunder."

Then Isaiah spoke again—

"Did not I rightly prophecy to you when I was alive on earth ?"

"The dead men shall live and they shall rise again who are in their graves, and they shall rejoice who are on earth."

"Then the mighty Lord appeared in the form of a man and lit up those places which had been before in darkness."

And "trampling upon Death, he seized the Prince of Hell, and deprived him of all his power."

It is also recorded that he dismissed "all the captives, and released all who were bound and all who were wont formerly

to groan under the weight of their torments" (chap. xviii.
v. 4).

The Buddhist universalism of this legend gives it, I think,
an early date. Peter evidently alludes to it when he records
that Christ "went and preached unto the spirits in prison" (1
Pet. iii. 19).

TRANSFIGURATION ON A MOUNT.

Buddha, like Christ, when he went up the steeps of Mount
Meru, was ministered to by his two chief disciples. Sâriputra
brought him food, whilst a double of the Great Teacher, perhaps his "diamond" or spirit body, was preaching to the
spirits in prison. Maudgalyâyana was at hand, too, and was
commissioned to tell the rest of the disciples that on a certain
day the Lord would descend to earth near a town called Sâm-
kaśya, which was situated some thirty yogunas from Śravastî.
A splendid staircase of diamonds and emeralds was constructed
by the spirits, and along this Buddha came; but at a certain
point he paused, and an astounding miracle was patent to the
vast multitudes who had assembled to greet his triumphal
return. The six glories of the Buddha shone out with
dazzling radiance on his head, and the splendid domes and
temples of the spirit cities were revealed. Men could see
spirits and spirits could see men. Sweet strains were in the
air from heavenly harps. And Indra the king of heaven and
Brahmâ were by the side of Buddha, with an innumerable
army of angelic beings. The light of all this glory illumined
even the hell Avîchi. A splendid canopy temple was afterwards erected on the spot where the King of Glory had
alighted.[1] Did not Peter wish to erect a "tabernacle" on the
spot where Christ was transfigured?

Another point is noteworthy. Sâriputra and Maudgalyâyana incurred, like the Sons of Thunder, the jealousy of the
other disciples by a similar request. They petitioned Buddha
that the one should sit on his right hand and the other on his
left.[2] The coincidence goes further. Sâriputra was also
called Upatishya (the "beloved disciple").

[1] Compare Bigandet, p. 208, and Rockhill, p. 81.
[2] Bigandet, p. 153.

The Triumphal Entry into the City of the King.

Bishop Bigandet points out that there is a "Précurseur de Bouddha" as well as a forerunner of Christ. When Buddha proceeds from the Desert of Uravilva to make his solemn entry into Râjâgriha, the Jerusalem of the Buddhists, a radiant young man, who was in reality Indra, appeared and cried out—

"Behold the great Buddha advances with a thousand disciples!" And when he was questioned about himself he said, "Sons of men, I am his humble servant. He alone merits the worship of men and spirits."

Dr. Rhys Davids also gives us an account of Buddha doing something the same sort of office to the great Buddha Dipañkara. In a previous existence he was the Brahmin Sumedha.

"If you clear a path for the Buddha, assign to me a place.

"I will also clear the road, the way, the path of his coming.

"Then they gave me a piece of ground to clear a pathway.

"Then repeating within me A Buddha, a Buddha! I cleared the road."

By-and-by the Buddha arrived, attended by a vast multitude of mortals and heavenly quiristers. Vast quantities of flowers were cast in his pathway, and Sumedha, who had on an antelope's skin, flung it in the mire with the grace of Sir Walter Raleigh.[1]

In the Gospel of Nicodemus, a herald goes before Christ into Pilate's presence, and throws his garment down for the Saviour to walk over. Râjâgriha means "the city of the king," and Buddha's solemn entry with a crowd of disciples, with banners and music and incense, his footsteps passing along a pathway of flowers, is only another version of the same story that was told in our last section, and which is told every Sunday in the Christian mass and the Buddhist temple—the passage of a human soul from the "wilderness" into the city of light, the city of the great king. The forerunner of the religion of Buddha was the religion of Indra ; and the teaching of John the Baptist preceded the teaching of Christ.

Whether either entry is pure history may be doubted.

[1] "Birth Stories," p. 12.

The ingenious author of " Rabbi Ben Joshua " holds that that
of Jesus was genuine, and rendered feasible by a popular movement, which awed for a moment the dominant party. He
holds, too, that Christ and his followers really broke into the
temple and overturned the stalls of the traffickers in doves.
But he says that this proves him an Essene, for the doves were
a necessity to the Jewish ritual.

I see great difficulties in the way of this interpretation. In
the first place, the followers of Christ would have had to deal
not with the dominant Jews, but the Roman soldiers, who would
have made short work of an unarmed multitude. In the
second place, the dominant party, who three times a day
called on God to send his curse on the Nazarenes, would have
been only too glad to set the Roman soldiers at their secret
enemies, and get rid of them at one fell swoop. And nothing
could have been more opposed to the genius and policy of
Christ than such a deed of violence. The overturning of the
money-changers is a beautiful trope, like the crown of thorns
and the rending of the veil of the temple.

THE LAST SUPPER.

Buddha, like Christ, sate down with his chief disciples to
a repast which he knew was to be his last. It is recorded
that a young pig was set before him, and knowing that this
would cause his death, he forbade his disciples to touch it,
and had the remainder buried after he had partaken of it.
He announced that this feast and the rice milk of Sujâtâ
were the two great feasts of his life. The one had given him
the Bodhi or Gnosis, and the other emancipation from the
flesh altogether.[1] Much of this, of course, is inserted in his
life to connect it with the two great festivals of the year : the
Harvest Festival or the Feast of Lanterns, and the Feast of
the New Year, which begins with the Feast of the Dead.
The pig is, I suspect, astronomical, like perhaps the boar's
head at a similar epoch in England. The Abbé Huc was
astonished to find the Tibetans sit up solemnly to see the

---

[1] Bigandet, pp. 280, 281.

O

old year out and the new year in. New year's cakes and
sweets and pantomimes abounded. Visits, as in France, were
made.[1]

"MY SOUL IS EXCEEDINGLY SORROWFUL, EVEN UNTO DEATH."

There is a passage in the life of Christ and another in the
life of Buddha that are puzzling. Perhaps, compared together, they throw some light the one on the other.

What was the "cup" that Christ had to drink in the
garden of Gethsemane, and what was the "garden?"

Turning to Buddha, it is recorded that shortly before his
death he and his disciples were invited by the courtesan
Amrapali to a feast in her beautiful garden. Almost immediately after the feast Buddha sickened.

"The sharp pains of a dire illness," he said, "have come
upon me, even to death." And when Ânanda, his attendant
monk, tried to comfort him, he added: "My body is as stiff
as if I had taken poison!"

Shortly afterwards, the Tathâgata repaired to the "village
of the earth" and partook of his last supper, a treacherous
disciple changing his dish. Great pains soon seized him, and
a dire thirst. Ânanda was by him on the banks of a little
river called the Haranyavatî, and the afflicted old man desired
his disciple to fetch him a sip of water. Carts were passing,
and the water was foul. The southern version says that by
a miracle Buddha clarified it; but in Mr. Rockhill's version,
the disciples, after Buddha's death, bitterly upbraided Ânanda
for giving the blessed one a foul cup of water. They were
angry, too, that he allowed courtesans to anoint Buddha's
dead body with their tears.[2]

Mysticism has an infinite number of symbols, but only one
truth; and that is that there is a spiritual state and a material
state.

The latter is frequently symbolized as a garden, an impure
woman, and so on. Each symbol is balanced by its opposite,

[1] "Voyages," vol. ii. p. 374.
[2] "Rockhill," pp. 130, 131, 133, 153.

for the two are only aspects of one truth. There is the garden of Gethsemane and the garden of Paradise; the "cup" of life and the "cup" of death; the "bread of life" that John the Baptist administers to the perfected novice; and the bread that the Judas, the treacherous disciple, "dips into."

And it is significant that Amrapali is not painted as a penitent Magdalene, for she represents the earth-life that the Buddha was leaving. It is quaintly announced that she was the most perfect woman in the world, and for this reason was forbidden by the king to become a wife, a fact which relegates her to the groves of the Brahmin Black Durgâ and her festival of the dead.

Christianity has cast out the seven devils of Mary of Magdala, the City of the Tower. But, for all that, her outlines still appear sharply limned, and her identity is unmistakable. She anoints Christ's body for the burial, and the unguent is human tears. She stays by Him at the foot of the cross when His disciples desert Him, and when for the hyssop of the Essene Sacramentum He is offered the hyssop which is presented on the point of a spear. Finally, in the sepulchre she is the first to greet Him, for, like Amrapali, her name is Death.

PORTENTS AT THE DEATH OF A BUDDHA.

In Mr. Rockhill's "Life of the Buddha" it is announced that portents and miracles always take place at the moment of a Buddha's death. These occur when Ânanda, who was a Buddha[1] after Sâkya Muni's death, and Mahâkâsyapa pass away.[2] When the great Tathâgata expired, a great earthquake terrified the inhabitants of the world, and the "drum of the gods" roared through the vault of heaven, whilst the angels in the sky covered their faces with their hands and rained down salt tears. The disciples were beside themselves with grief, and rolled with pain on the ground. Ânanda and a companion disciple saw numerous denizens of the other world in the city of Kusinagara, and by the river Yigdan.

---

[1] Page 165.   [2] Pages 162, 167.

Kâśyapa encountered a man carrying a mandârava flower, and he knew at once that the great teacher was at rest, for the mandârava flower blooms only in heaven.[1]

"THEY PARTED MY GARMENTS AMONGST THEM!"

The Abbé Huc tells us that the old garments of the Bokté, or incarnation of Buddha, are cut into little strips and prized immensely.[2]

"HE ROSE AGAIN FROM THE DEAD."

In the Chinese version, Buddha appeared after death:

"After his remains had been put in a golden coffin, which then grew so heavy that no one could lift it. . . . Suddenly his long-deceased mother, Mâyâ, appeared from above bewailing her lost son, when the coffin lifted itself up, the lid sprang open, and Sâkya Muni appeared with folded hands saluting his mother."[3]

This confirms what I said about Mâyâ Devî representing humanity as with the Hindoos. So clumsy an expedient as bringing her down from heaven to see her son who, according to early Buddhist ideas had joined her there, would not otherwise have been thought of.

TRINITY IN UNITY.

Professor Kellogg finds fault with all who draw a parallel between the Buddhist and Christian trinities. The Buddhist trinity is Buddha, Dharma, Saṅgha (Buddha, the law, and the order of the monks),[4] which is, of course, very different from the Three Persons of the Christian Trinity.

I will write down a very curious passage from the earliest history of the Christian Church, that of Hegesippus—

"In every city that prevails which the Law, the Lord, and the prophets enjoin."

As a monastery was called a school of the prophets in

---

[1] Foucaux, p. 419.   [2] "Voyages," vol. ii. p. 278.
[3] Eitel, "Three Lectures on Buddhism," p. 57.   [4] Page 184.

Palestine—and in the newly discovered "Teaching of the Apostles" the early Christian missionary is called a "Prophet"—is it possible to get a more literal translation of Buddha, Dharma, and Sangha than this?

But Professor Kellogg has not read every volume of the long list of Buddhist books that he gives in his preface with very great attention, or he would have known that Buddha, Dharma, and Sangha on earth have their prototypes in the sky; and that these divine beings were at any rate thought so like the three persons of the Christian Trinity by early missionaries and travellers in China and elsewhere that they pronounced that this "trinity in unity" was evidently derived from St. Thomas.[1] Father Tachard makes a similar announcement. The Buddhist triad in his view "renferment presque l'idée de la Trinité, car ces trois paroles signifient Dieu, le verbe de Dieu, et l'imitateur de Dieu."[2]

This triad figures in the rituals of both northern and southern Buddhism.

BUDDHA.

"He is the creator of all the Buddhas. He is the creator of Prajnâ, and of the world, himself unmade."

"He is the form of all things, yet formless."

"Âdi Buddha is without beginning. He is perfect and pure within the essence of wisdom and absolute truth. He knows all the past. His words are ever the same. He is without second. He is omnipresent."[3]

The next citation is from the ritual of Ceylon.

"We believe in the blessed one, the holy one, the author of all truth, who has fully accomplished the eight kinds of supernatural knowledge, . . . who came the good journey which led to the Buddhahood, who knows the universe, the unrivalled who has made subject to him all mortal beings whether in heaven or on earth, the teacher of gods and men,

---

[1] Picart, citing Purchas, "Ceremonies," etc. vol. vii. p. 203.
[2] Ibid., p. 59.
[3] These are cited by Mr. Hodgson from the "Nâma Sangîti."

the blessed Buddha. Through life till I reach Nirvâna will I put my trust in Buddha."[1]

This latter passage is from Ceylon, where every day the following sentences are ejaculated in the temples :—

"I bow my head to the ground and worship the sacred dust of his holy feet.

"If in aught I have sinned against Buddha,

"May Buddha forgive me my sin!"

"I bow my head to the ground and worship Dharma.

"If in aught I have sinned against Dharma,

"May Dharma forgive me my sin!"

"I bow my head to the ground and worship Sangha.

"If in aught I have sinned against Sangha,

"May Sangha forgive me my sin!"[2]

DHARMA OR PRAJÑÂ (WISDOM).

"I salute that Dharma who is the wisdom of the unseen world (Prajñâ Pâramitâ), pointing out the way of perfect tranquility to mortals, leading them to the paths of perfect wisdom, who by the testimony of the sages produced all things."[3]

"Whatsoever spirits are present either belonging to the earth or living in the air, let us worship Tathâgata Dharma, revered by gods and men, may then be salvation."[4]

SAÑGHA.

Sañgha, the third person of this trinity, sprang from the union of Sophia the mother and Buddha (Spirit). The relations between the transcendental Buddha and the mortal Buddha I have already shown to be the same as those between En Soph of the "Kabbalah" and the Heavenly Man. Philo's God the Father and the Logos his son is based on the same idea.

Our Holy Spirit was at first a woman, Sophia, the mother. The great cathedral in the first capital of Christendom is

---

[1] "Buddhist Credo in Ceylon," Dickson.

[2] "Patimokkha," p. 5.   [3] Hodgson, p. 142.

[4] "Sutta Nipâta," p. 39, Fausbol.

named after her. God made the world by means of the Word and Sophia,[1] says Irenæus, with whom she is also a woman.

I will draw attention here to a singularly neglected portion of the Jewish scriptures, the Apocrypha. I say singularly neglected, as it formed part of the scriptures known to Christ and the higher Judaism, and was most of it composed at Alexandria. The Buddhist inner teaching was set forth in compositions entitled Prajnâ Pâramitâ (the wisdom of the other bank). The higher Judaism also had its book of Wisdom. I will make an extract.

"O God of my fathers and Lord of Mercy, who hast made all things with the Word.

"And ordained man through thy Wisdom that he should have dominion over the creatures that Thou hast made.

"Give me Wisdom that sitteth by Thy throne, and reject me not from among Thy children. . . .

"Wisdom was with Thee which knoweth Thy works, and was present when Thou madest the world. . . .

"O send her out of thy holy heaven, and from the throne of Thy glory, that being present she may labour with me.

"For the corruptible body presseth down the soul, and the earthly tabernacle weigheth down the mind that museth upon many things.

"And Thy counsel who hath known, except Thou give wisdom and send the Holy Spirit from above."

In this passage we see Sophia personified as the Holy Spirit. She was in existence before God created the world. This He did by the aid of the Logos, as in the fourth gospel.

Immediately following the passage quoted it is narrated what Sophia did for the seven great prophets, Adam, Noah, Abraham, Lot, Jacob, Joseph, Moses. These are supposed by some to be the seven messengers of the Apocalypse.

Here are a few more verses about Sophia—

"She is the breath of the power of God.

"She is the brightness of the everlasting light, the unspotted mirror of the power of God.

[1] "Hær.," iv. 20.

" Being one she can do all things, and remaining in herself she maketh all things new." [1]

" She is privy to the mysteries of the knowledge of God." [2]

She appears constantly in the catacombs. The figure, known as the Orante, is a representation of her, not praying, but supporting the Kosmos; as in India, it is similarly supported by Krishṇa, or Hanumân. A female, with arms in a similar attitude, is seen constantly in the old Buddhist bas-reliefs. We see her here standing on the kosmical lily or lotus (Fig. 15). She is the " Bride " of the Apocalypse.

In the Indian religion it was feigned that the ecliptic, or circle of the year, was a great serpent with his tail in his mouth—Ananta, the Endless.

This serpent was supposed to be cut in half, and to become

Fig. 15.

two serpents which represented Summer, or the period of life, and Winter, or the period of death. These two serpents, as Ketu and Râhu, also represented good and evil with the Buddhists and Brahmins.

The word " union " is the keystone of all ancient mysteries. With the Brahmins this was yoga. With the Buddhists it was saṅgha. In early Christianity it was the mystic " marriage." Buddha (heaven, spirit, the universal father) was allied to Dharma (earth, matter, the universal mother), and from the union was born the mystic child.

The favourite way of representing these two mystic serpents was as twined round the " Rod of Hermes " (Fig. 2,

PLATE VIII.

Fig. 1.

Catacombs.

Fig. 2.

Sanchi.

Fig. 3.

Triratna.

Fig. 4.

Sanchi.

Fig. 5.

Burmah.

Fig. 6.

Tibet.

TRIRATNA OUTLINE.

[*Page* 200.

PLATE IX.

Fig. 2.

I. A. ω.

Fig. 3.

Serapis.

Fig. 1.

Jamalgiri.

Fig. 4.

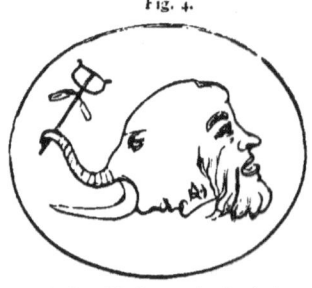

Father, Mother, and Mârttânda.

Fig. 5

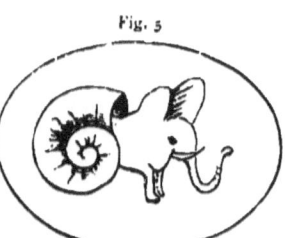

Serapis Shell and Mârttânda.

THE GNOSTIC TRIAD.   [Page 201.

Plate VIII., from the early Buddhist tope of Sanchi). In an ornamental form (Figs. 3 and 4) this became the Trisul or Triratna outline, the most holy symbol of Buddhism. Buddha's head (Fig. 5) has, I think, its very long ears to make up the same outline. Fig. 6 is a magic tortoise from Tibet, and here we have the same outline in another form. In Buddhism it is everywhere. Fig. 1, a head of Christ from the catacombs, whether by accident or design, makes up the same symbol of the mystic "union." In Greece it was feigned that Jupiter and Rhea, disguised as serpents, had produced this symbol. This was the explanation of the Rod of Hermes.

The two serpents in Alexandrian Gnosticism were the legs of the mystic I. A. ω. Compare Fig. 2, Plate IX., with Fig. 1, from the Buddhist tope of Jamalgiri. In Figs. 4 and 5 we see Buddha's symbol of the elephant as one limb of the triad, a strong proof that Buddhism was in Alexandria. Fig. 3 is Serapis, whose head is said to have suggested the conventional Christ. According to Gibbon, Christianity and Serapis worship in Alexandria were at one time scarcely distinguishable.

CHAPTER XVII.

Ritual—Saint Worship- Cosmology—Progress of Buddhism—Indulgences—Dispensations—Councils to put down Heresy—Close similarities in the Election of the Grand Lâma and the Pope.

RITUAL.

In my work, " Buddha and Early Buddhism," occurred
the following passage :—

" The French missionary Huc, in his celebrated travels in
Tibet, was much struck with the similarity that exists
between Buddhist and Roman Catholic rites and customs.

" The crozier, the mitre, the dalmatic, the cope or *pluvial,*
which the grand lâmas, wear on a journey, or when they
perform some ceremony outside the temple, the service with
a double choir, psalmody, exorcisms, the censer swinging on
five chains, and contrived to be opened or shut at will, benediction by the lâmas with the right hand extended over the
heads of the faithful, the chaplet, sacerdotal celibacy, lenten
retirements from the world, the worship of saints, fasts, processions, litanies, holy water—these are the points of contact
between the Buddhists and ourselves." The good Abbé has
by no means exhausted the list, and might have added " confessions, tonsure, relic worship, the use of flowers, lights,
and images before shrines and altars, the sign of the cross,
the Trinity in unity, the worship of the queen of heaven, the
use of religious books in a tongue unknown to the bulk of
the worshippers, the aureole or nimbus, the crown of saints
and Buddhas, wings to angels, penance, flagellations, the
flabellum or fan, popes, cardinals, bishops, abbots, presbyters,
deacons, the various architectural details of the Christian

temple," etc.[1] To this list Balfour's "Cyclopædia of India" adds "amulets, medicines, illuminated missals;" and Mr. Thomson ("Illustrations of China," vol. ii. p. 18), "baptism, the mass, requiems."

Mr. Pfoundes, a gentleman who has resided for eight years in a Buddhist monastery, tells me that when the monks enter the temple for the first time of a morning, they make the precise gesture which Catholics call the sign of the cross. They mean by this to invoke the four cardinal points as a symbol of God.

Listen, also, to Father Disderi, who visited Tibet in the year 1714—

"The lâmas have a tonsure like our priests, and are bound over to perpetual celibacy. They study their scriptures in a language and characters that differ from the ordinary characters; they recite prayers in choir; they serve the temple, present the offerings, and keep the lamps perpetually alight; they offer to God corn, and barley, and paste, and water in little vases, which are extremely clean. Food thus offered is considered consecrated, and they eat it. The lâmas have local superiors, and a superior general."[2]

The lâmas told the father that their holy books were very like his.[3] When he asked them whether Buddha was God or man, they replied god and man. He furthermore describes the high altar of a temple covered with a cloth and containing a little tabernacle, where Buddha was said to reside. Cross-examined by the father, the lâmas said that he lived in heaven as well.[4]

The Catholics use a "tabernacle" for the sacred elements; and whilst they are there, a lamp is perpetually burning, which, like a similar Buddhist light, represents God's presence. "Âdi Buddha is light," say the Buddhists.

Father Grueber, who, with another priest named Dorville, passed from Pekin through Tibet to Patna in the year 1661, published an interesting narrative of his journey, with ex-

[1] "Buddha and Early Buddhism," p. 180.
[2] "Lettres Edifiantes," vol. iii. p. 534.
[3] Ibid., p. 534.   [4] Ibid., p. 533.

cellent illustrations. Henry Prinsep thus sums up the points that chiefly attracted the father—

" Father Grueber was much struck with the extraordinary similarity he found, as well in the doctrine as in the rituals of the Buddhists of Lha Sa, to those of his own Romish faith. He noticed, first, that the dress of the lâmas corresponded with that handed down to us in ancient paintings as the dress of the apostles ; second, that the discipline of the monasteries, and of the different orders of lâmas or priests, bore the same resemblance to that of the Romish Church ; third, that the notion of an incarnation was common to both, so also the belief in paradise and purgatory ; fourth, he remarked that they made suffrages, alms, prayers, and sacrifices, for the dead, like the Roman Catholics ; fifth, that they had convents filled with monks and friars to the number of thirty thousand near Lha Sa, who all made the three vows of poverty, obedience, and chastity, like Roman monks, besides other vows ; and sixth, that they had confessors licensed by the superior lâmas or bishops, and so empowered to receive confessions, impose penances, and give absolution. Besides all this, there was found the practice of using holy water, of singing service in alternation, of praying for the dead, and of perfect similarity in the costumes of the great and superior lâmas to those of the different orders of the Romish hierarchy. These early missionaries further were led to conclude from what they saw and heard that the ancient books of the lâmas contained traces of the Christian religion which must, they thought, have been preached in Tibet in the time of the apostles." [1]

The Abbé Prouvéze, in his biography of the French missionary, Gabriel Durand, says that the points of similarity between Tibetan Buddhism and Christianity are far too minute to do away with the ideas of plagiarism. " The government of Tibet is borrowed from the ecclesiastical government of the States of the Church." [2] The Delai lâma is like the pope, and his election very similar. " The gospel has already passed into the hands of the Tartars, with the

[1] Prinsep, " Tibet, Tartary," etc. p. 14.   [2] Vol. ii. p. 365.

PLATE X.

THE BUDDHIST VIRGIN AND CHILD.   [*Page* 205.

Christian hierarchy and celibacy." St. Hyacinth of Poland and St. Oderic of Frioul, who visited Tibet in the fourteenth century, may have effected this propagandism.[1] "The cross,' pursues the Abbé, alluding perhaps to the Buddhist Swastika, " has remained enshrined amongst the arid rocks of Tibet as a sign of salvation."[2] But greater proofs of Christian propagandism are in reserve. The Abbé points out that the Chinese know all about the Virgin Mother. A " missionary of Kiang Si " reports that he has seen statues of her holding an infant child in her arms, and treading down the serpent with her feet. By this statue stood a solemn man surrounded by ten smaller statues. These, he thinks, were St. Joseph and the shepherds, though I fear that they were the disciples and Buddha. Other statues of Kwan ,Yin have each a descending dove on the head and a child in her arms. They bear for inscription, "The Mother who delivers the world." This mother is declared to be ever virgin. The Abbé Prouvèze is aware, however, that Kwan Yin is much earlier historically than the Virgin Mary, for he starts a second theory that the idea was plagiarized from an old Testament in the synagogue that the Jews had in China two hundred years before Christ.[3]

Here is a passage from the life of Gabriel Durand—

" There [in the pagoda of the Bell Pekin] we saw a Buddhist priest dressed almost exactly like a Benedictine, a kind of arch of alliance, shewbread (pains de proposition) on the altar, vases like our holy water, and censers."[4]

Let us now consider the Buddhist ritual a little more closely, selecting a liturgy given to us by Professor Beal—

" The form of this office is a very curious one. It bears a singular likeness in its outline to the common type of the Eastern Christian liturgies. That is to say, there is a ' Proanaphoral ' and an ' Anaphoral ' portion ; there is a prayer of entrance ($\tau\tilde{\eta}\varsigma$ $\varepsilon\grave{\iota}\sigma\acute{o}\delta ov$), a prayer of incense ($\tau o\grave{v}$ $\theta v\mu\iota\acute{a}\mu a\tau o\varsigma$), an ascription of praise to the threefold object of worship ($\tau\rho\iota\sigma a\gamma\acute{\iota}ov$), a prayer of oblation ($\tau\tilde{\eta}\varsigma$ $\pi\rho o\sigma\theta\varepsilon\sigma\varepsilon\omega\varsigma$), the Lections, the recitation of the Dharani ($\mu v\sigma\tau\acute{\eta}\rho\iota ov$), the Embolismus or

---

[1] Vol. ii. p. 363.   [2] Vol. ii. p. 263.
[3] Vol. i. p. 422.   [4] " Gabriel Durand," vol. i. p. 493.

prayer against temptation, followed by a Confession and a Dismissal." [1]

This similarity is so close, that the Professor believes it to be a Christian liturgy imported by the Nestorians at an early date.

In the pathway of this theory there are, however, considerable difficulties. In every other Buddhist country visited by early Christian missionaries were found traces of a similar propagandism. The services were all alike—incense, flowers, oblations, praise of the Trinity, confessions, hymns. This active "Nestorian," if he converted one Buddhist country, must have converted all, presenting thus a striking contrast to modern preachers who, even in Buddhist countries that have been one hundred years under Christian sway, make no impression at all. Besides this, the Nestorians were Unitarians.

In the central "mystery" the Buddhists use water and not wine, and condemn the Christian bloody atonement symbolized by the latter. How is it that this mysterious teacher, if he could effect so much, stopped short where he did?

Another point suggests itself. Ritual has one indelible record—the temple. The tope in the plain and the rock temple in the bowels of the mountain are exactly fitted for the Buddhist rites ; and the dates of these are long before the birth of Christ.

Mr. James Fergusson was of opinion that the various details of the early Christian Church, nave, aisles, columns, semi-domed apse, cruciform ground plan, were borrowed *en bloc* from the Buddhists.[2] He adduces the rock-cut cave temple of Karli, in the west of India, whose date he fixes at 78 B.C.

"The building resembles to a great extent an early Christian church in its arrangements, consisting of a nave and side aisles, terminating in an apse or semi-dome, round which the aisle is carried. . . . As a scale for comparison, it may be mentioned that its arrangements and dimensions are very

---

[1] Beal, "Catena of Buddhist Scriptures," p. 397.

[2] "Indian and Eastern Architecture," p. 117. "Rude Stone Monuments," p. 603, etc.

PLATE XI.

THE CAVE-TEMPLE OF KARLI.

similar to those of the choir of Norwich Cathedral, and of the Abbaye aux Hommes, at Caen, omitting the outer aisles in the latter buildings. Immediately under the semi-dome of the apse, and nearly where the altar stands in Christian churches, is placed the Dâgopa."[1] The Dâgopa is the Baldechino or canopy containing, as Mr. Fergusson points out, in both religions the relics of a saint.

Here we have already, many years before Christ's birth, an apparatus plainly adapted for early Christian rites. These were divided into two sections. There was a "mass of the catechumens," which took place in the body of the cathedral. Then these were expelled, and what is called the "Liturgia Mystica" was used. This was the Oblation of Bread, as Tertullian calls it; the Bloodless Sacrifice, as it is termed in the Liturgy of St. James, which is considered by scholars the earliest Christian ritual. The Bema was now approached by the chanting choristers. This represented heaven; and the marriage of the bread and wine, the birth of the mystic Christ, the word made flesh.

Into what the Buddhists call the "main court of the temple," which represents earth and earth life, the first procession of chanting monks comes. This is called the "Lesser Entrance." The second entrance, after the expulsion of the catechumens, is called the "Greater Entrance," when the Buddhist monks march slowly and reverently to the sanctuary, and march round it three times. "I will compass thine altar," said the Psalmist (Ps. xxvi. 6).

I give the Buddhist high altar with its lower altar in front, like that of the Catholics, with its lamp perpetually burning like theirs, its artificial flowers, thurifers, and tall candlesticks with wax candles made out of a vegetable wax. Votive tablets like doll's tombstones crowd it with offerings to the dead. In the Middle Ages, Catholic churches were similarly choked. In front of Buddha is the Sambo, a three-sided box, hollow behind. Always in front of it is represented the cross, made up of four circles, the four stages of spiritual growth. "I regard the sacred altar as a royal gem, on which the

---

[1] "Indian and Eastern Architecture," p. 117.

shadow (spirit) of S'akya Tathâgata appears" (See Plate XIII., p. 210).[1] This is from the Chinese ritual, and the accompanying bas-relief from Amarâvatî reminds one of the Armenian collect which describes Christ with His saints as also descending in the chariot of the four fiery faces.[2]

SAINT-WORSHIP.

I now come to a very important point, saint-worship. The Jews, as we know, believed that soul and body were inseparable, that both went to sheol (the cave); and later on came the idea of a universal resurrection of the dead, and a universal judgment, ideas that have been transferred to Christian creeds.

I will first of all cite a passage from the Persian scripture, the Boundehesch—

"After that the angel Sosiosch will raise the dead, as promised, by the power of Ormuzd. This resurrection will be certainly seen. Veins will be restored to the body; and this resurrection once made will not be repeated." This resurrection is called in a previous passage, "the resurrection of the dead, and the re-establishment of the body."[3]

After this resurrection of the body will come, as we learn from the same scripture, a last judgment.

"Then will appear on earth the assemblage of all the beings of the world with man. In this gathering each will see the good and the evil that he has done. . . . Then the just will be separated from the darvands. The just will go to Gorotman. The darvands will be precipitated into the Douzakh. . . . The father will be separated from the mother, the sister from the brother."[4]

We see from this where the Lower Judaism got its ideas about a resurrection of the material body, and the last judgment.

But on the top of this has been superposed a second idea, which contradicts and stultifies the first in every particular—saint-worship.

---

[1] Beal, "Catena of Buddhist Scriptures," p. 243.
[2] See ante, p. 13.
[3] "Boundehesch," chap. xxxi.   [4] Ibid., ch. xxxi.

PLATE XII.

THE BUDDHIST HIGH ALTAR.

[Page 208.

In 2 Maccabees xv. 15, the dead prophet Jeremiah revisits earth. He appears to Judas Maccabeus holding a sword. " Take this holy sword, a gift from God, with the which thou shalt wound the adversaries."

White-robed saints and their heaven figure conspicuously in the earliest scripture written by a personal follower of Christ, the Apocalypse. Plainly, too, Christ knew nothing of the idea that the soul after death dwelt in a torpid state with the worms and decomposing matter of its body in the sepulchre, as proved by the promise to the penitent thief, the story of Lazarus and Dives, the appearance of Moses and Elias. Also He promised to go and prepare places for His disciples in the "many mansions " of heaven ; and adjudicated in the squabble of His disciples for the privilege of sitting on His right or left hand. Had He held the popular Jewish views, He would have had to explain that the figures seen on the transfiguration mount could not possibly be Moses and Elias, for these will remain unconscious until the sound of the great trumpet.

Saint-worship emerges conspicuously in the earliest Christian monuments. In the Catacombs each chapel was the shrine of a saint, and each altar the lid of a sarcophagus. Immense exertions were made at a martyrdom to save the dead body, or at least a few bones, or a sponge dipped in blood. The Council of Carthage, cited by Cardinal Wiseman, decreed that all altars should be " overturned by the bishop of the place which are erected about the fields and roads as in memory of martyrs, in which is not a body nor any relics." [1] " God dwells in the bones of the martyrs," says St. Ephrem ; "and by His power and presence miracles are wrought." He further asserted that when St. Ignatius " laid down his life, he returned again crowned." [2]

On the grave of the martyr Sabbatius in the catacombs is this inscription : " Sabbatius, sweet soul, pray and entreat for thy brethren and comrades." [3]

This saint-worship, tomb-worship, corpse-worship was con-

---

[1] Can. XIV., Conc. Gen., tom. ii. p. 1272.   [2] Ibid., tom. v. p. 340.
[3] Wiseman's " Lectures of the Catholic Church," ii. 105.

spicuous in early Buddhism. Its first temple was the tumulus
containing a relic of Buddha, or the charred ashes of the body
of Śariputra, Ânanda, or other of the saints. Conspicuous
saints had each his tumulus, or tope, in many cities, and his
saint's day, when the devout offered him flowers and food.
The Great Vehicle, or school of nihilism shook this saint-
worship, but only superficially. When the P. Morales visited
Manilla, he was told that the saints had enormous power, that
they "were seated to the right and left of God."[1]

We have seen that many hold that all that is like Christianity in Buddhism was derived from Christian sources. I
think that this question of the status of saints is therefore
very important. For we see at the very source of Christianity
two internecine eschatologies struggling together, the Jewish
and Buddhist. Illogically the church eventually adopted
both. Now, if Buddhism had been derived from Christianity,
we should have seen similar contradictions. The Buddhist
monks would have announced that the good man after death
is at one and the same time—

1. Unconscious in the tomb awaiting the sound of a trumpet.
2. Conscious in the sky at the right hand of God.

The earliest Christian liturgies were called "Laudes."
The earliest Buddhist liturgy was called "Sapta Buddha
Stotra" (the Praise of the Seven Buddhas). Oddly enough,
in the Catholic "Litany of all the Saints," seven principal
beings are addressed—the angels Michael, Gabriel, and
Raphael, the Three Persons of the Trinity, and the Virgin.
Plainly these last have been substituted for the other four
angels of Kabbalistic worship. After these seven there is a
general invocation to "angels, holy angels, and happy spirits,"
and to the minor saints, as in Buddhism.

PURGATORY.

I have asked Catholics how it is that saints can be residing
in heaven before they can possibly have been judged and
pronounced saints. They say that it is a miracle. This, to

[1] Picart, "Ceremonies," etc. vol. vii. p. 216.

PLATE XIII.

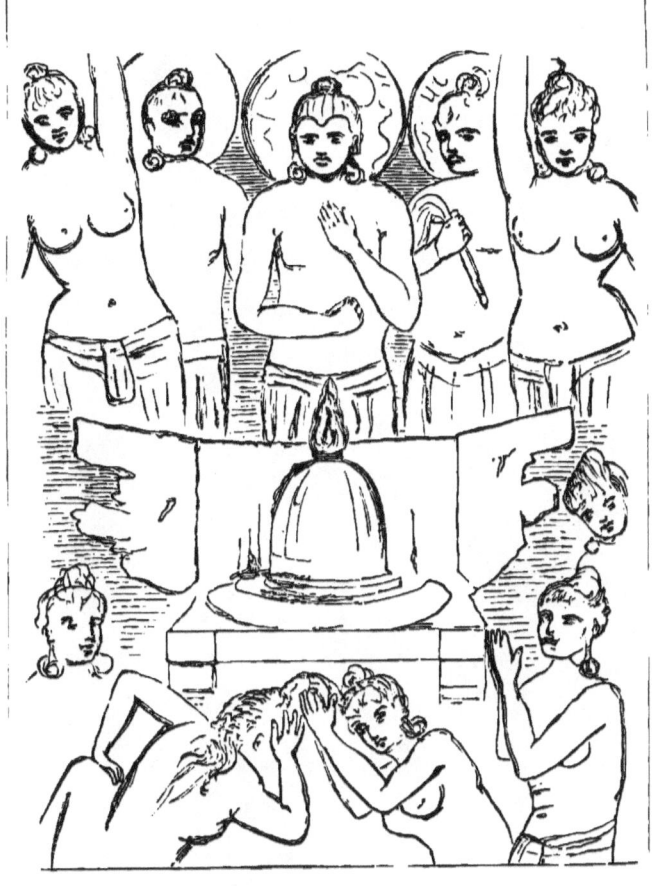

BUDDHA APPEARING AT THE ALTAR DURING WORSHIP.   [*Page* 210.

From Amarâvatî.

my mind, fails not only to explain, but to appreciate the difficulty. Besides, it is not only the question of saints that stultifies the Apostles' Creed. Much, indeed most, of the mechanism of the Catholic Church is designed to extricate the souls of laymen from purgatory as soon as possible after death. It is the same in Buddhism, but in that Creed we know how the doctrine was built up. In early Vedic days folks believed in an eternal heaven but no hell. By-and-by the notion of a place of expiation was added. Then the priests of India or Egypt invented the doctrine of the metempsychosis to account for their caste privileges. It was taught that the Karma, or causation of good or evil actions, ushered a man into a new birth as a parrot or a princess, a jackdaw or a banker, according to its quality. But an early creed is not easily superseded in the mind of a people, and it was found necessary to tack on the Vedic hell and heaven as temporary places of reward and expiation as well; men not inquiring too nicely why, if the causation of a bandit's crimes plunged him into the hell Avîchi for three centuries, it should be at all necessary after that to bring him back to earth as a pilfering jackal. These Buddhist contradictions are of value to our inquiry. Given the gross absurdity of an unintelligent causation sentencing people to be boiled in hot oil, the Buddhist system has its logic. Not so that of the Catholics. My grandfather died three weeks ago. He is in purgatory, I am told, but masses for his soul may much shorten the period of his stay there. Who sent him to purgatory? Not Christ, for He has not yet come to judge the quick and the dead. Not Karma, for the Catholic Church ignores Buddhism.

In point of fact we again see two conflicting eschatologies, the Jewish and the Buddhist; and their union brings about many necessary contradictions.

COSMOLOGY.

In Vedic days, the Indians had seven heavens, as Colebrooke teaches. The highest was the unchangeable Heaven of Brahma.[1] The Buddhists took over these seven heavens,

[1] Colebrooke, " Essays," vol. i. pp. 129, 130.

including the heaven of Brahma, where spirits enfranchised from returns to earth, for ever dwell.

In the " Testimony of the Twelve Patriarchs," a Christian work of a very early date, we get the seven Jewish heavens—

1. A heaven of sadness, owing to its proximity to man.

2. Full of fires and scourges, and ice and snow. Scourges and fire in paradise is very Jewish.

3. Celestial cohorts, destined to triumph over the spirit of evil.

4. Heaven of the saints enthroned in glory.

5. Heaven of the angels, offering a reasonable, not a bloody, sacrifice, and interceding with God.

6. Heaven of the high angels. They carry the messages of the angels of the Face of God.

7. The Most High, surrounded by "powers," "thrones," etc. In this heaven is the great throne and the heavenly temple.

Here, again, we get Buddhist derivation. To a Jew, who believed that the soul remained wedded to the disintegrating chemicals, which he miscalled the body, until a universal judgment, of what use would be heaven number four, the heaven of the saints? Plainly there could be no saints until after this universal judgment had settled who were the saints.

In point of fact, in Christian cosmology, these saints promptly usurped the functions of the earlier mythological beings. The earth was supposed by early Christians to be a large, flat, rectangle, twice as long as it was broad. In the centre of the earth was hell, with its circles of fire, sulphur, ice, dung, vipers, red-hot iron for heretics, and so on. Moses, talking of the tabernacle, which he says is the image of the earth, says that its length was two cubits, and its breadth one. That gives us the proportions, says Flammarion ; who gives also the map of the world by Cosmas in the sixth century. A guardian is depicted at each side of the parallelogram.[1] These in Buddhism are the four Mahârâjas, in Christian cosmology, they soon became Matthew, Mark,

---

[1] "Histoire du Ciel," p. 301.

Luke, and John. Around the rim of heaven, figured as a mountain, the holy Zion, were the twelve apostles, figuring as the twelve æons, a Greek term for the Buddhas who stand at the twelve points of space. St. Peter became Janus, the celestial door-keeper, with his key and beard. St. Anthony presided over the Palilia, the feast of the cattle, the Indian Pongal. By-and-by, there was a saint for every infirmity of the body, as in Pagan Rome there had been a god for every disease ; St. Petronella, for gout and ague ; St. Romanus, for those that were possessed ; St. Valentine, for the falling sickness.[1]

The heaven of Indra, as described in the Buddhist writings, is very like the heaven of St. John. There is a "high mountain," and a city "four square," with gates of gold and silver, adorned with precious stones. Seven moats surround the city, and beyond the last range is a row of marble pillars, studded with jewels. The great throne of the God stands in the centre of a great hall, surmounted with a white canopy. Trees that bear constant fruits are there, and the gem lake, with the peaches of immortality. Round the throne are seated subordinate heavenly ministers, who record men's actions in a "golden book."[2]

THE SIGN OF THE CROSS.

In the account of the "Churning of the Ocean," in the Mahâbhârata, the Indian signs of the zodiac are covertly detailed. The fish figures as Chakra, the terrible projectile of Vishnu, as of Thor. In all the epics it is being constantly alluded to as one of the treasures of the Sun-God, like the horse, the boar, the kaustabha gem, etc., which are all zodiacal. In early coins this cross (the Swastika) is formed by two serpents, the great Father and Mother. A similar idea is expressed in passages of the Mahâbhârata.

Fig. 16.

"Beneath the trenchant Chakra he saw guarding the Amrita two immense and terrible serpents, strong,

---

[1] See Burton's "Anatomy of Melancholy," part ii. sect. i.
[2] Upham, "History of Buddhism," pp. 56, 57.

venom-threatening, with fiery eyes and throats, and tongues of forked lightning."[1]

Here is another passage—

" Here dwell two serpents, the terror of enemies, Arvouda and S'akravâpî. Here are the sublime palaces of Swastika and Maninâga (jewel snake)."[2]

Bentley[3] puts forward a plausible explanation of it, and that is that it was "feigned that a dragon was cut in two by the ecliptic," and that Rahu was the ascending node, and Ketu the descending node. This would give the two serpents the positive and negative principles.

In India, when the fish are used, they always cross each other. In Japan, the constellation that has this sign)((our symbol for the fish), is called Tsing (beams in the form of a cross).[4] It is oddly enough, the only cross in the catacombs, and it was the only symbol on the drapery on the high altar in the first Japanese temple at Knightsbridge. It is the sole symbol that figures in the text of Asoka's inscriptions. It is called the "Seal of the Heart of Buddha."

This gives a new meaning to such words as "Take up thy cross," pronounced before Christ's hearers knew anything about the crucifixion. It is the symbol of the four stages of the soul's progress.

In the catacombs, the fish likewise make the form of a cross. The early Christians were called "The Fish," and the Christ monogram seems to have been built up gradually from the symbol which was the "seal," alike of Christ and Buddha (Rev. vii. 3).

Fig. 17.

Fig. 18.

[1] Mahab. Adi Parva, v. 1500, 1501.
[2] Ibid., Sabha Parva, p. 806.
[3] "Hindu Astronomy," p. 24. "Flammarion," p. 156.
[4] Balfour, "Indian Cyclopædia."

All these crosses are early forms. I take them from Smith's
"Christian Antiquities." To the two serpents
symbolizing the great Father and Mother, the
jod or rod of Christ was added, the whole
making the Alexandrine "I A ω" Oddly
enough, the Swastika cross, the Indian fish,
has dominated the year all through the epoch
of Buddhism and Christianity. A.D. 2000, it will be succeeded
by the Man with the Vase of Ichor.

Fig. 19.

BUDDHA'S MOVEMENT.

We shall perhaps make matters more intelligible if we take
up the story of Buddha's movement from the date of his death.
The creed, as I have shown, struggled on in obscurity and
probably in secrecy until the advent of a powerful monarch
250 B.C. King Aśoka ruled India—on this point we have the
evidence of his inscriptions and incised stones—from Peshawur
to Cape Comorin, and from Girnar in the Gulf of Cutch on
the east coast of Hindustan to Ganjam on the west coast.
When he made Buddhism the official creed of India he was
met with a difficulty. The teaching of Buddha was simply
the awakening of the spiritual life of the individual.

"Who speaks and acts with the inner quickening has joy
for his shadow!" This was his motto.

For the vulgar something more was required ; and the king
was obliged to graft on to it some of the outside worship of
Brahminism, for the people required some cultus that they
could venerate and understand. That cultus consisted in a
sort of saint-worship. The dead rishi or saint of the past
had his ashes casketed in a little stone chamber in the centre
of a huge mound like Avebury, or the Maes Howe in Orkney.
Round this, tanks and groves and tall columns were erected,
to which pilgrims resorted in shoals to see the ashes of the
saint coruscate with magic light, and to be healed of bodily
and spiritual infirmities. India had an arch Brahmin, the
high priest of the creed, and Aśoka changed him into a
Buddhist monk, called in the Mahâwanso the " high priest of

all the world." In process of time this pontiff dwelt in the great monastery of Nalanda, not far from Buddha Gâya. He was the Âchârya of Buddhism, the "teacher" par excellence. Hwen Thsang has left us a description of his pomp, and the splendour of his great monastery on the hills, the tanks, the gardens, the jade and the gold. He describes the architecture as like that of the Chinese ; red pillars and roofs that scale the sky. Ten thousand monks were dwelling in the court of the great Âchârya.

These days of the ascendancy of early Buddhism continued until A.D. 10, when another great Indian emperor arose who defiled Buddhism with the teachings of a bad school of Brahminism, the religion of the followers of Śiva.

This brings us to the two great schools of Buddhism—

1. The earliest school, the Buddhism of Buddha, taught that after Nirvâna, or man's emancipation from re-births, the consciousness of the individual survived, and that he dwelt for ever in happiness in the Brahma heavens.

2. The second, or innovating school, taught that after Nirvâna the consciousness of the individual ceased. The god of the first school was Buddha, which can have no other meaning than "intelligent." The god of the innovating school was Śunya (unintelligent causation).

Some readers will judge that this statement differs considerably from the teaching of St. Hilaire, Oldenberg, and Rhys Davids. In point of fact, when I first brought it forward in my "Popular Life of Buddha,"[1] one or two critics, notably one in the *Athenæum*, found fault with me for venturing to differ with so great a Pâli scholar as Professor Rhys Davids ; the critic himself having unconsciously ventured to differ quite as widely. He was plainly under the impression that without a vast and accurate knowledge of Pâli roots no decision could be come to in Buddhist eschatology. In point of fact the question is a piece of history as pure and easy of solution as the question whether the religion of Leo X. preceded or followed that of Luther. In the seventh century, A.D., a Chinese monk named Hwen Thsang visited India,

---

[1] Vol. i. pp. 150, 151.

and he was appointed president of a great convocation expressly summoned by King Silâditya, to put down the Buddhism of the Little Vehicle altogether. No better witness can be conceived. He has recorded the following facts :—

1. The council of King Kaniśka (summoned about A.D. 10) was the first occasion on which the innovating Buddhism of the Great Vehicle was introduced.[1]

2. This was done in spite of such strong opposition on the point of the Âchârya of the great monastery of Nalanda (the high priest of Buddhism), that the king was afraid to hold his convocation in the Buddhist Holy Land as he had at first intended.[2]

3. That the official representatives of genuine Buddhism at Nalanda asserted in the most positive terms that the innovating Buddhism did not come from Buddha at all, but from a sect of the followers of the Brahman god Śiva (the Kâpâlikas).[3]

4. On the nature of the innovating teachers the Chinese traveller is equally explicit. They were what is called in India Śunyavâdis.

As early as the Brahmin Gautama, who compiled a code of laws centuries before the Code of Manu, these philosophers existed. This is what he says of them—

" The Śunyavâdis affirm that from nonentity all things arose, for that everything sprung to birth from a state in which it did not previously exist : that entity absolutely implies nonentity, and that there must be some power in nonentity from which entity can spring. The sprout does not arise from a sprout, but in the absence or non-existence of a sprout. . . . The Sunyavâdi admits the necessity of using the terms "maker," etc., but maintains that they are mere words of course, and are often used when the things spoken of are in a state of non-existence, as when men say, ' A son will be born.' "[4]

---

[1] Hwen Thsang, " Mémoires," vol. i. p. 173, *et seq.*
[2] Ibid., p. 174.   [3] Ibid., p. 220.
[4] Sutras of Gautama, cited by Ward, " The Hindoos" vol. i. p. 420.

In an Indian drama called the " Prabodha Chandra Udaya," there is a sketch of one of these atheistic priests of Śiva.   In a dispute with a Buddhist he is made to say—

> " With goodly necklace decked of bones of men,
> Haunting the tombs, from cups of human skulls
> Eating and quaffing, ever I behold,
> With eyes that meditation's salve hath cleared,
> The world of diverse jarring elements
> Composed, but still all one with the Supreme.

" *The Buddhist.* This man professes the rule of a Kâpâlika.   I will ask him what it is (*going to him*).   O ho, you with the bone and skull neck-lace ! what are your hopes of happiness and salvation ?

" *The Adept.* Wretch of a Buddhist ! Well, hear what is our religion :—

> With flesh of men, with brain and fat well smeared.
> We make our grim burnt offering—break our fast
> From cups of holy Brahmin's skull, and ever
> With gurgling drops of blood that plenteous stream
> From hard throats quickly cut ; by us is worshipped
> With human offerings meet the dread Bhairava.
>
>   *   *   *   *   *   *   *
>
> I call at will the best of gods, great Hari,
> And Hara's self and Brahma.   I restrain
> With my sole voice the course of stars that wander
> In heaven's bright vault ; the earth, with all its load
> Of mountains, fields, and cities, I at will
> Reduce once more to water ; and, behold,
> I drink it up ! " [1]

The mock Mahâtmas that the notorious Madame Blavatsky professed to be in communication with were credited with similar pretensions.   They affirmed that there was no God, and that the divine powers usually credited to him were in their hands.   Has she not helped us to the secret of the atheism of the Kâpâlika ?   Greed steps forward to secure the homage and the oblations that man's nature pays to God.

The main position of writers like Dr. Oldenberg is that the atheistic literature of Ceylon represents the earliest Buddhism, the Buddhism of the Little Vehicle.   Hwen Thsang contradicts this in toto.

" In Ceylon," he says, " are about ten thousand monks who

---

[1] *Journ. Ben. As. Soc.,* vol. vi. p. 15.

follow the doctrines of the Great Vehicle."[1] He says, moreover, the controversy raged fiercely for a long time before the
Great Vehicle was successful over the Little Vehicle. He
tells as that one of the chief apostles of the Great Vehicle was
Deva Bodhisatwa, a Cingalese monk.[2] At Kanchipura the
Chinese pilgrim came across three hundred monks that had
just fled across the water from Ceylon, to escape the anarchy
and famine consequent on the death of the king there.[3] Hwen
Thsang was a sort of Lord High Inquisitor at the Convocation of Kanouj, that suppressed the Little Vehicle a short
time afterwards. If a vessel containing three hundred mixed
Christians from the Low Countries had been wrecked on the
coast of Spain in the reign of Philip II., we may fairly presume that any of them released after due inquiry by the Holy
Office might be considered Catholic, and not Protestant.

Although more wild theories are abroad concerning
Buddhism than any other old creed, it has oddly enough the
most trustworthy archives of all. Within two hundred and
fifty years of the death of the founder, Aśoka carved his credo
on the rocks—

" Confess and believe in God, who is the worthy object of
obedience. For equal to this belief I declare unto you ye
shall not find such a means of propitiating Heaven "—First
Dhauli Edict (Prinsep).

" Among whomsoever the name of God resteth, this verily
is religion "—Edict, No. VII. (Prinsep).

" I have appointed religious observances that mankind
having listened thereto shall be brought to follow in the right
path, and give glory to God "—(Ibid.).

No cavilling can explain away the word Iśâna. To the
Brahmin of Aśoka's time it meant the Supreme. And on
the subject of eternal life of the individual the king is equally
explicit.

" I pray with every variety of prayer for those who differ
with me in creed, that they, following after my example, may

---

[1] Hwen Thsang, " Histoire," p. 192.
[2] " Mémoires," vol. i. pp. 218, 277.
[3] Hwen Thsang, " Histoire," p. 192.

with me attain unto eternal salvation "—Delhi Pillar, Edict VI. (Prinsep).

" May they, my loving subjects, obtain happiness in this world and in the next "—(Burnouf.)

I have gone fully into this question in my "Popular Life of Buddha,"[1] but I have come across a fresh piece of evidence. The whole question of the nature of early Buddhism is quite set at rest by a work called the "Śatasáhasriká" (the Hundred Thousand Verses) also the "Rakshá Bhagavatí." It is in the collection of Nepalese scriptures ; and an abstract of it has been given to us by the invaluable scholar, Doctor Rajendra Lala Mitra. "It is pre-eminently," says the Doctor, "a work of the Mahâyâna class, and its main topic is the doctrine of Śunyavâda, or the evolution of the universe from vacuity or nihility."[2]

The work is alleged to have been delivered by Buddha in person on the hill Gṛidhakûṭa (Vulture's Peak). It was attested by many miracles, lambent flames, in which were seen many gold lotuses and other portents.

The disciples of the earlier Buddhism, the " Little Vehicle " (Hinayâna), are specially attacked in this treatise, and " refuted repeatedly," says the Doctor. "The terminology," says the same authority, "is borrowed from the Hindu philosophy." This quite confirms what the earlier Buddhists said of the innovating Buddhism, according to the testimony of Hwen Thsang, that it was borrowed from the Śunyavâdis of Brahminism.

The Buddhists of the Little Vehicle, according to the same authority, composed a neat sarcasm upon their opponents, who had somewhat arrogantly called themselves the Buddhists of the "Great Vehicle." They called this vehicle, Śunya Pushpa (the vehicle that drives to nowhere).[3]

This lets in a flood of light on the perplexities and contradictions of modern Buddhism. Plump in the way of the reckless charioteers of Śunya Pushpa were two formidable

---

[1] Page 275, et seq.   [2] "Napalese Buddhist Literature," p. 178.
[3] Hwen Thsang, "Mémoires," p. 220.   See also "Popular Life of Buddha," chap. xi. p. 171.

PLATE XIV.

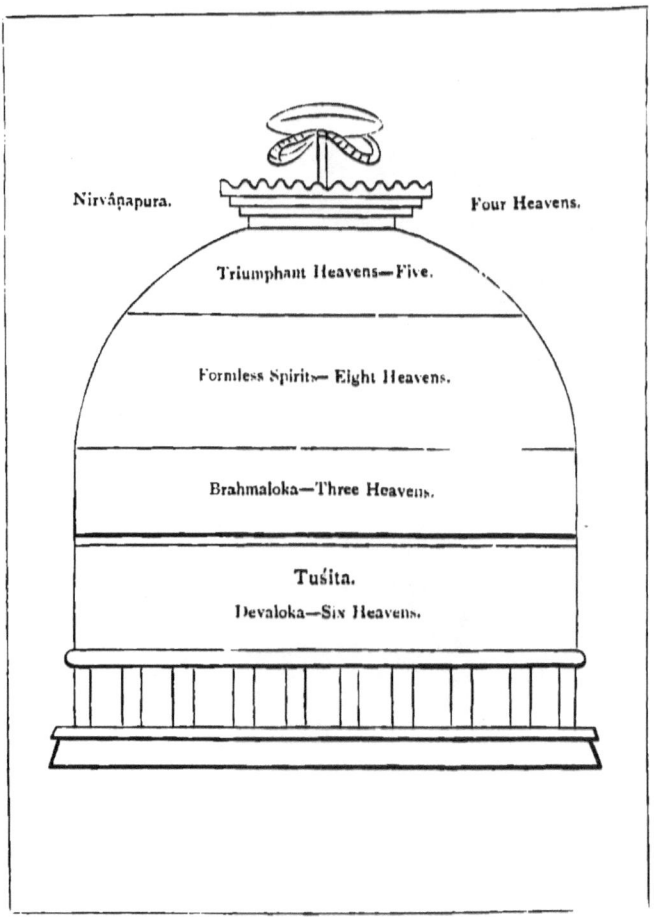

Nirvâṇapura.

Four Heavens.

Triumphant Heavens—Five.

Formless Spirits— Eight Heavens.

Brahmaloka—Three Heavens.

Tuśita.

Devaloka—Six Heavens.

THE HEAVENS AS CONCEIVED BY THE BUDDHISTS OF CEYLON.

[*Page* 221.

obstacles. The temples of Buddhism, whether carved in fine Indian woodwork, as at the date of Hwen Thsang, or built of solid masonry like the old tope whose outline I here give (Plate XIV.), represented the heavens to which the Buddhas and Jinas repaired after attaining emancipation from re-births. Secondly, on entering the temple, the spectator was confronted with a colossal figure of Śâkya Muni in the centre of the high altar, and by this were smaller Buddhas that had got to mean his Great Disciples. These were fed every day with oblations ; and Buddha was prayed to for spiritual and temporal blessings, and asked to forgive the sins of his humble votaries. How did the travestied followers of Śiva, the Śunyavâdis, get over all this ? They tried to substitute the Buddha and the saints of the future for the Buddha and the saints of the past. The eternal heavens got to be tenanted by saints about to be born on earth for the last time, although the life of Buddha had taught everybody that Tuśita, the sixth heaven of the Devaloka, was the highest region that these saints could reach. And on the altar they tried to set up the Great Buddha of the Future, Maitreya. He was to be asked to forgive sins, although he had yet to receive pap from his nurse. He was to be prayed to for spiritual light, although he had yet to learn his catechism. The fancy seems at first the dream of a madman, but a moment's reflection shows that it was the best of many bad roads. Also the plan has been most brilliantly successful. The Śunyavâdis defiled all the Buddhist scriptures, and deceived millions upon millions of Buddhists in many lands. They have also hoodwinked our Pâli professors, and through Schopenhauer, Parsvika, the leading teacher, is becoming the instructor of all Europe. In the matter of the Buddhist temple and its rites the new school were only partially successful. Buddha and his great disciples still figure on the altar, even in Ceylon, the hotbed of the innovating school of Buddhism that dethroned God and demolished heaven. But he is worshipped as a non-God. Flowers are flung daily to this non-God. Morning and evening meals are proffered to him. Daily the non-God is asked to forgive sins. We need not pursue these absurdities any further.

Unfortunately, too, the marriage of Church and State, as in Christendom later on, killed the life of the movement. It seems a law that all great spiritual movements shall promptly crystallize into formalism.

The starving and naked wanderer, with no thought save of heaven, was a mighty force for changing the creeds of the world. Christ likened His followers to a leaven with which He proposed to leaven the mass of humanity. But when victory is in sight, and in place of martyrdom the mystic is rewarded with prosperity and praise, then greed and self-interest are attracted to his ranks ; and the hungry Therapeuts become a fat abbey of lazy priests. To Aśoka and to Constantine the same problem presented itself. Given an army of idle ascetics, how are they to be lodged and fed ?

The answer, unfortunately, was the same in both cases. From the terrors and greed of the ignorant laity. And the processes by which these were stimulated—relics, pilgrimages, indulgences, dispensations, saint intercessions, the burning of candles to obtain supernal aid, the fears of purgatory, and the promised joys of a material heaven—are too like in both creeds to be the result of mere chance.

The Buddhist had taken over from the Brahman the doctrine of Karma and the metempsychosis. This is without doubt a priestly invention. It was proclaimed that the Buddhist Śramaṇa, having become as nearly as possible one with the divine Ruler of the Sky, had necessarily considerable influence both in this world and in the next. Karma, or the causation of deeds done in the body, carries a soul after death to regions of joy or pain, according to its merits. The lustful man may become a goat, the cruel man a tiger or a jackal. But if there is a Karma powerful for evil, there is also a Karma most potent in the opposite direction, and that is the Karma that results from a pure life and from ascetic practices. This is the mystical force that the priest of Buddha is able to set in motion. My avaricious father is a jackal. My daughter is in the hell Avichi. She is being gnawed by the lovers she deceived, who now assume the form of dogs. But the priests of Buddha can nullify these evil results. One hundred prayers before this statue, will release your father. It represents Śariputra, the beloved disciple of Buddha. The saints of the past remain for ever on the right hand and on the left hand of the King of Heaven. They have power to perpetually intercede. Build a temple. Feed fifty priests daily. These offerings to us are in reality offerings to Tathâgata. For your evil deeds you will be born slaves, women, rats, and partridges; but we have the power to convert you into rich merchants and princes shining with emeralds.[1]

INDULGENCES. DISPENSATIONS.

Father Froës, who visited Japan in 1574, announces that dispensations and indulgences, "much after the usages of the Catholic Church," were sold by the Buddhist monks there. The efficacy of pilgrimages was much insisted on; and one old lady had made so many of the latter, and bought so many indulgences, that she was able to make up a dress of them. The monks told her that if she were buried in this precious paper suit, she would go direct to Amitâbha, the supreme Buddha, and live for ever with the saints.[2] The Jesuit Father d'Entrecolles bears similar testimony. He describes a nun in China, "a devotee of Buddha much given to prayer (à longues prières). She was inscribed in the muster-roll of a famous temple, to which pilgrims came from great distances. These pilgrims, on reaching the foot of the mountain, kneel and prostrate themselves at every step during the ascent. Those who cannot make the pilgrimages, get their friends to buy for them a sheet of paper printed and marked all over by the Buddhist priests. In the centre is a figure of Buddha, surrounded by many small circles. The devotees, male and female, pronounce one thousand times this prayer, Namo-Omito-Fo (Praise be to Amitâbha Buddha!) which they have received from India, and which they do not understand. They then kneel one hundred times. They are then allowed to mark one of the many small circles with a red mark. The

[1] Consult Picart, vol. vii. pp. 145, 149, 216, 226, 232.
[2] Froës "Epist. Japonican," lib. iv.

Buddhist priests are invited to come and authenticate these red marks, after uttering certain prayers. The paper, sealed carefully up by the priests, is called Lou-in, and is carried after death in a casket, during the funeral rites. It costs many taëls, but it is a certain passport to the next world." [1]

CONFESSION.

Confession in the early Church was public, as in Buddhism. The dangerous innovation of auricular confession was due to Leo the First. [2]

FOOTPRINTS.

The footprints of Christ are shown in Palestine, and the footprints of Buddha in India. The traces of the feet of the former at the spot of the Ascension were long famous. [3]

THE COWL.

The cowl is common to the monks of Buddhism and Christendom. Gibbon, in his thirty-seventh chapter, says of the latter, "They wrapped their heads in a cowl to escape the sight of profane objects."

PRESENTATION OF CANDLES TO THE IMAGES OF BUDDHA.

Picart, in his account of the Buddhism of Siam, drawn chiefly from the Fathers La Loubére and Tachard, announces that the laity there make offerings of candles to the idols of Buddha. All offerings must be made through the instrumentality of the talapoins, or monks. [4]

PRAYER AS A CHARM RATHER THAN A PLEADING.

In the Buddhist and Christian rituals are many beautiful prayers. But it is plain that a repetition many hundreds of times of a mantra or paternoster on a rosary is not purely

---

[1] "Lettres Édifiantes," xiii.
[2] Rev. G. Waddington, "History of the Church," chap. ix. p. 126.
[3] "Jortin," vol. iii. pp. 87, 88.
[4] Vol. vii. p. 65. See also p. 140.

praying. It seems to me unmeaning without the Buddhist doctrine of Karma to explain it, namely, that by it a stored-up merit or magic is accumulated. And this seems practically the Catholic conception as well as the Buddhist.

FUNERALS.

The Buddhist funeral is partly the merry-making of an Irish wake, partly the solemn ceremonials of Catholic Europe. Comedians are hired whose farces have no reference to death. Fireworks sputter, and food is lavished on all. But Catholic missionaries have been struck on these occasions with the close similarity of the Buddhist and the Catholic rites. A chapelle ardente is erected; and candles burn incessantly before it, and incense smokes. Each night a choir of tala-poins comes into the mortuary chamber and chants in Pâli the sacred hymns, much after the fashion of Italy and Spain.[1]

THE EPOCH OF BUDDHA.

The Buddhist chronology dates from the epoch of Buddha, as the Christian from the epoch of Christ. The Nirvâna commences the Buddhist epoch.

FESTIVALS.

The earliest Christian festivals were simply the Jewish ones.[2] The Feast of the Nativity was not celebrated until the fourth century," says Riddle.[3] The three great Jewish festivals—the sowing, reaping, and Pentecost—were the same as the Buddhist. Of course, the Passover or Easter originally began the year. On "the fourteenth day of the first month" (Numb. ix. 5) it was celebrated. Many of the Easter rites still exhibit this derivation, witness the taper-lighting, a symbol of the birth of the new sun-god. The Easter

Fig. 20.

---

[1] See La Loubère, "Description," etc. vol. i. p. 371.
[2] Riddle, "Christian Antiquities," p. 607.   [3] Ibid., p. 618.

Q

eggs were unintelligible to me until I came across the
Buddhist mystical egg.

The legend is that at the beginning of each dispensation
or mystical year, the angel with the diamond spear strikes this
egg, left like Brahma's egg behind by the dead race, and at
once the yolk and the white divide as exhibited. One part
represents the unrevealed Buddha, the other the conceivable
Buddha, the eternal dualism of all mystics.

COUNCILS.

More important are the ecumenical councils introduced
into the early Christian Church to suppress heresy. Where
did they come from ? Such an idea is foreign to the genius
alike of the dominant Roman and Jewish religions. Both
were religions of outside ceremonial, and as long as this was
complied with, their priests were satisfied. They did not
pursue their scrutiny into the recesses of the worshipper's
brain to see if his metaphysics kept proper pace with orthodox
changes and fashions. In the records of Buddhism five
principal ecumenical councils are noticed. The first took
place at Râjâgriha, three months after Buddha's death. The
second, a rather mythical convocation, is said to have taken
place at Vaisâlî, one hundred years after the first. The third
was summoned by King Asoka. The fourth took place, as
I have mentioned, under the patronage of King Kaniska
(A.D. 10), and introduced the doctrine that man, after his
emancipation from re-birth, becomes unconscious. The fifth,
under King Silâditya, tried to suppress early Buddhism altogether. These two last convocations established the pernicious
originality that a creed is more commodiously turned topsy-
turvy from within than from without. Men are the slaves
less of ideas than words, especially such words as " orthodoxy " and " heresy. Irenæus and Pope Victor profited by
this lesson. A heretic in Christianity, as in Buddhism, got to
mean a man born two or three hundred years too soon to
adopt orthodox innovations.

HIERARCHY.

We have seen that more than one Catholic writer has drawn attention to the similarity between the Buddhist and Christian hierarchy. Bishop Bigandet has pointed out that in independent Buddhist countries like Burmah, there is a Superior-General, and under him Provincials. Then come the abbots, or heads of monasteries, and so on, "a distinct hierarchy, well marked with constitutions and rules." [1]

THE POPE.

Father Grueber, on visiting Lha Sa, the capital of Tibet, A.D. 1661, was very much shocked to find that the devil had struck at Christianity in its most vital part. He had invented a mock potentate, to whom were offered honours that are due alone to the vicar of Christ.[2] The faithful were required to fall flat before the grand lâma of Tibet, to knock their heads upon the ground, and to crawl forward and kiss his feet.[3] Like the pope, he was the acknowledged head of the Buddhist Church all over the world.

We have seen that at the great monastery of Nalanda, when Hwen Thsang visited it, there was a sovereign pontiff of Buddhism. That monastery was destroyed by the Brahmins in the eighth century, and the Buddhists were driven out of India. The grand lâma is, as it seems to me, this great pontiff, driven to take refuge amongst the mountains of Tibet. China and Japan and Tibet acknowledge him as the head of Buddhism; and the other day, when Lord Dufferin was reluctant to nominate the Tsaia-dau or "archbishop" of Burmah, China threatened to put in her right. The Pontiff of Nalanda was so sacred, that none dare pronounce his name. He was called the Âchârya, and the pontiff in Tibet has a similar name, the "Master of Doctrine."[4] Mons. de Remusat tells us that in a Japanese encyclopædia it is announced that Buddha, from the earliest days, was accustomed to come

---

[1] "Vie de Gaudama," p. 477.
[2] See "Histoire des Voyages," vol. ix. p. 130.　　　　[3] Ibid.
[4] De Remusat, "Origine de l'Hierarchie Lamaique," p. 27.

back to earth as a "teacher of kings."[1]   This is confirmed
by Mr. Rockhill's "Life of the Buddha," where Ânanda,
Buddha's favourite disciple, and Upagupta, had the title of
" Buddha " given to them,[2] when each became in succession
the head of the Church.   Also, when Hwen Thsang visited
the Âchârya at Nalanda, he was obliged to perform the same
prostrations, crawlings, head knockings against the ground,
etc., that shocked Father Grueber in Tibet.[3]

And when we come to consider the method by which a
grand lâma and a pope is each elected, the points of similarity increase.   When the grand lâma dies, all the faithful
devote themselves to prayer and meditation.   Prayer barrels
revolve, and search is made for the infant in whom the soul of
Buddha is once more to be born.   The list of candidates is
finally narrowed to three.   Then, as we learn from the Abbé
Huc, the whole body of cardinals (chutuktus) is assembled.
They are shut up in a temple of Buddha-La, and pass six
days in retreat, in prayer, in fasting.   The seventh day, the
names of the three candidates are written on gold plates and
placed in an urn.   The senior chutuktu draws the lot, and
the child whose name is drawn is immediately proclaimed
Delai Lâma, and carried in state through the town.[4]

All this reminds one of the election of a pope, on which
occasion cardinals of the Church erect a little lath and plank
monastery in the splendid Loggia of the Vatican, and
masquerade as humble Therapeut monks in pink satin.   Each
humble monk has two servants, one civil, one religious.   They
fetch him his food, like the Sramanero of a Buddhist convent.
The food when brought is inspected by certain prelates to see
that the ortolans contain no missive from the French ambassador, and that Austria has not sought to bias the election by
a surreptitious note inserted in the Johannisberger or Chateau
Yquem.   Three times a day the silken monks are summoned
to the Sistine Chapel to pray for divine guidance in their
choice.   The special mass on these occasions is called the

---

[1] De Remusat, "Origine de l'Hierarchie Lamaique," pp. 24, 25.
[2] Ibid., pp. 164, 165.   [3] Hwen Thsang, vol. i. p. 144.
[4] Huc, "Voyages," vol. ii. p. 244.

" Mass of the Holy Ghost." The special costume for each cardinal during these celebrations is a cope of crimson silk made exactly like a monk's cloak. Voting papers with fantastic scrolls are given to each, and an urn is sent round to any cardinal who has been pronounced too sick to be walled up in his little lath and plank cell. When the pope is elected, guns roar out and silver trumpets sound, and his holiness passes along in solemn procession, like the lâma in his vimâṇa, with umbrellas and smoking incense and waving fans He is placed on the great altar of St. Peter's, and worshipped like the lâma of Tibet.[1]

The grand lâma is chosen by lot, chance, the Holy Spirit ; the pope by chicane. Plainly the elaborate apparatus at the Vatican is not in harmony with its pitiful work. It is a copy, reproduction, the histrionics of something else. What? Matthias was chosen by lot by the Church at Jerusalem, and John the Baptist, Christ, and St. James, each ruled the whole of mystical Israel, the Church of the West. If Palestine at the date of Christ, and as I believe for one hundred and fifty years before and after, was in close communication with the Âchârya of Nalanda, this and the thousand other points of close contact between Buddhism and Christianity may be accounted for. I know no other manner.

[1] Picart, " Cerem.," vol. i. p. 34.

CHAPTER XVIII.

How did Buddhism Reach the West?

WE now come to the question, How did Buddhism reach the West? And here Professor Kellogg is triumphant. He cites Professor Kuenen, who it appears has announced that he can " safely affirm " that Buddhism had no influence at all on the origin of Christianity.[1] He cites Bishop Lightfoot, who has stated that there is " no notice in either heathen or Christian writers which points to the presence of a Buddhist within the limits of the Roman empire till long after the Essenes had ceased to exist." He cites Professor J. Estlin Carpenter, who has committed himself to the somewhat extreme statement that from the date of the preaching of Buddha until the advent of Christianity "no channel of communication " existed between Buddhist countries and the West.[2] But he ignores Deans Mansel and Milman, and is silent about Colebrooke, and Lassen, and Prinsep. Also he has not a word to say about the testimony of Aśoka, and the flood of light let in upon the intercourse between India and the West by recent Orientalists.

By the early Phœnicians the commerce of the East was carried across Arabia from the port of Gerrha in the Persian Gulf. It was then shipped on the Red Sea and carried up the Ælanitic Gulf on its road to Tyre. That some of the commodities must have come from India is proved from the fact cited by Herodotus, that cassia and cinnamon were amongst them, which articles could not be found nearer than

---

[1] " Light of Asia, etc.," p. 251.
[2] *Nineteenth Century*, Dec., 1880, p. 979.

Ceylon or the Malabar coast.[1] To reach Tyre, these goods had to pass close to the haunts of the Essenes near the Dead Sea.

"The Phœnicians," says Mr. Cust, the Hon. Secretary of the Royal Asiatic Society, "were in contact with India at least as early as the time of Solomon. . . . Then, as now, India had intercourse with the Western world through two channels, by land and by sea." Mr. Cust proceeds to show that, from the tenth to the third century B.C., Yemen was the great central mart in which Indian products were exchanged for merchandize of the West. For a prolonged period this lucrative traffic was in the hands of the Sabeans, and was the main source of their proverbial opulence. The trade between Egypt and Yemen began as early as 2300 B.C.; that between Yemen and India was established not later than 1000 B.C. Even in the time of the Ptolemies the Indian trade was not direct, but passed through the hands of the Sabeans, who possessed extensive commerce and large vessels. Their ports were frequented by trading vessels from all parts : from the Red Sea, the Persian Gulf, the coast of Africa, and especially from the mouth of the Indus. From the Periplus we learn that Aden was a great entrepôt of this commerce, while at the beginning of the second century B.C. the island of Socotra was the centre of exchange for Indian products. Mr. Cust argues that the Indians got their alphabet from the hieratic form of the Egyptian hieroglyphics.[2]

But Alexander's expedition gave a great spur to the intercourse between India and the West. Bactria and Persia were in the hands of the Seleucidan dynasty, until Persia revolted.

This brought Antiochus the Great into the field to restore the authority of the Greeks. According to Polybius, he led his army into India and renewed his alliance with Sophagasenes, king of that country. As the Aśoka edicts were incised on rocks some six years after Antiochus came to the throne, Prinsep and Wilford believe this to be an allusion to him.[3]

---

[1] Bunbury, " Hist. Ancient Geography," vol. i. p. 219.
[2] *Journ. Royal As. Soc.*, July, 1884. " Origin of Indian Alphabet."
[3] Prinsep, *Journ. Ben. As. Soc.*, vol. vii. p. 162.

Meanwhile the building of Alexandria had given a powerful fillip to the intercourse with India by sea. Alexander had designed it to be the capital of his vast empire, and the bridge between India and the West. This project was ably carried out after his death by his lieutenant, the first Ptolemy. Under his wise government, and that of his successor, Alexandria soon became the first commercial city in the world. Of more importance even was his large tolerance of creeds, whether Egyptian, or Grecian, or Jewish. In the year 209 B.C., Ptolemy Evergetes was on the throne. He conquered Abyssinia and a greater part of Asia, including Syria, Phœnicia, Babylonia, Persis, Media. His conquests extended to Bactria, and he had a large fleet on the Red Sea. This placed him in contact with India from two different directions.

He married the daughter of Magas, king of Cyrene. Macedonia was ruled by Antigone at this particular date.

This brings us to the celebrated rock inscriptions of King Aśoka, surnamed Devânampiyo, the beloved of the devas or spirits. They have set at rest for ever the question whether Buddhism was propagated westwards.

On the Girnar Rock, in Gujerat, the name of Antiochus the Great occurs four times. This is one passage—

"And moreover within the dominions of Antiochus, the Greek king, of which Antiochus's generals are the rulers, everywhere Piyadasi's (Asoka's) double system of medical aid is established, both medical aid for men and medical aid for animals, together with medicaments of all sorts, which are suitable for men and suitable for animals."[1]

This is the second inscription :—

"And the Greek king besides, by whom the four Greek kings Ptolemaios, and Gengakenos, and Magas . . . (have been induced to permit) . . .

"Both here and in foreign countries everywhere (the people) follow the doctrine of the religion of Devânampiya, wheresoever it reacheth."[2]

Now, here we have, indelibly carved in the rocks, a pure piece of history. It shows that the Buddhist king Aśoka

---

[1] Prinsep, *Journ. Ben. As. Soc.*, vol. vii. p. 159.   [2] Ibid., p. 261.

was closely associated with the Greeks, and that he sent missionaries to Egypt. It shows, furthermore, that at any rate he was under an impression that the Buddhist religion had been there established. One more piece of evidence I may notice here. In the "Mahawanso," or old history of Ceylon, it is announced that on the occasion of the building of the Buddhist tope of Ruanwelli, enormous numbers of Buddhist monks came from all parts, including thirty thousand "from the vicinity of A'lasadda, the capital of the Yona (Greek) country." In the same history is a statement that Aśoka did send a missionary named Maharakkhita to Greece.[1]

A'lasadda is agreed by all Orientalists to be Alexandria. Bishop Lightfoot considers that the passage refers to Alexandria ad Caucasum, a not very important town some twenty-five miles from Cabul. Koppen, on the other hand, and Helgenfeld, consider that "Alexandria, the capital of the Yona country," must be Alexandria in Egypt. The Buddhist history states that the monks—all Indian histories exaggerate numbers—came from "the vicinity" of Alexandria. This word, I think, is important. It was in the vicinity of Alexandria that convents of monks, practising rites precisely like those of the Buddhists, existed in large numbers in the days of Philo. It is to be observed that it would be more easy to get to Ceylon from Alexandria in Egypt than from Alexandria ad Caucasum (Beghram).

It may be mentioned here that the *Saturday Review*, in its onslaught on the "bold assertions" of Professor Kellogg, points out that Nâgasena, a Buddhist, had a discussion with Menander in the capital of Syria.[2]

But even if no Buddhist came to the West, without doubt Buddhism did. For about this time there arose in Alexandria a teaching called "Gnosticism." This word is the exact Greek equivalent of "Buddhism" (Sans., Bodhi), and it simply means interior or spiritual knowledge. That the anti-mystical section of the early Christian Church was quite aware whence Gnosticism came is shown by the form of

---

[1] "Mahawanso," p. 171.
[2] *Saturday Review*, February 6, 1886.

adjudication prescribed for those who renounced it. It expressly mentions Βόδδα and Σκυθιανός (Sâkya).[1]

Attempts have been made to put forward the date of the introduction of Gnosticism to the second century A.D., but an able article in the new "Encyclopædia Britannica," by Principal Tulloch, shows how futile these attempts have been. He says that at the date of Christ, Egypt and Syria were so saturated with it that it was "in the air." It is to be found "especially in the theology of the Alexandrian Jews." It is "represented in the writings of Philo and in the influence flowing from the Persian and Buddhist religions." It is in the Septuagint and the Book of Wisdom. He cites also a number of texts showing Gnosticism in the New Testament. In this he follows Herder, Mosheim, Hammond, and Brucker, who, as Mutter shows, "discover Gnosticism and the eastern philosophy on almost every page" of that sacred volume.[2]

According to Principal Tulloch, the Gnostics taught that the universe "does not proceed immediately from a Supreme Being." The god of the Gnostics, like En Soph of the "Kabbalah," is formless, inconceivable, inactive, and, being perfect, is incapable of imperfect work. This god is called by Basilides "The Unnameable," and by Valentinus "Buthos" (the Abyss).

"From this transcendent source," says Principal Tulloch, "existence springs by emanation in a series of spiritual powers. It is only through these powers, or energies, that the infinite passes into life and activity, and becomes capable of representation." To this higher spiritual world is given the name of Πλήρωμα (Pleroma), and the divine powers composing it in their ever-expanding procession from the highest are called αἰῶνες (Æons).

The Buddhist words Nirvritti and Pravritti are the Buthos and Pleroma of the Gnostics. It was held that for countless millions of ages Swayambhu brooded in Nirvritti, rayless, quiescent, unfashioned matter, or perhaps I should write spiritual substance. Then from him emanated Padmapâni

---

[1] Hunter's "India Gazetteer," citing Weber.
[2] "Histoire Critique de Gnosticisme," vol. i. p. 124.

and the four other Dhyani (heavenly) Buddhas. In Gnosticism, from "The Unnameable," the inactive unborn God, dwelling in Buthos, proceeded five Beings as Æons, Νους, Λόγος, Φρόνησις, Σοφια, Δυναμις, who peopled the spaces with bright spirits dwelling in luminous worlds. This fashioned, organic, luminous matter, was the Pleroma, or Buddhist Pravritti ; Nous and Padmapâni being the active artificers in either case. The luminous world systems were called Ogdoads. In Buddhism they are called Buddha Kshetras, luminous counterparts of the starry dome of heaven, with the Great Dragon for apex and the zodiac for base. Padmapâni means bearing the lotus, a bud from the great cosmical emblem. In Gnostic gems and Buddhist sculptures the Divine Child is usually represented either seated on a lotus or holding a bud in his hand.

Here is a representation of the Child Christ taken from the catacombs. He also is emerging from a lotus or lily.

Padmapâni is also called Manas, a complete equivalent for Nous, the head Æon of the Gnostics.[1]

We have shown that Buddha, as the elephant issuing from the mighty fish, symbolized the active God ruling in Pravritti, or the Pleroma. The same is said of Christ.

"It was the Father's good pleasure that in

Fig. 21.

Him the whole *pleroma* should have its home" (Col. i. 19).

"In Him dwells the whole *pleroma* of the $\left\{ \begin{array}{c} \text{Godhead} \\ \text{Deity} \end{array} \right\}$ in bodily shape, [*i.e.* 'corporeally']" (Col. ii. 9).

[1] Hodgson, "Languages, etc., of Nipal," p. 78.

"The Church which is His body, the *pleroma* of Him that filleth all in all" (Eph. i. 23).

"That ye may be filled unto all the *pleroma* of God, unto the measure of the stature of the *pleroma* of Christ" (Eph. iii. 19).

"Of His *pleroma* we all received" (John i. 16).

In the great controversy carried on by the Gnostics, these texts were considered most important. Their works have been burnt ; but we see from Irenæus that they also relied on the frequent mention of the Gnostic Æons in the New Testament.

"Even the mystery which hath been hid from the Æons and generations, but now is made manifest to his saints" (Col. i. 26).

"According to the purpose of the Æons, which He purposed in Christ Jesus our Lord" (Eph. iii. 11).

The Gnostics, too, pointed out in the "giving" (communion), the prayer to "the Æons of the æon."[1]

Perhaps the following passage, from the Liturgy of St. James, is what is alluded to—

"O beneficent King of the Æons, and Maker of the whole creation."[2]

The same Gnostics, in their controversy with Irenæus, cited (Eph. ii. 21).

"To all the generations of the Æons of the æon." They asserted, too, as I have shown, that the twelve disciples signified the twelve mystical months of Christ's life, the twelve Æons residing in the pleroma ; that the twelfth was Christ's death, the "suffering Æon ;" that the woman with the issue of blood twelve years, meant also the mystic cured at last.[3]

They asserted, too, that all created things were images of the Æons, and a shadow of the pleroma.[4]

The words "Gnosis" and "Sophia" are used for mystical or interior knowledge all through the New Testament.

---

[1] Iren., "Hær.," bk. i. 3.
[2] Neal, "Liturgies of the Greek Church," p. 32.
[3] Iren., "Hær.," lib. i. 3.   [4] Ibid., ii. 7, 8.

"Wisdom is justified of her children," says Christ (Matt. xi. 19).

"Walk in Sophia," says St. Paul (Col. iv. 5).

"And thou, child, shalt be called the prophet of the Highest: for thou shalt go before the face of the Lord to prepare His ways; to give the Gnosis of salvation unto His people" (Luke i. 76, 77).

"But grow in grace, and in the Gnosis of our Lord and Saviour Jesus Christ" (2 Peter iii. 18).

"O the depth of the riches both of Sophia and Gnosis of God" (Rom. xi. 33).

Now it seems significant of the extreme distance that we have travelled from the great spiritual thought of the epoch of Christ, that a candid and acute writer like Principal Tulloch should finish his article on Gnosticism in the way that he does. He admits the Buddhist derivation of it. He admits that Philo and the Septuagint and the New Testament are full of it; but he holds, if I read his article aright, that when Christ's disciples described their Master as the King of Æons, and Lord of the Pleroma, the Son who alone could reveal the Father, whom no man has seen, they somehow spoke not as missionaries, but victims of a phraseology that they did not understand.

Instead of the Gnosis of the mysteries of the kingdom of heaven being the quintessence of Christianity, it was a foreign and indeed a hostile accretion. A dull monk, named Irenæus, has so pronounced, and his doctrine is final.

Of course, the poor Gnostics of Alexandria might have replied, "If you think, like Irenæus, that the idea of an invisible Father, dwelling in Buthos, is an absurdity; if you think, like him, that the world was created by the Father, and not the Son, why base your Christianity exclusively on our writings? You must either discard the Fourth Gospel, or allow its authors to explain its meaning."

In point of fact, the notion of a Divine Son being born from the Eternal Father, by the help of Sophia, though the breath of life of the religion of the Gnosis is an unmanageable accretion in the lower or temple Christianity. On the plane

of matter the tritheism of the Council of Nice has been judged
by the thought of modern Europe and condemned.   This is
the case within, as well as without the Church, and in England most conspicuously.   The trinity idea is nominally
accepted, but Broad Churchmen are monotheists who worship
the Father, Low Churchmen are monotheists who worship the
Son, and High Churchmen are monotheists who worship the
Holy Ghost.

"O God the Father of heaven : have mercy upon us miserable sinners."

"O God the Son, Redeemer of the world : have mercy upon
us miserable sinners."

"O God the Holy Ghost, proceeding from the Father and
the Son : have mercy upon us miserable sinners."

Unitarians maintain that whatever the Athanasian Creed
may be, this liturgy is either pure polytheism or pure nonsense,
and it is difficult to find a flaw in their reasoning.

Man comes into the world and schemes and dreams.   He
grows grey prematurely, to hand down his name as a statesman, poet, soldier, founder of a house.   But athwart his
schemes and dreams comes a universal experience—failure.
The inner life and the outer life can never correspond.   Years
pass, and the hard facts of existence, famines and spoliation, and
wars and misery perplex the dreamer's mind.   Alone at night
new thoughts crowd upon him.   He dreams of a God distinct from the God of priests and creeds.   Beyond the
Pleroma, beyond the million twinkling Ogdoads, the starry
Buddha Kshetras of the Buddhist, sits the Unnameable, a
God that evades alike philosophers and workers in marble.

To such a dreamer, a trinity is a necessity.   Only through
the anthropomorphic God can he get at the Unseen.   And
that, not by the aid of brain and Bible, but by the aid of
Sophia, the Holy Ghost.

It is a relief to turn from modern polemical writers to the
fine Gnosticism of Clement of Alexandria.   Kaye, the late
Bishop of Lincoln, has a chapter in his work, " Clement of
Alexandria," which gives, chiefly from the Stromata, a good
analysis of what the father calls the teaching of the " Christian

Gnostic." Clement declares that there is a "twofold know-ledge." The first is the "milk for babes" of St. Paul. The second is the "strong meat" of the Gnosis. The first is "common to all mankind, irrational as well as rational, being derived through the senses ; " and the other, called the Gnosis, receives its character from mind and reason.[1] The higher knowledge was "not designed for the multitude, but com-municated to those only who were capable of receiving it orally, not by writing."[2] Peter, James, John, and Paul, specially received this Gnosis from Christ.[3] John the Baptist and Job are conspicuous examples of Gnostics under the old law. The Gnostic "alone possess the true and spiritual mean-ing of the scriptures." To him "the sayings of our Lord, though obscure to others, are clear and manifest."[4] The words—the "Elect," the "Seed of Abraham," the "Called," the "Spiritual Levite," the "True Israelite," the "Friend and Son," the "King," do not refer to literal Hebrews, but to the winnowed group of earth's high mystics.[5] Gnosticism is the "divine science." It is "the light that comes into the soul." It is a "rational death, separating the soul from the passions."[6] It is not born with men ; it is a growth, a "mystical habit," acquired by degrees.[7] By it "man becomes assimilated to God."[8] He gains the privilege of being called "brother" by Christ. He is the friend and son of God ;[9] he is the "God-bearer ;" he is God, walking in the flesh.

The Unnameable of the Gnostics is very like the God of Fichte's fine prayer—

"Exalted and living Will, whom no name can express and no idea embrace, I yet may raise my heart to Thee! for Thou and I art not divided. Thy voice is audible within me. In Thee, the Incomprehensible, my own nature and the whole world become intelligible to me ; every riddle of existence is solved, and perfect harmony reigns in my soul. I veil my face before Thee, and lay my hand upon my lips. Such as

---

[1] Kaye, "Clement of Alexandria," pp. 239, 247. See also Clement, S. L. 6 D. ccxxxvii. 1.

[2] Ibid., p. 241.   [3] Ibid.   [4] Ibid., 240.   [5] Ibid., p. 253.
[6] Ibid., 240.   [7] Ibid., 239.   [8] Ibid., 233.   [9] Ibid., 242.

Thou really art—such as Thou appearest unto Thyself—
I can no more behold Thee than I can become like Thee.
After thousands of thousands of lives such as superior spirits
live, I should be as little able to understand Thee as in this
house of clay. What I understand is, from my very understanding it, finite, and by no progression can ever be
transformed into the infinite. Thou differest from the finite,
not in degree, but in kind. I will not attempt that which
my finite nature forbids. I will not seek to know the nature
and the essence of Thy being. But Thy relations to myself and
to all that is finite lie open before my eyes. Thou createst
in me the consciousness of my duty—of my destination in
the series of rational beings; how, I know not, nor need I to
know. Thou knowest my thoughts and acceptest my inten-
tions. In the contemplation of this, Thy relation to my finite
nature, I will be tranquil and happy. Of myself I know not
what I ought to do. I will do it simply, joyfully, and without
cavil, for it is Thy voice that commands me, and the strength
with which I perform my duty is Thy strength. I am tranquil under every event of the world, for it is Thy world.
Whatever happens forms part of the plan of the eternal world
and of Thy goodness. What in this plan is positive good,
and what only means of removing existing evil, I know not.
In Thy world all will end in good—this is enough for me, and
in this faith I stand fast—but what in Thy world is mere
germ, what blossom, and what the perfect fruit, I know not.
The only thing which is important to me is the progress of
reason and of morality through all the ranks of rational
beings.

"When my heart is closed to all earthly desires, the
universe appears to my eye in a glorified aspect. The dead
cumbrous masses which served only to fill space, disappear,
and in their place the eternal stream of life and strength and
action flows on from its source—primeval life; from *Thy*
life, Thou Everlasting One!"—Fichte, "Bestimmung des
Menschen."

CHAPTER XIX.

CHRISTIANITY AT ALEXANDRIA.

I NOW come to a very important question. Was there any connection between the Therapeut monasteries of Alexandria and the subsequent Christian monasteries in Egypt and elsewhere? Smith's "Dictionary of Christian Antiquities," denies this unhesitatingly, and dates the Christian monasteries not earlier than the fourth century. On the other hand, Catholic writers maintain that it is quite impossible to make any historical gap or line of severance between the Therapeuts, "the monks of the old law,"[1] as St. Jerome calls them, and the Christian monks of Alexandria. Eusebius, St. Jerome, Sozomenes, and Cassien, all maintained that monasteries in Christendom were due to the Therapeut converts of St. Mark, the first Bishop of Alexandria. Eusebius, in point of fact, has an elaborate chapter to show that Philo, in his book "The Contemplative Life," made a mistake, and sketched a community of Christians, believing them to be Jews. St. Jerome makes the same assertion; and it is well known that the poet Racine, in a fit of piety, translated Philo's treatise to be used as a Catholic book of devotion. It is important that no writer in the early Christian Church could see any difference between a Therapeut and a Christian monastery. Without doubt the three grades of Christian ecclesiastics—the ephemereut or bishop, the presbyter, and the diakonos, were derived from the three grades of Therapeut monks.

[1] Epist. IV. ad Rust.

R

If, too, there was no connection between the Therapeuts of Alexandria and the early Christians, why was the word " Therapeut " first used to name the new sect ?   " The Christians," says Bingham, citing Epiphanius, " were at first called Therapeutæ and Jessians." [1]   The word " Jessians," by the same Father, was pronounced an equivalent of " Essenes." [2] St. Dionysius the Areopagite furnishes us with another important fact.   The word Therapeut, in the early church, was used to describe the third and highest grade of Christian initiation, the perfected adept.

The other names given to Christians in the earliest times are important.   The school of philosophy at Alexandria was called, by the outside world, " The Eclectics," and so were the early Christians.   They were also named " Brethren," " Believers,"   " Saints,"   " Temples   of   God,"   " Temples   of Christ," [3] all strange names for professed anti-mystics.   It must be remembered that the perfected Essene was called " The Temple of the Holy Ghost."

Another important name was made use of.   The early Christians were called "Gnostics."   Clement of Alexandria calls himself a Christian Gnostic.   Athanasius and Evagrius Ponticus also make use of the same term.   Socrates cites a passage from the writings of the latter which describes "a monk of great renown, of the sect of the Gnostics ; " and he shows that this alludes to "a monk in a village called Parembole, near Alexandria, whom Evagrius and the rest called by the then known name of Christian Gnostics." [4]

The monks of the Greek Church still retain traces of the Therapeut influence.   The strictest, those of the " Great Habit," content themselves with four, and even two hours' sleep.   They eat no flesh ; they never drink anything but water.   They are cenobites ; and some, in a little garden with figs, grapes, and cherries, still attempt to be anchorites, like St. Anthony.   In the Greek Church the consecrated

---

[1] " Antiquities of the Christian Church," vol. i. p. 1.
[2] " Hær.," ii. 29.
[3] Bingham, " Antiquities of the Christian Church," vol. i. pp. 3, 4.
[4] Bingham, " Antiquities of the Christian Church," p. 4.

bread (pain bénit) is almost as much esteemed as that of the communion table, and the holy water is drunk eagerly by the sick, etc., plain echoes of early Essenism. The poorer monks cultivate the land as in an Essene monastery. In the centre of the monastery is the sanctuary detached with its "holy gate." The cells are ranged around as in a Buddhist convent.[1] The monasteries send out their begging friars.[2]

Bishop Bigandet has pointed out that there are "numerous points of close similarity" between the Christian and Buddhist ceremonies when a novice is received into a monastery.[3] The main rite in both cases seems to consist in what Christendom calls "casting off the old man," as symbolized by the secular dress, and donning the new, the dalmatic, alb, and other monkish garments, identical, as we have shown, in Christianity and Buddhism. With the Buddhists the head is clean shaved on the occasion, with the Christians a rim of hair is left to represent the "crown of thorns."[4] The Christian postulant appears bearing a lighted taper. In Buddhism a light is also kindled. The Buddhist postulant has a ring placed on his finger, and so does the abbot in a monastery.[5] In the Greek Church the "Contacium"[6] is produced, in the Buddhist the "Patimokkha," both works being the regulations of monastic life. A fan is given alike to the Buddhist and to the deacon in the Greek Church.[7] Vows of poverty, chastity, and obedience are pronounced in both cases after much cate-chizing, bell-ringing, incense-burning, hymns to the Buddhist or Christian Triad, etc. At one moment the Bible is placed on the head of the postulant. In Buddhism the same cere-mony is performed with the Pancha Rakshâ Śâstra.[8] The head of the monastery (abbot from *abba*, father), with crozier and mitre, conducts the proceedings in both religions. A feast terminates the proceedings with the Buddhists, after the neophyte has been allowed to offer the food oblations to

---

[1] See Picart, "Cérémonies, etc.," vol. i. pp. 67–71, 100–109
[2] Ibid., vol. iii. p. 136.   [3] "Gaudama," p. 488.
[4] Picart, "Cérémonies," vol. ii. p. 130.
[5] Compare Hodgson, p. 140, and Picart, vol. ii. p. 143.
[6] Picart, vol. iii. p. 132.   [7] Ibid., p. 131.
[8] Compare Picart, vol. iii. p. 132, with Hodgson, p. 143.

the statues of Buddha and his saints.[1] At the ordination of a priest the same power is given by the ceremony of touching the communion chalice and pattine.[2] In a Greek monastery is an interesting ceremony. At the termination of the chief meal in the refectory, the presiding monk blesses a small portion of the food and drink, and it is handed round to all, quite reproducing the Therapeut "mysteries" of Philo.[3]

THE CHURCH OF JERUSALEM.

This brings us to the Church of Jerusalem ; and the hastiest glance at the first popular work that describes it shows us that it was closely modelled on a Therapeut community. Renan, in his work "Les Apôtres," calls it "a monastery without iron gates."[4] Migne, "Dictionnaire des Abbayes," brings it forward to overthrow the Protestant position that monasteries were unknown in the early church.[5] Its members were cenobites, as Renan shows.[6] "No one possessed anything that he could call his own. On becoming a disciple of Jesus, he sold his goods and gave the proceeds to the society. The officers of the society distributed this as each had need. All lived together in one quarter of the city."[7]

There were other points of close similarity. The disciples lived in groups of houses, with a central house as a place of meeting, making the resemblance to a Therapeut or Buddhist monastery as close as was practicable in a hostile city.[8] "Long hours were passed in prayer. Ecstasies were frequent. Each one believed himself constantly under the influence of divine inspiration."[9] The breaking of bread was mystical and sacramental. "The bread itself became in a certain sense Jesus, conceived as the sole source of human strength."[10] These repasts, which Renan calls the "soul of Christian mysteries," took place first of all at night, as with the Therapeuts. They

---

[1] Hodgson, p. 142.   [2] Picart, vol. ii. p. 133.
[3] Ibid., vol. iii. p. 137.   [4] Renan, "Les Apôtres," p. 75.
[5] Ibid., p. 970.   [6] Ibid., pp. 75, 86.
[7] Ibid., p. 76 ; see also Acts ii. 44, 46, 47.
[8] Ibid., p. 76 ; Acts xii. 12.   [9] Ibid., p. 76.   [10] Ibid., p. 76.

were then restricted to evenings of Sunday, and by-and-by
were celebrated in the morning. The temporary chef de table,
as Renan calls him, broke the bread and blessed the cup.
Here we have the ephemereut of the Therapeuts.[1] Into these
poor houses of holy beggars the commonest beggar found
admittance. This was, as Renan suggests, the great engine
of propagandism. Penury found clothing and food and
sympathy. The proud exclusiveness of the high caste Jews
was denounced. The doors of heaven were thrown open to
the poor man.[2]

We see, too, that within a year or two of Christ's death
seven deacons were chosen. This is a Therapeut title, and a
Therapeut office. "Sisters" also have their holy functions,[3]
a Therapeut custom, but one that went completely counter to
the genius of the Lower Judaism.[4] Renan, an impartial judge,
says that the Protestants in modernizing nuns, beguines, brides
of heaven, cenobites, socialism, fail to appreciate the very
earliest institutions of Christianity.[5]

And as we read his glowing pages describing these days,
we are a little surprised that English bishops should seriously
state that the ἀσκητής, or mystic, was unknown in them. Far
from being anti-mystical, the little church at Jerusalem has
inspired and parented all the highest mysticism that the West
has since known. "All the secrets of the great knowledge of
the interior life, the most glorious creation of Christendom, were
there in germ."[6] St. Basil, St. Arsenius, St. John the Mystic
were then rendered possible. Quakers, Irvingites, Shakers,
Mormons, and "Spiritists" have looked back upon and been
developed by that one church.[7] All were possessed of the
spirit, and exhibited all the phenomena of illuminism. All
had the baptism of the spirit, the baptism of fire, which took
the outside evidence of tongues of flame.[8] The risen Saviour
constantly appeared in person, as He has since appeared in

---

[1] Renan, "Les Apôtres," pp. 81, 82. He cites 1 Cor. x. 16 ; Justin,
"Apol.," i. 65–67 ; Acts xx. 7–11 ; Pliny, "Epist.," x. 97 ; Justin, "Apol.,"
i. 67.

[2] Renan, "Les Apôtres," pp. 116, 117.   [3] Rom. xvi. 1 ; 1 Cor. ix. 5.
[4] Renan, "Les Apôtres," p. 122.   [5] Ibid., pp. 123, 125.
[6] Ibid., p. 73.   [7] Ibid., p. 62.   [8] Ibid., p. 59.

times of spiritual fervour to other visionaries. "In an island near Rotterdam," says the French scholar, "which has a population of austere Calvinists, the peasants believe that Christ comes to the bed of death to assure the elect of their justification. Many see Him in point of fact."[1] The visions of the Church of Jerusalem were produced like all other visions, by a "life of fasting and austerity."[2] For this they had the example of their Divine Master, who went through a similar preparation, and "who more than once presented in His person the ordinary phenomena of extasia."[3]

The Church of Jerusalem, the Church of the Nazarenes, as it was called, started with a high priest of Christendom.

Eusebius, on the authority of Hegisippus, informs us that James, the brother of Christ, was appointed high priest there after His death. Epiphanius confirms this, and states that as high priest he went once a year into the holy of holies.[4]

I will write down the passage from Hegisippus about James—

"He was consecrated from his mother's womb. He drank neither wine nor strong drink, neither ate he any living thing. A razor never went upon his head. He anointed not himself with oil, nor did he use a bath. He alone was allowed to enter into the holies. For he did not wear woollen garments, but linen. And he alone entered the sanctuary and was found upon his knees praying for the forgiveness of the people, so that his knees became hard like a camel's through his constant bending and supplication before God, and asking for forgiveness for the people."[5]

This passage is rejected as unhistorical by Bishop Lightfoot, not on the grounds that the writer is reputed untrustworthy, but on account of the ascetic character assigned to St. James. But the early fathers believed in Hegisippus. Epiphanius, in commending the passage, adds the sons of Zebedee to the list of ascetics.

[1] Renan, "Les Apôtres," p. 22.
[2] Ibid., p. 72 ; see also St. Luke ii. 37 ; 2 Cor. vi. 5 ; xi. 27.
[3] Ibid., p. 70 ; citing St. Mark iii. 21, *et seq.;* St. John x. 20, *et seq.;* xii. 27, *et seq.*
[4] "Hær.," lxviii. 13.   [5] Eusebius, "Hist. Eccl.," ii. 23.

"For John and James together with our own James embraced that same plan of life. The two first of these were the sons of Zebedee; and the last, being the son of Joseph, was called the Lord's brother because with Him [the Lord] was he [James] nurtured and brought up, and by Him [the Lord] was he [James] always held as a brother, on account, of course, of Joseph's well-known connection with Mary, who was married to him. Moreover, to this latter James only was that honour assigned: once yearly to enter the holy of holies, because he was both a Nazarene and related by descent to the priesthood."[1]

The father adds that James ate no animal food, and also wore the bactreum or metal plate of the high priest. Let us see also what Clement of Alexandria says of St. Matthew—

"It is far better to be happy than to have a demon dwelling with us. And happiness is found in the practice of virtue. Accordingly, the Apostle Matthew partook of seeds, and nuts, and vegetables without flesh."[2]

This picture given of himself by St. Peter in the Clementine "Homilies" is equally Essenic—

"However such a choice has occurred to you, perhaps without your understanding or knowing my manner of life, that I use only bread and olives and rarely pot-herbs; and this is my only coat and cloak which I wear."[3]

Here is another passage—

"The Prophet of the Truth, who appeared on earth, taught us that the Maker and God of all gave two kingdoms to two [beings], good and evil, granting to the evil the sovereignty over the present world. . . . Those men who choose the present have power to be rich, to revel in luxury, to indulge in pleasures, and to do whatever they can. For they will possess none of the future goods. But those who have determined to accept the blessings of the future reign have no right to regard as their own the things that are here, since they belong to a foreign king, with the exception only of water and bread and those things procured with sweat to

---

[1] Epiphanius, "Hær.," lxxviii. 13, 14.   [2] "Pædag.," ii. 1.
[3] Clem., "Hom.," xii. 6.

maintain life (for it is not lawful to commit suicide) ; and also only one garment, for they are not permitted to go naked, on account of the all-seeing Heaven." [1]

The popular theory of the day is that Christ and His earliest disciples were orthodox Jews who proposed to fulfil every jot and tittle of the law as interpreted by the dominant party. Baur is the leading exponent of this theory. He holds that Christianity, which is the direct opposite of Mosaism, came from St. Paul.

But in judging ancient creeds there is an infallible test— rites. What were the rites of the early Church of Jerusalem ?

Plainly those of the Essenes. They had baptism and the bloodless oblation. James, the first high priest, abstained from meat and wine. He was consecrated from his mother's womb, that is, he and the other members of his Church were called Nazarenes, because they were Nazarenes. "We are they of whom it is written, Her Nazarites were whiter than snow !" says Tertullian.[2] St. James was plainly bound by a vow to abstain from wine for life. He shunned the use of oil. This, as I shall show, meets Bishop Lightfoot's argument that the Christians could not have been Essenes because they used oil. Renan cites many passages to show that tribute was sent to the high priest of Christendom from distant churches.[3]

If we could bring these questions, some will say, from the misty realms of polemics into the region of exact historical knowledge, how happy we should be. It so happens that we can bring this question into the region of exact historical knowledge. A most valuable document has survived. It is a statement of the case of the Ebionites, or the disciples of the Church of Jerusalem, against St. Paul. This document is known as the Clementine "Homilies."

In it St. Peter and St. Paul appear and argue out the various points of Christian teaching. St. Paul is Simon Magus, and the main points against him are that he "rejects

---

[1] Clem., "Hom.," xv. 7.   [2] "Ver. Marcion," iv. c. 8.

[3] "Les Apôtres," p. 78 ; Acts xi. 29, 30; xxiv. 17 ; Gal. ii. 10; Rom. xv. 26, *et seq.*

Jerusalem,"[1] and believes in his own "visions."[2]   He is also
accused of announcing that he is Christ in person.[3]   That he
never was the Prophet of the Gentiles is held as proved from
the text Matt. xxviii. 19.

But more crucial questions arise.   In this work are bloody
sacrifices forbidden or enjoined?   Is mystic communion with
the next world a crime punishable with death or the first
duty of man?   Is the shewbread of the temple to remain
the food of the priests exclusively, or is it to be given to
every citizen of the New Jerusalem?   One glance at such
a work will settle such questions for ever.

That glance shows us that the author of the Clementine
" Homilies " is a disciple of mystical Israel, detesting the
ruling of the Sadducees and the anti-mystical expositors.
Against the sacrifice of blood he is especially moved.   The
rites of the Ebionites also are the rites of the Buddhists,
Essenes, and the Christians, as we know them.

In the arguments that are carried on between Simon
Magus and Simon Peter, the latter boldly cites the passage
about the " jot or tittle."   He gives it, in fact, in a form
slightly varying from St. Matthew's Gospel, which seems to
point to the fact that he is citing the lost Gospel of the
Hebrews, which is known to have been the Gospel of the
Ebionites.   The passage runs thus : " The heaven and earth
shall pass away, but not one jot or tittle shall pass from the
Law."[4]   This fact is important, as it shows that the passage
upon which such a large superstructure has been erected was
intended to bear nothing of the sort.   It was framed to
condemn the Mosaism of the bloody sacrifice, and not to
announce that it was the ultimate revelation of God to man.
St. Paul is strongly condemned in the argument for neglecting the Hebrew scriptures ; but canons of interpretation are
laid down which practically annul them.   It is announced
that the Law was given by Moses orally to the seventy wise
men, and that in writing it down " many chapters " have been
added.

[1] " Hom.," ii. cap. 22.   [2] Ibid.   [3] Ibid., xvii. 7.
[4] Ibid., iii. cap. li.

The Gospel is cited to show that the legitimate expositors, the Sadducees, have erred, "not knowing the true things of the scriptures." Here again we seem to have a citation from the Gospel of the Hebrews.[1] Another saying of Christ is recorded, "Be ye prudent moneychangers" (in the matter of scripture interpretation). The canon laid down in the Clementine "Homilies" is that the only test of a true scripture is whether or not it coincides with the teaching of Christ. This, of course, practically supersedes the Old Testament with the new one.

The way in which the bloody sacrifice is explained away gives us a good idea of the Essene allegorizing. St. Peter argues thus against St. Paul—

"But that He is not pleased with sacrifices is shown by this, that those who lusted after flesh were slain as soon as they tasted it, and were consigned to a tomb, so that it was called the grave of lusts. He then, who at the feast was displeased with the slaughtering of animals, not wishing them to be slain, did not ordain sacrifices as desiring them, nor from the beginning did he require them. For neither are sacrifices accomplished without the slaughter of animals, nor can the firstfruits be presented. But how is it possible for Him to abide in darkness, and smoke, and storm (for this also is written), Who created a pure heaven, and created the sun to give light to all."

The first Epistle of Clement to the Corinthians, an epistle read in the primitive church, confirms the account of the status of the Christian high priest of Jerusalem—

"Seeing then these things are manifest to us, it will behove us to take care that, looking into the depths of the divine gnosis, we do all things in order whatsoever our Lord has commanded us to do. And particularly that we perform our offerings and service to God at their appointed seasons, for these He has commanded to be done, not rashly and disorderly, but at certain determinate times and hours. And therefore He has ordained by His supreme will and authority both when and by what persons they are to be performed,

---

[1] Comp. Matt. xxii. 29.

that so all things being piously done unto all well pleasing, they may be acceptable unto Him. They therefore who make their offerings at the appointed seasons are happy and accepted because, that obeying the commandments of the Lord, they are free from sin. And the same care must be had of the persons that minister unto him. For the chief priest has his proper services, and to the priests their proper place is appointed. And to the Levites appertain their proper ministries. And the layman is confined within the bounds of what is commanded to laymen. Let every one of you brethren bless God in his proper station with a good conscience and with all gravity, not exceeding the rule of his service that is appointed to him. The daily sacrifices are not offered everywhere, nor the peace-offerings, nor the sacrifices appointed for sins and transgressions, but only at Jerusalem. Nor in any place there but only at the altar before the temple ; that which is offered being first diligently examined by the high priest and the other minister we before mentioned " (ch. xviii. ver. 13, *et seq.*).

Now it is impossible to confuse this Christian " high priest " and the Jewish one. It is stated distinctly that the first has been established by God through Christ (xix. 7). It is also stated that Christ has laid down what " offerings and service " must be performed (xviii. 14). Indeed, St. Clement, misquoting Isaiah (lx. 17), finds a passage promising Christian bishops in the works of that early prophet (1 Clement xix. 6).

There is a passage in the Gospel of the Hebrews that throws additional light on the head of the Christian Church at Jerusalem. The author of the later portion of the Acts and Luke's Gospel is an author who, in the view of modern scholarship, is not very trustworthy. He writes with a purpose, which is to throw a veil over the sharp controversies of St. Peter and St. Paul, which are very patent in other parts of the New Testament. His motive also is, I think, to give an undue prominence to those apostles, and to the Roman Church which they are said to have founded. He gives Peter what Renan calls a "certain precedence," [1] though we see

" Les Apôtres," p. 98.

from St. Paul's Epistle to the Galatians, that when James the
high priest sent a messenger forbidding Peter to eat meat
with the Gentiles, he felt bound to obey.[1]   I think it is quite
certain that if we had the earliest gospel, the Gospel of the
Hebrews, we should see the status of St. James represented
in a far different light.   It was written in Hebrew, the language of the disciples at Jerusalem, and was used by the
Nazarites and Ebionites when, after the destruction of the
temple, they took refuge in Palla, beyond Jordan.

Fortunately a very important passage from this Gospel
has been rescued to us by St. Jerome, in his work, " De Viris
Illustribus."   In it we see that the first apostle that Christ
appeared to was St. James, and that as early as the night of
the crucifixion.   That this circumstance should be mentioned
in the earliest gospel and suppressed in the later ones, enables
us to appreciate more justly such passages as that of Matthew,
where Christ announces that Peter is the rock on which the
Church is founded.

" The Lord, after giving His shroud to the servant of the
priest, went forth and appeared unto James.   Now James,
since he had drunk in the cup of the Saviour, had made oath
not to eat bread until he had seen Him risen from the dead.
The Lord then said, ' Bring me a table and some bread ! '
And when He had received that which He commanded, He
took the bread and blessed it, and brake it, and gave it to
James saying, ' My brother, eat this bread, because the Son of
Man is risen from the dead.' "

" Maranatha ! "—" The Lord is risen ! "   This was the
great catchword of the early Christians, and this passage
looks very like the first institution of the communion service.
At any rate the account of the last supper in the Gospel of
the Hebrews was manifestly quite different from the accounts
given in our present gospels.   There we see nothing about
James drinking out of Christ's cup, a fact which proves that
the contents of the cup must have been water, for St. James
was bound by the vow of the Nazarite to drink water for life.
" The Ebionites," says Robertson, " abstained from flesh, and

[1] Gal. ii. 12, 13.

from wine even in the sacrament."[1] As the Gospel of the Hebrews or Nazarites was the gospel used by them, it is difficult to see how the passage about the "fruit of the vine" could have been in it when they used it.

This brings us to the "temple" where St. James ministered as high priest. It is plain that it would have been quite impossible for him to have entered the holy of holies of the regular temple, if only for the obstacle of the temple guards. This gives a significance to the passages in Revelations, describing the temple of the mystic Jerusalem, which of course would be modelled on the temple familiar to the white-robed saints of the material New Jerusalem, the "angel" taking the "golden censer," and "filling it with the fire of the altar," the "lamps," the "candlesticks," the "golden altar," the "incense." Dean Stanley pronounced that the catacombs were modelled on the sepulchral crypts of Palestine.

Keim points out that the command given in chap. xi. ver. 2 to leave out the court of the bloody sacrifices in the ideal temple of the New Jerusalem, is an additional piece of evidence in favour of the Essenism of early Christianity ; and that ver. 15, chap. vii. points to Essene night-worship.

Perhaps the rites of the Greek Church may help us here. At eight o'clock in the morning, on the day after Good Friday, the Greeks at Jerusalem put out all lights, including those burning in the holy sepulchre. They then act like madmen, wrestle, kick each other, yell, howl, and roar with meaningless laughter, at least, they did one hundred years ago. Plainly, the general idea was that the Light of the World was in the tomb, and the demoniacal host rulers. It lets in some light on the orgies which the different sections of early Christianity accused each other of committing, the lights put out, etc. It shows also the meaning of the buffoon mass in the cathedrals during the Middle Ages, when students, attired in mitre and cope, holding the scriptures upside down, preached mock sermons, and turned every detail of the Christian ritual into wild tomfoolery.[2] At three o'clock in

---

[1] " History of the Christian Church," vol. i. p. 33.
[2] Hone, " Ancient Mysteries," p. 159.

the afternoon, the Patriarch of Jerusalem comes with a large procession, and marches three times round the holy sepulchre. He then enters it (the solitary time during the year), taking with him a bundle of tapers. All these ceremonies are based on the legend that fire from heaven descends miraculously to the holy sepulchre the day after Good Friday. Out comes the patriarch with his bundle of tapers all lit, and the mob scramble for them, and wrestle to light their own tapers, and blow out those of their neighbours.[1] After this, all call out, "Christ is risen!" In every Greek church at this time they give the kiss of peace; and the consecrated bread (pain bénit), the truest relic of the Essenic love-feast, is distributed. The sacrament taken at this time is considered, beyond measure, more efficacious than at any other. Indeed, many pious people communicate only at this season.

Whether in this little picture of the head of the church at Jerusalem, going alone and once a year into the holy place, we get any key to the similar action on the part of St. James, I cannot tell. The sepulchre of the Founder of Christianity would probably be an object of paramount veneration from an early date.

As a centre for great pilgrimages, holy offerings, miraculous cures, etc., the sepulchral mound of a great saint in Buddhism had already acquired the highest importance. In the earliest catacombs, we see that the sepulchres of Christian saints were similarly utilized. Pilgrimages were of great importance in the early religions. They supported the priesthood. Also they were a form of initiation into the mysteries, Eleusis being simply an Indian feast. The pilgrim, as in Buddhism, trod the footsteps of some great teacher, visited the Bo Tree, the Deer Park, and the many caves and rocks where Buddha sate during his spiritual progress. In Christendom, the pilgrimage was once a very serious thing. The Armenians prepare for one for seven years, fasting forty days in each year. The early pilgrim, like the modern Greek, splashed no doubt in the Jordan, visited Christ's cell in the

---

[1] Picart's "Cérémonies, etc.," iii. p. 143.

Quarantania Monastery. Perhaps, also, he kissed the holy stone near Bethlehem, which is still white with the milk of the Virgin, carried away specimens of the rose of Jericho, so useful in childbirth and peril from lightning, measured out his future shroud on Christ's sepulchre, and had the record of his pilgrimage tattooed on his body.[1] Rome, with its feet-washing, step climbing, and its "stations of the cross," gives us probably other reminiscences. To this day the Jordan cures all diseases, mental and bodily. Without doubt, the holy city was the focus of all early pilgrimages.

But it may be said that this high priest of the Christian Hebrews dwelling in Jerusalem, with his sacrifices, his Levites, and his holy of holies, is purely a Hebrew, and not a Buddhist derivation. On the surface this is so. But if we look below the surface, it is impossible to conceive two more dissimilar entities than Caiaphas and St. James. They differ as much as the Messiah, as conceived by the Pharisees, and the Messiah, as conceived by the humble Nazarites. The one is supreme in the realm of matter, the other is supreme in the realm of spirit.

St. Denys the Areopagite, whatever his date, throws considerable light on this point. The higher mystics have always held that there are two worlds, the one of matter, and the other of spirit; and that the spiritual world, instead of being far away, is here. The one world is a dead world, the other a living world; for all the life in this our seen world is borrowed from the world of spirit. They held that the Kosmos is single, not dual, and that the army of thrones, dominations, cherubs, and seraphs mingles with and interlaces with the higher souls of the human hierarchy, the object of all being one, namely, to get nearer and nearer, and every hour more in harmony with the Great High Priest of the sky. He sketches the point of contact thus—

Human Order.				Celestial Initiators.
High Priest ...	...	...	...	Perfector.
Priests	...	...	...	Illuminator.
Levites	...	...	...	Purifier.

[1] Picart, vol. iii. pp. 145, 221.

It will be seen by this that the priests, at the date of St. Denys, were an army of initiated mystics, and that he never could have sanctioned the absurdity of a hierarchy of non-initiated officials, such as the pope and Church of Rome by-and-by became. The vital flaw of that religion is not so much that it discountenances mysticism, as that it gives to a mystic an instructor not himself a mystic, as the court preacher Bossuet was given to Madame Guyon. Such a proceeding has also killed the spiritual life of modern Buddhism. The Abbé Huc and Colonel Olcott, tell us that the cultivation of mysticism has passed away.

CHAPTER XX.

Dr. Lightfoot, in his work, "Epistles to the Galatians," has given a vivid picture of the Church of Jerusalem. He admits that they were Essenes and Ebionites, water-drinking ascetics, who rejected flesh meat.[1] They were pure Gnostics[2] like the other Essenes. This seems at first sight the very proposition that I am seeking to establish. If the earliest Christian church were Essenes, it affords a strong presumption that Essenism and Christianity were connected together.

But Dr. Lightfoot will not allow this. The Church of Jerusalem were "heretics." At some time between Christ's death and the Epistle of St. Paul to the Colossians,[3] a sort of pre-historic Anglicanism ruled in Jerusalem, without monks, nuns, monasteries, mysticism. The views of these believers in the matter of the Trinity approached "the Catholic standard;" whereas the Essene Ebionites regarded Christ as a prophet. Christ, this seems a necessary inference, though baptized an Essene, effected a root-and-branch revolution, and carried His followers into the camp of anti-mystical Israel. And then the Ebionite heretics retraced this long and difficult pathway step by step. This, of course, involves two root-and-branch revolutions, and that in a very small space of time; the first to establish this opposing creed, and the second to overthrow it.

As Bishop Lightfoot is the leading advocate of the proposition that between Essenism and Christianity there was no

---

[1] Page 313. [2] "Epistle to the Colossians," p. 98.
[3] Lightfoot, "Epistle to the Galatians," p. 313.

connection whatever, and that the two religions are pure antagonisms, we will now consider his arguments at some length. In his "Commentary on the Colossians," he draws up the following points of what he considers radical difference between Essenism and the teaching of Christ :—

1. The Essenes refused to take part in the ritual of the bloody altar at the temple of Jerusalem, at the risk of being stoned. Christ and his disciples went up to all the feasts and attended the bloody sacrifices.

2. Essenism is based upon asceticism which "postulates the false principle of the malignity of matter." The Son of man "came eating and drinking, and was denounced in consequence as a glutton and wine-bibber." [1]

3. The Essenes were extra strict Sabbatolaters. Christ strongly condemned the superstitious respect for the Sabbath.

4. The Essenes added constant lustrations to the law of Moses. Christ strongly condemned these.

5. The Essenes went beyond the most bigoted Jews in their avoidance of strangers. Christianity threw open Judaism to the Gentiles.

6. The Essenes considered oil a defilement, and Christ was anointed with oil by the Magdalene.

7. The Essenes denied the resurrection of the body.

8. The Essenes were not prophets but fortune-tellers.

I think we are all indebted to Bishop Lightfoot for his industry and acumen. He has collected a number of passages of scripture which convey, and I think purposely convey, the idea that Christ and his companions were not Essenes. I for one have to thank the bishop for helping me in a difficult research. It is remarkable that almost all these passages occur in one gospel, the Gospel of St. Luke.

A second curious fact emerges. The Gospel of St. Luke is generally thought to be more tinged with pure Essenism than any other gospel.

In St. Matthew, Christ says, "Blessed are they that hunger and thirst after righteousness ; " in St. Luke, He says, "Blessed are ye that hunger now."

---

[1] "Epistle to the Colossians," p. 170, etc.

Then in St. Matthew, Christ is made again to say, " Blessed
are the poor in spirit ; " but in St. Luke, He says, " Blessed be
ye poor." This is plainly a more correct version of His words,
for they were followed by " Woe unto you that are rich."

They are further illustrated by the thoroughly Essene
parable of Dives, who is not described as a wicked man at all,
only a rich man, and by the story of the ruler—

" And a certain ruler asked Him, saying, Good Master, what
shall I do to inherit eternal life ? And Jesus said unto him,
Why callest thou Me good ? none is good, save One, that is,
God. Thou knowest the commandments, Do not commit
adultery, Do not kill, Do not steal, Do not bear false witness,
Honour thy father and thy mother. And he said, All these
have I kept from my youth up. Now when Jesus heard these
things, He said unto him, Yet lackest thou one thing : sell all
that thou hast, and distribute unto the poor, and thou shalt
have treasure in heaven : and come, follow Me. And when
he heard this, he was very sorrowful : for he was very rich.
And when Jesus saw that he was very sorrowful, He said,
How hardly shall they that have riches enter into the kingdom
of God ! For it is easier for a camel to go through a needle's
eye, than for a rich man to enter into the kingdom of God."

This is the pure Essene doctrine that no admission is
possible to the roll of Christ's followers without the poverty
and communism of the Essenes, and all through the gospel
the teaching of Christ and of the Nazarite John is set forth
as identical, and it is expressly announced that this teaching
has superseded the Law and the prophets. All this being the
case, how is it that we suddenly find, side by side with this
teaching, another set of texts which, in the view of one of the
most acute and honest writers of the church, set forth the
doctrine that Christ cancelled the teaching of John ; that
having joined mystical Israel by accepting its baptism, that
having taken part in the Essene fastings and communings
with what Philo calls the Divine Essence, having denounced
anti-mystical Israel for keeping the key of the gnosis unused,
and having trained a large following to accept beggary, con-
tumely, hate, and martyrdom, in a sublime crusade against

anti-mystical Israel, how is it that the Great Captain should have suddenly marched off into the enemy's camp, allowing the key of the mystical gnosis once more to rust unused in the hands of Annas the high priest, and binding again on the shoulders of his emancipated followers the ceremonial that was so grievous to be borne ?

Surely we have here two distinct gospels, due certainly to two distinct writers, and most probably to two distinct periods of Christendom.

The question then that arises is : Which is the early gospel, and which is the one that has been superadded ? To help us to answer this question we have valuable historical data at our disposal.

1. The testimony of the other gospels.

2. The other writings of St. Luke.

3. The early rites and customs of the Christians. This last is the most valuable testimony of all, for ritual is far less easily altered than scriptures.

I propose to discuss this question at some little length, for the views of Bishop Lightfoot are very widely spread.

The early chapters of St. Luke's Gospel seem at first sight to bear out the bishop's thesis. The parents of Jesus go up every year (from A.D. 1 to A.D. 12) to the Feast of the Passover, and we see incidentally (chap. ii. 24) that they belonged to that section of Israel which adhered to the bloody sacrifice, as distinguished from the bloodless sacrifice, for they sacrificed doves in the temple. Mary, the mother, is brought into close contact with Zacharias, the father of John the Baptist, and Zacharias is said to be a "priest" who ministered in the "temple of the Lord " (chap. i. 9).

But a few moments of careful scrutiny show us that even in these chapters two distinct hands have been at work. Zacharias could not possibly have been of that section of Israel which piously exclaimed three times every day, "O God, send thy curse upon the Nazarenes." For when he hears that his son is about to become one of these hated Nazarenes, separated even from his mother's womb (Luke i. 15), and that he is to preach the Essene doctrine of " salvation by the remission of sins " (Luke i. 77), the good priest, instead of cursing, is filled with joy. Plainly the words "priest" and "temple" did not mean the priest and the temple of dominant Israel, for Zacharias further alludes to that section as, "those that hate us," our "enemies," they "that sit in darkness and in the shadow of death " (Luke i. 79), which he could scarcely have done had he belonged to their body. In the Revised Version, the word "temple" has given way to "sanctuary." Of Zacharias more hereafter.

There remains, then, the solitary historical statement that the parents of Christ (from A.D. 1 to A.D. 12), went up every year to Jerusalem to the Feast of the Passover, and took part in the bloody sacrifices there offered up. This statement is contradicted *in toto* by Matthew's Gospel. That distinctly announces that when the Child Christ was a baby its parents carried it to Egypt to save its life from Herod ; that they remained there until that monarch's death ; and that on their return they avoided Judæa altogether, for fear of Archelaus, Herod's successor.

Let us now consider the only other passage on which Bishop Lightfoot can have based his somewhat sweeping statement, that Christ and his disciples went regularly to Jerusalem each year for the three great festivals, and celebrated them according to the edicts of Moses with bloody rites. In Luke xxii. we read—

" Then came the day of unleavened bread, when the passover must be killed. And He [Jesus] sent Peter and John, saying, Go and prepare us the passover, that we may eat."

It is further stated that these disciples accosted a man, who took them into a house within the walls of Jerusalem, and "they made ready the passover," thus plainly, and I think intentionally, inferring that this "passover" was a slaughtered lamb. To all who have not studied Jewish ritual, this is a strong statement. But in point of fact, if the description of the passover in Luke is historical, Christ and His disciples infringed the Jewish ritual in almost every particular. Before I go into this question, however, I wish to draw attention to the individual that St. Luke calls the " good man of the house." Supposing for a moment that Christ and His disciples were members of non-mystical Israel, it is perfectly plain that this house-owner was not. He has a guest-chamber in his house, like the other Essenes, and on receiving the pass-word from the " Master," is ready to risk his life and harbour the brethren. It would make very little difference to the inquisitors of the dominant party whether a lamb was killed in his house, or the Bloodless Oblation was offered up. Rites instituted for the profit of the dominant priesthood should have been performed in the great temple. And it is the neglect of these rites that would have constituted the capital offence, not their falsification.

For the sixteenth chapter of Deuteronomy explicitly lays down that the Paschal lamb must be killed "at the place which the Lord thy God shall choose to place His name in." Like all other bloody sacrifices, it must be slaughtered in the temple, and the priest must receive the shoulder, the two cheeks, and the maw (Deut. xviii. 3). " Thou mayst not sacrifice the passover within any of thy gates " (Deut. xvi. 5). The edict is very distinct. " The assembly of the congregation of Israel shall kill it in the evening" (Ex. xii. 6). The slaughtering must be done in public by the recognized slaughterers. Also the lintels of the door-post must be smeared with the blood, and the worshippers must eat the flesh with their loins girded, with shoes on their feet, and with a staff in their hands, they remaining all day within doors. None of these injunctions were complied with on this occasion. It was impossible that Christ's disciples could have complied with some of them, for they were forbidden shoes and staves.

But a valuable test is in our possession, for this last supper was made the model of the daily sacrifice in the early Christian Church. Was this sacrifice bloody or bloodless? From the earliest days, according to St. Luke himself (Acts ii. 42), it consisted not of a lamb but of bread. In the earliest rituals it is called the " Bloodless Oblation."

But perhaps the bishop may have in his eye a chapter in the Fourth Gospel. Let us consider two separate accounts of the feasts, as observed by Christ's disciples in that Gospel.

"After these things Jesus went over the sea of Galilee, which is the sea of Tiberias. And a great multitude followed Him, because they saw His miracles which He did on them that were diseased. And Jesus went up into a mountain, and there He sat with His disciples. And the passover, a feast of the Jews, was nigh. When Jesus then lifted up His eyes, and saw a great company come unto Him, He saith unto Philip, Whence shall we buy bread, that these may eat? And this He said to prove him: for He Himself knew what He would do. Philip answered Him, Two hundred penny-worth of bread is not sufficient for them, that every one of them may take a little. One of His disciples, Andrew, Simon Peter's brother, saith unto Him, There is a lad here, which hath five barley loaves, and two small fishes: but what are they among so many? And Jesus said, Make the men sit down. Now there was much grass in the place. So the men sat down, in number about five thousand. And Jesus took the loaves; and when He had given thanks, He distributed to the disciples, and the disciples to them that were set down; and likewise of the fishes as much as they would. When they were filled, He said unto His disciples, Gather up the fragments that remain, that nothing be lost. Therefore they gathered them together, and filled twelve baskets with the fragments of the five barley loaves, which remained over and above unto them that had eaten. Then those men, when they had seen the miracle that Jesus did, said, This is of a truth that prophet that should come into the world" (John vi. 1–14).

Let us now consider the seventh chapter of John's Gospel.

"After these things Jesus walked in Galilee: for He would not walk in Jewry, because the Jews sought to kill Him. Now the Jews' feast of tabernacles was at hand. His brethren therefore said unto Him, Depart hence, and go into Judæa, that Thy disciples also may see the works that Thou doest. For there is no man that doeth anything in secret, and he himself seeketh to be known openly. If Thou do these things, shew Thyself to the world. For neither did His brethren believe in Him. Then Jesus said unto them, My time is not yet come : but your time is alway ready. The world cannot hate you ; but Me it hateth, because I testify of it, that the works thereof are evil. Go ye up unto this feast : I go not up yet unto this feast ; for My time is not yet full come. When He had said these words unto them, He abode still in Galilee. But when His brethren were gone up, then went He also up unto the feast, not openly, but as it were in secret."

In the Synoptics, between the date of Christ's disputation with the doctors and His great entry into Jerusalem, there is no mention of His going to Jerusalem. This has induced critics to view with suspicion the many visits to Jerusalem of the Fourth Gospel. In any case, if we piece the two accounts together, it is evident that they tell against the bishop's theory. The passover was plainly celebrated with Essene rites far away from Jerusalem. This creates a strong presumption that the "feast" that the disciples went up to was of the modest pattern described in the early Church of Jerusalem, an Essene breaking of bread in some secluded house, but this is unimportant. Supposing the narrative to be historical, the great question is, Did Christ go up as a partisan of the bloody altar, or as an apostle of the bloodless altar? Did He content Himself with contributing a shoulder, two cheeks, and a maw of a slaughtered beast to enrich and support the priesthood, or did He attempt to subvert that body? But one answer is possible. It is announced that the chief priests sought to kill Him, and sent officers to take Him. It is also recorded that in the midst of the feast He stood up in the temple and told the most strict and superstitious observers of a written scripture that the world has ever seen, " None of you keepeth the Law."

From their lips we get an instructive commentary. They said of His followers—

" This *people* who knoweth not the Law are cursed."

This shows that the legitimate interpreters of the Law of Moses were well aware that they were dealing, not with a man, but a multitude ; whose interpretation of the Law of Jehovah was so subversive in their view, that it merited His malediction. Much accentuated, we here get again the eternal *malentendu* between mystical and anti-mystical Israel on the meaning of the word "law."

If the narrative of the chief priests being compelled to bribe Judas before they could take Christ is correct, it is difficult to see how the account contained in this chapter can be historical. Certainly the answer of the bloodthirsty myrmidons sent to seize Him in the temple seems an impossible one, "Never man spake like this man!"

Had they given this excuse for neglecting their chance of seizing Him, they would have been executed.

From the didactic point of view, the meaning of the two narratives is more obvious.

"For the bread of God is He which cometh down from heaven, and giveth life unto the world. Then said they unto Him, Lord, evermore give us this bread. And Jesus said unto them, I am the Bread of Life, he that cometh to Me shall never hunger; and he that believeth on Me shall never thirst."

These are the words of Christ regarding the first feast.

"In the last day, that great day of the feast, Jesus stood and cried, saying, If any man thirst, let him come unto Me, and drink. He that believeth on me, as the scripture hath said, out of his belly shall flow rivers of living water."

This is the pith of the second ; and the two together are a sanctification of the "bread of God" and "living water" of the Essene mysteries.

We now come to the two texts most relied on by those who hold, with Bishop Lightfoot, that mysticism and asceticism are "inconsistent with the teaching of the gospel."[1] On these a vast superstructure has been raised from the date of Irenæus and Pope Victor to modern times. Let us read each with its context.

"And when the messengers of John were departed, He began to speak unto the people concerning John, What went ye out into the wilderness for to see? A reed shaken with the wind? But what went yet out for to see? A man clothed in soft raiment? Behold, they which are gorgeously apparelled, and live delicately, are in kings' courts. But what

[1] "Epistle to the Colossians," p. 173.

went ye out for to see? A prophet? Yea, I say unto you, and much more than a prophet. This is he, of whom it is written, Behold, I send My messenger before Thy face, which shall prepare Thy way before Thee. For I say unto you, Among those that are born of women there is not a greater prophet than John the Baptist, *but he that is least in the kingdom of God is greater than he.* And all the people that heard Him, and the publicans, justified God, being baptized with the baptism of John. But the Pharisees and lawyers rejected the counsel of God against themselves, being not baptized of him. *And the Lord said, Whereunto then shall I liken the men of this generation? and to what are they like? They are like unto children sitting in the marketplace, and calling one to another, and saying, We have piped unto you, and ye have not danced; we have mourned to you, and ye have not wept. For John the Baptist came neither eating bread nor drinking wine; and ye say, He hath a devil. The Son of man is come eating and drinking; and ye say, Behold a gluttonous man, and a winebibber, a friend of publicans and sinners!* But wisdom is justified of all her children " (Luke vii. 24–35).

It is a singular fact that this short passage has been made the chief armoury of the disciples of gastronomic, and also of interior Christianity. Thus Migne's " Dictionnaire des Ascétes" cites it to show that Christ approved of the asceticism of the Baptist. Does not this at starting seem to argue two teachings, and, as a corollary, two distinct teachers? If we omit the passages that I have marked in italics it is difficult to find a more eloquent eulogy of ascetic mysticism. The Buddhist mystics are called the Sons of Wisdom (Dharma or Prajñâ) and Christ adopts the same terminology. Plainly the gist of the passage is that the children of the mystic Sophia have no rivalry and no separate baptism. The lower life of soft raiment and palaces is contrasted with John's ascetic life amongst the " reeds " that still conspicuously fringe the rushing Jordan. John is pronounced the greatest of prophets, and his teaching the " counsel of God." Then comes my first passage in italics, the statement that the most raw catechumen of Christ's instruction is superior to this the greatest of God's prophets. It completely disconnects what follows from what precedes, and involves the silliest inconsequence, as shown by the action of Christ's hearers. It is said that they crowded to the "baptism of John." Had that speech been uttered, of course they would have stayed away from it.

The subsequent insertion of the gospel of eating and drinking and piping and dancing involves a greater folly. It betrays a writer completely ignorant of Jewish customs. The fierce enmity of anti-mystical Israel to the Nazarites pivoted on the very fact that the latter were pledged for life to drink neither wine nor strong drink. This was the Nazarite's banner, with victory already written upon it. Hence the fierce hatred of the Jewish priesthood. If Christ in their presence had drunk one cup of wine, there would have been no crucifixion, and certainly no upbraiding.

This is the second passage that anti-mystical Christianity builds upon—

"*And they said unto Him, Why do the disciples of John fast often, and make prayers, and likewise the disciples of the Pharisees; but Thine eat and drink? And He said unto them, Can ye make the children of the bridechamber fast, while the bridegroom is with them? But the days will come, when the bridegroom shall be taken away from them, and then shall they fast in those days.* And He spake also a parable unto them; No man putteth a piece of a new garment upon an old; if otherwise, then both the new maketh a rent, and the piece that was taken out of the new agreeth not with the old. And no man putteth new wine into old bottles; else the new wine will burst the bottles, and be spilled, and the bottles shall perish. But new wine must be put into new bottles; and both are preserved. *No man also having drunk old wine straightway desireth new: for he saith, The old is better*" (Luke v. 33–39).

I have again resorted to italics. I think we have here a genuine speech of Christ, and a very important one. His doctrine was "new wine" and it was quite unfit for the "old bottles" of Mosaism. The gravity of this speech was felt by the Roman monks who were trying to force the new wine into the old bottles (with much prejudice to the wine), so they tried to nullify it with flat contradiction let in both above and below.

" For the old is better."

This completely contradicts Christ's eulogy of the Christian's "new wine." Moreover, the words are not found in Matthew's version, which makes the cheat more palpable. There, too, we have the gospel of eating and drinking, a gospel that did not require an avatâra of the Maker of the Heavens for its promulgation.

But supposing that we concede the two passages to be genuine, I do not see that the priests of materialism will gain very much.

These texts are internecine, involving contradictions due either to more than one author, or to an interpolator singularly deficient in logical consistency and common sense. The statement, as far as it is intelligible, is that Christ, having determined to forsake mystical for anti-mystical Israel, made the following enactments :—

1. That the ascetic practices that He had taken over from John the Baptist and the Nazarenes, and which in other gospels He enjoins under the phrase of "prayer and fasting" as the machinery for developing miraculous gifts, interior vision, etc., shall be discontinued by His disciples during His lifetime and then again renewed.

2. That feastings and the use of wine, which as Nazarites He and His disciples had specially forsworn, should be again resumed, with no restrictions in this case in the matter of His death. So that by one enactment His disciples after His death were to remain jovial "wine-bibbers" by the other fasting ascetics. It is scarcely necessary to bring forward the true Luke to confute the pseudo Luke.

A valuable historical transaction is recorded by the real Luke which throws a strong light on the relations between Christ and John the Baptist. Towards the close of the Saviour's career, at Jerusalem itself, the chief priests accosted Him and asked Him by what authority He did what He did. Now if the relations between Christ and John the Baptist had been what the pseudo Luke would have us believe, Christ had only to state all this and He might have saved many valuable lives. He had only to plainly announce that His movement was not from anti-mystical to mystical Israel, but from mystical to anti-mystical Israel; that He had introduced wine and oil as a protest against Essenism; that He had forbidden its ascetic fastings, and brought many disciples back from "the baptism of John" to the orthodox fold. If He had stated all this clearly, the high priest and elders would have hailed Him as a friend instead of slaying Him as a foe. But the Saviour, evidently quite unaware that He had led a great movement against the Baptist, takes refuge behind John instead of condemning him. He asks the pregnant question, Was he a prophet of God, or was he not? inferring, of course, that he was, and that the prophetic gift was "authority" enough (Luke xx. 1, *et seq.*). "For I say unto you, Among those that are born of women there is not a greater prophet than John the Baptist" (Luke vii. 28). Here again we have the real Luke confronting his unskilful interpolator.

Point 2 has been dealt with all through this book. Asceticism was the Greek word for mysticism at the Saviour's date, and Dr. Lightfoot seems to include all mysticism in his attack. He talks of a "shadowy mysticism which loses itself in the contemplation of an unseen world,"[1] as part of the "false teaching" of the Colossians; also of the "monstrous developments" and "and "heresy" of Gnosticism. It is plain that he assails not the abuses of mysticism, but the thing itself.

This involves two distinct questions—

1. Was Christ a mystic, Gnostic, Nazarite—one of the type that the writers of His day ranked under the generic name of ἀσκητής? I have, I think, already shown that He was. At any rate, I will not say more on this point at present.

2. If Christ was a mystic, does such a man make himself and his surroundings more or less happy than the proclaimer

---

[1] "Epistle to Colossians," p. 73.

of the gospel of eating and drinking—the materialist, in point of fact?

Let us first of all see if the materialist is so very happy. Recently his creed has had many eloquent exponents, especially in France. Two days ago I was reading some powerful essays by Paul Bourget,[1] a sympathetic materialist, notably one on Dumas Fils, the poet-laureate of the cultus. Materialism, as I gather from these teachers, holds that there is no God, but Evolution, and that science is promptly suppressing the creeds. The idea of any life after death is not only a dream, but a morbid dream. We must find all usefulness and all enjoyment in the present, and be true and honest; but the ordinary ideas of morality are also visionary. Man is a tiny cog-wheel in a vast mechanism, and his acts depend chiefly on his surroundings, the sin of his father, the virtue of his grandmother. He may plunge into the modern popular pastime of money-making, but this means simple dishonesty, with its accompanying self-contempt. He may strive to be a poet, an artist, a statesman, careers in which originality means heart-breaking neglect, and a wave of unmerited popular favour, a back action that is still more trying. There is the squirrel-cage of fashion, a little wearying, and the actual pleasures of the gospel of eating and drinking, marred a little in modern days by gout and dyspepsia. There remains the absorbing passion of man and woman, and it can be considered under three aspects—

1. Venal love, which ruins the greater number of votaries. Even its factitious blushes and blandishments never conceal the idea that it is strict barter.

2. Adulterous love, which promptly means a vast contempt on the part of the male, and a bitter hate on the part of the female. It is perdition, with the smallest amount of pleasure.

3. There remains conjugal love, which, in the case of a few sparse "ideals," may mean happiness; but the conditions of modern life render such ideals almost impossible. Woman is educated to be not so much a wife as a gainer of

[1] "Psychologie Contemporaine:" Nouveaux Essais.

husbands. Her training is perfect up to a certain point, the altar. Every detail of physique, dress, and deportment, has been studied. The result on the wedding morning is a shrinking ideal of charming girlhood, at least exteriorily. It is when the arts of the mother and the milliner, the governess and the barber, the tailor and the dressmaker, have been stripped off, that the pair see their real selves, and not their counterfeit presentments. The sixteenth century lady is confronted with the nineteenth century man, and he finds that all he believes to be truth she believes to be fiction ; and all he believes to be fiction, she believes to be absolute truth. The result is a duel, more terrific in its rancour and hate than any stand-up fight between man and man. It is a duel prolonged through bitter days and nights for many years, a duel that must end in death.

This picture is too French, some will say. In England we are not all materialists ; and even the most materialist of our bishops promise us, from their pulpits, a paradise, when a trumpet shall summon us from our coffins. But, unfortunately, in these days of exegesis, both preacher and flock know quite well that this trumpet was promised in the lifetime of the apostles, a fact that has brought it into some discredit. At any rate, on the Monday the preacher and his flock act as if the trumpet of Sunday were a very, very shadowy thing.

Now, the Gnostic maintains that this dark picture is due not to the landscape, but the eye of the beholder. He holds that the material world, instead of being an abyss of hopeless pain, is the most perfect mechanism that could be conceived for the express purpose for which it was designed. That purpose is to open the spiritual eye, about which the most paradoxical misapprehensions are constantly being enunciated in modern pulpits. This means not to plunge us into an abyss of gloomy pessimism, but to rescue us from it ; not the abdication, but the discovery of happiness and joy ; not to encourage monkish idleness and fanatic selfishness, but to train and husband the individual man's powers for the extreme of work. By work is here meant the only work that is of any value in the world—spiritual work. The illuminati, instead of fattening in idle convents, have marked their passage through the world by many notable monuments, the ruins of overturned tyrannies and superstitions. Where is the iron Brahminism of early India? Where is the policy and atheism of Cæsar? Where is the Inquisition, the Star Chamber, the Bastille? Amongst the sheaf of fallacies about Buddha is the fancy that he passed his life watching his navel. As Bunsen puts it, "he renounced in despair the actual world which Christ sought to raise to godlike purity." These are words without meaning. In point of fact the labours of Christ and Buddha were identical. Each, without rest, travelled about teaching the spiritual life.

"The Gnostic makes his whole life a festival," says Clement of Alexandria. And a very intelligent modern Buddhist has written a little work, called " Christ and Buddha contrasted," which deserves to be studied here. He says that there is an Ego, which means spiritual ignorance and un-happiness, and a non-Ego, which means joy and God. With the intelligent Buddhist, heaven is a state resulting from domination of the Ego. The English expand their com-merce by war and slaughter ; and deem money-making happi-ness. Their heaven is as material as their life here, a sort of opera, with music, singing, and even eating and drinking. The good Buddhist seems to forget that the heaven of Amitâbha is also sensuous ; but, at any rate, he reads a valuable lesson to our materialism. The secret of the unhappiness of poet and preacher, of the fine lady and the pious money-seeker is, I think, laid bare. Each strives to build up a world to suit his own blind and petty ego, instead of moulding the ego into harmony with God and his world.

But here, perhaps, it may be urged that although material-ism is making gigantic strides in the Church, still, in Protestant Christianity, there are many excellent ladies, and some men, who have attained a high spirituality, far higher, as thinkers like Professor Kellog argue, than the fanciful inner light of the "lost" Buddhist, or the "shadowy mysticism" of the heretic Ebionite. Such people go regularly to church, give much money in charity, attend to all the ordinances of their spiritual advisers, believe that they have "grace" and "faith." They are of the "elect" who have gained atonement through the blood of the Lamb. This systematic restriction of Christianity to the external religion, the religion by body corporate, shows what a tremendous gap there is in thought and feeling between the epoch of St. Paul and the epoch of Professor Kellog.

St. Paul, in his earlier life, was perhaps the most illustrious votary in the world of the religion of exteriors. Modern duchesses and serious bankers would stand aghast if they knew all that this involved, A.D. 20. Instead of languidly visiting God's house twice or three times a week, and advertising his liberality in the pamphlets of a few charitable institutions, St. Paul, like all contemporary pious Jews, went to the temple three times a day. On awaking in the morning he exclaimed fervently, " Blessed be Thou, O Lord God, King of the World, for spreading out the dawn on the mountains ! " And he repeated similar ejaculations for every pleasant sensation, pleasant dish, pleasant drink, pleasant smell. No strict Jew ever terminated a day without the orthodox, " One hundred benedictions." On the right folding-door of his house was inserted a reed containing the passage in Deuteronomy that promised a land of milk and honey, abundant rain, and grass and fodder for cattle, the oil of fatness, and corn and wine, to those who obeyed the eternal edicts of Jehovah. In this passage was an injunction that these words should be written upon a Jew's house and his gates. He was commanded to lay up the words on his heart and his soul, and to bind them for a sign on his hands and on the frontlets between his eyes. All these commands St. Paul religiously complied with. Whether by compulsion, or of his own free will, he also was mulcted of many trespass offerings, burnt offerings, Sabbath offerings, tithes, and firstfruits to support the priests ; and like all Jews, ancient or modern, he gave away a considerable proportion of his wealth to the poor. Moreover, he looked for propitiation to the blood of a slain lamb.

Also the fact must not for a moment be lost sight of that

T

St. Paul at this stage of his existence was no hypocrite, no dull formalist. He has left on record ample proof that he was both zealous and sincere. If the religion of externals—by which I mean the religion of rites, prayers, propitiation, as distinguished from the religion of interior development, could do anything, it never found a worthier subject than St. Paul. And yet, instead of being proud of what modern popular theology must consider the most healthy period of his life, he can scarcely find language strong enough to express his abhorrence of it. He talks of "beggarly elements" (Gal. iv. 9), the "curse of the law" (Gal. iii. 13) of "bondage," of being "under a curse" (Gal. iii. 10).

And all this time it is not his own shortcomings that he assails, but the shortcomings of the system. Cogs and wheels and elaborate mechanism can make a good automaton whist-player, but not a man with a human soul.

Modern Christians talk freely about "salvation" and "Christ's blood," about "grace," "the elect," and the "new birth." If one of these could be suddenly confronted with the shade of St. Paul, he would hear language that would astonish him. He would be told that he was using the terminology of the mysteries without the least idea or even the faculty to understand what they meant. He would be told that his ideas about "Christ" and "salvation" were purely material; and that the spiritual estate of the real "Elect" compared with his own, could only be suggested to him by the symbols of nature that express extreme contrasts, light and darkness, life and death, the condition of a venal woman, and of one as pure as the evening star when it has just bathed in the ocean. He would be told that in the "Hidden Wisdom" the word "grace," instead of meaning a rejection of mysticism, meant "the whole body of mystic teaching sprinkled along the Jewish scriptures in such a manner that none but mystics could read it."[1] He would learn, too, that until he could find the mystic "Key of David," that unlocked the "open door," he was still in hell, in the gloomy world of torment, presided over by the prince of evil spirits, Samael and the Whore.

[1] Ginsburg, "The Kabbalah," p. 4.

3, 4. Two points brought forward by Bishop Lightfoot may be considered together. It is alleged that Christ condemned the extra strict sabbatolatry of the Essenes, and their lustrations added to the Law of Moses. But here an objection suggests itself at starting. Bishop Lightfoot is the keenest and most learned disputant in the English Church. It is, therefore, important to respectfully consider all that such a writer can bring forward on a subject where his following is so enormous. But it must be borne in mind that his leading thesis is not alone that Jesus was not an Essene, but that He was a strict observer of the Laws of Moses, as interpreted by their recognized exponents, the dominant section of the Jews. Supposing that we grant all that he says about the Essene sabbaths and their lustrations, is it not plain that his argument likewise demolishes his own theory, unless he can show that the numerous passages of the New Testament where Christ was adjudged guilty of death for the offence of sabbath breaking are spurious? If one of these accounts is genuine, it is perfectly plain that Christ was not an observer of every jot and tittle of the law. When the bishop retorts that he was Lord of the Sabbath, that argument concedes at once the very point at issue. It relegates him to the ranks of mystical Israel, which held that the voice of God was in the breast of the living Nazarite and not in the worm-eaten records which the Saviour contemptuously called that " which hath been said by those of old time."

But it is not until we consider the important question of the rites of the early church that we can appreciate the full force of the case against the bishop. The Christians, as we see from the earliest record, celebrated their Sabbath on Sunday, not Saturday. This was plainly done with Christ's sanction, and no conceivable piece of evidence could more plainly show that He did not accept the ruling of the dominant party. It has been suggested that Sunday was the Essene Sabbath, and that that was the reason of the change.

No two institutions could be more different than the Sabbath of sacrificial and the Sabbath of mystical Israel.

The Sabbath of the dominant party was a holy convocation, a " day of blowing of trumpets " (Numb. xxix. 1). It was a compulsory feast and holiday rather than holy day, on which two lambs had to be offered up, with strong wine, and a tenth part of an ephah of flour, mingled with a fourth part of a hin of beaten oil.[1] As a considerable portion of these offerings went to the priests, the savage laws about the very strict observance of the Sabbath are rendered intelligible. It was a weekly tax for the support of the priesthood.

" This is the law of the meat-offering : the sons of Aaron shall offer it before the Lord, before the altar. And he shall take of it his handful, of the flour of the meat-offering, and of the oil thereof, and all the frankincense which is upon the meat offering, and shall burn it upon the altar for a sweet savour, even the memorial of it, unto the Lord. And the remainder thereof shall Aaron and his sons eat : with un-leavened bread shall it be eaten in the holy place " (Lev. vi. 14–16).

On the other hand Philo, in his treatise on " The Contem-plative Life," gives us the rites of the Essenes and Therapeuts. Once a week they met, " clad in white and of a joyful coun-tenance," for " prayers," " allegorical " explanations of the scriptures, hymns, and the breaking of bread. All this, including the white garments, made up the earliest Christian rites, so it is plain that Christ's followers knew little of His great anti-Essene movement. Dr. Lightfoot says that Christ fulfilled the Law ; also that He " enunciated the great prin-ciple, as wide in its application as the Law itself, that man was not made for the Sabbath, but the Sabbath for man."[2] The Jews had certain rites for Saturday. Christ appointed quite different rites for another day. If this is " fulfilling " a law, how can a law be broken ? It must be remembered, too, that according to the eternal and unchangeable covenant of Jehovah (1 Chron. xvi. 17), " the priests, the Levites," were to be the sole interpreters of the Jewish law. To enunciate great principles of expansion or change was in consequence

---

[1] Numb. xxviii. 1, *et seq.*
[2] Lightfoot, " Epistle to the Galatians," p. 286.

a worse violation of that law than mere disobedience. Death was the penalty (Lev. xxii. 8–12).

4. On the subject of the "lustrations added to the Law of Moses," the bishop seems to get upon still more dangerous ground. Surely the first question that at once suggests itself is that, if Christ wished, as the bishop thinks, every jot and tittle of that Law to remain intact, why did He introduce the Essene baptismal lustration into his religion at all? Also, if He uttered the words attributed to Him, His disciples that He left behind Him to spread His religion seem to have paid very little attention to them, for the Church has always used lustrations at child-naming, adult baptism, exorcisms, entering a temple, at burial, three times during the mass, many times during the consecration of a church, and so on. It is to be remarked, too, that in the gospels Christ is invariably depicted as condemning the lustrations of anti-mystical Israel. These passages [1] are either historical or unhistorical. If the bishop detects an unhistorical element in them, they are worthless to prove his case. If they are historical, they depict Christ as an opponent, not a partisan of anti-mystical Israel.

5. In the matter of "extra Jewish exclusiveness," I fail to follow the logic of Bishop Lightfoot. Philo knew nothing of any rabid Essene exclusiveness. He calls the Jewish mystics "citizens of heaven," and says significantly, that they had abandoned "fatherlands" as well as children, wives, parents, brethren. He claims that they were akin with the Pythagoreans, "Mages," and the "Gymnosophists of India," who abstained from the sacrifice of living animals, thus plainly connecting, I may point out, the Gnosticism of Alexandria with Indian Buddhism. [2] On the other hand, Mosaism forbade missionary labour. The prohibition, says Gibbon, of receiving foreign nations "into the congregation, which in some cases was perpetual, almost always extended to the third, to the seventh, or even to the tenth generation." [3]

The fact that Christianity seeks to bring humanity into

---

[1] Luke xi. 37 ; Mark vii. 1, etc.
[2] "Every Virtuous Man is Free."
[3] "Decline and Fall," chap. xv. ; Deut. xxiii. 3.

"one fold" is adduced by Dr. Lightfoot to prove that Christ belonged to the non-proselytizing section. Surely, the inference is exactly the reverse.

6. To prove his position that Christ was anointed with oil, which the Essenes considered a defilement, Dr. Lightfoot brings forward the story of the woman anointing Christ. It is told in a very different way by Mark, Luke, and John. Mark says that Christ's head was anointed with "spikenard very precious," Luke with oil. John, on the other hand, says that Christ's feet alone were anointed, and that with spikenard, whilst Luke tells us that the feet were anointed "with tears." This last is the most beautiful story, and seems to fit in best with the sequence that the tears of even the Magna Civitatis peccatrix can move the Ruler of the Sky to compassion. Probably the word "oil" was by-and-by put in to give a sanction to extreme unction. That a prostitute should anoint a man in good health "to the burying" (Mark xiv. 8) seems improbable. That she should guess that a zealot of anti-mystical Israel was about to be put to death by His own partisans seems impossible.

The word anointing, in the early church, was applied to its baptism.[1]

7. "The Essenes," says Bishop Lightfoot, "denied the resurrection of the body." So did Christ, who has shown us that Lazarus, the penitent thief, Moses and Elias, instead of being wedded to their rotting bodies in the tomb awaiting the sound of a trumpet, are in skyey "mansions," the two latter certainly in spirit bodies. Paul also denied this physical resurrection. So does chemistry, a science of which the framers of the doctrine of the resurrection of the material body were quite ignorant. The human body is so much water, lime, gas, etc., and in the six thousand or six hundred thousand years that the human race has endured, some of these ingredients must have formed part of more than one dying individual. This makes it impossible for every one to claim the exact chemicals that made up his body at the moment of death.

[1] Riddle, "Christian Antiquities," p. 442

8. The question whether the Essenes were "prophets" or fortune-tellers belongs chiefly to philology. Was the Baptist an Essene, and was he a prophet or a fortune-teller?

Perhaps I may here mention one point more. The narrative of Jesus turning water into wine is believed by almost all independent scholars to be didactic rather than historical. Bishop Lightfoot favours the latter idea, and bases much of his argument upon it. Dr. Giles, however, gives some overwhelming reasons why it cannot be pure history. Christ is baptised in the Jordan. The next day, according to the narrative, he converts Andrew and Philip. "And the *third* day there was a marriage in Cana of Galilee" (John ii. 1).[1] Cana is seventy miles from the Jordan near the Quarantania. This is a long distance for a Nazarite, who had just taken the vow to abstain from wine, to go in one night for the purpose of breaking his vow and supplying the wine of a festival. Also it is completely contradicted by the other gospels, which announce that after Christ's baptism He remained forty days in the wilderness.

I think that chronology also explodes this theory of a double revolution. Supposing it to be historical, at what date did Christ carry the disciples, whom, as we have seen, He had admitted into His fold with what He called the "Baptism of John," into the camp of John's murderers? Supposing we give His movement an early date, we can scarcely conceive such a movement would be reversed by the disciple appointed by the Divine Spirit to succeed Him as head of the Church. James was martyred A.D. 44, and twenty-two years afterwards pure Essenism was not only the religion of the Church of Jerusalem, but, as Bishop Lightfoot shows, this "heresy" had been spread by this Church in Colossæ in the heart of Asia Minor. Accepting the doctor's dates, is not this a very short time for two root-and-branch revolutions?

By a brief comparison of Mosaism and Christianity, it will be seen how sweeping must have been each of these changes. The institutions of Mosaism seem plainly to have been

[1] " Hebrew and Christian Records," vol. ii. p. 178.

devised for a very small tribe. This is proved by the fact that it sanctioned only one temple ; and to this temple once a week every Israelite, under pain of death, was required to repair, to enrich and support the priesthood by the sacrifice of two lambs.[1] For the three great yearly festivals, pilgrimages to this temple, and larger offerings, had to be made ; an edict that became very burdensome when the nation increased. The world, to a savage tribe, consists of its own wigwams and a few neighbouring tribes, who it fancies will slaughter if not slaughtered. Hence the bloody edicts of the Jewish code.

"But of the cities of these people, which the Lord thy God doth give thee for an inheritance, thou shalt save alive nothing that breatheth : but thou shalt utterly destroy them ; namely, the Hittites, and the Amorites, the Canaanites, and the Perizzites, the Hivites, and the Jebusites, as the Lord thy God hath commanded thee" (Deut. xx. 16, 17).

To similar archaic civilization must be attributed the narrow laws against marriage outside the tribe, commerce, and propagandism. The theology is also the theology of early races. God resided not in the heavens, but in an ark of shittim wood, covered with "beat out" gold, in the midst of the tribe. The eschatology was the eschatology of the cave man. The soul, after death, went with its body to the cavern where it was entombed, went to Sheol. It is true that the prophets learnt from the Babylonian priests more noble ideas, but these were discouraged by the priests, who wanted God still to be conceived as residing in His little "ark." It must be remembered too, that slavery, polygamy, and the duty of private murder, as in Corsica, were parts of this eternal covenant.

I fail to see, with some modern writers, how this code can be due to the epoch of King Hezekiah, although it may have been codified in his reign. It seems quite unsuited to the reign of a civilized king, whose policy made it necessary for him to court the alliance of Egypt against Assyria. In this code the priest is absolute. He administers as well as makes

---

[1] Numb. xxviii. 9.

the laws; and taxation is entirely in his interest. Tithes, firstfruits, exactions of flour, the weekly and four-monthly slaughter of beasts all profit him. He exacts a ransom for the first-born son. The number of purifications is excessive. Then there is the greedy exaction for what is entitled the "sin through ignorance" (Lev. iv. 13), which seems practically to have placed the property of the layman in the hands of the priest; for he could be mulcted of "a young bullock" at any moment for an offence against a code of which, as Mr. Stanley puts it, "he was expected to be ignorant, as the documents were in the priests' hands."[1] It is scarcely to be thought, too, that the puerile laws about stoning oxen, slaughtering a perfumer who made a smell like the temple smells, putting to death the man who ate fat and blood in his meat, could be due to a king as civilized as Hezekiah. I think even a brief sketch like this shows what a tremendous undertaking it would have been to carry the Nazarites bodily into the fold of Caiaphas.

For without doubt Mosaism and Christianity are pure antagonisms; and Renan is right in giving to Marcion the credit of first emphasizing this fact. The one held that the spiritual world was the only real world, and that the seen world was a mere dream and hint of it. The other, as interpreted by the dominant party, held that the seen world was the only real world, and that the unseen world was visionary. The God of Mosaism was the God of a small tribe, with the prejudices of a small tribe against the rest of mankind. The God of the Christians had for motto, "One Fold under One Shepherd." The rewards promised to good deeds by the God of the Jews took the form of matter. The active merchants who in Christ's day were already the great traffickers of the world were promised grain and shekels as a recompense for ritual obedience. Their favourite text promised a full basket and store (Deut. xxviii. 5). The Christians, on the other hand, asserted that all the grain and shekels of the world could not secure moral happiness. This hinged on the absence, not the presence, of

[1] "The Religion of the Future," p. 285.

shekels.   In short, one was the religion of the spiritual world, and it enjoined communion with that world as the highest duty of man.   The other was the religion of the seen world, and it pronounced such intercourse a capital offence.   A leading thought of one was to spread brotherly love through the wide world.   With the other, God's blessings would have lost all savour if he thought that they were enjoyed outside Palestine.   The one was the religion of the individual with conscience for high priest, the other was religion by body corporate with conscience suppressed.

One argument of Bishop Lightfoot I had nearly forgotten, although perhaps it is too purely theological for these pages. He relies on the alleged fact that an advanced Christology distinguished the earliest religious thought of the Church of Jerusalem, which the "heretics" altered.   But is there any evidence of this advanced Christology at an early date ? German scholars say, No!   Jerusalem had the earliest Gospel, the original of the Synoptics, and in it Christ utters the cry of abandonment on the cross, fears the cup of agony, receives the Holy Spirit at baptism, "grew and waxed strong in spirit" (Luke ii. 40), which two last facts scarcely bear out the theory that the original writer of the Gospel held the notions of many modern pulpits that Jesus was the Ruler of Heaven, that had for a time abrogated His omnipresence, but not His omniscience.

Recently a valuable light has been thrown on this question by the discovery of a very early Christian book, the "Teaching of the Apostles."   In it Christ is only mentioned once, and that as "Jesus Thy Servant.   The *Saturday Review* of July 19, 1884, speaks thus of it—

"The importance of such a work as this, exhibiting to us in such plain, unvarnished fashion a portion of the Christian Church in its earliest development, as we have said, can hardly be exaggerated.   Its value is enhanced by the unexpected and, we may almost say, the startling character of the picture. The authenticity of the work is guaranteed by its complete unlikeness to anything which any one forging a document for party purposes—doctrinal or ecclesiastical—would have conceived. The large additions made to it at a later date in the so-called "Apostolical Constitutions" and in the "Epitome," to support the definitely formed system of Church polity and ritual by that time elaborated, are a warrant for the genuineness of the bare and cold original, in which we look in vain for any trace of specifically Christian doctrine, Christian fervour, or Church organization according to the platform universally established at the close of the second century. Of all the books of the New Testament it has the greatest relationship to the Epistle of St. James. Like that, it deals with moral and practical subjects, and is entirely devoid of dogmatic teaching, and has a certain Jewish colouring, easier, perhaps, to feel than to specify. Like that, too, there is in it a complete silence as to the leading facts of the Christian faith. There is nothing in it from beginning to end to indicate that the compiler had any acquaintance with the Incarnation, the Crucifixion, the Resurrection, or the gift of the Spirit, and the bearing of those great facts of Redemption on the spiritual life."

The critic adds that the "Agape" had not yet been separated from the Lord's Supper, and that the "cup" signified not Christ, but His teaching. Itinerant "prophets" figure conspicuously in the work. The word "prophet" was another name for the travelling "apostle."

One fact must not be lost sight of, and that is that if Jesus accepted Mosaism in its entirety, it follows that the rites and philosophy of Jesus and His apostles were diametrically opposed to the rites and philosophy that were accepted as Christianity about the end of the first century. Writers like Renan and Bishop Lightfoot deny this conclusion; but Gibbon has pressed it home with all the emphasis of his most brilliant irony. If on the other hand Christ was an Essene, the theory of Baur, that St. Paul invented Christianity, falls to the ground. For the question at once suggests itself, Why did St. Paul use the name of Jesus at all? Why did he not put himself forward as leader of the movement? The answer is plain enough. By the sect of the Nazarenes one conspicuous leader was already accepted. An historical character, sublime beyond all

previous Western experience had appeared in the world. He
had given it laws and rites, and newer and grander concep-
tions of life. He had told the Hebrew that forgiveness was
more noble than retaliation, poverty than riches, the ignominy
of the gibbet in the cause of enlightenment than crowns of
gold. He had announced to the death-dealing zealot that
even in the presence of outrage and treachery it was better
to sheathe than to draw the sword. He had taught that to
perform such menial offices as feet-washing was more Godlike than to accept them.

Renan opposes Baur on the question of the origin of
Christianity ; but even he is of opinion that it is St. Paul who
has "assured an eternity" to Christ. Without him the "little
conventicle of illuminati" would have passed away like the
Essenes, almost unremembered.[1] This depends upon the
question whether Christ's religion was an education or a
recruiting office. The scheme of Jesus was to slowly leaven
the world by means of a secret society of mystics rigorously
winnowed by beggary, celibacy, hunger, and persecution.
Have such little "conventicles of illuminati" been always so
contemptible ? Was Buddha insignificant when he stood
with his sixty disciples at Mrigadiva, and the proud priesthoods of Asia were already to the divine eye a thing of the
past ? Was Wieshaupt contemptible when he and the other
members of the "family of the human race" brooded over
the wings of society, and were in travail of the convulsion
by-and-by to be christened "French Revolution"? Was
Madame Guyon despicable in her dungeon, or George Fox,
or Swedenborg, or any other recipient of spiritual forces that
change empires? Certainly the sublimest spectacle of history,
if "Exegists" and "Apologists" would allow us to see it,
is the historical Jesus standing amid the grey limestone hills
of Palestine and planning the greatest battle of the world.
In one army were a few beggars—naked, shoeless, with no
shelter but the caves of the "foxes," no protector except the
mephitic air that depopulates the shores of the Dead Sea.
In the other army were the invincible legions of Cæsar.

[1] "Les Apôtres," p. 187.

Their weapons were death, stripes, torture, and obloquy. To these were opposed patience, long-suffering, courage, martyrdom, by a Captain who was determined that the warfare should be waged by spirit forces alone.

Modern bishops and duchesses masquerading in Christian communism and beggary may lament its present want of influence. They know quite well that if the genuine Christianity were revived it would tear the shams of modern society to pieces.

CHAPTER XXI.

Pope Victor—Rome supersedes Jerusalem—The Introduction of Religion by Body-Corporate—Marcion—He represented the teaching of St. Paul—His Gospel—Accused and Accusers changing places—Testimony of Marcion against Roman innovators.

POPE VICTOR.

AT the close of the second century of the Christian era a fierce controversy raged in Christendom. The East was pitted against the West. On the surface this controversy pivoted on a very petty matter ; which was, however, merely used in the light of a flag or party badge. The question was whether Christ was crucified on the day or the day before the Passover. Pope Victor summoned a council and threatened to excommunicate all the churches of Asia Minor who accepted the gospel account and the early church traditions. It is plain that a revolution in leadership had been effected in Christendom since St. James, as Christian high priest, received tribute from the other churches.

Many influences had been at work. At first the Church of Jerusalem was recognized as the leading church of Christendom. But the capture of Jerusalem by Titus deprived it of its commanding position. All Christians were banished from the holy city. The church of the Nazarenes took refuge in Pella beyond Jordan. From that point it still asserted its claim to be the leading church in Christendom, but its influence waned.

Whilst the Church of Jerusalem was thus on the decline it was in the necessity of things that another church should rapidly gain influence, Rome was the centre of the political world ; and the rapid progress of the new creed by-and-by rendered possible the dream of a Christian Pontifix Maximus. But across such dreams many pregnant questions would crowd. Were the institutions of the humble Ebionites with their communism, their celibacy, their uncomprising unworldliness, a form of religion fit for a great empire ? Would the rich Roman patrician consent to a community of goods with the Roman beggar ? Would the proconsul tolerate an allegiance that superseded allegiance to the civil power ? Were the fastings and solitary communings of St. Antony and St. Jerome a fit form of religion for the humble artisans of a work-a-day world ? Could women and children and men of weak intellect be safely permitted to trust alone to the God within the breast ? The Christian religion had proved itself an irresistible missionary force. But was it not more adapted for battle than peace ? The uncompromising Nazarite could grind into small pieces all priestly and pagan creeds, but did he present a suitable substitute ?

I do not think that this despiritualizing of Christianity was due to conscious priestcraft in the first instance, but rather to the force of circumstances. The fall of Jerusalem had far-reaching and indirect effects, not all of which are fully appreciated. Christianity was specially a Jewish religion worked by Jews. This was a source of strength, for it was thus kept outside the vigilance of the imperial inquisitors. All the early persecutions came from Jews alone. These were bitter in Jerusalem, but outside Palestine the Jews had less power. This enabled the barefooted missionaries to overrun Europe before the priests of paganism knew their danger. In the presence of the pertinacity of Jewish hate the poor Nazarite showed an equal pertinacity of passive endurance ; but it was natural that endeavours should be made to conciliate his great enemy. But until the fall of Jerusalem the arguments of the Nazarite were not likely to have much effect on an educated Hebrew. Such a man, if told that the execution of Christ by the Sanhedrim was a complete substitute for the ceremonies and sacrifices instituted with painstaking minuteness by Jehovah Himself, would have hailed the statement as an unmeaning quibble. He would have pointed out that these ordinances were pronounced to be of eternal duration, and to criticise them was more culpable even than to disobey them.

But when Titus put an end for ever to the Jewish rites of the temple, the poor Nazarite would have more chance of a hearing. Plainly the rites of Moses had not proved eternal ; that was a bewildering fact. But to convert a Jew to Christianity peculiar arguments were necessary. His main postulate was that God could be only propitiated by the shedding of blood. Hence the prominence that Christ's death began to assume in Christian polemics. In the earliest writings crept in the trope that Christ by His death had made a perpetual propitiation. This was at first only put forth as a trope ; but it contained a great danger to the religion of interior gnosis. By it could be brought in once more the conception of remission of sins by the daily bloody sacrifice of the priest. By it religion by body corporate could be reintroduced. This was the meaning of the immense excitement in the eastern churches when Pope Victor proposed to change the day for celebrating Christ's death to the day of the Passover. By the change Christ was made the Paschal Lamb.

But another great danger had come upon Christendom. The early church took over from the Essenes the Jewish scriptures, read with Essene interpretations. Under the title of " the law and the prophets " they figure in the writings of the fathers, and were, in fact, the only writings deemed inspired until the end of the second century. When all Christians were mystics there was little danger in this ; but when the lower Judaism was being largely recruited, matters changed. The peril of having, as it were, two bibles bound up in the same cover, began to assert itself. With commonplace minds, like that of Irenæus, the lower and literal reading began to swamp the spiritual meaning altogether. The more spiritual teachers in Christendom perceived this peril.

The real leader of this opposition was plainly Marcion. For this the vials of theological wrath have been poured upon him from the date of Irenæus to modern times. His answers have been burnt, but even without them accusers and accused have now changed places in the dock and the witness-box. Marcion represented what in modern days are called the Ethnico Christians, the party that, under the banner of St. Paul, had been so conspicuous in the previous century. Marcion had nearly half Christendom at his back, hence the bitterness of the Roman monks. " Of churchly organizations," says the latest edition of the " Encyclopædia Britannica," " the most important next to Catholicism were the Marcionite communities."[1] Tertullian affirmed that they swarmed and increased like wasps : " Faciunt favos et vespœ, faciunt ecclesias et Marcionitæ."[2]

Perhaps the Roman movement was in the first instance a mere squabble for precedence with the Nazarite Church in Jerusalem. But as the latter became insignificant in all but title deeds, the rising priestly party turned their attention to the Pauline party.

The Church of Rome, says Irenæus, was "organized by the two most glorious apostles, Peter and Paul. · For it is a matter of necessity that every church should agree with this church, on account of its pre-eminent authority."[3]

Perhaps it was also a matter of necessity that the disciples of these two most glorious apostles should be proved heretical in the same interest.

The disciples of Marcion were celibates who enjoined sexual abstinence as the condition of their receiving even the married .in their fold. They dressed simply, and fled theatres and public spectacles. They ate no meat except fish, and lived on bread, milk, honey, and water. They used the latter in their communion service. They bore great persecution heroically. Their leader pathetically called them, " companions in suffering, and companions in hate."[4]

It is to be observed, also, that it is dangerous to take writers like Justin or Tertullian as safe guides in dealing with

---

[1] Article, " Marcion."   [2] Cited by Gibbon, ch. xv.
[3] Iren., " Hær.," bk. iii. ch. 3.
[4] Heim, " Marcion, sa Doctrine et son Évangile," pp. 27, 29.

the transcendental metaphysics of a rival. The latter calls Marcion "anti-christ," and his section of the church "scorpions ;" and Justin declares that "'wicked demons' put forward Marcion to deny that God made all things," and also to assert the existence of "some other god greater than the Creator." Yet he himself declares that the "ineffable Father and Lord of all" made use of the Logos to create the world. The two statements seem so very similar, that it is difficult to understand how, if one is an "atheistical doctrine" and a doctrine of "devils," the other is not so likewise.

But the most prominent charge against Marcion is, that he mutilated St. Luke's gospel and St. Paul's epistles, to make these books fit in with his heresies.

"Moreover," says Irenæus, "he mutilated the Gospel according to Luke, taking away all that is recorded of the generation of the Lord, and many parts of his discourses in which he recognizes the Creator of the universe as his Father." [1]

He is accused, too, of attacking the Jewish scriptures, and prejudicing the three other canonical gospels by ignoring them.

The controversy about what is called Marcion's gospel has been renewed with great vigour recently. Neander, Sanday, Gratz, and Arneth, have supported the views of Tertullian, Epiphanius, and Jerome. On the other hand, Eichhorn, Löffler, Baur, and the author of "Supernatural Religion," maintain that Marcion can never have seen our version of St. Luke at all. Marcion's gospel is the original, and the present Gospel of St. Luke was composed from it not earlier than the end of the second, or beginning of the third century. [2]

This controversy throws much side-light on the subject I am investigating.

Many common-sense arguments at once suggest themselves, which make it difficult to accept the theory that Marcion cut about Luke and Paul for the reasons put forward by Irenæus.

---

[1] Iren., bk. i. c. 27, sect. 2.
[2] See Heim, "Marcion, sa Doctrine et son Évangile," p. 40.

1. The first that strikes me is the apparent aimlessness of most of the alleged omissions.

2. Marcion sometimes cuts out texts that strongly support his views. He leaves a vast quantity of others that are thought to confute them. Irenæus, Epiphanius, and Tertullian exult at this, failing to see how much it tells against them.

"But because," says Irenæus, "he alone has dared openly to mutilate the scriptures, and has gone beyond all others in shamelessly disparaging the character of God, I shall oppose him by himself, confuting him from his own writings, and with the help of God will effect his overthrow by means of those discourses of our Lord and His apostle [St. Paul], which are respected by him, and which he himself uses."[1] The good monk fails to perceive that a very astute confuter may sometimes "confute" himself.

3. Many of the omissions, including four Pauline epistles, are pronounced ungenuine by leading modern experts who have taken no part in the Marcion controversy.

4. If there have been any intentional excisions, they must be thrown very much further back than Marcion, as Cerdon, the previous leader of the Ethnico Christians, also used a "mutilated Luke."[2]

5. Why does Justin Martyr, in his fierce attack on Marcion, say not a word about these excisions, and nothing at all about there being four canonical gospels in his day? If there were four such gospels, he has disparaged them by his silence quite as much as Marcion.

6. On the hypothesis that there then existed four canonical gospels, and that Marcion was the fanciful independent teacher that he is now described, why did he not take John's gospel instead of Luke's? Strauss shows that its anti-Jewish dualism would have suited him perfectly.

7. The alleged falsification of St. Paul's epistles is still more perplexing. The Cerdonites and Marcionites had one distinguishing feature. They almost worshipped St. Paul and his writings. It was the first instance of Christian

---

[1] Iren., bk. iii. c. 12.
[2] Article, "Cerdon," "Encyclopædia Britannica."

bibliolatry. Supposing that Marcion had arbitrarily deprived them of large portions of their favourite scripture, would they have tamely submitted, or would they not have risen up and expelled the despoiler from the community? The Roman doctors, using a favourite polemical weapon of the day, accused Marcion of having been excommunicated for seducing a virgin ; but they have neglected to explain how it was that the most spiritual and self-denying half of Christendom followed such a man with enthusiasm.

8. The replies of the Marcionites have been burnt with their authors, but one little piece of evidence has been preserved. One of them, named Megethius, affirmed that Luke's gospel, in its present form, is full of errors and self-contradictions.[1] We see, too, from their bitter adversary Irenæus, that the Ebionite Church of Jerusalem gave a similar testimony. They pronounced Luke full of spurious additions. As Irenæus puts it, "they reject the other words of the gospel which we have come to know through Luke alone."[2]

The gospel of Marcion began abruptly. " In the fifteenth year of Tiberias Cæsar, Jesus came down to Capernaum, a city of Galilee, and taught them on the sabbath day." It will be seen by this that it cut out nearly the whole of the first four chapters of our present gospel, the statement that the parents of Jesus went up to Jerusalem every year at the Feast of the Passover, and celebrated it with bloody rites. Irenæus makes this the main point against him ; but the poor "Heresiarch" suddenly finds himself defended by all the learning of critical Europe. These chapters are now generally believed to have been added to the gospel by a Greek writer quite ignorant of Jewish history. He announces that, at the date of Christ's birth, a decree had gone forth from the Emperor Augustus that the whole world should be taxed. There is no mention in history of any such decree ; and if there had been, it would not have affected Galilee, which at this time was ruled, as Luke states, by Herod, an independent sovereign.[3]

---

[1] Heim, " Marcion et la Doctrine," p. 44.

[2] Iren., " Hær.," bk. iii. c. 15.

[3] Giles, " Hebrew and Christian Records," vol. ii. p. 190.

But a graver matter is behind. The details about Zacharias and the birth of the Baptist have been shown by Ewald and others to have been borrowed from the Protevangelium of James, which records further the tragical death of Zacharias. Why has pseudo Luke omitted this striking incident? Plainly because he wanted to show that the relations of Christ and the Baptist sacrificed doves and belonged to anti-mystical Israel, a theory which would be a little disturbed by the fact that Zacharias was the Zacharias that Christ announced as the last of the martyred "prophets." His death, when the Baptist was a boy, connects the latter with Essenism, because it is only as an Essene that Zacharias could have been executed.

Perhaps the strongest text that Marcion could have found to support his anti-Jewish views would have been Christ's saying about the folly of placing new wine in old bottles (Luke v. 37). Will it be believed that Marcion is accused of having excised this strong text?

In ch. vi. he is also supposed to have cut out Christ's fine protest against the lex talionis of Leviticus. Why should Marcion have cut out these injunctions to love our enemies and forgive insult and violence (vv. 27–31)? They quite proved that the Saviour was no supporter of the Old Testament bibliolatry of Irenæus and Justin.

The twenty-second verse of ch. x. is a fine statement of transcendental Gnosticism. It affirms that no gnosis of "the Father" can be obtained except through the Christos, the awakened soul. This is the quintessence of St. Paul's preaching. At a time that Irenæus was setting up the rival doctrine that knowledge of God must come from without, not from within, and be sought in "Scriptures," that is, the Old Testament, this text, one would have thought, would have been the most powerful support that Marcion could have found; and yet he is accused of tampering with it.[1] With Marcion, Christianity was a growth, an inspiration. On the other hand, Irenæus detected its mysteries in texts like the following :—

[1] See Migne, " Dict. des Apocryphes." I have also consulted for this chapter, Giles, " Codex Apocryphus," Heim, " Marcion," etc., and " Supernatural Religion."

"And Moses stretched out his hand over the sea, and the Lord caused the sea to go back by a strong east wind all that night." Plainly Moses, with outstretched hands, typified the mysteries of the cross.[1]

From ch. xi. 49–51, and from ch. xiii. 29–35, we get some more inexplicable excisions, texts where Christ condemns the priest party for slaughtering apostles and prophets. The beautiful passage commencing, "O Jerusalem, Jerusalem, which killest the prophets," is amongst these. Here was quite an armoury for Marcion to use against adversaries committed to the same sinister pathway. Is it to be believed that, instead of using these texts, he excised them?

I must confess, however, that the complete doctrinal aimlessness of many of the excisions is the strongest reason, in my mind, for disbelieving the excision theory. The pretty Buddhist parable of the prodigal son is as unknown to Marcion's gospel as it is to Matthew, Mark, and John. The innocent apologue of the widow's mite (xxi. 1–4); the parable about the son sent to the vineyard (xx. 9–18); the parable of the fig tree (xiii. 1–9), form part of the alleged excisions. Why, too, should Marcion (xvii. 5–10) erase the thoroughly Pauline teaching that "faith" could tear up a sycamine by the roots? And certainly the parable about uppermost seats (xiv. 1–11) seems, on the surface, scarcely so favourable to Pope Victor and his party that fraud should be called in to suppress it.

In Marcion's gospel Christ's triumphal entry into Jerusalem and cleansing of the temple is not to be found. Most readers will agree with that acute divine Dr. Giles, that this account is didactic rather than historical. Dr. Giles says: "Let us picture to ourselves a single man entering a throng of merchants in London or any other of our populous cities, and forcibly ejecting them from their usual haunts, that some hundreds of tradesmen should have been driven by the force of a single arm. It is inconceivable that such a scene could be real. The guards and constables of the city would have interposed, even if the traders themselves had not been firm in

[1] "Apology," cap. 90.

defending their property from destruction. It is painful to imagine such a scene passing in reality before our eyes. We cannot conceive that the Son of God and Saviour of men should create a tumult in that temple which he wished to purify."[1]

In the Lord's Prayer for " Hallowed be Thy name," the words " Pour Thy Holy Spirit upon us " are found. " How much more shall your heavenly Father give His Holy Spirit to them that ask it," says Christ just afterwards, meaningless words unless Marcion's version is the correct one. Verbal changes have been much made of by Marcion's opponents. " It is your Father's good pleasure to give you the kingdom " (xii. 32) has been changed into " It is *the* Father's," etc. " You know the commandments " (xviii. 20) figures as " *I* know the commandments." In the verse commencing " Then entered Satan into Judas surnamed Iscariot " (xxii. 3), the word Satan is omitted, a strange change for one whose philosphy was dualism. More may be said for verse 28 in ch. xiii. where the words " Ye shall see Abraham, Isaac, and Jacob, and all the prophets in the kingdom of God," have been changed to " all the just." Marcion apparently perpetrated a grim joke, if pleasantry were possible in those ferocious times, that when Christ descended into hell he released all except Abel, Enoch, Noah, and the leading prophets of the old law, " though Cain and the Sodomites and the Egyptians,"[2] were set free, says Irenæus, quite as much shocked by the last as the first statement. In chap. xxiv. Marcion's gospel leaves out all about Christ expounding the prophets, and seems to imply by the use of the word phantasma (ver. 39), that Christ's appearance to his disciples was in a spirit form.

But the most important "excisions" by far are the texts (Luke vii. 29–35) announcing that " the Son of Man came eating and drinking " and was called a " wine-bibber," (v. 36–39), the text about the " old wine " being better (xxii. 16–18). These verses are also omitted, " For I say unto you, I will not any more eat thereof, until it be fulfilled in the kingdom of

<hr>

[1] " Hebrew and Christian Records," ii. p. 251.
[2] " Hær.," xxvii. 3.

God. And He took the cup, and gave thanks, and said, Take this, and divide it among yourselves: For I say unto you, I will not drink of the fruit of the vine, until the kingdom of God shall come."

I have said enough elsewhere to show, I think, that there was no dishonesty in Marcion here.

We now come to the epistles of Paul, and the great question is, Supposing that the Marcionites excised the epistles to the Hebrews, Titus, and Timothy, whence have they been restored to us? Dr. Giles has pronounced that, until the date of Irenæus, Catholic Christendom knew nothing about St. Paul's epistles at all. Of the literature of the first two centuries, this writer has been the most profound student in England. He has translated the most important relics of the Apostolic Fathers of the first century, and brought out the text of the Codex Apocryphus. In his "Hebrew and Christian Records," he declares that St. Paul's epistles are "not mentioned by the Apostolic Fathers, by Justin Martyr, or by any other writer until the end of the second century, when the whole canon of Scripture comes at once into notice and is extensively quoted by Irenæus and others."[1]

Dr. Giles makes an exception in favour of three passages in the apocryphal epistles of Clement and Polycarp, but it is much doubted he adds, whether these writings are genuine.[2] "Justin Martyr seems to have been wholly ignorant that such an apostle as St. Paul ever existed, and Theophilus of Antioch, whilst he quotes the first chapter of St. John's gospel, does not even name or remotely allude to the great apostle to whom the Christian religion is so much indebted, and who resided so often and so long in his own city of Antioch."[3]

As regards Marcion, this silence of Justin Martyr is of the highest importance. If that writer had known that the most formidable opponent of Roman ascendancy had suppressed four epistles of Paul, he would have certainly not neglected so good a weapon against him.

Another curious fact emerges. I think I can show that

---

[1] Giles " Hebrew and Christian Records," vol. ii. p. 386.
[2] Ibid., p. 397.   [3] Ibid., p. 399.

the first sheaf of arrows that Irenæus has aimed at Marcion come from the Clementine "Homilies." He says distinctly that Marcion derived his system from Cerdo, and that Cerdo was taught by the followers of Simon Magus.[1]

I will make an extract from the Clementine "Homilies"—

Simon Magus, "I promised to you to return to-day and in a discussion show that He who framed the world is not the highest God, but that the highest God is another who alone is good and who has remained unknown up to this time."[2]

This is exactly what Irenæus says in the first instance of Cerdo, who taught that "the God proclaimed by the law and the prophets is not the father of our Lord Jesus Christ, for the former was known but the latter unknown, while the one also was righteous, but the other benevolent."

He says, too, that Marcion taught that Jesus "being derived from that Father who is above the God that made the world, and coming into Judæa in the times of Pontius Pilate the governor, who was the procurator of Tiberias Cæsar, was manifested in the form of a man to those who were in Judæa, abolishing the prophets and the law and all the works of that God who made the world, whom also he calls Cosmocrater."[3]

Other curious points of resemblance occur. The "Homilies" assert that Simon Magus does not believe that the dead will be raised.[4] Irenæus declares that Marcion denies the resurrection of the actual body, or, as he puts it, "the body as having been taken from the earth is incapable of sharing in salvation,"[5] the good father forgetting that the "glorious Apostle Paul" had announced the same views : "It is sown a natural body. It is raised a spiritual body" (1 Cor. xiv. 44).

Then, like Marcion by Irenæus, Simon Magus was accused by St. Peter of attacking the authority of the Jewish scriptures.[6] And it is a curious fact that the real Paul advocates complete continence (1 Cor. vii. 1, 8), and rules that they that have wives "be as though they had none" (1 Cor. vii. 29). This is the "heresy" of Marcion, who enacted sexual conti-

---

[1] Iren., "Hær.," xxvii. 2.   [2] Clem., "Hom.," xviii. 1.
[3] Iren., "Hær.," xxvii. 2.   [4] Clem., "Hom.," ii. 22.
[5] "Hær.," cap. xxvii. 3.   [6] Clem., "Hom.," iii. 50.

nence even with the married. The theological controversy
seems to have rolled very much on 2 Cor. iv. 4, where St.
Paul talks of a " God of this world."

All this is puzzling. Did Irenæus know that the sketch
of Simon Magus was an attack on St. Paul ? If he did, he
has put himself out of court by dishonestly using that attack
to prove another guilty of altering St. Paul's teaching. If he
did not, he practically confirms Dr. Giles, for he shows that
the partisans of Pope Victor knew very little about Paul and
his controversies.

Baur, from internal evidence, saw that the Epistles to
Timothy were an attack on Marcion.[1] Dr. Giles detected that
in the Epistle to the Hebrews the "tenour and tendency"
were quite different from the teaching of "the other less
doubtful of St. Paul's epistles."[2] Must we not carry these
deductions further, and conclude that it is to the Marcionites
that we are indebted for the preservation of St Paul's epistles,
and that the encroaching Church, obliged to take them over,
added four new ones to destroy their influence.

There are two Pauls, the one put forth by Catholics of the
type of St. Vincent de Paul, and Fenelon as the ideal of
the Christian ascetic. They cite his watchings, mystic communion, and " fastings," his assertion that for the mystical
life he would that all men were bachelors (1 Cor. vii. 7).
This Paul announces that he was separated from his mother's
womb, a phrase which with John the Baptist and St. James
meant vows of water-drinking for life. This Paul states also
that the spiritual drink of Christians in the communion
service was the water that flowed from the rock of Moses.
This Paul strives to keep his body under subjection by the
ordinary processes of the mystic. He announces that he has
the resultant spiritual gifts (1 Cor. xii. 1). His motto is,
" Walk in Sophia !" the phrase with mystics for the interior
life (Col. iv. 5).

The other Paul is the champion of anti-mystical Anglicanism. Bishop Lightfoot puts him forward, as we have seen.

[1] Baur, " Life and Work of St. Paul," vol. ii. p 100.
[2] " Hebrew and Christian Records," vol. ii. p. 396.

This Paul held that "asceticism postulates the malignity of matter and is wholly inconsistent with the teaching of the Gospel."[1] This Paul held that Gnosticism was "false teaching," and "monstrous developments," "heresy,"[2] "a shadowy mysticism which loses itself in the contemplation of an unseen world."[3] This Paul is a Paul that specially cautions his disciples against the "gnosis that puffeth up" (1 Cor. viii. 1); a Paul singularly solicitous about bishops' wives, though he cared so little for the bishops themselves; a Paul who considers the "stomach" of Timothy before his soul, and, forgetful of his own Nazarite vows, recommends him wine; a Paul the apostle of eating and drinking, who, it must be added, seems to have made singularly little impression on his personal followers, for they emerge in the light of history water-drinking mystics of the most ascetic type.

Let us first judge St. Paul, not by his writings, but his acts; that will test his ideas. Was he a Gnostic?

Professor T. M. Lindsay, in his article on Irenæus, in the "Encyclopædia Britannica," gives from that father the definition of true gnosis.

"True gnosis, not the false gnosis of the Gnostic, comes from the Holy Scriptures," meaning those of the Old and New Testament, and also from "the Church." This means: Suppress conscience and reason, and take A B and C, three widely divergent spiritual guides. Also it is a mere verbal quibble, for the word "gnosis" was selected by mystics to denote not external but internal knowledge.

For the early years of his life St. Paul conformed to the ideal of Irenæus. It is difficult to find in history a more perfect specimen of the "true Gnostic." He sought spiritual knowledge in his Church and Scriptures, two guides that, in his day at any rate, had the advantage of not being divergent, whatever they may have been at the date of Irenæus. He learnt that the sin of sins was independent thought. It was clearly laid down in the eternal covenant of Jehovah that

[1] Lightfoot, "Epistle to the Colossians," p. 173.
[2] Ibid., "Epistle to the Philippians," p. 41.
[3] Ibid., "Epistle to the Colossians," p. 73.

"the priests, the Levites," were the sole judges in matters of "controversy" (Lev. xvii. 8, 9). It was as clearly laid down that "divination," consulting with spirits, sabbath-breaking, prophesying anything except what the priests pronounced to be true, were crimes to be summarily punished with stoning. In the heart of Israel was a body of men who, in the view of "the priests, the Levites," infringed these laws. In consequence, St. Paul "persecuted" them "unto the death" (Acts xxii. 4). He "made havock of the Church, entering every house, haling men and women committed them to prison" (Acts viii. 3). But one day, on the road to Damascus, his interior vision was opened, and he began to see himself in a completely new light. And then he knew that there is an offence even more hateful than that of Barabbas on the highway, or of Mary of Magdala bartering her shame for shekels, and that is the infamy of the priestly zealot, who hunts down liberty and proscribes conscience.

·After this, for three years St. Paul was in Arabia, alone with his remorse, seeking to develop the Christ within his soul.

This brings us from Saul to Paul. Was he a Gnostic in the Alexandrian and Buddhist sense? It is quite impossible in the whole history of Christendom to find a mystic who regulated his life so purely by interior light. In the new Church he says he "conferred not with flesh and blood," and "withstood" its high priest and its apostles (Gal. i. 12). Throughout his second life he had but one guide, the Christ of his mystical reveries.

The great conflict between St. Paul and the historical apostles is, as German critics tell us, the one solid and incontrovertible fact in the Christendom of the first century. This is giving to the Apocalypse and the Epistle to the Galatians title deeds of early authenticity that most other books of the New Testament are gradually ceasing to be credited with. This controversy pivoted on two points—the authority of the Essene high priest and his apostles, and the authority of the Jewish scriptures interpreted, of course, in the Essene sense. From the bitterness of the Clementine writings it seems that St. Paul the preacher strongly opposed both from the very first. As Simon Magus he is made to point out many inconsistencies in the Jewish scriptures, and to affirm that they "lead us astray."[1] In his own epistles he is equally plain spoken. He calls the law "weak and beggarly elements" (Gal. iv. 9).

He talks of "blotting the handwriting of ordinances that were against us," of "nailing" the law "to the cross" (Col. ii. 14). He talks of the "curse of the law" (Gal. iii. 13). His visions are mercilessly attacked in the Clementine "Homilies."

Now it certainly seems a little strange that this high mystic has recently been made the great apostle of what he himself calls "meats for the belly. Migne's "Dictionnaire des Ascétes" cites the following texts to prove that he was just the reverse. The first is 1 Cor. ix. 27—

"And every man that striveth for the mastery is temperate in all things. Now they do it to obtain a corruptible crown ; but we an incorruptible. I therefore so run, not as uncertainly ; so fight I, not as one that beateth the air : but I keep under my body, and bring it into subjection : lest that by any means, when I have preached to others, I myself should be a castaway."

It cites also Gal. v. 4—

"And they that are Christ's have crucified the flesh with the affections and lusts. If we live in the Spirit, let us also walk in the Spirit."

And again, 2 Cor. vi. 4—

"But in all things approving ourselves as the ministers of God, in much patience, in afflictions, in necessities, in distresses, in stripes, in imprisonments, in tumults, in labours, in watchings, in fastings ; by pureness, by knowledge, by longsuffering, by kindness, by the Holy Ghost, by love unfeigned."

The highest stage of Christian mysticism was called the "perfect man," a phrase taken over from Pagan mysteries :

"Till we all come in the unity of the faith, and of the Gnosis of the Son of God, unto the perfect man" (εἰς ἄνδρα τέλειον) (Ephes. iv. 13).

---

[1] Clem., "Hom.," xvi. 9.

"Now concerning spiritual gifts, brethren, I would not have you ignorant. Ye know that ye were Gentiles, carried away unto these dumb idols, even as ye were led. Wherefore I give you to understand, that no man speaking by the Spirit of God calleth Jesus accursed : and that no man can say that Jesus is the Lord, but by the Holy Ghost. Now there are diversities of gifts, but the same Spirit. For to one is given by the Spirit the word of Sophia ; to another the word of the Gnosis by the same Spirit. To another faith by the same Spirit ; to another the gifts of healing by the same Spirit ; to another the working of miracles ; to another prophecy ; to another discerning of spirits ; to another divers kinds of tongues ; to another the interpretation of tongues " (1 Cor. xii. 1–10).

This is the passage from pseudo Timothy that Baur thought to be an attack on Marcion—

"Now the Spirit speaketh expressly, that in the latter times some shall depart from the faith, giving heed to seducing spirits, and doctrines of devils ; speaking lies in hypocrisy ; having their conscience seared with a hot iron ; forbidding to marry, and commanding to abstain from meats, which God hath created to be received with thanksgiving of them which believe and know the truth " (1 Tim. iv. 1–3).

It must be said, too, that Hebrews is a polemical pamphlet on Pope Victor's side of the paschal controversy. All critics reject it. In it we get warm eulogies of an "unchangeable priesthood " (vii. 24); of "ministers of the sanctuary" (viii. 1, 2); the theory that "without shedding of blood there is no remission " (ix. 22); the theory that a "testament " for some reason or other must be sealed in blood—all the "beggarly elements" and "ordinances" which the real Paul thought he had nailed to the cross. With pseudo Paul, Christ's death is important for its blood effusion. With Paul the Gnostic it was important as an emblem of the crucifixion of the lower and material life. Dr. Giles points out that in this epistle there are more citations from the Hebrew scriptures than in all the other epistles of St. Paul put together.

Enough has been written to put the reader in a position to

judge whether Marcion has curtailed or the anti-Gnostic encroaching Church enlarged the writings of Luke and St. Paul. Of immense importance to our inquiry is the key that it gives us to the principle on which the Roman doctors acted in dealing with the scriptures of opposing Churches. They took them over and added contradictory matter.

To sum up: is there any evidence for the two root-and-branch revolutions on which modern ideas are based? Can it be proved that Christ abandoned the baptism of John for wine and eating, and for every tittle of the law of sacrifices, slavery, polygamy, Corsican vendetta? Can it be shown that between 33 A.D. and 62 A.D. there was a period of nunless, monkless, Anglican orthodoxy before the "heresy" of the "Essene-Ebionites"? All evidence is in the contrary direction. Christ plainly knew nothing of the first revolution two or three days before His death, for He based His miracles on the baptism of John instead of repudiating it. St. James, His successor, knew nothing of the movement, for he was a water-drinking ascetic to the day of his death; and moreover celebrated Essene sacramental rites with the risen Christ on the day of the crucifixion. St. Peter, St. Matthew, St. James the son Zebedee, were also ascetics, and so was St. John, who has given us the earliest document of the historical Church, the Apocalypse. In it is a picture of Christ's kingdom on earth, with its virgin saints, and, for drink, "the water of life" (Rev. xxi. 17); with its communism, its baptism, its fastings, the "monastery without iron gates" of Renan. Rites are crucial, and the early Church adopted those of the Essenes. And to the vigorous rancour of Irenæus and his companions we are indebted for another authentic piece of history, namely, the rites of the two great antagonists of the first century, the Pauline and the Petrine parties, as they appear in the middle of the second century. Both emerge water-drinking mystics of the most ascetic type. Facts are before forged documents.

CHAPTER XXII.

Ráma—The "Grove of Perfection"—Early Brahmin Rites—Bow-shoot-
ing—Marriage of Ráma—Palace Intrigues—Banished to the Forest
—Rape of Sîta—Hanuman—Passage of Adam's Bridge by Monkeys
—Fight between Ráma and Ravana.

BEFORE BUDDHA.

I PROPOSE to give the lives of Ráma, Ceres, Osiris, Krishna,
and the five sons of Pandu. Considered together they will
show—

1. That the chief ancient scriptures represented the mysteries. These, under the symbolism of the growth of the
people's food, represented the twelve stages of the soul's progress in interior knowledge, the one important "mystery"
that man can learn. This progress was veiled by the scaffolding of the ecliptic.

2. They will show further that the story of Buddha has
not, as Mr. Kellog and his many followers imagine, been
stolen from the Nestorian Christians. The ideas of a divine
child born of spirit and an earthly mother is common to all
these stories. I shall begin with the story of Ráma, which
was certainly written before that of Buddha; indeed, some
writers have traced the rape of Helen and the battles of
Achilles, Ulysses, etc., to its inspiration.[1] Colebrooke believed
that the narrative of Buddha's life was largely derived from
the story of Ráma. I shall treat this in consequence at some
length.

[1] Dr. Hutchinson's "Literary Works," p. 298.

The Avatâra of Râma.

In the autumn of the year 1854, when serving in India, I was sent on my first detachment duty. Lieut. Turnbull commanded the party. We left the military station of Dinapore, crossed the Sone river, and encamped in the extensive thicket of trees through which the road to the civil station of Arrah passes. We were the only English officers, and we occupied the same tent. We reviled our sad fates, I recollect, at having to serve in India when the epoch of romance and adventure had closed. In three years, poor Lieut. Turnbull was lying in the terrible well that served as a cemetery to the ill-fated garrison of Cawnpore. And the thicket of trees where our camp-kettles simmered was fated at the same moment to be red with the blood of a gallant British force, which had attempted to relieve my friend Mr. Wake at Arrah. Vincent Eyre was then to reach the same thickets and fight his gallant fight with Koer Singh and the sepoys. And, eventually, I myself, whilst serving with the little column of Lord Mark Kerr, had the honour of taking part in another severe action against these my old Dinapore comrades, when Lord Mark Kerr defeated Koer Singh at Azimgurh. The poor torn colours of the 13th Light Infantry were exposed to a fire on that day, according to the Duke of Edinburgh, such as few other English regiments have ever witnessed.

These thickets of Arrah, in ancient days, were the scene of the first exploit of the god Râma, when he visited earth. Here was the "Grove of Perfection," tenanted by holy anchorites. Here he conquered the ferocious demon Marichi. The word Râma represented to our sepoys very much what the word Christ did to us. Writers in England who announce that the Indians ignore what they call the higher truths of Christianity, namely, trust in a personal god made man, make a great mistake. Every Hindoo sepoy in our detachment believed that if he died with the name of Râma on his lips, he would go to Swarga. His scriptures and his miracles are

X

as much a matter of fact to them as Christ's miracles to their
English officers.

Our tents shone out against the dark trees ; horses neighed,
and the water-carriers brought swollen skins from a neighbouring spring ; belts and cartouche-boxes were slung on the
branches.   The silent elephants, who had carried the tents of
the sepoys, glided away with their keepers to bring in spoils
of branches and leaves.   Anon the loud conch of some high-
caste Rajput sepoy was heard as he fortified a poor little altar
of mud or dust against the spirits of evil, with an invocation
to Râma, as a preparation for cooking and dinner.   And
through the night went up the not unmelodious nasal chant
of a Brahmin, who narrated the conquest of the mighty
demon Marichi, who, some hundred years before the siege of
Troy, marred the pious cultus of a congregation of rishis
assembled in this " Grove of Perfection," and how the shaft of
the intrepid young Râma laid him low.   What the psalms of
David were to the old Jew and the English Ironside, that are
still the warlike speeches of the Râmâyana to the Hindoo.   For
at least three thousand years they have incited him to battle.

The birth of Râma was miraculous.   At a great horse
sacrifice a spirit appeared and gave a magic nectar, which
his mother, Queen Kauśalyâ, drank.   Thus his father, King
Daśaratha, had nothing really to do with his parentage.
Three other queens grew pregnant with smaller portions of
this magic liquor distilled from the roasted horse, a symbol
of the dying year.

The demon Marichi was interfering with the rites of the
Brahmin rishis.   What were those rites ?   From the date of
Râma to the date of Earl Dufferin the Brahmin rites have
scarcely altered.

The savage believed, like the Christian Fathers, that the
earth was an enormous flat plain, rich with grain and cattle
for food.   He believed the cold stars, the homes of his dead
forefathers, to be comparatively tiny and destitute of food.
Hence arose the sacrifice, a *bonâ fide* feeding of ancestors and
gods.   Three meals were offered in Vedic days, and are still
offered every day—at matins, noontide, and evensong.   Gar-

lands and incense form part of the rites,—processions, lights, vestments. Chant and response are provided for as early as the hymns of the " Ṛig Veda." It was thus quite unnecessary for the Buddhists to derive their rites, as Mr. Kellogg holds, from the Nestorian Christians. Food, from an early date, was taken as a symbol of God Almighty, rice, and milk, and barley, and the intoxicating soma.

Considerable light is thrown on the early Indian worship by some papers by Dr. Stevenson that appeared in the *Asiatic Journal*.[1] In the Dekhan and in the Maratha country, a simple worship still prevails which he believes to have been the original worship of the Hindoos. The "Great Spirit" (Vetâl) has no statue, and the gods are never represented as animals. "The place where Vetâl is worshipped is a kind of Stonehenge, or enclosure of stones, usually in somewhat of a circular shape. The following is the plan after which these circles are constructed. At some distance from the village, under a green spreading tree, is placed Vetâl. If, as sometimes happens in a bare country like the Dekhan, no tree at a convenient distance is to be found, Vetâl is content to raise his naked head under the canopy of heaven, without the slightest artificial covering whatever. The principal figure where the worship of Vetâl is performed is a rough unhewn stone of a pyramidal or triangular shape, placed on its base, and having one of its sides fronting the east, and, if under a tree, placed to the east side of the tree. A circle is formed with similar, but smaller, stones placed one or two feet from each other. The number of stones varies, but I have generally found them about twelve, or multiples of twelve."[2]

This number twelve represents, says the doctor, the twelve Âdityas, the sons of Aditi the great mother, the twelve Dii Majorum Gentium of the Romans, the "different manifestations of the sun in his passage through the ecliptic." The stones are rudely fashioned like flames, with red paint at the base and a white spire. Fire-worship is evidently the leading idea. In the full moon of Ashvini a tree is planted and worshipped under the title of the Holi goddess.

[1] Vol. v. pp. 189, *et seq.*   [2] Page 193.

The same volume of the *Asiatic Journal* gives from Ceylon a ground plan and sketch of some of these monoliths found in deep jungle by Mr. Simon Chitty. He affirms them to be a portion of the ancient city of Tamana Nuwera or Tambapanni, founded by the first king of Ceylon 543 B.C. To come upon a dead city choked with the rich growth of an Indian jungle, and to see its dead gods strangled in ferns and parasite figs, whilst through the fine gothic tracery of pandanus boughs and those of the Indian fig the slanting sun sparkled, must have been a solemn sight. Behar is the garden of India, and some such splendid leafy cathedral was no doubt in existence in this "Grove of Perfection," when the young Râma came to this spot.

Not far from Arrah and the military station of Dinapore, is the district of Tirhoot, famous for pig-sticking and hospitable indigo planters. The latter used to entertain our officers. It appears that in the ancient days a king named Janaka was monarch of Mithilâ, its chief city. This monarch possessed two rarities, a daughter whose beauty was quite unrivalled, and a bow that no one could bend. The history of the bow was a little remarkable. A great sacrifice was once instituted, and all the gods were bidden except Rudra. This made him as angry as the fairy in the tale of the sleeping beauty; and he came, uninvited, and shot terrible shafts at all the divine guests.

"Because you have not given me my share of the sacrifice," he cried, "I will slaughter you all." The terrified gods prayed for mercy, and Rudra relented. His mighty bow became an heirloom in the family of King Janaka of Tirhut. Many kings desired the beautiful Sîtâ in marriage, but King Janaka gave the same answer to all, "My daughter is the prize of the strongest. Try and bend the bow of Rudra!" Each monarch did try, and each monarch failed. When the two young princes left the Grove of Perfection they crossed the Ganges and came at length to a large encampment where King Janaka was celebrating a great religious festival. Then Râma heard of the bow and the beautiful princess. Mithilâ is the modern Janakpur.

It was suggested by Viswâmitra, his guru, that his young pupil should try his prowess. The king immediately sent for the bow. It reposed in an iron case. Eight hundred athletes and eight wheels were required to bring it along.

"This," said the king to Râma, "is the Shining Bow. Many kings have tried, but all have failed even to lift it. I have ordered it hither, young prince, according to your wish. Who can hope to string it and shoot with it !"

Buoyed up by the wise Viswâmitra, the young sun-god opened the iron case. A breathless crowd looked on. Râma took up the bow and fixed a string to it. He adjusted an arrow, and using all his force he bent the mighty weapon. It snapped with a terrible uproar. The spectators fell to the ground stunned. It seemed as if the thunder-clap of Indra was reverberating amongst a thousand hills. The king was astonished.

"Venerable prophet," he said to Viswâmitra, "I have heard of the brave young Râma. But what he has now done transcends mortal strength. I have promised my daughter Sîtâ as a prize to the strongest. With her let him raise up a mighty race to be called the "Sons of Janaka."

Swift messengers were sent to King Daśaratha to tell him of Râma's luck.

King Daśaratha came to the wedding accompanied by his two younger sons. It was arranged that the marriage should be quadruple, a necessity in the presence of a quadruple sun-god. A sister of Sîtâ was given to Lakshmana, and two nieces of Janaka were betrothed. to the other brothers. The meaning of the four brothers is unfolded in this part of the great epic. It is distinctly confessed that the four brothers are like the guardians of the four points of space.[1] It is plainly stated also in another passage that the "four sons born of one body are like the four arms of Vishnu,"[2] another presentment of the same idea. A gift of cows was a leading feature of an early Aryan marriage. Pompous rites

[1] " Simili ai quattro Custodi del mondo," Gorresio, " Adi Kaṇḍa," 74.
[2] " Nati d'un corpo solo siccome le quattro braccia di Visnu," " Ayodhyâ Kâṇḍa," 1.

were performed to the Pitri or slumbering ancestors. The cows were then given to the Brahmins that the goodwill of the ghosts might be still further secured.

And now in the "place of sacrifice," in a leafy cathedral perhaps, with its twelve huge unhewn columns, the four moon-faced, large-eyed brides came tinkling along with their leg bangles and mincing in their gait like the daughters of Zion who irritated the prophet Isaiah. Their clear brown skins contrast with their fleecy muslins. Their jewels, it is said, made them sparkle like dancing flames. The sons of King Dasaratha were also bravely decked. Brahmins muttered their incantations and chanted their hymns. The offerings smoked up in the clear air. Each prince advanced and gave his hand to his bride. The four couples then marched round the flaming altar with measured steps. Three times this rite was repeated. A prodigy crowned the feast. Flowers not grown in earthly gardens were showered upon the young couples and the soft strains of the Gandharvas gave the mortals present a taste of heavenly minstrelsy. When the new married couples had disappeared, King Dasaratha also departed, accompanied by Vasishtha the rishi. But ere he reached his capital he was disturbed by sinister auguries observed on the journey. Birds flew away to the left-hand side, and wild beasts appeared in the same unlucky quarter. And before the monarch and the rishi reached their journey's end another shadow of coming misfortunes was encountered. Suddenly the skies grew black as ink and the fierce Indian sun was blotted out of the sky. Winds moaned and a huge storm of choking black dust burst upon them. A similar phenomenon, called by flippant officers a "devil," was encountered by the present writer whilst making the same journey. When the king arrived at Ayodhyâ the winning manners of pretty Sitâ made him forget his sad fancies for a time.

Perhaps the worst evils of polygamy are the cruel rivalries of the palace. Each queen strives to get her son nominated heir to the royal umbrella. To effect this, the murder or mutilation of his rivals is considered quite lawful. And the

interests even of the father are made quite secondary to those
of the boy. When the English government got into difficulties with Shere Ali of Afghanistan, it is no secret in
diplomatic circles that one of his queens volunteered to
murder him if the succession were secured by the English
government to her son. A zenana is of necessity a divided
house, and a state ruled from the zenana a divided kingdom.

The poet of Ramâyâna has based the dramatic interest
of his story on these truths. It was the misfortune of King
Daśaratha that his favourite son was not the offspring of his
favourite queen. This was the hidden calamity that made
the birds of the air fly to the left and the dust whirl in
darkening circles about the skies.

One of the brown-skinned, large-eyed queens of King
Daśaratha was named Kaikeyî. She was beautiful and attrac-
tive, silly and jealous. This jealousy was fanned by a malicious female slave. She accosted her mistress one day.
"Awake, O foolish queen. See you not that you are lost.
Râma is pronounced the heir of the king." Outside, the city
streets were noisy with preparations for the coming consecration.

"What is the meaning of these words, Mantharâ?" said
the queen, with much surprise.

"You are nursing a serpent," said the slave, "and a serpent stings. See you not that the rise of Prince Râma means
the disgrace and ruin of your son, Prince Bharata. The king
has befooled you with sterile blandishments and empty dreams,
and will now give you a prison for a portion!" With speeches
like these the jealousy of pretty and silly Queen Kaikeyî was
fanned. The slave pointed out also a substantial danger that
exists in all Indian courts. When a young prince comes to
the throne, he banishes or assassinates his younger brothers.

Queen Kaikeyî was soon beside herself with rage and
fear. "What is to be done?" she said, with breathless excitement.

"Do you not remember, O queen, a promise of the king?
In ancient days, when he came back wounded from a war, you
tended and cured him. His Majesty then pronounced these

words, 'Ask me a boon, two boons, and I will grant them!'
That promise has not yet been fulfilled. Demand that Bharata
shall be consecrated as heir to the throne, and Ráma banished
to a desolate forest!"

The boldness of this proposal took the queen by surprise.
But the persevering slave was not to be baulked. She
arranged a clever comedy for the ill-fated king.

In the women's apartments of an ancient Indian palace
was a Chamber of Pouting. If any queen grew out of temper
or jealous, this chamber was always ready to receive her whilst
the fit lasted. By the advice of the slave, Queen Kaikeyi
prepared what modern husbands call a "scene" in the palace
of Ayodhyâ. King Daśaratha was summoned thither in hot
haste, and what did he see? His favourite wife, the lovely
Kaikeyî lying on the bare ground, and weeping scalding tears.
Her splendid tiara of pearls and diamonds was flung at her
feet. Her glittering ankle bangles and armlets were also
scattered around. Silks were tossed hither and thither and
the rarest muslins. The pretty nails of the queen were no
longer anointed with rare unguents of sandal powder. The
fine artistic touches of kohl that were wont to make her eyes
sparkle like the eyes of a nymph of Indra, were now blurred
with salt tears. The monarch, seeing the queen that he loved
dearer than his life in this pitiable position, sought to comfort
her, as a noble beast when his consort in the forest is smitten
with a poisoned arrow.

"I know not, dear queen," he said, "the cause of this
anger that you show me. Who has outraged you, that you
lie thus in the dust on the ground? If there is an enemy to
punish, a wrong to be righted, a poor man to be made rich,
if you want more pearls, diamonds, emeralds, tell me, O
woman of the heavenly smile. I am the king of kings. Name
but your wish, and it is granted!"

"No one has insulted me or vilified me," said the queen;
"but in old days you made me two promises. Those promises
I now wish to see fulfilled."

"They are granted," replied the monarch. "With the
exception of Prince Ráma, you are all that is dear to me in

the world. Ask what you wish, and the boon is granted. I swear this on the integrity of all my past acts."

"When a king swears before Indra and the heavenly hosts," said the queen, "before the Gandharvas and the spirits that watch over the homes of us all, we may be sure that he will keep his word. In lieu of Râma consecrate my son Bharata, and banish Râma for fourteen years to the forests!"

"Oh, infamous fancy," said the king in his horror; and, torn between his love for Râma and his integrity, he fell senseless upon the cold ground. When he recovered, his remorseless wife was still at his side. He stormed at her, he railed, he entreated. He flung himself at her feet and prayed her to withdraw her ungenerous demand. "If for a moment I were deprived of the sight of my dear son Râma, my mind would not bear the shock. The world would be without its base, the grass without rain, my body without the breath of life!"

"Once you were celebrated amongst just men as a man of truth, a man of integrity," answered the queen. "You promise, and now you refuse."

"The banishment of Râma, O ignoble woman, means my death," and the painful reflection came into the king's mind that his memory would for ever be execrated as the dotard slave of a vain woman and the slaughterer of his son. And when, thought he, the holy masters call me to a solemn account and say, "Where is Râma? What shall I say?"

"You speak as if I were the malefactor," said the queen, with persistent cruelty. "What fault have I done? The promises came from you, not me."

Thus, through a painful night the poor king fretted in "chains of fraud." At times he flung himself at her feet, and tried senile blandishments and flatteries: "Save a poor old man, whose mind is getting unhinged. Sweet Kaikeyî of the gentle smile, take my life, my kingdom, my treasure, everything but Râma! Spare me, save me!"

The poet records that once a king, having promised to save a fluttering dove that flew for protection to his bosom, engaged himself to give the pursuing hunter any other boon.

"Cut out your heart," said the hunter. The king complied.
Our poor, loving, senile old dotard has much now in common
with that afflicted monarch.

Morn came, but it brought no solace. The king's charioteer, who was poet-laureate as well as coachman, woke him up
with a madrigal. Outside were courtiers and citizens in gala
dress. They were collected to see the consecration of Râma.

The king sent for his son.

Forth drove the charioteer to the palace of the prince.
Râma, summoned, started after exchanging a bridegroom's
farewell with Sitâ at the doorway. Strong demonstrations
from the citizens greeted him in the streets. The populace
idolized him. In his father's palace he found the king with
Kaikeyî. The piteous condition of the former quite startled
him. The poor old king could only just articulate the words,
"Oh, Râma," and burst into a convulsion of sobs. Râma
demanded of Kaikeyî the meaning of the king's grief. She
told him bluntly the history of the two promises and her
choice—

"My son Bharata is to be consecrated. And you will be
banished to the forests for fourteen years."

"If it makes my father any happier, I am ready to go,"
said the prince simply.

Soon the terrible news that the prince was to be banished
spread through the palace. Kausalyâ heard it. The brothers
heard it. All were in consternation. A trial greater than
the long banishment was the task of breaking the painful
intelligence to poor Sitâ. Râma told her what had occurred.
He exhorted her to bear his absence bravely, and comfort his
mother. This was the answer of Princess Sitâ—

> "Brave prince in mortal life
> Men singly battle ; good and evil deeds
>   Are theirs ;
> And each man reaps the harvest of his acts,
>   His own and not another's.
> But woman clings to man,
>   For she is weak ;
> His lot is her's, and wheresoe'er he goes,
> In briary paths or weary tanglements
>   She follows gladly.

By my great love I swear that reft of thee,
Protector, Master, Refuge, Patron Saint,
    E'en Brahma's heaven were dull.
  Fathers and mothers eke,
Beloved sons and daughters, what are they?
A wedded spouse lives only in her lord.
    Blind malice plots and wounds,
    Laugh at her wiles, sweet prince,
The shining towers of golden battlements,
    Halls hung with silks galore,
    Couches and odours sweet,
These without thee were as a desert waste.
    In paths of banishment
    I hang around thy feet,
    Thy weary feet, dear spouse,
And the rude home of tiger, snake, and pard,
The thorns, the stony steep, the cataract
That bellows with the water of the storm,
And e'en the realms of anguish mortals feign,
As the grim goal of earthly infamies—
    These by thy side were bliss—
    Thou art my universe,
    Thou art the form benign,
    That speaks to me of heaven,
    That speaks to me of love.
In wildernesses dank our holy men
    Clad in the bark of trees,
    Dream holy dreams of God,
Thus will we live, and I will deck my spouse
With chaplets plundered in the hidden dells."

Râma remonstrates, and points out how little the silken days of her past life have fitted her for the terrible ordeal of the yogi in the forest. His other friends try to dissuade her. The spectacle of this old-world, brown-limbed, bold-hearted young woman, this high ideal of wifehood, at the date of the poem, is quite extraordinary.

A crowd of citizens accompany the poor exiles as they are driven by the faithful poet-charioteer out of Ayodhyâ. Râma is the idol of the populace. Lakshmaṇa has obtained leave to bear him company. The fond old king went out for a short distance with his son. He then watched him departing in a cloud of dust. Râma's mother tried to comfort him in the palace. "Râma is gone," said the king. "Some men are happy, for they will one day see him return.

Not so his poor father. Touch me, Kauśalyâ, I see you not." The eyesight of the afflicted monarch had departed with his son.

The first halt of the exiles was on the banks of the Tamasâ. Here was a thick wood, and Râma and Sîtâ slept under a tree on a litter of leaves. Each wore the apron of bark tied with a cord round the waist.

Râma escaped furtively next day from the banks of the Tamasâ, for the citizens still hung on his track. He made his way to the Gomatî (now the Goomtee) and by-and-by reached the Ganges at Śringavera in the district of Allahabad. The poet-charioteer was here dismissed with a loving message to the old king. He was enjoined to be kind to Kaikeyi and to forgive her. They then reached the hermitage of the holy saint Bharadwâja, at the junction of the Jumna and Ganges. At this very sacred spot is the modern Allahabad. By the advice of the sage they took up their quarters on the hill of Chitra Kûṭa, which is about two days' march from Allahabad, and situate on the river Pisúni. The holy hill of Chitra Kûṭa is now to the followers of Râma what the Lion hill of Gâya is to Buddhists.

" How many centuries have passed," says Professor Monier Williams, "since the two brothers began their memorable journey, and yet every step of it is known and traversed annually by thousands of pilgrims! Strong, indeed, are the ties of religion when entwined with the legends of a country. Those who have followed the path of Râma from the Gogra to Ceylon stand out as marked men amongst their country-men. It is this that gives the Râmâyana a strange interest ; the story still lives : whereas no one now in any part of the world puts faith in the legends of Homer." It is added that every cavern and rock round Chitra Kûtra is connected with the names of the exiles. The heights swarm with monkeys. The edible wild fruits are called "Sîtâ's fruits."[1] Valmiki, the author, lived here, and he has given his poems local colour.

To cross the holy Yamunâ (or Jumna) a raft was made by the brothers of logs and bamboos. Sîtâ trembled at the

---

[1] " Indian Epic Poetry," p. 68.

sight of the gurgling current, and Râma held her in his strong embrace. Near the banks where they landed was a holy fig tree (Śyâma). "Having adored that sacred tree, Sîtâ thus prayed to it with pious reverence, 'May my step-father live for a long time, lord of Kosala. May my husband live a long time, Bharata, and my other kinsmen. And may I see once more Kauśalyâ living!' With these words uttered near the tree, Sîtâ prayed to the holy fig-tree, which is never invoked in vain ; and having duly worshipped it by tripping round it from the right hand side, the three exiles went on their way."[1]

The India of Prince Râma has very little altered in the India of to-day. Then, as now, perhaps folks already dwelt in tiny brick houses, with arabesques of vermilion and rich purple like those of Pompeii. Delicate wood carvings, like those that have recently astonished us at South Kensington, were no doubt abundant both in the bazaar and in the palace. Heavy hangings, with rich browns and pale yellows and subdued reds, showed that a bright sun can teach harmony of colour as well as M. Chevreuil or the great Veronese. White draperies and coloured turbans and rich arms and jewels flashed in the sunshine. Tiny little half-naked children were "nursed at the side" like the biblical Israelites. Isaiah describes the women weeping for the god Tummuz. This is the lament of the women of Ayodyâ for the god Râma. It has echoed in India for perhaps three thousand years.

"THE LAMENT OF THE WOMEN.

"Weep, husbands weep,
For what are homes and wives and riches now
   With Râma fled ?
   Afar the forests smile,
   The brake with dainty flowers,
   The lotus-covered mere,
The trees that climb the mountain, hiding fruits
   And honey, Râma's food.
Blessed rocks and thicket tangles ye that hold
   The gentle Lord of Worlds,
The Owner of the Mountains, and the Prop,

---

[1] "Ayodhyâ Kaṇḍâ," cap. lv.

The Champion of the Right.
Days follow weary days,
Each brings its guerdon sad ;
Our sons grow up within our rayless homes
Our homes bereft of hope,
And full of woman's tears.
Fraud reigns, the wicked queen
Yokes us like weary beasts ;
Soon the blind king will die.
O Râma, come again !
The shadow of his feet
Worship ye men, ye women bow your heads,
To Sîtâ, blameless wife ! "

The fugitives slept that night on the banks of the river, and sped the next morning through the forest.

"See," said Râma to his wife, " the kinśuka with flowers that shine like flames of fire.   See the pippala, and the champaka.   We have reached Chitra Kûṭa, and can live on fruits. The bees hum around and offer us their honey.   Cuckoos sing to the peacocks.   Here, O woman of the dainty waist, is joy for man and brute ! "

The brothers immediately set to work and constructed a rude hut for Sîtâ.   It was made of supple boughs broken down by the wild elephants and covered with leaves.   This rude hut, the pansil, is very prominent in Buddhism.

When the hut was completed, Râma sent Lakshmaṇa to slaughter a stag with his bow.   A rude altar was erected. Râma bathed to purify himself.   The carcase of the stag was placed on the holy fire, and the proper incantations were recited.   Offerings were then made to the dead ancestors. In this way the new domicile received the protection of the unseen intelligences.   Portions of the deer were then eaten by the two brothers ; and then the woman, Hindû fashion, contented herself with the broken victuals.   Thus commenced their life in the green woods of Chitra Kûṭa.   Round the rude huts the flowers clustered and the birds sang.

Meanwhile the charioteer returned to the palace and announced that Râma had crossed the Ganges.   The news was too much for the blind old king.

" Touch me, queen," he said to Râma's mother, " touch me,

and I shall know you are there. If this hand were the hand of Râma, perhaps it would heal a malady that nothing else can cure. In fourteen years you will see him return with the mystic earrings. Like an old torch, my life is burning low!" That night he died, and his body was embalmed, to delay his cremation until Râma's return.

On the death of the king, Bharata was summoned to reign in his place ; but instead of being pleased with the machinations of his mother, he stormed and raved. He refused to accept the crown, and started off with an army of four corps (infantry, horsemen, chariots, and elephants) to bring Râma back. They stayed one night at the hermitage of Bharadwajâ, and that great adept, by the power of his magic, was able to regale them all with flesh meat and wine.

The necessity of a rigid observance of a promise, no matter what the consequences, is perhaps the noblest teaching of this fine old-world song. Râma summoned to the throne, refuses proudly, "Have I not pawned my word," he answers, "to the dead king, to remain fourteen years in the forest ? "

A curious compromise is effected. Bharata consents to return as viceroy, taking with him Râma's two shoes. These are to govern until Râma's fourteen years of banishment are completed. The chhattra, or royal umbrella, is hoisted over them when Bharata returns. They are placed on a royal throne. Obeisances and royal honours are paid to them, and no public business is transacted without first consulting them. Analogous, as it seems to me, is the custom of the Buddhists to worship the two footprints of Buddha. From Chitra Kûta Râma repairs to the forest Daṇḍaka, and there a mighty bird Jaṭâyus, offspring of Garuḍa, promises to watch over Sîtâ.

The action of the drama is now quickened. In the forest Panchavatî is a beautiful demon, named Śûrpa-ṇakhâ. She chanced to see the splendid figure of Râma in the green wood. His arms were long. His brow flashed with a heavenly shimmer. His eyes beamed like the lotus. His limbs were the limbs of Kandarpa, the Indian cupid. Instantly she plunged deeply in love with him.

"Who art thou with the matted hair?" said the demon.

" Thou bearest a bow and a quiver. Why hast thou sought these woods ? "

" I am Râma, the son of Daśaratha," said the prince.

" I love thee," said the female demon.   " My power is immense.   It can transport thee to distant steep, to hidden flowery dell.   Fly with me, and taste joys unknown to mortals."

" I have a wife already," said Râma, " and must be true to her.   Here is my brother Lakshmana.   Love him."

The female demon had power to change her shape at will. " Thy wife is misshapen and puny.   In me you behold a worthier bride.   I can thy wife destroy."

Śûrpa-nakhâ is the sister of Râvana, and, baffled in her love, she makes an attack on Sîtâ. Lakshmana, to punish her, cuts off her ears and nose. Two of her brothers also, who try to avenge her, are slaughtered by Râma and his brother.

The enraged fiend hurries away to Lanka (Ceylon), to her terrible brother Râvana.   She narrates the slaughter of the two brothers ; and judging that lust is as strong a motive power as revenge, she paints the charms of Sîtâ in warm colours—

> " A wife Prince Râma owns,
> With large round eyes and cheek divinely fair,
>   Pure as the moon her brow ;
>   The locks that fall adown her neck
> Outshine the clustering locks of Indra's nymphs ;
> Her waist is supple, and her shapely arms
>   Around a lover's neck
>   Were guerdon richer far
> Than all the wealth that Indra can bestow ;
>   Sîtâ, her name. Away,
>   Away, and seize the prize—
>   Her beauty worthy thee.
>   Lakshman hath marred my face,
>   Our brothers in the earth,
>   Dâshan and Khara, lie,
> Their silent lips call mutely for revenge,
>   My wit shall aid thy strength,
>   A woman's wit,
> And we will spoil Prince Râma."

The ferocious Râvana falls easily into the meshes of the

subtle fiend Śûrpa-ṇakhâ. He goes off with her to the Daṇḍaka wood.

This is the description of Râvaṇa—

He had "ten faces, twenty arms, copper-coloured eyes, a huge chest, and white teeth. His form was as a thick cloud, or a mountain, or the God of Death with open mouth. . . . His strength was so great that he could agitate the seas and split the tops of mountains. He was a breaker of all laws, and a ravisher of other men's wives. . . . Tall as a mountain-peak, he stopped with his arms the sun and moon in their course, and prevented their rising. The sun, when it passed over his residence, drew in its beams with terror."

Professor Monier Williams thinks that this "wild hyperbole" contrasts most unfavourably with Milton's description of Satan;[1] but the Indian poet, having Rudra as the storm cloud and the many-armed scorpion to depict, was of necessity a little confused in his metaphor. The plot of the sister is that one of the crew of Râvaṇa shall assume the form of the most beautiful antelope ever seen. This deer skips through the wood near Sîtâ, and she thinks it so beautiful that she sends Râma off to secure it. Soon cries of help are heard in the distance. The fiends are counterfeiting Râma's voice. Sîtâ sends off Lakshmaṇa to his assistance; and a holy mendicant appears before her. This is Râvaṇa disguised. He seizes her in his arms and places her in his chariot. Soon she is flying through the skies in the direction of Lanka. Gods and the saints of the past are astonished at this bold iniquity. Brahma himself calls out, "Sin is consummated!"

The faithful Jaṭâyus, the vulture who had promised to guard Râma's wife, was witness of the queen's flight. He opposed the terrible Râvaṇa with beak and talons, receiving shaft after shaft in his faithful breast. At last, after a terrible contest, he receives a death-blow. Libra is killed by Scorpio.

Râma and Lakshmaṇa are in woeful plight when they discover the loss of Sîtâ. The dying Jaṭâyus reveals the name of the ravisher. Râma is assisted in his quest by seven

---

[1] "Indian Epic Poetry," p. 73.

Y

adepts. These friendly spirits are able, by the power of their magic, to assume any shape, but they usually figure as apes. The ape is a very holy animal in India. The most active of these spirits is the famous Hanumân. Hanumân witnessed the flight of Sîtâ, and was able to produce for Râma's inspection some jewels and a garment that she had dropped in her flight. Sugriva, the king of the monkeys, forms an alliance with Râma, and promises to help him to recover Sîtâ. In return, Râma slaughters some of that monarch's foes. An army is equipped, and Hanumân marches south to try and discover the whereabouts of Râvaṇa.

Meanwhile, Râvaṇa has reached Lanka, and has shown Sîtâ the wealth and splendour of his capital. Warmly he urges his suit, and promises to make her mistress of all his gold and jewels. Our missionaries are shocked when they hear some of the primitive language of these old Indian epics. But the lofty moral tone that pervades the treatment of this difficult topic, the rape of Sîtâ, is quite noteworthy. Râvaṇa uses cajoleries, threats, intimidations. Sîtâ is dignified, simple, brave. She speaks as if Râvaṇa's safety was the only pressing point involved—

> "O giant king give ear,
>   Free me and save thy soul!
> Within thy breast a guilty hope abides
>   To hold me in thine arms
> And seize a joy that ends in agony.
>   Thus in his fevered dream
>   The madman hopes to still
>   His pangs with poison,
> Release the wife of Râma while you may,
>   Not long his vengeance stays,
>   Implacable as fate
> It traverses the hills and seas and plains
> That part the culprit and his punishment ;
>   Soon shall his twanging bow,
>   His arrows flecked with gold,
>   His dart of glistening steel,
>   Grim as dread Yama's mace,
> Disperse thine inky legions as the wind
> Pursues the racing cloudlets white with fear,
>   Legions on legions press,
>   Their serried ranks shine out,

With gold and burnished brass,
And axe, and sword, and bow,
They hurl defiance to my lion spouse ;
Thus shall it ever be,
His shining bolts, through the complaining air
Shall speed to mar thy panoply and show.
In old wife lore the Indian fable runs,
That dying men see phantom trees of gold,
Look up, thy doom is near !
Not far the horrid regions red with lakes
Of human gore, the brake with thorns of steel
Prepared by Yama's justice for red hands,
And breasts surcharged with lust.
Thy threats and hopes are vain !
My death an easy feat ; a harder task
To shirk my Râma's unrelenting bolt."

Baulked in his passion, Râvaṇa hands her over to certain furies. Brahma sends Indra to the rescue, and he gives her a vase of holy ichor.

As the backbone of the great Indian epic is the invasion of the island of Ceylon by an army of monkeys, the dramatic interest suffers as the climax nears. The "Beautiful Book," *par excellence* in the view of the Hindûs, is full of the marches and countermarches of these unusual warriors. Professor Monier Williams laughs at this idea, failing to see that the pure totemism of the epic traverses his modernizing theories. The Aryan cave man, face to face with many difficult problems of nature, had to guess what was the function of the scorpion and the cobra that still infest the cave temples. These creatures, with bewildering capriciousness, could inflict death and horrible tortures. What wonder that animals got to be worshipped superstitiously, and that they crept into the Indian zodiac as an aspect of God ? It must be remembered that an ancient religious story had to be presented to the people dramatically, hence the value of monkeys' heads, dragons' heads, etc. Scenes from the Râmâyana enacted on the old Thespian car are still prominent at the great festival of Durgâ. The demon crew, too, are an army of grotesques. Some are excessively fat, some comically thin. Some have heads of elephants, some heads of donkeys. Humpbacks and very crooked thighs are the rule rather than the exception.

Some have three legs, like pre-historic Manxmen. The teeth of some of them would puzzle the limited instruments of modern dentistry, if extraction were necessary. The giants and dwarfs of modern fairs date perhaps from the early Bactrian invasion of India, and the pig-faced lady has probably as illustrious a pedigree.

Besides this, anthropology in the mysteries of modern savages is getting valuable hints as to how the earlier mysteries developed. These savages wear hideous masks of white beads and red paint. They personate pale death and monsters with heads of birds and beasts. They smear the novice with filth ; and their floggings and torture quite transgress the regions of pure mime and pantomime. They have, as Mr. Lang has shown, the bull-roarer, the ρόμβος of the mysteries of Eleusis. This is a flat oblong piece of wood which whirled round with a string produces a hideous sound. Death is the penalty of showing this to a woman. This means that it was seriously schemed in early days that the hideous noises in the mystic groves, the dread figures with masks and beads should be believed to belong to the supernatural. Râvana means "the noisy one," and Rudra "the roarer."

When Râma and his allies find themselves arrested by the sea in the vicinity of the now-celebrated Adam's Bridge, the exceptional accomplishments of Hanumân are brought into requisition. He can swim, he can fly, he can swell his form to gigantic proportions or make it as small as the body of a cat. He passes the straits by swimming, and raises up the mountain Mainâka in the very middle of them. Certainly it is there to this day, so the story must be true. He has a tremendous encounter with the queen of all the Nâgas or mighty submarine monsters. She opens her huge cavernous jaws to swallow him and the mighty aperture is ten leagues across. Hanumân distends himself to twenty leagues and puzzles the monster. Her monstrous jaws grow capable at last of compassing this huge swallow, and then Hanumân increases his bulk to forty leagues, and eventually to one hundred leagues as the swallowing capacity of the Nâga proportionately increases. Then Hanumân suddenly contracts himself to the size of a thumb and darts through her huge carcase. Professor Monier Williams half apologizes for mentioning such "wild exaggeration." [1] But the student of mythology may take a different estimate of its importance. At the date of the Sanchi temple (500 to 100 B.C.) the sign for Capricorn [2] was a huge sea monster with a gigantic elephant in his mouth. Symbol and narrative are plainly connected. In discussing the antiquity of the Indian zodiac the story of Hanumân and the Nâga has its manifest value.

Hanumân discovers Sitâ in a grove of trees amongst the splendid palaces of Râvana's infernal kingdom. She was plunged in sad dreams. She wore the garb of a widow. Her hair was collected in a simple braid. She appeared like "memory clouded, like prosperity ruined, like hope abandoned." Hanumân reveals himself as Râma's messenger, but she distrusts him. He exhibits Râma's ring, which had been entrusted to him, and gains her confidence. He offers to transport her through the skies to Râma, but she says that she cannot touch the person of any one but her husband. Hanumân then has a great fight with the demons. He kills many, but is in the end taken prisoner, and they set alight to his tail. He escapes and creates a great conflagration. By-and-by he returns to Râma, and exhibits a jewel sent by Sitâ as a token.

The bridge built between Ceylon and the peninsula of Hindustan by the monkeys will be famous for ever. This was the prophecy of the Pitris, or dead saints of the past, as they witnessed the operation of building. The son of Visvakarman was the architect. The mighty boulders that have been scattered about the plains of India by ice or other action are believed to this day to have been dropped by the monkeys when collecting rocks for their gigantic bridge. The line of rocks that cross the straits and figure in modern maps as Adam's Bridge, are called Râma's Bridge in India. And the island half-way across is called Râma's Pillar.

The terrible Râvana, having learnt from his spies that a

---

[1] "Indian Epic Poetry," p. 78.   [2] See p. 7.

mighty army of monkeys had crossed, made one more supreme effort to beguile poor Sitâ. By the power of his magic he produced a phantasmal head exactly like Râma's head. He flung it at her feet—

"There," he said, "is your husband and your avenger, and there is his bow. I have put his army to the rout."

Poor Sitâ was plunged in the depths of despair; but by-and-by a benign spirit appeared to her and told her that the story was false.

"Listen to yonder distant rumbling. Hear you not the drum and the conch. Râma is not dead. There is his army." Soon the noise of battle draws nearer. The single combats are of course numerous, and detailed at great length. Cohorts of doughty warriors bite the dust. Even Râma and Lakshmana are by-and-by overthrown, and Râvana forces Sitâ to come with him in his chariot to view their dead bodies, as he believes them to be. But the bird Garuda heals them.

At length the crucial battle takes place between Râma and Râvana. Râvana is seated in a magic car, drawn by horses with human heads. Indra sends Râma his own car, driven by charioteer Mâtali. As during the fight of Achilles and Hector, the gods range themselves on each side of the combatants, and the armies cease fighting to witness the crucial encounter. The tactics on both sides seems to have been skilful bow-shooting and rapid whirls of the cars. Râma cuts off a hundred heads in succession, but, Hydra-like, a fresh one takes the place of the last one. The fight lasts for seven days and seven nights. At length the mighty chakra is brought into play. This has the wind for its feathers, the fire for its point, the air for its body, the mountain of Meru for its weight. This is, I think, stating very plainly that it is the swastika, the symbol, the four seasons, the four elements. In one part of the poem it is said that the weapons of conquering Indra take the form of serpents; and in a book, the "Hanumânataka," it is explained that these weapons change to serpents when they reach an enemy. Râma overthrows Râvana, and his wives set up doleful lamentations.

CHAPTER XXIII.

THE ZODIAC OF INDIAN MYTH.

THE root idea of this story is to reveal and conceal the mysteries.

For the initiates we have the story of an ascetic acquiring magical powers and the twelve stages of interior progress symbolized by the Indian zodiac.

For those who are only fit for St. Paul's "milk for babes" we have the conceivable anthropomorphic God Purusha, whose life is made to fit in with the festivals and monthly worship of the twelve stone gods.

Under the second aspect is presented the growth of rice, the material food, under the first the growth of the bread of life.

"They [the Brahmins] have always observed the order of the gods as they are to be worshipped in the twelvemonth," says the "Rig Veda." [1]

"The year is Prajâpati" (the Divine Man), says the "Aitareya Brahmana." [2]

"Thou dividest thy person in twelve parts," says a hymn in the "Mahâbhârata," "and becomest the twelve Adityas." [3]

"These pillars, ranging in rows like swans, have come to

[1] "Rig Veda," vii. p. 103.   [2] Haug, vol. ii. p. 6.
[3] "Vana Parva," v. 189.

us erected by pious rishis to the East. They proceed resplendent in the path of the gods." [1]

"The body is like a town with eleven gates, through which the soul enters. The soul dwells in the heavens as the divine bird." [2]

Let us consider these mystical gates. Mr. Burgess and an American Orientalist named Whitney asserted a few years back that the Indians knew nothing of the zodiac until they borrowed it from the Greeks, A.D. 500. Of the Greek zodiac perhaps not. The Indian zodiac is detailed, with a little disguise, in the episode of the "Mahâbhârata," entitled the "Churning of the Ocean." Narâyaṇa, to gain for mortals the amṛita or immortal drink, coils the serpent Vâsuki or ecliptic round the mountain Mandar (the Indian symbol for the Kosmos), and makes it spin round and "churn" the ocean (unfashioned fluidic matter). This action is opposed by the spirits of darkness, and in the little story the signs of the Indian zodiac, as they figure in the earliest monuments, are somewhat clumsily brought in.

1. "The Deva Dhanwantari in a human shape came forth, holding in his hand a white vessel filled with the immortal juice amṛita" (Aquarius).

2. "Chakra," the disc with the swastika symbol (Pisces).

3. "The White Horse, called Uchîsrava" (Aries).

4. "Surabhi the Cow, that granted every heart's desire" (Taurus).

5. Gemini represents the positive and negative principles symbolized here by Narâyaṇa and Râhu the Sura (Spirit of Light) and the Asura (Spirit of Darkness).

6. "Kûrma Râja" (King Tortoise) who has, like the Crab, the mystic outline of the Rod of Hermes.

7. "The Lion" (Leo).

8. "Śri, the goddess of Fortune, whose seat is the white lily of the waters." Virgo is also symbolized by the "Parijataka, the Tree of Plenty."

9. The Jewel Kaustubha (Libra).

---

[1] Translated by Max Müller, "Rig Veda," iii. 8.
[2] Cited by Mrs. Manning from Kattra Upanishad "A. Ind." i. 138.

10. " Rahu the Asura," beheaded by the quoit of Narâyaṇa (Scorpio).

11. "Immortal Indra" (Sagittarius) who pierces the cloud with his lightning.

12. "In the mean time Airâvâta, a mighty elephant, arose, now kept by the god of thunder. And as they continued to churn the ocean more than enough, that deadly poison (the elephant) issued from its bed burning like a raging fire, whose dreadful fumes in a moment spread through the world, confounding the three regions of the universe with its mortal stench, until Śiva, at the word of Brahma, swallowed the fatal drug to save mankind, which drug remaining in the throat of that sovereign Deva of magic form, from that time he hath been called Nilkanta, because his throat was stained blue."

As early as the date of the Sanchi tope the sign for Capricorn was an elephant sticking in the throat of a makara or leviathan. This is, of course, the same story as Hanumân and the Nâga.

The career of the sun-god begins, as I have shown, at the last octave of February, the feast of the Black Durgâ. As the symbol for this month is the swastika, we have in Râma's case a quadruple birth. The horse is Agni. Agni, in the "Rig Veda," is constantly called the messenger of the gods, the medium of communication between the seen and the unseen worlds. This brings in a second piece of symbolism.

"Thou art born, majestic Child, of Heaven and of Earth. Thou hast come forth from the wood of the Aranî (fire-churn). With noise thou appearest on the breast of thy mother. Darkness and Night flee away.

"He is born majestic and wise, under the name of Vishṇu." [1]

As the Aranî, or fire-churn, was also shaped like the swastika, we get from another source the meaning of that symbol. Its two limbs, as early as the "Rig Veda," meant heaven and earth, the two mighty serpents, the father and the mother.

I wish here to notice a subtle principle of construction that seems to have been followed in framing the twelve

[1] "Rig Veda," 7. 5. 15.

Adityas. These in reality are only six. Each god of the summer half-year has his counterpart in the wintry half-year. In the instance of the black and the white Durgâ this seems patent enough. The higher Brahminism at bottom has always been an idealism and not a dualism.

ARIES. THE HORSE. AGNI.

"I honour the steed Dadhicrâs, strong and victorious.

"Praise the swift Dadhicrâs! Honour heaven and earth.

"An humble servant, I honour the great Dadhicrâs, generous, adorable, shining like Agni.

"In his ardour to attack (the Dasyous), he leads the war-chariot. With a panoply of flowers, a friend of the people he shines, beating the dust and champing his bit." [1]

The special symbol of Agni in the Hindu Pantheon is the horse. The following passage, from the "Satapatha Brâhmana," describes him under eight different aspects, Rudra, Isama, etc. I give the opening verses.

"The Lord of Beings was a householder and Ushas was his wife. Now these 'beings' were the seasons. That Lord of Beings was the year. That wife Ushas was the daughter of the Dawn. Then both these beings and that Lord of Beings, the year, impregnated Ushas and a boy (Agni) was born." [2]

In this passage we plainly see that the young sun-god, or year, Agni is the daughter of Ushas, our Black Durgâ. He opens the year in Aries, and has a complicated quaternity of seasons for a father like Râma, and, as I shall show, the five sons of Pânda. The passage of the year was imaged as the flight of a horse round the world. Hence the horse sacrifice. A selected horse was cast loose like the scapegoat of the Jews. For an entire year he roamed free, and then was sacrificed with great pomp.

Another Vedic hymn explains the wings—

"Thine arms, O shining god, are like the wings of the sparrowhawk. O horse, thy birth is noble and worthy of our praise." [3]

[1] "Rig Veda," 3. 7. 6 ; portions of hymns 6, 7, 8.
[2] "Satapatha Brahm.," 6. 1. 3. 8.   [3] "Rig Veda," ii. 3. 6.

The wings of the horse are the flames, the wings of the heavenly bird, the doves of Agni, as one hymn calls them. On the other side of the zodiac, Agni is Garuḍa, the divine spirit, as I shall show.

This explains the first stage of Râma's life. He is the year born from the ichor of the horse sacrifice,

Fig. 22.

the dead year. I copy a winged horse from Buddha Gaya (Fig. 22).

THE BULL.

That there are in reality only six year-gods, each figuring in the wintry half-year as well as the six months of summer, might be inferred from the Bull alone.

Vriha, the Bull. Root word, *vrish*, to rain. Whence also Vritra, the Scorpio, as I shall show, of the " Rig Veda."

"*Rudra*, one who roars. The name of Śiva as the god of the tempests." Thus Benfey in his " Sanskrit Dictionary."

Rudra in the summer half-year roars like a bull. In the wintry half-year he roars like the terrible Indian tempest. In the one he is Taurus, in the other Scorpio. In the " Rig Veda" the demon Vritra is being constantly slaughtered by the arrow of Indra (Sagittarius). The modern Vritra figures as the terrible Bhairava. This last was an avatâra of Śiva, as the god of cruelty. He wears his terrible chaplet of skulls, and rides upon the bull Nandi. " Let us invoke the terrible Rudra with the Maruts "[1] (winds). Human sacrifices were offered to Rudra at the date of the Mahâbhârata.

In the " Rig Veda " Vritra is always represented as having carried away the cows or clouds to his cavern (the wintry half-year). He is constantly being called a thief, like Rudra the Prowler, the Lord of Woods, the Lord of Thieves. In the epics the evil principle, the villain of the story, as moderns would say, has always an excessive number of limbs, like Ravaṇa. The noisome insect that, like Rudra, "assails with

[1] " Rig Veda," x. 126. 5.

poison," and has, moreover, a superfluity of eyes and legs, was a fit emblem for Nature under her most unbenign aspect. In the East, scorpions are sometimes a foot long, and their sting fatal.

But in the summer half-year he is the fructifying shower—

"May the fruitful cows with their tongues caress the plants. May they drink those waters which give strength and life. Rudra, spare these moving creatures which give us our food!

"These cows who give up their bodies to the devas. Soma knows their forms. Bring them, Indra, to our pasturage. Let them give us their milk. For us let them become fruitful."

The bull in Râma's life is the demon killed in the " Grove of Perfection."

GEMINI.

The great Indian festival of the Twins, represented in India by a too homely word, means nature procreative. It is the festival of the waters, when from the days of Râma to the days of Lord Dufferin, young maidens pelt each other with red water and broad mirth ; and they dance round the Indian maypole, the tree of the Holi. The red water represents nature's fecund juices. The rice buried in the earth is now to be fertilized by the rains. The festival is the Indian Olympia, where Buddha and Râma win a bride by their athletic prowess. At midnight, Sagittarius, the celestial bow, is shining.

The pair, Aditî and Daksha, matter and spirit, the male and female symbol, are they not the keystone of the old religions. They represent procreation, life, summer ; and opposite to them in the zodiac is the wintry arrow of death.

"Of these two gods, which is the oldest? Which is the youngest? How were they born? O poets, who can tell? They carry the world whilst Day and Night roll along like two wheels.

"Calm and motionless, they contain beings endowed with activity and life. As parents protect a beloved child, preserve us, O Heaven and Earth, from evil.

"Sisters, always young and complete counterparts, they follow each other by their parents, and gliding through the centre of the universe. O Heaven and Earth, deliver us from evil.

"I invoke in the sacrifice imploring the aid of the gods these two mothers, colossal, solid, beautiful, containing immortality. Heaven and Earth, deliver us from evil. . . . Heaven and Earth, our father and mother, grant to us the favour which we ask of thee."[1]

In this hymn they are two sisters, and also husband and wife. In the following they are male twins, and also inferentially husband and wife. Sex is of small account in stars. "They (the Ribhus, or ancient prophets) have constructed for the truth-loving Aswins (the Indian Twins) a car of good omen that glides round the world. They have produced the cow that gives milk.

"The Ribhus, powerful by their prayers and justice, have restored youth to their father and mother."[2]

I will now quote some other passages that throw light upon the subject.

"Two mothers of different colours, rapid in motion, give birth each to a babe. From the womb of one is born Hari (the Blue One), honoured by libations. From the womb of the other is born Sukra (the Shining One), with the dazzling flame."[3]

"I invoke Night which covers the universe. I demand the succour of the divine Savitri. Divine Savitri returning to us with his dark face establishes every one in his right place, gods and mortals. . . . He will follow two roads, the one ascending and the other descending (during the night). . . . His black horses step out with their white feet. And on the chariot with the golden wheels they bring light to men. The noble god called the Asura (Rayless One) rises by imperceptible movement, and comes, wing borne, to reveal himself in the sky. Where in this minute is the sun?[4] What regions are lit up with his rays?"[5]

---

[1] "Rig Veda," v. 2.   [2] Ibid., ii. 1. 34.   [3] Ibid., vii. 1. 1.
[4] At the moment of the Hindoo sacrifice, just before sunrise.
[5] Ibid., iii. 2.

"Beneficent Aswins, the same immortal chariot bears ye across the ocean (of their air).

"Of this chariot one wheel touches the unscaleable mountain, the other rolls along the sky." [1]

"Travellers, to form the light you drive along the sky one of the shining wheels of your car. The other also rolls grandly across the worlds that belong to the children of Night." [2]

"Aswins, we invoke to-day your swift and mighty chariot . . . . which on its seat transports the daughter of the sun." [3]

These passages tell us pretty plainly all we want to know about the Aswins. As Yasca and the scholiast assure us, they are plainly the father and mother, the positive and negative principles. Savitri, the sun-god, has two roads, the ascending and descending nodes of the ecliptic. In the summer he is Sukra, the Shining One. In the winter he is the Asura.

CANCER. LEO. VIRGO.

The signs Cancer, Leo, Virgo, and the Balance, are closely connected. The wicked queen of the material world and the crooked slave (perhaps Cancer) drive Râma to spiritual life under the mystical tree that in Buddhism has the lion throne at its base and the pearl Mani, also imaged as the bird Garuda, in its branches. This is why that bird watches over Sîtâ. Sîtâ marching round the tree is Virgo in her double aspect. We have reached the "Black Gate" of the Buddhists that separates the earth life from the heavenly life. It is the Indian gate crested with the bird Garuda. Sîtâ (a furrow), as her name implies, is the Indian Ceres; and in the Dekhan Peshwa and all his followers move out into camp on the twelfth day of her festival, the Dasara, as it is called by the Marathas. Sir John Malcolm describes the ceremonies. Elephants and cannon and sepoys and nobles are all dressed and decked out in gala array. The whole population moves in solemn procession towards the Holy Tree, the object of

[1] "Rig Veda," ii. 11. 18. 19.   [2] Ibid., iv. 11. 3.
[3] Ibid., vii. 12. 1.

adoration. The Peshwa in person plucks a few leaves from it, after the Brahmins have gone through the prescribed sacrifices and prayers. Cannon and muskets are discharged, and bows shot off; and the whole population, headed by the Peshwa, decorate themselves with stalks of jowri, or the rice stalk. Sîtâ is, of course, the earth, and Râma the rice. Our sepoys in the old days used to make Sîtâ's festival their great holiday. I saw on the drill ground of Dinapore two colossal wicker giants, built up to represent Râvaṇa and Kumbhakarna. Then the sepoys, disguised as demons and as the monkeys of the army of Hanumân, executed a pantomime in which many a sounding stroke was delivered. The giants, stuffed with crackers, were then exploded with a loud noise.

Assisted by the missionary Ward's excellent "History of the Hindoos," let us consider the great festival of Durgâ, or the full-grown tree. It took place at the same period of the year that the great Eleusinian mysteries were celebrated. They also had the Sacred Way to the Fig Tree. Durgâ is Ceres. Durgâ is Aditî. The Great Mother has seen many rivals contest her throne, Indra, Vishṇu, Śiva, Allah, etc. She has seen many creeds wax and wane. She preceded them by many centuries, and has eclipsed them all. Her festival, with Vaishṇavas, as well as with the worshippers of Śiva, is still the great religious feast of the year. One of her names is Vana-devi, the goddess of forests.[1]

The festival of Durgâ is the great holiday of the year. All business is suspended for many days. Poor and rich devote themselves to piety and pleasure. One of the most important early ceremonies is the consecration of the image of the goddess. The officiating Brahmin has to give eyes and life to it. With the two forefingers of his right hand he touches the breast, the two cheeks, the eyes, and the forehead of the image. He says, "Let the soul of Durgâ long continue in happiness in this image!" He then takes a leaf of the vilwa tree, rubs it with clarified butter, and holds it over a burning lamp until it is covered with soot. With

---

[1] Ward, vol. ii. 115.

this soot he touches the eyes, filling up with soot a small white place left in the pupil of the eye. This ceremony is called chakshûr dâna. Giving eyes to the idol, with all early religions, meant divine obsession. In the days of Râma the representation of a god was a shapeless stone. Stones, especially the Shâlagrâma, are still worshipped by the Brahmins of India.[1]

Proceeding with his worship, the officiating priest now throws himself into the mystic trance (dhyâna).[2] He becomes, in fact, full of the divine spirit, like a Quaker at a meeting-house. He places a tiny square piece of gold for the goddess to sit upon. He offers rice, plantains, flowers, and leaves. For a drink-offering the soma wine is presented, or aromatic water, the flavouring medium of which is usually the sesamum Indicum. Handbells ring, gongs sound, incense rises. The priest says, "O goddess, come here, stay here. Take up thine abode here and receive my worship!"[3] He then addresses her as if she were now occupying the tiny piece of gold as a seat. He asks her if she has arrived happily. A voice from the priest's throat, supposed to be the goddess, makes reply, "Very happily!" Water to bathe her feet, water to wash her mouth, water for a bath, clothes, jewels, arm bangles, ankle bangles, nose rings, earrings, even coins of money, are provided for her. Flowers are offered, each with a separate incantation. A lamp is lighted before the image. The Brahmin walks round her seven times.

But Durgâ is not a vegetarian. She was in existence many years before Buddha forbade flesh meat and Krishṇa confirmed his edict. Therefore, if you want her to come down and sit on a tiny golden throne, you must give her something more substantial than rice. For the bloody sacrifice, the Brahmin takes a sheep or goat and bathes it in the river. He marks its horns and forehead with red lead. He recites an incantation : "O goddess, I sacrifice this goat to thee that I may live in thy heaven to the end of ten years." He then whispers another incantation in the ear of the victim, and puts flowers and sprinkles water on its head. The

[1] Ward, vol. ii. xxxiv   [2] Ibid., p. 89.   [3] Ibid., p. 47.

instrument with which the animal is killed is also consecrated with red lead, flowers, and incantations. A blessing, in the shape of a flower, is given to the poor victim. Mr. Ward (an eye-witness) gives a graphic description of one of these animal sacrifices: " In the area were the animals devoted to the sacrifice, and also the executioner. About twenty persons were in attendance to throw the animal down and hold it to the post whilst the head was being cut off. The goats were sacrificed first, then the buffaloes, and last of all two or three rams. In order to secure the animals, ropes were fastened round their legs. They were then thrown down and the neck placed in a piece of wood fastened into the ground, and made open at the top like the space between the prongs of a fork. After the animal's neck was fastened in the wood by a peg which passed over it, the men who held it pulled forcibly at the heels, while the executioner, with a broad heavy axe, cut off the head at one blow. The heads were carried in an elevated posture by an attendant (dancing as he went), the blood running down him on all sides, into the presence of the goddess. . . . . The heads and blood of the animals, as well as different meat offerings, are presented with incantations as a feast to the goddess, after which clarified butter is burnt on a prepared altar of sand. Never did I see men enter so eagerly into the shedding of blood, nor do I think any butchers could slaughter animals more expertly. The place literally swam with blood. The bleating of the animals, the numbers slain, and the ferocity of the people employed, actually made me unwell. I returned about midnight filled with horror and indignation." [1]

Durgâ is worshipped as the smiling goddess of summer in September. Indeed, Mahâ Lakshmî,[2] the great goddess of fortune, is one of her names. Her offerings are more bloody as Kâlî, or the black half-year. A native told our good missionary that he had sacrificed as many as 108 buffaloes to her. Mr. Ward records also that 65,535 animals were butchered at one feast by the father of the then reigning King of Nadîya.

Similar ceremonies take place all through the festival.

[1] Ward, vol. ii. p. 123, also p. 90. [2] Ibid., p. 115.

Each day, the goddess, during her supposed visit to earth, is fed, washed, etc. Each day, dancing girls go through certain sedate pantomimic gestures in her presence. They raise their hands. They turn slowly round. They bow gracefully to the goddess from time to time, according to the cadences of the rude native music. Mr. Ward and the old missionaries used to pronounce their dances very indecent; modern Anglo-Indians cannot see why. All rites, no doubt, in old days signified the mystic marriage of spirit and matter. Other dances in this feast, of a Bacchic type, are performed by naked men smeared with the bloody mud of the sacrifice ground, and lashed into a mystic frenzy with spirits and bhang. On the last day of the festival, the goddess is shipped on board two boats lashed together and manned with musicians, singers, and naked male dancers. The priest addresses her—

"O goddess, I have to the best of my ability worshipped thee. Now go to thy residence, leaving this blessing, that thou wilt return the next year."

The tinsel idol of the goddess is then drowned in the sacred Ganges.

This allows us to understand a hymn of the "Rig Veda." The half-year is addressing her rival—

"I tender that vigorous tree by means of which one kills her rival and gains a spouse.

"Strong and happy tree, fostered by dêvas (spirits), thou puttest forth thy broad leaves. Let me see my rival leave my house, and my husband be all my own.

"Great tree, I also am great, greater than all that is great, as my rival is baser than all that is base. I name her not. She is not of our race. We will speed my rival to a far-off land."[1]

In these few verses we have many epics in epitome.

THE BALANCE.

The Balance in the earliest times in India was, I feel convinced, the bird Garuda depicted like the winged sun and serpents in Egypt and Persia, as the following passage in the

[1] "Rig Veda," viii. 8. 3. 1.

" Mahâbhârata " shows :—" Carried on the back of Garuḍa, the glad serpents bathed in the clouds of Indra promptly alighted on the shores of an island."[1]   This by-and-by with the Buddhists became the maṇi or trisul outline.   (See the Scales in the old Buddhist zodiac, Plate IV. p. 119).

Fig. 23.

In the " Rig Veda," Garuḍa is Garatman.

I give from Buddha Gayâ a bas-relief of Garuḍa changing from one to the other.

I give also from the " Asiatic Researches " the maṇi changing into the scales.

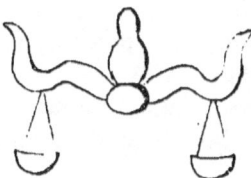

Fig. 24.

SCORPIO AND SAGITTARIUS.

Sagittarius is Indra, and the myth is that Vṛitra (Scorpio) had stolen the celestial cows (Taurus) and had hid them in a cavern (the wintry half-year).

" Maghavan [Indra] has taken the lightning, which he is about to let fly like an arrow."[2]

---

[1] " Adi Parva," v. 1305.　　　　[2] " Rig Veda," ii. 13. 3.

"Indra has struck Vṛitra, the most cloudlike of his enemies." [1]

"Surrounded by his army [the maruts, or winds], Indra has taken his quiver and his arrows. He is the Arya who conducts his cows whither he will. . . . This is why thou hast smitten with thy weapon Vṛitra, the robber charged with his booty. This is why thou hast attacked him, the maruts being at hand. Under the shafts from thy bow the Sanacas have died many deaths. They have perished, those foul men who perform no sacrifices. . . .

"He has beaten in the door of that cavern where Vṛitra held the waters shut up. Indra has torn to pieces Suchna with his horrid horns." [2]

"These waters, the celestial cows, were imprisoned by the miserly one (Pani). They had become the wives of a vile enemy." [3]

The rainbow is called Indra Dhanus (the bow of Indra).

It is worthy of remark that the upanishads, which the "Atharva Veda" [4] calls the higher wisdom of Brahminic teaching, are constantly using this simile of the bow—

"Seizing the bow found in the upanishads, the strongest of weapons, man shall draw the arrow (of the soul) sharpened by the constant application of mind, to God." [5]

The word O.M., signifying God, is represented as the bow. The soul is the arrow, and the Supreme Being its aim. [6] Buddha is said to have attained to the state of jinendra (Indra the Conqueror) in the "Sapta Buddha Stotra." The Buddhist sign of the bow is made with the vertebræ of the fleshless mystic.

Amongst the early Christian mysteries or miracle-plays is a pretty little drama where Abraham and Ephrem are hermits in a forest. A beautiful young girl, named Mary, is entrusted to the care of the former, her uncle, who points out to her that the word Mary means the star of the sea. It is ever aloft in the sky as a guide to mariners. This means that it

---

[1] "Rig Veda," ii. 13. 5.   [2] Ibid., iii. portions of hymn 1.
[3] Ibid., 13. 11.   [4] "Rammohun Roy," trans. p. 28.
[5] "Mundaka Upanishad," cited p. 34.   [6] Ibid.

never sinks into the contaminating earth, as do the other stars, at least in appearance. Therefore Mary must mean chastity. A small hermitage is constructed for the young girl ; but one day it is found empty. Abraham is in consternation, for he has had a terrible dream. A beautiful white dove was attacked by a serpent, and slain and eaten. The dove, of course, is the pure white soul of Mary. Ephrem is also in great straits ; but Abraham has been consoled by a second vision. Again the white dove was seen, but this time the serpent lay dead beside it. Abraham, in disguise, goes off in quest of Mary, and by-and-by discovers her at a house of infamy. His gentleness wins her to penitence, and she returns with him to the hermitage. Here we have all the ancient mysteries of the world in epitome. Far from being meaningless, as some modern writers contest, they were designed to inculcate a truth, the highest that man is capable of receiving. This was that it is impossible to know God without an experience of the non-god. It is impracticable to try to know the spiritual life without an experience of the material life. Lofty ideals must be prefaced by low ideals. All progress comes from reaction. Without the conviction of error we cannot gain knowledge. Without sin how can we gain purity and compunction? The mission of Sorrow, a name of Ceres and also of the Indian Mother, is to teach us happiness. The old mystics viewed the soul as "buried in a sepulchre," [1] the body. It had to "descend to Hades," to "be plunged in matter." [2] Hades was the wintry half-year, presided over by Rudra or Typhon. The crucial ordeal was necessary before the divine wisdom could be attained. "Men," said Ficinus, cited by T. Taylor, "were engaged in the delusion of dreams, and if they happened to die in this sleep before they were roused, they would be afflicted with similar and still sharper visions in a future state." [3]

It will be seen that in all the Indian mystery stories the progress of the mystic is from the light half-year to the dark

---

[1] "Clement of Alexandria," Strom. bk. iii.
[2] "Plotinus Ennead," 1. bk. viii.
[3] T. Taylor, "Eleusinian Mysteries," p. 13.

half-year, and that the higher presentments of divinity, Hari (the Blue One), or Vishnu, Râma, Krishna (the Black One), Kali or Krishnâ (the Black Female), Varuna and Indra, and Śiva or Rudra, are all in the black half of the zodiac, and most of them are painted blue-black, the colour of night. It means that the daylight of the material eye is the darkness of the soul. At night, heaven's own lamps glitter.

CHAPTER XXIV.

ELEUSIS.

THE sun is aglow in bright September, and a vast procession is issuing from the "Sacred Gate" at Athens. This "Sacred Gate" leads along the "Sacred Way," and the "Sacred Way" conducts over a low hill covered with oleander bushes to the little town of Eleusis, which sparkles on the cobalt rim of the sea at a distance of ten miles. It is the period of the Eleusinian mysteries, celebrated every four years. The copper drums sound out, and the trumpets and flutes are loud.

The crowd is immense, thirty thousand at least; all initiates. Death is the penalty of appearing in the procession without having trodden on the Dios Kodion. The μύσται march along proud of their garlands. More proud are the ἐπόπται, those who know the aporrheta, or secret meaning of the rites. They have eaten out of the mystic "Drum." They have held the "Vase" in their hands. They have perused the secrets of the Petroma, the two tables of stone. They flaunt their white robes and bear proud myrtle on their brows. A monotonous low chant, such as we hear in Indian festivals, goes up into the balmy air, recounting the woes of the goddess whose mystic name is "Sorrow." Dancers dance. Actors play pantomimes on the car of Thespis. On goes the vast crowd to the "Sacred Fig Tree," the first solemn stage of the mystic pilgrimage.

And now, amid a louder clash of cymbals and the blare of

trumpets, comes a solemn car, preceded by chanting priests. On it is the statue of a young man cut out in the whitest Pentelica marble. His limbs are the limbs that we know later as those of Apollo, not those of the tippling Bacchus. His face is of rare beauty. In his hand is a lighted torch, and nothing else. The crowd call out his name. It is the young Bacchus, the son of Jove, he who, torch in hand, sought his mother, Proserpine, in the regions of gloom. He is the "divine child" of all mysteries, the son of spirit and matter, the awakened soul. At the date of the holy festival of the Sacred Fig Tree, he leaves the rich temple of Athens for the gloomy caverns of the rock-cut temple of Eleusis.

Sir William Jones, in the "Asiatic Researches," vol. ii. p. 132, has pointed out that the Greek Bacchus is Râma. It is recorded of him that he conquered India with an army of satyrs, beings half-men half-goats, led by Pan. These are plainly Hanumân and his monkeys, who also conquered India. Ceres is the Indian Śri. Jove, according to Max Müller, is the Sanskrit Dhyaus (Gk., Zeus), with the Sanscrit Pitar (father). May we not add that Demeter is probably Divâ Matrâ, the divine mother?

The stories of the rape of Sîtâ and the rape of Proserpine are practically the same, the two narratives supplementing each other. This latter goddess was the daughter of Jupiter and Ceres. One day, as she was gathering flowers, she was seized by Pluto and carried to his gloomy cavern. This was conveniently placed by the ancients close to the mountain in Sicily that belches subterranean flames. Her cries of agony were heard by Hecate and Helios, but the mother only heard the echo. Instantly she forsook her husband and went off in search of her daughter. Iris was despatched to bid her return to Olympus, but she refused. Soon a mighty famine began to rage, for the angry mother forbade the earth to bear fruit. In this desperate strait, Zeus commanded Pluto to restore Proserpine. The God of Darkness complied, but he gave her a pomegranate to eat to force her to return to his kingdom from time to time. It was fixed at last that for six months of the year she should dwell with

Pluto, and for six months she should visit the realms of light. During her sojourn on earth, Demeter dwelt at Eleusis, and taught the mysteries in that city.

This story, according to Clement, was told dramatically at the Eleusinian mysteries. They seem to have been more like the great pilgrimages to Chitra Kûṭa than real initiations. It was the pantomime of a pantomime of Râma's life. We hear of seven caverns of darkness and seven caverns of light, but these were probably for more serious occult training. The author of the article on the mysteries in the new "Encyclopædia Britannica" suggests that the real flashing of light was the entry to the great temple. A moonless night was selected, and the crowd stood in the gloom of the great sea. Then millions of tapers were lit, and the hill paths glittered with them. Then came the splendid interior of the temple, a vast pile, with its lights, music, statues, pantomime. Beautiful women presented Proserpine and her train as in India; and we have hints that such episodes as Baubo denudata[1] and the divine hymeneals were too faithfully rendered. Does not the missionary Ward hint the same thing of the Indian festival? There are epochs of prudery and epochs before the epochs of prudery, and rites are stubborn things.

"I have fasted. I have drunk the cyceon. I have taken out of the cista and placed that which I took into the calathus. I have taken out of the calathus and placed that which I took into the cista. The bed I have entered!"

This was the supreme formula. The calathus was a basket containing the fruits of Ceres, or earth. The cista was a chest with an egg and the Indian symbols of natural reproduction. The meaning has been variously interpreted. It meant, I think, the birth of the torch-bearing Bacchus, the spiritual man, and the substitution of immortal food—the food of Proserpine for that of Ceres—barley cakes and a mullet. The Διος κωδιον, "Jupiter's skin," was the skin of a victim— a calf. An Indian rite may throw some light on this.

The Diksha ceremony may be called a drama in which the processes of nature are reproduced. The candidate is

---

[1] "Eleusinian and Bacchic Mysteries," by T. Taylor, p. 16.

smeared with water and butter, and placed in a spot that represents the mother's womb. They cover him with a cloth which represents the caul. Outside the cloth is wrapped an antelope's skin (the placenta). The initiates of Eleusis were enveloped in a calf's skin. The Dikshita Vimita, where the initiate lies, is probably the Pastos, the bed, the coffin of the old mysteries. In it the initiate lies with closed hands like a child in the womb. In his hands he is supposed to hold " all the deities." When the proper moment arrives he is taken out of the Dikshita Vimita, the antelope's skin, or placenta, is removed, and he is bathed.

CHAPTER XXV.

THE LEGEND OF OSIRIS.

" I AM Osiris, who led a large and numerous army as far as the deserts of India, and travelled over the greater part of the world." This old Egyptian inscription is important. The Greeks admit that they derived the story of Bacchus and the rape of Proserpine from the mysteries of Osiris ; and here again we have the conquest of India as the chief feature of a conqueror's life.

Osiris and Isis, according to Plutarch, were brother and sister. They were also husband and wife, for two stars, many millions of miles apart, can commit incest without shame. They were the twins of the zodiac, and so were Osiris and his wicked brother Typhon.

Osiris, leaving his brother in charge of his kingdom, like the Indian Râma, set out on his career of conquest. Everywhere he spread the knowledge of agriculture, and gave salutary laws. His conquering army was an army of satyrs, led by Pan. In his absence, his brother stirred up the people against him, and hatched an infamous plot. At a great feast given by the Queen of Ethiopia, Osiris was inveigled into making an attempt to get into a strange coffer that was brought into the banquet. He was then locked up in this and pitched into the Nile. Isis wandered away in search of her husband's body, and, guided by the doleful cries of the satyrs, discovered it near Byblos ; but Typhon stole it away from her and cut it into fourteen pieces. Of these pieces, Isis, by-and-by, recovered all except the genitals, and had a splendid pyramid built over each. "A temple unrivalled in the world," says Dupuis, "was erected in honour of the missing portion." This is the great pyramid, and in it is the mysterious king's chamber and the empty sarcophagus. The legend in this part is plainly framed to account for the worship of the Indian lingam. Sir W. Jones thought that the words Osiris and Isis were the Sanskrit Iswara and Isi. Other writers in the old days derived the Egyptian religion from India, notably M. Chevalier, an ex-governor of Chandernagore. Familiar with the ancient rock temples of India, he visited the similar rock temples that are to be found in Egypt, and pronounced that the similarity between them was too minute to be accounted for by any other theory than direct derivation.[1] It was held that both sets of temples must have been erected at least two thousand years before Christ.

These opinions have been altered by modern authorities. It is admitted that the rock temples of Philæ must have been erected at least two thousand years before Christ, but the similar temples in India were constructed two thousand five hundred years later.

As the mystical story of Buddha was thought by Colebrooke to be derived from the story of Râma, I will say a brief word on this, because, if we can connect thus closely Râma with the early Greek and Egyptian mysteries, the theory that the story of Buddha is derived from the Nestorian Christians falls through. Anthropology tells us that the earliest man was a cave-man. For hundreds, perhaps thousands, of years he knew nothing of agriculture, or how to clear the jungle. Like a beast, he dwelt in a natural cave and lived by hunting. His first attempt at architecture was to scrape and enlarge this natural cave.

This gives us the *raison d'être* of the rock temple. It takes the natural form of quarrying, as Mr. Gwilt has shown. And in his ignorance of the arch, man was obliged to carve his first detached temple inside a mountain, and then cut the mountain away. 'Tis thus that Mr. Gwilt accounts for the characteristics of the earlier Egyptian temples.

[1] Savary, "Lettres sur l'Egypte," ii. p. 178.

"The simplicity, not to say monotony, its extreme solidity, almost heaviness, forms its principal characters. Then the want of profile and paucity of its members, the small projection of its mouldings, the absence of apertures, the enormous diameter of the columns employed much resembling the pillars left in quarrying for support, the pyramidal form of the doors, the omission of roofs and pediments, the ignorance of the arch . . . all enable us to recur to the type from which we have set out."[1]

The colossal sphinxes and enormous obelisks were constructed also by cutting away rocks and hills. The obelisk was then moved in one solid piece. One obelisk, some 93 feet high, was brought to Karnac, a distance of 138 miles. Sculpture, too, throws its light on this early period. The earliest form of the art developed out of columns and blocks of stone. "The addition of heads," says Westmacott, "and then of feet and hands—the latter close to the sides, and the legs united like columns—formed probably the earliest attempts at giving such objects a human form."[2]

India is *par excellence* the land of cave temples, rock caverns in all stages of progress, natural caves smoothed and enlarged, temples without carving or statues, temples with plain octagonal columns, temples splendidly carved, enormous temples cut out of the mountain and detached. Also she has her stambhas or obelisks, her colossal bulls all formed by cutting away rocks and mountains; and her statues with legs united and arms glued to the side.

Such is the colossal statue at Sravana Belgula, seen by the Duke of Wellington. It is seventy feet in height, and a mountain was cut away to form it. Such are similar human statues at Karkala and Yannûr.[3] This seems to point to processes similar to those in Egypt and Greece. But here our Indian authorities step in. These dark caverns with enormous columns that take the form of quarrying, these colossal bulls cut out of a mountain, these masses of stone,

---

[1] Gwilt, " Encyclopædia of Architecture," p. 30.
[2] " Handbook of Sculpture," p. 87.
[3] Fergusson, " Indian Architecture," p. 268.

half column, half man, are not due in India to the tentative processes of the cave-man at least 2000 B.C. India first learnt to build temples in the plain about 500 B.C., to cut stone, and to carve a detached human figure as seen at Sanchi. After that, she adopted the crude art of the cavern-builder. A clever but self-opinionated architect, Mr. Fergusson, has ruled this, and all defer to him.

For principal evidence he points to the rails and gates of King Aśoka's dolmens or tumuli (Bharhut, 200 B.C. ; Buddha Gayâ, 250 B.C.). He gives elaborate drawings to show that their stone rails and gateways imitate woodwork. On this he builds up the somewhat large superstructure that India knew nothing of stone-cutting until a short time before this period, and that here we catch the art in the process of change. But I fail to see that Mr. Fergusson's inferences are warranted by his facts. The dolmen was the earliest building known to the Arya when he emerged from his cave. It was his dwelling, his tomb, his temple. With its circle of monoliths it was the Indian temple before Aśoka. The rails and gates represented the confines and gates of paradise in the rites. Nothing is so conservative as religious symbolism, and this pattern may have been settled a thousand years before Aśoka. Dr. Rajendra Lala Mitra, in his work on Orissa, has shown that the stone cutting of the pillars of Aśoka betrays not crudeness, but efflorescence. Indeed, the rails and gates of Bharhut and Sanchi remind one of the pattern of a Chinese card-case. Not an inch of marble can be found without lotuses, elephants, peacocks, winged horses. That Indian artists should have returned from such overdone efflorescence to a severe rock temple with no carving at all save one gigantic stone canopy for a high altar is inconceivable.

Most of the rock temples exhibit figures of Buddha. This perhaps, has chiefly produced the idea that they are modern, One or two points suggest themselves which make me think too much has been made of this.

1. The figure of Buddha, a naked man with woolly hair, is quite different from the Buddha of the early topes. Major Keith tells me that it is unknown at Sanchi.

2. These rock temples, said to be Buddhist, are far, far away from the Buddhist holy land. No such temples have been erected in any of the hilly country in the chief centres of the cultus.

3. The Brahmins assert that they erected these temples, and that the Buddhists took them over. They say that the figure presumed to be Buddha is Parisnâth.

4. The most conspicuous figures in some of the Buddhist topes are Brahmin gods.

5. Another important point remains.

Mr. Mackenzie gives from Lassen's "Indische Alterthum skunde" an account of the Indian initiation in the mysteries. It has this advantage, that it is written by a Freemason to show how close a likeness there is between the Indian initiation and that of Freemasons.[1]

At eight years of age, the child girded on the sacred cord. For the "Fellow-craft degree of the Mason," as Mr. Mackenzie calls it, the disciple "was led into a gloomy cavern in which the aporrheta were to be displayed to him. Here a striking similarity to the Masonic system may be found." Three chief officers or hierophants "are seated in the east, west, and south, attended by their respective subordinates. After an invocation to the sun, an oath was demanded of the aspirant to the effect of implicit obedience to superiors, purity of body, and inviolable secrecy. Water was then sprinkled over him, he was deprived of his sandals or shoes, and was made to circumambulate the cavern thrice with the sun. Suitable addresses were then made to him, after which he was conducted through seven ranges of caverns in utter darkness, and the lamentations of Mahâdevi, or the great goddess, for the loss of Śiva, similar to the wailings of Isis for Osiris, were imitated. After a number of impressive ceremonies, the initiate was suddenly admitted into an apartment of dazzling light, redolent with perfume and radiant with all the gorgeous beauty of the Indian clime, alike in flowers, perfumes, and gems. This represented the Hindu paradise, the acme of all earthly bliss. This was supposed to constitute the regenera-

[1] "Royal Masonic Cyclopædia," *sub voce* "Mysteries of Hindostan."

tion of the candidate, and he was now invested with the white robe and the tiara. A peculiar cross was marked on his forehead and the Tau cross on his breast; upon which he was instructed in the peculiar signs, tokens, and doctrines of his order. He was presented with the sacred girdle, the magical black stone, the talismanic jewel for his breast, and the serpent stone which guaranteed him from the effects of poison. Finally, he was given the sacred word, A.U.M."

To obtain the third degree, it was necessary to practise tapas in a forest. In the "fourth degree, the Brahmin was, by peculiar ceremonies, conjoined with the divinity."

It is plain that we have the seven dark and the seven light caverns of the mysteries of Ceres, and the question is, From what country did this idea come? The great temple of Eleusis was apparently a great cave temple, but it was solitary. "Egypt proper," says Mr. Fergusson, "has no rock-cut temples, only sepulchres." The rock-cut temples are in Nubia. In the west of India, on the other hand, there are cave temples innumerable.

It is to be observed also that these temples, though they were taken over by the Buddhists, were not pre-eminently fitted for Buddhist rites. Mr. Fergusson calls many of the caverns viháras or monasteries, and the side chapels or caverns cells for the monks. Each sanctuary has usually a number of these, seven on one side and seven on the other. These would do admirably for the caverns of initiation, but they are not at all like the cells of monks as described in Buddhist scriptures. A large convent had some ten thousand monks, and these were usually lodged in little huts of boughs.

To go back to Osiris, I must here point out, that whilst the stories of Buddha and Ráma fit in exactly with the zodiacal career of the mystic working-up through six stages of animal life to the mystical portal, the new birth in the womb of the Virgin with the Lion and the Fire Dove, the story of Osiris, misfits it completely. This is due to the fact that the Egyptian festivals were based on agriculture by the aid of the Nile inundation. This event takes place about June 30th. Then comes the sowing about the middle of October, when the waters have subsided. The harvest is in April, the great festival of Isis or agriculture, and this festival is described by Greek writers as having been like their festivals of Ceres, with lamentations and lights, instead of flowers and joy for the new year. Then came the festival of the Nile ; and when the mystic should be opposing Scorpio with the bow of Indra, the sowing festival took place.

To sum up, the stories of Râma, Osiris, and Bacchus, reveal the same mysteries. All three conquered *India* with an army of animals ; the pure totemism of the Indian story giving it priority. The zodiacal framework fits in exactly with the Indian rice culture, and the life of the Indian mystic. It misfits on all points corn culture by the inundation of the Nile. Its main features are in the hymns of the " Rig Veda," the earliest surviving hymns of the world ; hymns to the horse, to the bull, to the twins ; hymns to the mystic mother, the tree, and the fire dove ; hymns detailing the great battle of the mystic with the roaring storm-cloud, a feature unknown in Egypt at all. The cows shut up by the god of winter for six months in the cavern may point to the experience of the poor Aryan cave-man in his cavern on the steeps of Hindu Kush or Cashmere.

Also in the zodiacal framework of each story much illustrates and explains the others. The Indian feast of the Tree is the half-way house in the life of the mystic ; the feast of the Greater Mysteries at Eleusis. At this period we have the rape of Sîtâ, the rape of Proserpine, Osiris shut up in his box, incidents which the Greek story confesses to symbolize the entry to Hades, imaged as the six wintry months. At that period the mystic forsakes his animal life for his battle with the demoniacal host—a battle to terminate only under the sign chakra, the terrible discus that Râma finally flings at Râvana, the swastika, the only cross in the catacombs. *In hoc signo vinces.*

Another point is of the highest importance. We now know how the Indian seeks to gain psychic powers. The process is simply by the will-power of the yogi developed patiently in solitude. All concomitants, magic stars and talismans, food offerings and scent offerings to spirits, are nonessential, although perhaps the complete discernment of this truth may be due to Mesmer or some other modern investigator. The story of Râma is the simple story of a mystic practising yoga under a tree. The battles and sieges are mere symbol, and in the Buddhist version—for the Buddhists have made Râma an avatâra of Buddha—are omitted. The pilgrimage to Chitra Kûṭa is not yoga, but the histrionics of yoga. It stands to reason that thirty thousand people spending a week in visiting holy fig-trees, holy ghauts, the successive spots where Râma developed his powers, would not be thirty thousand adepts at the end of the week, although it might be argued that the pilgrimage was an institution useful in suggesting, and also in concealing psychic knowledge. Now at Eleusis we get not yoga, but simply the pilgrimage presentment of yoga. The mystics go to the fig-tree as a sight; Râma sits under it for fifteen years. The Temple of Eleusis is said to have been built 1330 years before Christ, This gives a very early date to Râma, if he suggested the mysteries to Egypt as well as Greece. The worship of Râma survives, although its pedigree may be so stupendous. In 1882, the Indian government, in collecting cholera statistics, discovered that three millions of pilgrims visited Allahabad for one festival in that year. More strange still is the fact that, although India throws such curious light on the distant past, no one hardly cares for these Indian subjects at all.

THE INITIATION OF THE NOVICE UTANKA.

I will here give an episode from the "Mahâbhârata." It gives the initiation of a simple ascetic, without the usual account of the conquest of evil propensities in the guise of mailed warriors. Utanka was a young Brahmin, dwelling in the forest with a guru, or spiritual guide, named Veda. The novice on these occasions has to choose a sort of patron god, like Râma or Krishṇa. He must then conceive his guru as an incarnation of the god, and perform the most menial offices to him. He must wash his feet and drink some of the water afterwards. He must offer him flowers and treat him as God Almighty walking on the earth.

One day, a king visited Veda and made him Archbráhmin of the palace. Veda left Utanka in charge of the hermitage and departed. Whilst he was away, the wives of the guru each tempted him as Joseph was tempted by Potiphar's wife. In the same way, the pretty daughters of Mâra try and distract the tapas of Buddha, and the phantom of Kotavî, the naked woman, tries to thwart Kṛishṇa. This ever-recurring incident in the great ordeal of the mystic may have been only psychological, as in the case of St. Augustine. When extasia supervenes it is well known that its visions often appeal thus grossly to the senses. But I cannot help thinking that when the great trial of the mystic became formalized into a scenic pantomime, this temptation by women was a prominent feature. Arjuna, in one episode of the "Mahâbhârata," is tempted in Indra's heaven by a beautiful Apsarasa. The woman in each case is man's lower nature.

By-and-by Veda returns, and somehow discovers that his pupil has resisted temptation. He praises Utanka, and offers to put a term to his noviciate. Utanka is very happy with his guru, and asks leave to remain with him. Veda consents for a season.

The higher initiation is introduced in this form. Veda orders his pupil to go and demand the earrings of the queen. As Libra in the account of the churning of the ocean is called the "Earrings of Aditî," the meaning of this is not far to seek.

" If you get them," says the guru, " you will gain supreme happiness. In what other way can you get it ? "

Utanka departs for the palace. On his way he meets a gigantic being mounted on a colossal bull.

" Eat the dung of this beast, Utanka, and drink its urine," said the giant.

" I cannot," replied the novice.

" Your master, Veda, once did the same thing."

This unsavoury initiation is still practised by Brahmins and the followers of Zarathustra.

Utanka obeys. He then pursues his path and reaches the palace.

"Give me, O king," he says, "the earrings of the queen, as a present to my guru."

" Enter the women's apartments, O holy man," replied the king, "and ask her yourself."

Utanka enters the harem and searches everywhere. He cannot find the queen.

" You have eaten flesh-meat, and your body is not pure," says the king in explanation. " That is why she is not visible."

Utanka went out to perform the ceremonial of purification. He sate down on the ground facing the east. He washed his mouth, his feet, his hands. He drank three gulps of pure water. He returned to the queen's apartment. This time the queen was visible.

" What are thy commands, O holy man ? "

" My master desires the queen's earrings," said the novice.

" He is a worthy Brahmin," said the queen graciously, " I cannot disoblige him." But in giving them, she cautioned him to beware of the serpent Takshaka. This serpent had a great desire to get the queen's earrings.

Utanka returned home overjoyed with his new possession. Passing near a holy tank he thought it right to purify himself. A naked Brahmin was near, who apparently possessed great powers of yoga or magic, for he appeared and disappeared in a most marvellous manner. Utanka plunged into the water. The Brahmin seized the earrings and fled. It was the wily serpent Takshaka in disguise.

Utanka sprung out of the water and pursued him. At the very moment that he was being overtaken, the Brahmin changed his form and became a serpent. Deftly he glided into a chasm in the earth.

The chasm was a very narrow one. Utanka tried to enlarge it with his staff, but was baffled. Indra on his throne witnessed his discomfiture, and sent his celebrated thunderbolt to open up the gap. Utanka descended into a cavern. There he saw the palaces and towers of Kuru Kshetra, the subterranean city of the serpents. The mystic earrings of Aditi (the purity of Utanka's soul) were not to be recovered easily. In their quest he has time to take note of the marvels of the mystic cavern. He sees two women weaving a veil, the one with white and the other with black threads. He sees a wheel with twelve spokes. He sees a man and a horse. He sings the following hymn :—

"Three hundred and sixty rays spring from the nave of this eternal wheel. Its movement is everlasting. To it are joined twenty-four lunar fortnights. Six youths [the six seasons] turn it for ever.

"This woof is woven by two women, who have the forms of the universe. They weave for ever with black threads and white. Adoration to the god who holds the thunderbolt, to the slaughterer of Vṛitra, who wears a blue garment, and has Agni for a charger!"

The man on the horse hearing this hymn, says to Utanka, "I am pleased with your praise. I will grant you a boon."

"Be pleased to make the serpents pass under my power," says the novice.

"Blow under the crupper of my horse," says the man.

Utanka obeys, and at once the snake palaces are over-whelmed with terrific fire and smoke. Takshaka, in consternation, offers the earrings to the novice.

"Mount this horse," says the man.

Utanka obeys, and is transported to the hut of his guru.

That holy man explains to him the significance of the sights he has seen. The man on the bull is Indra. The cow dung is the immortal ichor. The man on the horse is Indra also ; and the horse Agni. The wheel with the twelve spokes is the year. The two women are Dhatâ and Vidhatâ ; the white threads days, and the black threads nights. He might have added that the cave is the pastos, the coffin, the dark half-year. It is the "Cave of Indra," of all Indian initiations, even the Buddhist. Takshaka, man's lower nature, is subdued by the flaming Garuḍa, the dove of the Kabbalists, the baptism of fire. To subject the serpent is the secret of all magic, says the Abbé Alphonse Louis Constant.

I will here say a word about the secrets of the so-called "Theosophy." Some time back I earned considerable opprobrium from its votaries, by questioning the existence of Koot

Hoomi, but I think it can be shown that his existence is more prejudicial to Theosophy, viewed as a school of mysticism, than his non-existence.

In the year 1872, Madame Blavatsky earned her bread as a professional "medium." From a box, called a "cabinet," she could cause to issue a form with a beard and turban, the spirit, she affirmed, of a pirate who died more than two hundred years ago. In the year 1883, we find her at Adyar, in Madras. Again she has a box, which she calls this time a "shrine." Again a figure emerges with beard and turban. This time it is announced to be a "Buddhist" from Tibet, who some years back instructed Madame Blavatsky in the secrets of Esoteric Buddhism. She lived in Tibet for seven years under his roof. But she failed to notice in all these years that the Buddhist monks of Tibet do not wear long hair, but shave their heads. She failed also to remark that in climates like Lha Sa turbans are as little necessary as a parasol to a Greenlander. She failed also to notice that the language of Tibet is Tibetan, and not Chinese. She tells us in "Isis Unveiled," vol. ii. p. 59, that in Tibet Buddha, Dharma, and Sangha, are called "Fo, Fa, and Sengh." Our exoteric scholars tell us that Buddha is called Bchom-dan-hdas-Sangs-r-gyas, and Dharma and Sangha, T. Tchos and d Ge hdun.

An interesting report has just been published by the Psychical Research Society (December, 1885). They sent out to India a gentleman named Hodgson to investigate certain very damaging revelations put forward by a Madame Coulomb and her husband, confederates of Madame Blavatsky. In this report, we see that "Tibet" was Madame Blavatsky's well-curtained bed-chamber at Adyar. This through a pierced wall and sliding panels furtively communicated with the interior of the "shrine." And through this "Esoteric" passage all the "Buddhism" was pushed. The letters of Koot Hoomi have been examined by Messrs. Netherclift and Sims, and pronounced to be all in the handwriting of Madame Blavatsky, the early ones unskilfully, the later ones skilfully disguised. The matter was plagiarized wholesale from a lecture on spiritualism, by Professor Kiddle, in America, and from a French book of magic, by Eliphas Lévi, a dash of Orientalism having been added from notes furnished by a somewhat illogical Brahmin, named Mr. Subba Row,[1] From this same "Tibet" issued the "astral form" of the Mahâtma, seen by Mr. Sinnett, Mohini, and others. It was Mons. Coulomb, with false beard, turban, shoulders and mask, made up like the picture of the Mahâtma within the "shrine." This picture was painted in America for Madame Blavatsky, who wanted an "ideal Hindoo." It was scarcely necessary for Mr. Edwin Arnold, in his recent visit to Ceylon, to get from the Buddhist high priest there a categorical statement that there were no Mahâtmas in Tibet. More noteworthy is the statement that the atheism and nihilism of "Esoteric Buddhism" were unknown to him.

I have said that the existence of Koot Hoomi is more prejudicial to theosophy than his non-existence. The object of Indian mysticism was to bridge the worlds of matter and spirit, and pilot the novice through the demoniac host which were believed to infest the mystic portals. This was to be effected, as in the case of Utanka, under the supervision of a flesh and blood guru. It was held that man's usefulness on earth could be thus inconceivably increased, for all knowledge of God must come from within, not from without.

Theosophy proclaims the direct opposite of all this. It says that, owing to the danger from evil spirits, all yoga must be practised under the guidance of an adept in his "astral form." These adepts, owing to the gross aura of India are obliged to reside in Tibet. But how is this in any way union with the next world? Koot Hoomi is a mortal. Moriah is a mortal. Their teaching is as rigid a mundane dogmatism as that of Bishop Proudie. And how can I tell that evil spirits are not personating Koot Hoomi or Moriah? The phantom form of this last gentleman, conjured up from the "ideal Hindoo" of the American artist, is said to have appeared to many "Theosophists" in visions of the night. His gospel is a jumble of contradictions changed every day. Supposing

---

[1] See "Report Psyc. Res. Soc.," p. 274.

after a long course of asceticism I see this vision, how can I tell that it is not an evil spirit personating the holy man? Also, how can I tell which gospel I am to pick out of his basket?

THE STORY OF HIRAM ABIF.

Has any one ever puzzled over the fact that the only modern representatives of the initiates of the ancient mysteries should occupy themselves entirely with the practical business of the hodman and the builder. What is the connection between the mysteries of the kingdom of heaven and matter-of-fact mortar, **T** squares, trowels? Mr. H. Melville, a Royal Arch Mason, in a work entitled "Veritas," has given us an answer to this question. Esoteric masonry occupied itself in reality with a temple built without any sound of hammer, axe, or tool of iron.[1] It was the temple in the skies, the Macro Kosmos in point of fact. And the true mason was seeking to construct the micro cosmos, the temple of the soul.

"According to the grace of God, which is given unto me as a wise *master-builder*, I have laid the foundation."[2] It has been deduced from this passage that St. Paul was an initiate of these rites. Masonry has its fellow-craft mason and its royal arch.

Modern researches are suggesting, as it seems to me, another point of contact between the trade of the builder and the trade of the astro-mystic. This even Mr. Melville has failed to see. The earliest astronomical instruments were the square, the level, the compass, the rule. By their aid a temple was oriented. This meant that important feast days, the periods of the sowing and reaping, could be thus accurately told by the stars.

Recent writers have shown how much the Pleiades had to do with ancient rites and feasts. In Hesiod's day, corn was cut "when the Pleiades rise," and ploughing commenced when the Pleiades set.[3] These two periods were the occasion of the two great festivals of the old world.[4] The first observatory was

---

[1] 1 Kings vi. 7.　　　　　[2] 1 Cor. iii. 10.
[3] J. F. Blake, "Astronomical Myths," p. 120.　　　　[4] Ibid, 115.

the temple of standing stones astronomically arranged. The dolmen, with its chamber of rough stones, is thought to be the first building of the cave-man in the plain. It imitates cave architecture.

The primitive astronomy of the Chinese was able to obtain the solstitial and equinoctial points at the solstices by fixing on a horizontal platform a rule marking the point of sunrise, and another at night marking the point of sunset. A mean taken between these two lines would give the meridian. But to get the two other cardinal points was the difficulty. Hence the importance of **T** squares, plummets, masonry secrets. The early priest was scientist as well as theologian, and the twelve unhewn stones an observatory.

The story of Hiram Abif need not detain us long. He was the master-builder of Solomon's temple. It is recorded that three apprentices murdered him because he would not disclose the lost word. Hiram made three efforts to escape. He ran to the eastern gate of the temple and found himself confronted by an assassin. It will be recollected that Buddha made his first effort to escape from the material pleasures of the palace of summer by the eastern gate, and that he was there arrested by the old man. The second and third journeys of Hiram were from west to south and south to west, each arrested by an assassin. Buddha's journeys were by the southern and western gates, during which he encountered the sick man and the corpse. Hiram was then slaughtered, and the body was carried out by the northern gate and buried. The conspirators had at first been fifteen. Twelve had repented, and much of the ritual of masonry goes on the discovery of the body by these twelve craft masons. A sprig betrayed the secret, and they planted a sprig of acacia at the grave whilst they hurried away to inform King Solomon. That king had a sumptuous tomb prepared for the body as near the holy of holies in the temple as was permissible by Jewish law.

Masonry is plainly a Jewish version of the mysteries, with Buddhism and Osiris worship superadded. It is, I think, an echo of the Therapeut secrecy and precautions. The entered apprentice, even in England, is stripped of his sovereigns, breast-pin, and watch. His eyes are blinded, and certain formalities which menace "stabbing and strangling" are gone through. Vows of secrecy, fidelity, and obedience are enacted —obedience which must extend, if required, to the sacrifice of a son like that of Abraham. All this is Buddhist, although the gold and money is promptly returned, and marquesses and royal dukes are told that the vows of obedience will never be stretched so far as to force them to compass the overthrow of the House of Lords and the British Constitution. " Endow him with a competency of Thy divine Wisdom " is a portion of a prayer offered up, and it is explained to the aspirant that knowledge of self is the prime desideratum. "The light of a Master-Mason is darkness visible." [1] All these are profound mystical truths.

The imaginary temple of Solomon has a royal arch made by two columns, Jachin and Boaz. Through this the fellow-craft mason must pass to become a master. Here we have another form of the Indian mysteries—the zodiac divided into Jachin and Boaz, the black and white halves, at the feast of the Tree. The candidate pretends to fall dead to imitate Hiram's death, in England, but in some lodges he is placed in a tomb with a tree by it.

In England, masonry is thought to be an unmeaning farce. Abroad, by clericals and republicans alike, masonry in its various forms is pronounced the most formidable force in Europe. Lord Beaconsfield declared that the secret societies and the papacy were the only two institutions endowed with permanency. It was introduced by James II. during his exile in France. It was designed to prop up the Stuart. Instead, it pulled down the Bourbon ; for its main principle is the apocalyptic maxim that the individual must be made a priest and a king. The Albigenses were masonic mystics. So were the Hussites. That it produced the Reformation is the belief of all clerical writers abroad. It is asserted that the discovery of the " Kabbalah " had spread mysticism and gnosticism. The Templars, leaving Europe to attack the

---

[1] Carlile, p. 9.

Moslem, had returned with the secret tenets of the Sufis, which they again had derived from the Buddhists. In the fourteenth century, as Mons. Jannet has shown, numerous guilds and corporations existed, and mystic societies were in the heart of Catholicism. "Social order was attacked, and the legitimacy of political power, the rights of property, and the institution of the family. . . . The Albigenses borrowed their grades and organization, as well as their doctrine, from the Freemasons."[1]

In the matter of the French revolution the influence of Freemasonry was very great. Historians like Louis Blanc on the one side and the Père Deschamps are there agreed. The Baron d'Haugwitz, at the Congress of Verona, used these words: "I acquired then a firm conviction that the drama which commenced in 1788 and 1789, the French Revolution, the regicide, and all its horrors had not only been resolved in the lodges of the illuminati, but was due to the association and oaths of the Freemasons."[2] Mirabeau was sent in the year 1785 on a diplomatic mission to Prussia. There he was initiated in German illuminism. He brought the institution to France, and five hundred lodges were promptly formed. The famous lodge of Les Amis Réunis in Paris had all the chief agents of the revolution on its lists, Robespierre, Barnave, Petion, Talleyrand, etc. It was debated whether the great explosion should occur in Germany or France, and decided for the latter country.[3]

In the days of Wieshaupt and the illuminati of Germany a striking scene was enacted. The novice who had been brought in blindfolded, was shown an altar on which was a sceptre and crown, some gold pieces, and some valuable jewels. Above was a picture of the "Founder of Illuminism"—an Ecce Homo that was solemnly unveiled.

"Here are the attributes of virtue," cried the Grand Master "here are the attributes of tyranny. Choose!" It was explained to the aspirant that the masked brothers around were quite competent to push his career for him in court or

[1] C. Jannet, "Les Sociétés Secrètes," p. 51.
[2] Ibid., p. 74.　　　　[3] Ibid., p. 69.

camp. It was explained also to him that the aim of the society, "the Family of the Human Race," was very far-reaching, and exacted extremes of devotion and self-denial. It was directed against all despotism and class-privileges, secular and religious.[1]

[1] Victor Huriot, " Mystères des Sociétés Secrètes."

CHAPTER XXVI

AFTER a dispensation or Day of Brahma has continued a certain time, says the "Vishnu Purâna," the human race deteriorates. Kings despoil their subjects instead of protecting them. "Property alone confers rank. Wealth is the only source of devotion. Passion is the sole bond of union between the sexes. . . . Dishonesty is the universal means of subsistence. Fine clothes are dignity. The Brahminical thread makes the Brahmin. Presumption is substituted for learning." Treasures are sought, not at the shrines of the immortal dead, but in the bowels of the earth. But when the prospect is blackest the relief is at hand. The two first stars of the seven rishis (the Great Bear) are seen at night in the heavens with a certain lunar asterism between them, and then the star-gazers are made aware that the Deliverer is about to be born.[1] The nineteenth century should begin to watch the Great Bear.

Once upon a time the world groaned with the oppressions of a demon Kâlanemi, who was incarnate as King Kansa. In this strait, Earth repaired to Meru, and laid her complaint before Brahmâ. That god pronounced that Vishnu should be appealed to. Is it not a well-known fact that when his sacred feet have touched the earth, that globe is at peace for a hundred mystic years?[2]

The Avatâra of Krishna was in this wise. In Mathurâ (the modern Muttra) was a nobleman named Vasudeva, who had two wives, Devakî and Rohinî. Vishnu plucked two of

[1] Wilson, "Vishnu Purâna," pp. 482–487.   [2] Ibid., p. 485.

his hairs, a black one and a white one. From that black one sprang up, in the womb of Devaki, Krishna, The Black One, as his name signifies. From the white hair, in the womb of Rohini, Bala Râma (the boy Râma) was conceived. Now, the special sign of Krishna and Vishnu, is a holy emblem on the breast formed by curling hair. It is called the śrivatsa (holy breast, holy mark). I think this is plainly a later form of the swastika cross, the symbol of the commencing year. And the two hairs are the two principles— heaven and earth—the higher and the lower life— that the Nârâyana, or god-man unites.

Fig. 25.

A king of asuras, or spirits of darkness, has at his court Brahmins, soothsayers, and other holy institutions, just like a king of the spirits of light. Conspicuous at the court of King Kansa was a holy saint named Nârada. This seer, by his mystic insight, was able to discern that the son of Devaki would one day overturn King Kansa. The monarch, hearing this, was in a fury, and determined to destroy the child. He flung Devaki into a dungeon, awaiting the infant's birth. At midnight one evening the child was born. It had four arms and the mystic mark, śrivatsa, on its breast. Vasudeva begged the baby to veil his supernal "four-armed shape." He addressed him: "God of gods, who comprisest all the regions of the world in thy person!"

From this it appears that the four cardinal points were the express symbols to distinguish the universal from the anthropomorphic god.

A mystic sleep, called yoganidrâ (the magic sleep of yoga), is cast upon the jailers and warders of the great gate of Mathurâ by unseen agencies. This yoganidrâ must have been a sort of mesmeric trance. The holy infant is then carried out of the prison and the city. The dew being heavy, a portent occurred. A many-headed serpent, the mighty Śesha, spread out its hoods to shield the four-armed divinity. A similar portent occurred to Buddha. A nimbus of serpent heads is a divine symbol in all the old Hindû temples and Buddhist topes.

On this particular night, on the banks of the Yamunâ, or Jumna, was a poor cowherd, Nanda, and his wife Yaśodâ.

They were asleep on the cold ground under a waggon, after a weary journey. Nanda was bringing tribute to Kansa. Yaśodâ had just been confined. Babies were shifted, and the infant Krishna, "black as the dark leaves of the lotus," was placed by her side. In the morning, the infant of Yaśodâ was seized by the jailers and handed over to the delighted Kansa. He dashed it against a stone, but it changed into a gigantic being.

"He is born who shall kill thee!" said the apparition solemnly, and it vanished in the heavens. Kansa, alarmed, like Herod, ordered all the male children of Mathurâ to be put to death, but Krishna escaped with his putative father, Nanda. This poor cowherd dwelt at the village of Gokula.

One night, the infant had a terrible adventure. A wicked fiend, Pûtanâ, tried to suckle it with her poisonous nipples. The infant drained the life out of her. Diseases in the old days were all believed to be the work of individual fiends ; so Yaśodâ, alarmed, fenced about the little infant with many charms. She swished a cow tail over him. She placed powdered cow-dung on his head. She bound round his arm a rakshâ or amulet. It was the following inscription tied with silk :—

"May Hari from the lotus, of whose navel the world was developed, protect thee! May that Keśava, who assumed the form of a boar, protect thee. May that Keśava who, as the man-lion, rent with his sharp nails the bosom of his foe, protect thee. May Garuḍa[1] guard thy head ; Keśava thy neck ; Vishṇu thy belly ; Janârddana thy legs and feet ; the eternal and irresistible Narâyaṇa, thy face, thine arms, thy mind, thy faculties of sense. May all ghosts, goblins, and spirits unfriendly ever fly thee, appalled by the quoit, mace, and sword of Vishṇu, and the echo of his shell."

The ancients believed that diseases were the obsession by fiends, and different parts of the body had to be separately protected. Similar amulets to that of poor Yasodâ were called "knots," in ancient Babylonia.

"Knot, bind the head of the sick man, bind his forehead,

---

[1] These are all synonyms of Vishṇu.

bind the seat of his life," etc., says an ancient formula.[1] M. Lenormant points out that the phylacteries of the Pharisees and the "knots" patronized by mediæval duchesses were of the same pattern.

To differentiate Indian mythology and pure history is difficult. In the view of Indian scholars there was a real Krishna, a conqueror who enlarged the domains of the Aryas by victories over the aborigines, who figure always in Indian legends as giants and fiends. Mr. Garrett, in his excellent dictionary, fixes his date at the time when "the Aryans were still a nomad people, pasturing their herds of cattle at the foot of the Himalaya range and in the plains of the Punjab." The movement was towards "the interior and east" from the north-western corner of the peninsula.[2]

This geography would place him before Râma and the sons of Pându. It is significant that Krishna differs from the other incarnations in not being of royal birth. The story of the baby being found close to the waggon of a cowherd means, of course, that he was a peasant.

Krishna and his brother Balarâma grow up amongst the cowherds. Their infant sports are a never-ending popular theme in modern India. When they were quite tiny they "began to crawl about the ground, supporting themselves on their hands and knees, and creeping everywhere, often amidst ashes and filth. Neither Rohini nor Yaśodâ was able to prevent them from getting into the cow-pens or amongst the calves, where they amused themselves by pulling their tails."[3] On one occasion, the infant Krishna, being tied as a punishment to the mortar with which the Indians bruise unwinnowed corn, pulled it along with him against two large trees, overturning both in the process. On another occasion he upset the waggon which in those pastoral times seems to have been the paternal dwelling. By-and-by, the little colony emigrated to a pastoral district of Mathurâ, called Vrindâvana, where "new grass springs up even in the hot weather." Here

---

[1] Lenormant, "La Magie Chaldiénne," pp. 39, 43.
[2] Garrett, *sub voce* Krishna.
[3] Wilson, "Vishnu Purâna," chap. v.

the two boys romped in the forests. They made themselves crests of the peacocks' plumes, and garlands of forest flowers, and musical instruments of leaves and reeds. They piped to the cowherds. They sang in chorus and danced together. Sometimes they stained themselves of various hues with the minerals of the mountain. On his head each boy wore the Kâka-paksha,[1] or the hair trimmed like the outspread wings of a flying crow. The bird Garuda typifies spiritual light and fire.

In a pool on the Yamunâ, near Vrindâvana, was a terrible water serpent. Its name was Kâlîya, and it made the water poisonous to men and cattle. Young Krishna, reflecting that as the bird Garuda he had once before vanquished this snake, determined again to attack it. Climbing a kadamba tree, he leaped boldly into the pool. Immediately he was attacked by a vast number of serpents, male and female. They coiled themselves round every limb, and bit fiercely with their poisonous fangs. Nanda and Yasodâ and the young gopîs (cow-girls) wept bitter tears—

"Without Hari the forest will lose its delight. We have listened to his music, and now the serpents will kill him. Let us all plunge likewise into the fearful pool of the serpent king."

But Balarâma, listening to the words of the cow-girls, and seeing the cowherds themselves pale with terror on the bank, was filled with disdain. He at once "reminded" Krishna of his "real character," as the "Vishnu Purâna" somewhat quaintly puts it.

"God of gods, the quality of mortal is sufficiently assumed. Thou art the centre of creation, as the nave is of the spokes of a wheel. The gods, to partake of thy pastimes as man, have all descended in disguise. The goddesses have come down to Gokula to join in thy sports. Disregard not these sorrowing divinities, the cowherds and cow-girls, thy kith and kin. Thou hast put on the character of man. Thou hast exhibited the tricks of childhood. Subdue this fierce snake." Krishna obeyed.

The "fierce Kesin" was a demon haunting the woods of

---

[1] Wilson, "Vishnu Purâna," p. 510.

Vrindâvana. Kansa, alarmed at the death of Pûtanâ and other prodigies, sent him against the two divine boys. He assumed the form of a horse, "spurning the earth with his hoofs, scattering the clouds with his mane, and springing in his paces beyond the orbits of the sun and moon." The cowherds and their wives, hearing his neighing, fled to Krishna for protection.

"Away with these fears of Kesin," said the young hero. "He is but a galloping steed, ridden by the strength of the Daityas. His neighing is his only terror!"

The fierce steed galloped at Krishna with his mouth wide open. Krishna thrust his arm in it and tore out his teeth, as the wielder of the trident tore out the teeth of Pûshan. The arm in the throat of the demon now enlarged, like a malady that grows and grows and ends in death. From his torn lips the demon vomited foam and blood. He was rent asunder by the arm of Krishna as a tree is rent by the lightning's flash. The cowherds were delighted, and Nârada the Brahmin, invisible, seated on a cloud, exclaimed, "Well done, Lord of the Universe, thou hast destroyed Kesin, the oppressor of the denizens of heaven. Thou shalt be called the Slayer" (Kesa va)![1] After the fight Krishna returned to Gokula, the "sole object of the eyes of the women of Vraja."

Krishna had another adventure. This was with the demon Arishta, disguised as a savage bull. "His colour was that of a cloud charged with rain. He had vast horns. His eyes were like two fiery suns. As he moved, he ploughed up the ground with his hoofs. His tail was erect." The hump, which is a feature of Indian cattle, was enormous. Many hermits in the forest had fallen victims to his fierce rage.

Seeing Krishna, the fierce beast charged him with lowered horns. Krishna seized them deftly, and with gigantic strength tore them off. He beat the demon with them till he died. He pressed the bull with his knees. This feat reminded the

[1] Professor Wilson questions the etymology of Nârada, and gives "He of the hair" (Kesa) as the correct derivation. As the old Indians loved verbal quips, they perhaps had both root-words in view (" Vishnu Purâna," p. 540).

herdsmen of Indra triumphing over the Asura Jambha. Other feats were performed by this young boy.

Whatever the respective dates of the three great Indian legends, I think that an attempt has been made to blend them into one harmonious whole. Having taken the aspects of Nature as a great symbol of God, the Brahmins have tried to make Râma's story specially deal with the autumn of life, Yudhishthira's with summer and kingship, Krishna's with youth and spring. This last is quite proved by the kalendar. With Indian genius, as with Sanzio and Fra Angelico, the child god is the favourite idea expressed. Krishna is drawn suckling, or sprawling with playthings, or strangling a snake whilst yet a baby. But at one point the Christ and the Krishna palpably diverge. The Brahmins were plainly of idea that God considered as Nature could never be fully drawn unless the element of adult love was added. There is the Bala Krishna, or child Krishna, but there is also a Krishna arrived at puberty.

Krishna's celebrated dalliance with the milkmaids has been pronounced unchaste by missionaries, and been glossed over by some writers. Thus Miss Gordon Cumming suggests that when he hid their clothes when they were bathing he wished to read them a lesson of modesty.

I think both sets of writers fail to read the legend aright. The mystic cows of the Brahmin religion and the milkmaids are one, and we know from the " Mahâbhârata " that these cows are the days of the year. The sun-god in his yearly course lights up each in succession. "The drops of perspiration from Krishna's arms were like the fertilizing rain," says the " Vishnu Purâna." That Krishna's love has been pronounced platonic by so many readers shows that the subject has been treated with great delicacy.

In spring the air is perfumed with the white water-lily and the bees murmur. At this time Krishna and his brother sang sweet strains in various measures such as the women love. The milkmaids came forth from their huts. One sang a gentle accompaniment to the song. Another listened, a third called out his name, and then shrunk abashed. One girl, afraid of her father and mother, dared not come out, but meditated on Krishna with closed eyes, and emancipated herself from her lower nature. Some imaged him as the " Supreme Brahma," and obtained final emancipation. One fine moonlight night, the milkmaids and the god indulged in a pretty dance, the celebrated Râsa dance (" speech dance," " chain dance.")

In this dance, the girls form a ring and a phantom Krishna is at the side of each. The pretty comedians then personate the god. One pretends to hold up the mountain Govard-dhana. Another makes believe to pipe, a third sings. One slaps her round brown arms like a wrestler and challenges the serpent Kâliya with a quite imposing defiance. One affects to see the footprints of the god and a particular milkmaid on the ground, and pouts with pretty jealousy. Then one shows her rapture that Krishna is by her ; another her despair because she is abandoned. One mimics the higher happiness of the rishi who, with closed eyes dreams of the formless Vishnu. Bracelets jingle and round arms are flung aloft till at last all the poor girls, abandoned, feel that they can only sing Krishna's songs to the sound of the Vina and the musical sing-song of the women.

This dance was a temple dance when the Babylonian women wept for Tammuz, and probably many hundred years before. The chain represents the year and the girls the days. The sun-god visits each in turn.

The name of one milkmaid, Râdha, has been studiously kept out of the Purânas, but tradition has been too powerful. One night in the rainy season, Krishna, a wanderer, received shelter from one Nanda, a cowherd, and the cowherd's daughter became his mistress. Their lives are still sung in every bazaar.[1] The sculptures too of the temple of Jagannâtha, Krishna's temple in Orissa, are said to make plain the nature of Krishna's dalliance with the milkmaids.[2]

King Kansa having been unsuccessful with his zodiacal horse and his bull, determines to slaughter Krishna with a

[1] See " Gita Govinda " and Tod's " Rajesthan," vol. i. p. 540.
[2] " Garrett's " Dictionary," *sub voce* " Jagannâtha."

famous brace of athletes, and bids him in consequence to a
great summer festival. Akrûra is his messenger. When the
poor milkmaids hear that Govinda, the divine cowherd as
they call him, is going to leave them, they weep bitter tears.
The dames of Mathurâ are proud and seductive. The divine
cowherd is a rustic. "Their smiles and airs and meaning
glances will turn him from us. Bright is the morning for the
women of Mathurâ, for the bees of their eyes will feed upon
his lotus face. Delicious will be the great festival, for they
will see Krishna. Brahmâ has given us a great treasure.
He takes it away and we are blind. Despair shrivels our
beauty and makes our bracelets slip from shrunken limbs."

Akrûra was possessed of the Syamantika gem (the higher
initiation). On the journey he went down to the river for the
Sandhya or noonday rite. He threw himself into the Dhyâna
or mystic reverie, and saw Krishna transfigured before him.
Lightnings flashed as from a dark cloud. His body was
changed. The mystic four arms held the four great symbols.
The śrivatsa or mystic cross was on his breast. A gem was
on his brow, and the whitest of lotuses on his head. Emerging
from the water, the Akrûra was astonished to see the brothers
in their car, sitting like ordinary mortals. Again he went
into the stream, and again the phantasmal body of Krishna
visited him there. The holy man became convinced that
Balarâma was Śesha, the mighty serpent that supports the
Kosmos, and Krishna was the "the supreme Brahma, eternal,
unchangeable, uncreated."

Upon entering, Mathurâ, the divine cowherd, met a deformed girl, Kubjâ. She was carrying a pot of precious
ointment.

"Fair girl," said Krishna, "give me of that ointment, the
ointment of kings."

"Take it," said Kubjâ. Krishna smeared his body with
the Brakticheda anointing. This means that he put on the
various mystic nose, cheek, breast, and arm marks of the
followers of Vishnu, and the celebrated tridentine streaks on
the forehead. They symbolize Vishnu's three steps.

Then Krishna, who had the power of healing by touch,

put his thumb and two fingers under the deformed girl's chin and made her straight and beautiful.

The festival of King Kansa was very like similar festivals in the other epics. Pavilions, and tents, and platforms were erected. They were decorated with pictures, and garlands, and flags, and statues. Aromatic scents were everywhere. The octagonal columns that were put up for the horse sacrifice in the Ramâyana, were here likewise. The pavilions had each seven roofs, supported on four posts. Professor Wilson thinks that they must have been of the pattern of Chinese pagodas.[1] Coloured awnings, and carpets, and silks, and pretty women animated the scene. They were allowed to appear, as in the "Mahâbhârata," without curtains or conceal-ment.[2] Drinks were prepared for the common people, and a phrase that may mean "viands" is used.[3] This would carry the legend to days before Asoka, the Buddhist, forbade flesh meat.

Krishṇa, like Râma, breaks the bow that no one can bend. He and his brother then confront the two great athletes, Châṇûra and Mushṭika. At the sight of these strong men, Devakî mourns for her son, and fears that she will never see his lovely face again. The courtesans, too, under the bright awnings, cry out, Alas! The graceful, though light frame of the young cowherd, as he tightened his girdle and danced in the arena, had earned him their sympathies. As he slapped his arms in defiance to the mighty Châṇûra, all the women said, "How can the delicate form of Hari, the blue one, oppose that great giant?"

The Indians are unrivalled wrestlers. Officers who have learnt their grips have shone against English athletes. The fight between Châṇûra and Krishṇa has found an expert for a historian. "Mutual grips," "interlacing arms," "inter-twining the whole body," "pulling forwards," "pushing back;" these and a dozen other stratagems are detailed in long Sanskrit words. By-and-by, the wreath of flowers on Châ-ṇûra's head began to quiver, and his mighty strength to wane. At last Krishṇa lifted up his adversary and dashed him to the ground. His soul fled, and Balarâma disposed of the other

---

[1] "Vishṇu Purâna," p. 554.   [2] Ibid., p. 555.   [3] Ibid., p. 554, note.

wrestler. Then the two brothers danced in the arena in the Indian manner.

King Kansa was terribly incensed. He gave orders that Vasudeva should be horribly tortured, and Nanda, Krishna, and Balarâma seized. Krishna came to the defence of his kinsmen, and jumped up and dragged Kansa out of his regal pavilion. He knocked off his tiara, squeezed him to death, and dragged his body across the sand in the middle of the arena. It was furrowed as by a watercourse. He released Ugrasena, the father of Kansa, from prison, and placed him on the throne. A Brahmin, Sândîpani, was told off to instruct the youths in arms and magic. For a fee, Krishna promised to raise his son from the dead. He had been drowned when bathing at the celebrated temple of Somnâth, in Guzerat. A terrible demon, named Panchajana, who was in the form of a conch-shell, had swallowed him. Krishna plunged in the sea and rescued the boy. He slew the marine monster and made a conch-shell out of his bones. This is his celebrated Sankha, whose "sound fills demon hosts with dismay."

The great modern festival of Krishna, in India, takes place in Gemini-Cancer. Hence, the two wrestlers slaughtered by the two twins of the new year. The images of Krishna and his brother Balarâma, in the great Temple of Jagganâtha, in Orissa, have arms uplifted to form the Buddhist trisul.

This explains the upraising of the mountain Govard-dhana. Krishna is *stambha*, the Kosmos-supporter. Kansa is the Kosmos-supporter of the preceding year. Opposite Gemini is the arrow, and opposite Cancer the marine monster with the elephant in his mouth. Hence the incident of the bow, and the monster like a shell.

King Jarâsandha (who figures likewise in the "Mahâbhârata") was the father-in-law of King Kansa. Incensed at the death of the king, he marched from his capital, Magadha, with forty-six million fighting men. The men of Mathurâ were besieged; but Krishna, with the "bow of Hari," the magic double quiver, and the mace Kaumodaki, did prodigies of valour. He had recourse to the four strategic devices— bribery, negotiation, dissension, and chastisement. A feigned retreat is mentioned as another device.[1] "It was the pastime of the Lord of the Universe, in his capacity of man, to launch various weapons against his enemies."

After the defeat of Jarâsandha, a Greco-Bactrian king, Kâlayavana, whose "breast was as hard as the point of the thunderbolt," marched against Mathurâ. Krishna, reflecting that the Yudavas were much weakened by their long campaign against the king of Magadha, retreated westward, some six hundred miles to the sea. At the extremity of the peninsula of Guzerat, he begged from ocean twelve furlongs, and thereon constructed the city of Dwârakâ. Ramparts and gardens, and tanks and buildings, made this city like Amarâvatî, the city of Indra. In this city he placed the inhabitants of Mathurâ. Kâlayavana was enticed into a cavern and killed by Muchukunda ; and all his horses, and elephants, and chariots handed over to the men of Dwârakâ.

By the sounding sea, a shrine, called "Krishna's Shrine," is all that modern pilgrims can see of ancient Dwârakâ. Meanwhile Krishna runs away with the beautiful Ruckminî. A more difficult task is before him to gain the earrings of Aditi, the celestial virgin, like Utanka in the former legend.

There is a fine hymn to Aditî in the "Vishnu Purâna," which runs partly thus :—

HYMN TO ADITÎ.

Matter thou art unwelded and eternal ;
    And in the gloom
The Lord of gods celestial, and infernal,
    Lay in thy womb.

Then wert thou Speech ! The voice of the immortals,
    O Aditî,
Whispers to man through the well-guarded portals—
    Whispers through thee !

By thee the world was fashioned from the waters,
    At Brahma's call ;
The stars of heaven are thy shining daughters,
    Mother of all !

---

[1] According to the "Mahâbhârata," Krishna was driven westward by Jarâsandha.

In pursuit of his great task, Krishna calls to his aid the "eater of serpents," the bird Garuda. He mounts his back and proceeds to the city of King Naraka, which was defended by nooses with edges sharp as razors. Krishna, with the aid of his terrible discus, cuts in pieces the nooses, disperses the dark legions of the king, and slaughters that monarch. He lets loose sixteen thousand one hundred damsels, and comes back through the skies on Garuda, bringing the earrings of Aditî and the other treasures. The sixteen thousand one hundred damsels enter the hero's zenana.

Krishna had a wife named Satyabhâmâ, who desired to have the celebrated Pârijâta Tree (tree of life). This blooms in Paradise. Its bark is of gold. Its leaves of a rich copper colour. Its fruit is delicious.

"Why," said the queen, "should not this divine tree be transported to Dwârakâ? If I am really dear to you, fetch it. You say neither Ruckminî nor Jambavatî are so dear to you as I am. If this is not mere flattery, bring the tree from heaven and let me wear its flowers in the braids of my hair!"

Krishna having to return the earrings of Aditî to the universal mother, thought this would be a good opportunity to seize the Pârijâta Tree. He hurried to Swarga, the Indian Paradise, on the back of Garuda. He presented the earrings to their owner. He then seized the Pârijâta Tree and carried it off. Indra, indignant, attacked him with the heavenly legions, but Krishna triumphed. The Pârijâta Tree is another name for Virgo. And the episode is also brought in to exalt the Vishnu worship over the more ancient Indra worship.

The abundant imagery of the Scales being exhausted, let us now see whether a character with a superfluity of arms appears upon the scene. Krishna had a grandson, Aniruddha. A girl, Ushâ, saw him in a dream. She became melancholy, and at last gave up her secret to a confidante. This lady being possessed of magic powers, inveigled Aniruddha to the court of the girl's father, King Bâna.

King Bâna had for a patron deity the god with three eyes. This is Rudra or Śiva. He was possessed also of a thousand arms; and he prayed to Rudra, saying, "Peace is not good for a monarch with a thousand arms, give me war!"

"When thy peacock banner shall break," said the god, "thou shalt have that war that delights the wicked spirits that feed on the flesh of man!"

Krishna, hearing of the captivity of his grandson, started off with his brother and Garuda. As he neared the court of King Bâna, the "spirits that attend on Rudra" opposed him, but he vanquished them. Then Mighty Fever, an emanation from Rudra, having three feet and three heads, barred his path and afflicted Balarâma with a burning heat, who clung to Krishna for help. Anticipating Hahnemann, the "fever emanating from Siva was quickly expelled from the person of Krishna by fever which he himself engendered." Krishna next overcame the five fires. Then Rudra in person, with the Indian Mars on his right hand, advanced to protect Bâna. Kârtikeya, the war-god, was born of six nymphs, the six Krittikas (the Pleiades). Rudra was defeated by Krishna, and Kârtikeya by Balarâma. Bâna then, in his mighty car, advanced into the thick of the fight. He and Krishna shot arrow after arrow at each other, and blood flowed from both. At length, the Blue One took up the terrible discus that nothing can resist. As he was about to hurl the great chakra, a phantom appeared before him and veiled Bâna from his sight. This was the naked woman, Kotavî. Undeterred by the apparition, Krishna hurled the discus and lopped off in succession all the arms of Bâna. Rudra here interceded, and Bâna was spared.

The great value of the Purâna legend is the bold way in which the inner teaching is blurted out. In the circle of twelve stones, one in spring and one in autumn represented Rudra, and these were worshipped according to the position of the Pleiades. Thus Rudra, Siva, and Kârtikeya, the son of the Pleiades, figure without much disguise, and so does Bâna with his thousand arms. Bâna is spared, for the quaint reason that Krishna confesses that Rudra and Vishnu are one and the same person. The Indian triad is not three individualities, but three aspects of one God. Brahma creates, Vishnu preserves, Śiva destroys. The year is a day of Brahma in miniature, and Brahma is the four months of spring, Vishṇu the four months of summer, Śiva the four months of winter.

Other adventures occur to the two brothers. Pauṇḍraka assumes the insignia and style of Krishṇa. He is supported by the King of Benares. Krishṇa attacks them and sets Benares on fire with his discus. Balaráma kills the Asuru Dwivida, in the form of an ape.

The incidents of this portion of the legend, the five fires, the bird Garuḍa, the Pârijâta Tree, Bâṇa or Rudra, typify the struggle of the devotee with his lower nature. The serpent Sesha issues from the mouth of Râma. This is one form of the elephant issuing from the mouth of the sea-monster Makara. The ape incident is fresh proof, I think, that Cancer was once an ape.

Krishṇa now determines to practise yoga, or the initiation of the mystic. He sat under a tree meditating on the Supreme God. There is an attitude known to the higher initiates, the left leg is laid across the right thigh, and the sole of the foot is turned outwards. Buddha constantly figures thus in the sculptures. It is called, I think, the swastika attitude. Krishṇa was seated thus when a huntsman, Jarâ, mistook his foot for a deer, and fired an arrow at it tipped with iron from the celebrated club kaumaudaki. At this particular instant Krishṇa had solved the riddle of the universe, and merged his spirit into that of the universal Brahma.

When Buddhism was expelled from India in the seventh century A.D. the modern religion of Vishṇu, a form of Buddhism, stepped into its place, and as India was then vegetarian and water-drinking, accommodated itself to circumstances. But if the present religion of Vishṇu is modern, I think the actual story of Krishṇa very ancient. Krishṇa is a fighting herdsman. His virtues and his vices belong to a rude society. He treats woman as a spoil of war. He is brave, but cunning and cruel. The question of geography is also important. Râma's chief adventures are about Oude and the valley of the Ganges. Krishṇa, on the other hand, is born not far from the famous land of the seven rivers of the earlier Aryas. Indeed, his tribe is pushed westwards by the incursions of fresh hordes from Bactria. All the local colour of the legend is in keeping. We see nomad herdsmen sleeping under their bullock carts, and under the pressure of prolific neighbours wresting fresh pastures from the earlier races. Both legends were probably sung in short ballads by the people long before they were elaborated. And the legend of Krishṇa has one immense advantage over that of Râma, his death is described. His body is left on a tree to be devoured by carrion, an Aryan custom of the date of Zarathustra's secession. His relics are prized, and traditions of a Kshetra being built over them are preserved. We hear nothing of Râma's dead body. This is suspicious. The body of a genuine historical hero or saint was more prized after death than in life.

The story of Krishṇa is made very modern by writers who subordinate philology to theology. Thus a writer, Dr. Lorinser, has written an elaborate work to maintain that the idea of Krishṇa is plagiarized from Christianity. In parallel columns he shows the identity of much of the teachings of the "Bhagavad Gîtâ" with that of the New Testament, and notably of the Fourth Gospel. I have only room for a few of these citations.

They who honour me are in me and I in them.	Dwelleth in Me, and I in him (John vi. 56).
I am the origin of all. From me everything proceeds.	For of Him, and through Him, and to Him, are all things (Rom. xi. 36).
I am the beginning, middle, and end of all things.	I am the first and the last (Rev. i. 17).
Among letters I am A.	I am Alpha and Omega (Rev. i. 8).
From all sins will I free them. Be not sorrowful.	Be of good cheer. Thy sins be forgiven thee (Matt. ix. 2).
No one knows me.	No man hath seen God at any time (John i. 18).
Dwelling in the heart of every man.	Sanctify the Lord God in your hearts (1 Pet. iii. 15).
They who eat of the immortal food of the sacrifice pass into the eternal Brahma.	I am the living bread which came down from heaven. If any man eat of this bread he shall live for ever (John vi. 51).

Dead in me.   For ye are dead, and your life
                               is hid with Christ in God (Col.
                               iii. 2).

As opposed to this, an intelligent native convert, the Rev.
K. M. Banerjea, chaplain to the Bishop of Calcutta, has
shown how unwise it is to tell the natives of India that their
creeds are all borrowed from Christianity. He shows that the
ideas of the Incarnation, of Christ as the Creator of heaven
and earth, and of Christ offered up as a sacrifice for the whole
world, are familiar to all Hindoos in books admitted now
to be long anterior to the Bible.[1] Let us listen to the "Rig
Veda."

"Hiraṇyagarbha arose in the beginning. Born he was
the one Lord of all things existing. He established the earth
and the sky. To what god shall we offer our oblation ?

"He who gives breath, who gives strength, whose commands
all, even the gods, reverence, whose shadow is immortality,
whose shadow is death. To what God shall we offer our
oblation ? . . .

"Prajâpati, no other than thou is lord over all these created
things. To what God shall we offer our oblation ?"[2]

Mr. Banerjea shows that Prajâpati or Purusha, is the
divine Man, like Christ ; that he is the Lord of a kalpa or
dispensation—the maker of heaven and earth. Dr. Muir, too,
has shown that many of the phrases which Dr. Lorinser
imagines to have been taken from the Fourth Gospel, are in
the "Rig Veda."

"O Indra, we sages have been in thee."

"This worshipper, O Agni, hath been in thee ! O son of
strength."[3]

In point of fact, a triad like that of Philo and the Therapeuts has existed in India from the earliest days.

"The deities invoked," says Colebrooke in his "Essay on
the Vedas," "appear on a cursory inspection of the Veda to
to be as various as the authors of the prayers addressed to
them ; but, according to the most ancient annotations of the

---

[1] "The Relation between Christianity and Hinduism," p. 2.
[2] "Rig Veda," x. 121. 1.   [3] "Metrical Translations," p. 14.

Indian scripture, those numerous names of persons and things are all resolvable into different titles of three deities, and ultimately of one God."[1]

The triune nature of the Vedic divinity is accentuated all through the hymns with every conceivable play of fancy. Knowledge of God is called "triple knowledge;" his revelation the "triple Veda," the "triple speech." "May the soft wind waft to us a pleasant healing! May mother earth and father heaven convey it to us! . . . We invoke that lord of living beings," etc.[2] This lord of living beings is Purusha, the god-man, born of the inactive god and Aditi or Sophia. This birth was typified in every rite. The fire-churn was in the form of the swastika, the fish of the zodiac, and from it Agni was born, as Krishṇa from the black and white hairs, at every sacrifice. He was also the Siśur Jâṭah produced by the offerings of rice and milk.

I will give what the Scotch call a paraphrase of a fine hymn to Vishṇu, in the "Vishṇu Puraṇa," which seems to set forth Indian theosophy very clearly.

" Ruler of gods and kings,
Thou dost enfold the spaces near and far ;
System and shining orb and peopled star
　　With thy Garuḍa wings.

" For their fantastic creeds
Men fashion gods with legs and arms of stone ;
No legs nor arms hast thou of gods alone,
　　Though near all needs.

" Eyes hast thou not, nor ears ;
Yet hearest thou all sounds that shake the air,
The whispered villainy, the baby's prayer,
　　Man's uttered wants and fears.

" Seekers of heavenly light,
Two secrets know—the Higher Wisdom this—
The Lower Wisdom probes the blank abyss
　　Of earthly appetite.

---

[1] "Essays," vol. i. p. 25.　　　　[2] "Rig Veda," i. 89. 4.

" It learns how kings are crowned ;
How Brahmins chant, and what will fatten kine ;
Seeks gold in streams, and jewels in the mine ;
    Makes wealth abound.

" To the dim Far away
The Higher Wisdom turns with hungered eye ;
It scans the stars uncounted in the sky,
    It bursts its bonds of clay.

" It probes the heart of man ;
He forms the potent longing in his brain,
Desire deceives, and every hope is vain ;
    His life one baffled plan.

" He looks within to find
Ideas of life distinct from mortal scheming,
Fancies and wants transcending mortal dreaming.
    He sees thy mind.

" Both of these lores art thou !
We image thee a man with human breast,
Gored with the shaft of hate and love's unrest,
    A man with fevered brow !

" As God we view thee too,
All wise, all good ! with thy three mystic paces,
The welkin's unimaginable spaces
    Were overlapped, Vishnu !

" Thou art the formless Brahm,
The God that dwells in the awakened heart,
The state our mystic dreamers know in part,
    Pure, passionless, and calm.

" Earth's wailings sound afar,
Crime rules, and Cruelty is throned on high ;
Among the seven rishis in the sky,
    Glitters the mystic star.

" It heralds thy new birth,
Thy glorious avatâra come again !
To bring fresh comfort to the sons of men,
    Thy holy feet touch earth."

CHAPTER XXVII.

THE LEGEND OF THE FIVE SONS OF PÂNDU.

DR. J. VON HAHN, in analyzing the Aryan myth, sets forth amongst its characteristics the incident that the hero must found a city.[1] In the epic of the Five Sons of Pându this is a prominent event.

The country round modern Delhi is sad to the thoughtful. The step of the traveller is over crumbling civilizations and the overturned spires of dead nationalities. Here is a column on which Aśoka, the Buddhist, preached peace and toleration. There is a ruined fane where crowds of unarmed Hindus fell before the scimitar of the bloody Nadir Shah. Around for miles and miles are the ruins, pile upon pile, of many cities. In ancient days the enervated Indians of the plain always fell a prey to the hardier races that emerged from the direction of Central Asia, through the passes of Afghanistan. Elephants in thousands, and unwieldy crowds of horsemen and spear-men were hurried northward to oppose. But with Baber, Alexander, or Nadir Shah, the result was always the same. The onslaught of the hardier races resulted in a vast rout.

Here Lake won India, and Archdale Wilson reconquered it. But the legend of the Five Sons of Pându narrates a still more fierce struggle. On this field the Aryas gained a great victory over the Daisyas or black races, and then founded Indraprastha (ancient Delhi).

The Aryas came from fabled Meru, with its seven famous streams. Sir H. Rawlinson believes these to be the seven head streams of the Oxus. Other writers point to "the great

---

[1] "Sagwissenschaftliche Studien." Jena, 1876.

plateau, walled to the north by the Altai and to the south by the Himâlaya, from which the great rivers flow northward, eastward, and southward, through Siberia, China, and India, to the Arctic, Pacific, and Indian oceans."[1] It is asserted that the four great races of men, the Arya, the Semite, the Turanian, the Cushite, all came from this central table-land, as evidenced by their common legends.

"Not far from the foot of the colossal Dhawalagiri, and Nanda-devi, and near the little town of Gartokh, lies the group of lakes called Ravana-Rhada, or Manasarowar. From these, or within a radius of thirty miles from the central one of the group, the four greatest rivers of India take their rise ; the Indus flowing to the north, the Ganges and its chief branch the Gogra to the south, the Brahmaputra to the east, and the Sutlej to the west. The Ganges, Brahmaputra, and Sutlej rise in the lakes."[2] Mr. Stanley holds, with many other writers, that Cashmir and Tibet were the paradise of Moses, Manu, and Zarathustra ; and that the serpents who drove them forth were the foaming torrents of a great debacle. This region fits in with Zarathustra's description of the "delicious region," and that suggested by Sir H. Rawlinson does not.

"Ahura Mazda said to the holy Zarathustra, ' I made most holy Zarathrustra into a delicious spot, what was previously quite uninhabitable. . . . As the first and best regions and countries, I, who am Ahura Mazda, created Aryanam Vaêjo of good capability. Thereupon, in opposition to it, Angrô Mainyus, the death-dealing, created a mighty serpent and snow, the work of the devas.

"Ten months of winter are there, two months of summer. Seven months of summer are there, five months of winter. The latter are cold as to water, cold as to earth, cold as to trees. There is midwinter, the heart of winter."

This seems to mean, as Mr. Stanley plausibly suggests, that the region of the Aryas (Aryanam Vaêjo) was at first temperate, and then a great change of climate set in. Snows

---

[1] Stanley, " Future Religion of the World," p. 88.
[2] Ibid., p. 100.

that gave only two months summer instead of seven; a "flood" or inundation, typified in myths by the serpent. This flooding of the valley was the cause of the migration from this paradise, and is, perhaps, the deluge story common to the various legends of its inhabitants.

The Aryas, when they came to India, had five gods, and a friend of mine who has studied India is convinced that the Rishi Pându is in corrupted form Pan Deo (five gods).

Pându himself had nothing to do with the parentage of his five celebrated sons. Having accidentally killed a rishi, who had assumed the form of a deer, he had become an ascetic celibate. He had two wives, Kunti and Mâdri. Kunti, with an incantation given to her by an ancient rishi or adept, brought down three gods from the skies, one after another; Dhârma, who was the father of Yudhishthira; Vâyu, the wind, who begat Bhima, the Indian Hercules; the great Indra himself, who was the father of Arjuna. The other wife summoned the Aswins, or celestial twins, and they performed the impossible physiological feat of a double paternity.

The wives are plainly the black and white mother in the ecliptic, and the five gods the four seasons, the four points of heaven, one of which is Gemini. They are the five heavenly Buddhas, the five creative Æons of the Gnostics. As the Pleiades regulated early agriculture, perhaps they suggested the number five.

Shortly after the birth of his illustrious sons, Pându dies, and the widows draw lots which shall commit widow immolation in his honour. Mâdri mounts the pyre. It has been remarked by M. Senart that the mother of the demi-god, the Buddha, the Krishna, always dies in seven days. My explanation is that the year opens with the celebration of the festival of the Black Durgâ, and when the sun enters Aries, seven days later, she is drowned or consumed.

The five sons of Pându are brought up in the palace of their uncle Dhritarashtra, King of Hastinâpura. The throne belonged by right to Yudhishthira, the elder boy. A brood of a hundred first cousins, hatched of an egg like a scorpion, were the playfellows of the young princes. These cousins hated their playmates, and from their earliest years tried to poison them and otherwise get rid of them. Duryodhana was the name of the leading spirit amongst these hopeful infants. It was remarked at his birth that he at once gave forth discordant sounds like the braying of many asses. The vultures of the air and the foul jackals echoed these noises of ill-omen, and a terrible tempest began to roar. The sky was on fire. Duryodhana is plainly Rudra in the sign of Scorpio. This is confirmed by the fact that he had one hundred brothers, all born at a birth. Rudra, as we have shown, has a hundred arms.

Then certain soothsayers came to King Dhritarashtra and said to him: "The portents, O king, are terrible. Your nephew, Yudhishthira, is heir to the crown. This son of yours, born amidst the roaring of wild beasts, presages great calamities to your offspring. The wise have said, 'Sacrifice one man for the safety of a family. Sacrifice a family for the benefit of a village. Sacrifice a village for a nation. Sacrifice the whole world to save one's soul.' Make away with your son to save his brothers. If he lives, they will be destroyed."

This allusion to human sacrifices shows the great antiquity of the legend. At the date of the "Yagur Veda" the form of tying the human victims to posts was alone gone through. No actual immolation took place.

Dr. J. von Hahn sets down that another token of the hero of Aryan legend is that he must be driven forth from his home at an early age, owing to tokens and warnings of his future greatness. In the case of the five sons of Pându this quickly came about. Arjuna learnt the use of the bow, and Bhima that of the club. They became so expert, that the soothsayers were alarmed, and this time recommended the king to make away with them. Alarmed, he consents to an infamous plan set on foot by Duryodhana to burn the five sons of Pându. But Vidura, the uncle of the youths, was an adept in occult wisdom. By means of his arts he became acquainted with the peril that menaced them. He packed off silently the mother and her five sons in a large boat on the Ganges. Although this occurred, as some have said, before the siege of Troy, the large boats of the Ganges are as archaic now as then. In their boat, the fugitives, aided by the current, dropped down to Vâranâvata, the modern Allahabad.

But the malice of a young man like Duryodhana can go faster than a boat drifting with the stream. He despatched an agent, named Purochana, to Vâranâvata. This man was entrusted with the details of an infamous plot. He summoned workmen to erect a palace of great magnificence, to be called the House of Delight. This palace had four great halls. It was erected at some little distance from the town. Hemp, and resin, and shellac were plentifully used in its construction. The shellac was mixed with oil and grease and other inflammable materials. The palace, which it is announced was erected very rapidly, was probably of the pattern of the veneered wooden structures of Chinese architecture. All things likely to inflame quickly were left carelessly lying about. "Of a truth," said an observer, "this is not the House of Delight, but the House of Calamity."

The fugitives were dwelling in another building. They were invited by Purochana to occupy the House of Delight. The inhabitants of Allahabad had been very civil to them, especially the better-to-do folks. The Aryas of those days drew a line between "carriage company" (rathinâm) and company that had no carriages. The Aryas of Cheltenham and Torquay are credited with formulating similar distinctions.

The subtle Purochana did his best to lull the victims into a false sense of security whilst he waited for a propitious day for his crime. Exquisite food and delicious drinks, soft couches and royal thrones were provided; silver vases, gold dishes, and sumptuous furniture.

But Vidura afar, by means of his occult arts, detected the great danger that threatened his nephews. He sent an emissary to give them warning.

"I am a miner," said a stranger one day. "I come from Vidura. On the fifteenth day of the dark half of this month, Purochana will try to burn you all alive." It was arranged that this expert miner should secretly prepare a subterranean passage for the escape of Kuntî and her five sons.

When this was finished, one night, a Nishâdî woman, one of the wild tribes of the Vindhya mountains, "vexed by Famine and pushed on by Death," as the poem tersely puts it, arrived at the House of Delight with her five barbarian sons. They were feasted, and became very intoxicated. It seemed to the five sons of Pâṇḍu that the moment of escape had come.

At once Bhîmasêna the Hercules applied a torch to the room where the treacherous Purochana was sleeping, and promptly disposed of him. He also set a light to the four doorways of the House of Shellac. In a short time the whole building was a vast conflagration. The citizens of Vâranâvata arrived in great terror. Afar the tempest muttered hoarsely.

Kuntî and her five sons hurried rapidly through the sub-terranean passage. They escaped unseen in the darkness of night to a forest. The mother grew weary, but her strong son Bhîmasêna carried her in his arms like an infant. The poor drunken Nishâdî woman and her five sons were con-sumed. Their corpses were found, and the inhabitants of Vâranâvata wept for the death of the five sons of Pâṇḍu. By-and-by the fugitives grew thoroughly exhausted, and they slept on cold mother earth. Bhîmasêna alone kept awake to watch over them. The sight of his queenly mother sleeping like a beggar under a tree vexed this stout-hearted youth.

"The poem of the 'Mahâbhârata,'" says the missionary Ward, is deemed so holy, "that it purifies the place in which it is read." [1] He adds that a Brahmin may not enter a village where a copy of it is not to be found.

On the other hand, our Sanskrit professors are constantly pointing out to us that this celebrated poem, far from being very holy, is often very much the reverse. Thus Professor Monier Williams has some virtuous indignation at the five sons of Pâṇḍu for their treacherous conduct in leaving the poor Nishâdî woman and her sons to burn. [2] Plainly, he

---

[1] "The Hindoos," vol. iii. p. 279.
[2] "Indian Epic Poetry," p. 54.

would never send for a copy of the volume if he wished to deodorize his native village morally. How is it that these Pundits differ so radically? Simply because the literal English mind cannot get beyond the letter of the scripture, and the Hindus declare that the letter is only for the vulgar.

In the Muṇḍaka Upanishad of the "Atharva Veda," Śaunaka, a wealthy householder, questioned the Rishi Angiras, who told him that there were two sorts of knowledge. There were the four Vedas, the "Rig Veda," the "Yagur Veda," the "Sâma Veda," and the "Atharva Veda ;" these were the scriptures of the "inferior knowledge." But the "superior knowledge" is not to be gained in books. It evaded "rites and rules of grammar." It was the interior knowledge of the Omniscient.[1] The object of scriptures was to conceal as well as to inculcate the highest truths. It was judged that most men could not receive them. Can we get at the secret meaning of this episode?

On the surface, the story of the "House of Shellac" is mystical. The apparatus of villainy and the expedients to foil it are suspiciously elaborate. Why build a sumptuous palace, if you want to murder half a dozen unbefriended fugitives? Why construct toilsome subterranean galleries, if you want to run away from an assassin? But if, as I have suggested, Kunti and her sons mean the new year and the four seasons, then Nishâdi and her sons mean the old year and the four seasons. It was necessary to destroy these by fire, as it is the appearance of Agni as Aries that puts an end to them. It was necessary that Kunti should escape through a cavern, the symbol of earth-life.

The fugitives escape to a forest and slaughter a mighty demon, who falls headlong "like an ox." They then attend a great festival, where the beautiful princess Draupadî appears as a matchless prize if any competitor can bend a mighty bow. Duryodhana and the wicked cousins try and fail. Arjuna comes forward and succeeds. Draupadî became the common wife of the five sons of Pâṇḍu. In reality, the five sons were one man.

When the Kuru faction returned to Hastinapura, they

[1] Colebrooke, "Essays," vol. I. p. 94.

talked over the striking events of the Swayaṁvara and came to the conclusion that the successful strangers, for they were in disguise, could be no other than Bhima and Arjuna escaped from the old snares. Many schemes were proposed in the crisis. Duryodhana was in favour of assassination, Karna proposed manly and open warfare, Vidura and the holy men suggested compromise. This last proposal was adopted, and half the kingdom was given to the five sons of Pâṇḍu. In the terrible jungle of Khandava Prastha they were now to found the city of Indraprastha, or Delhi.

The table-land by Indra's heavenly mount. This is the literal meaning of Indraprastha. Indraprastha is heaven, and Kuru Kshetra, the real head-quarters of the Kurus, is called hell in one or two of the legends, without any disguise. The sun each year builds up a celestial kingdom, the kingdom of summer.

The account of Indraprastha states that " it was adorned like paradise." After preliminary sacrifices a propitious spot had been measured out. Soon upsprang mighty ramparts and towers like the gorged clouds of autumn. White palaces pierced the skies like the pinnacles of Meru. The great gates were like the bird Garuḍa with its wings outspread. The ditches in front of the ramparts were like the ocean. The streets were broad. In many gardens the aśoka and the feathery pippala, the branching palm and the bamboo, the sweet pink laurel and the bignonia were heavy with bright and musical birds. Upon the broad surfaces of the lakes, which were fringed with the blue lotos, swam red geese and white swans. Cunning pictures were in the halls of the palaces. Indraprastha sparkled like a city in the clouds, like the heaven of Indra.

The city of the poet's dream, the Atlantis, the Indra-prastha, is generally the exact opposite of the city wherein he dwells. Applying this test to the " Mahâbhârata," we might get a great deal of insight into the actual India of the period. In Indraprastha, every poor man had a settled occupation, for all enemies were exterminated, and truth was maintained. Agriculture flourished. Indra sent rain exactly as it was called for, and the reason is a curious one. The rich nobles gave plenty of gifts to the Brahmins. Commerce flourished also, thanks to the supervision of the king ; and no favourite could obtain an unjust decree. Drought was unknown, and inundations, pestilence, and fever, for the department of priestly meteorology was well worked. A poet who sees everywhere around him suborned justice, and violence, and spoliation ; and who is liable at any moment to be himself offered up to Rudra as a captive of war might well indulge in such happy dreams.

Seated on thrones, the founders of Indraprastha dispensed patriarchal justice to all who sought it. They also enlarged their domains by successful war. One day, a Brahmin had his cows stolen from him. He appealed to Arjuna, but the arms of the community were in the king's house, and it was the turn of the king to possess the beautiful Draupadî for a week. It had been arranged that any son of Pâṇḍu who disturbed his brother under these circumstances should be banished to the forest for twelve years. Arjuna, balanced between duty and exile, chose the path of duty. He righted the wrongs of the poor Brahmin, and then went into voluntary exile in the forest, like Râma. When there, he puts out a burning wood, and rescues an Undine in a lake—the fire and water ordeals of the mysteries. Then, assisted by Kṛishṇa, the five sons of Pâṇḍu capture Magadha after a severe fight. As Kṛishṇa, acting as charioteer, drives Arjuna along, the bird Garuḍa comes down and perches on his banner.

An episode of the "Mahâbhârata" illustrates the crisis of the story. It is recorded that Nala, King of Nishâda, fell in love with the beautiful Damayantî, and won her at a Swayamvara held by her father the King of Berar. Sani, a baffled suitor and a malevolent being, cozens Nala out of his kingdom at a game of dice. The lovers, stripped of their possessions, repair to a forest ; and the king, finding the life too hard for his delicate wife, leaves her sleeping under a tree, hoping that that will induce her to return to her father's house. Lamenting, she seeks her husband over many a weary mile, and eventually becomes maid of honour to a certain queen. Nala repairs to the same court, but he has become so black that no one can recognize him. He engages himself as a cook. Eventually Damayantî recognizes her husband, and the pair recover their kingdom. Here we have the backbone of the "Mahâbhârata;" for the heroes also disguise themselves as menials. A king becomes a slave at the constellation of Libra. Whether this probably very old legend was the original form of the Mahâbhârata legend would be a curious inquiry.

This gives in epitome the story of the five sons of Pându. They are invited to a great feast by the treacherous Kurus who have hatched another plot. This is to inveigle Arjuna into a gambling bout with a noted cheat. He stakes his gold, his jewels, his dominions. He stakes his people, his brothers, his wife. He loses at every bout. The feast of course is the feast of Durgâ, who is also worshipped as Lakshmî (whence our word "luck") at this season, and all the natives still gamble immensely at the game of Pasha. The gambling is really the mysterious destiny that mortals see around them, which gives us health, life, joy, friends, loved ones, and then destroys our air-built castles.

When the five sons of Pându have become the chattels of the sons of Kuru, their clothes are torn off their backs. It is proposed to subject the beautiful Draupadî to the same indignity. Isis must be unveiled. Duhśâsana drags her into the midst of the assembly by the hair of her head. This rouses the terrible Bhîma, and the spoils won by cheating seem likely to be lost again through his great rage. Eventually matters are compromised. The kingdom was given up to Duryodhana for twelve years. The five sons of Pându agreed to pass twelve years as ascetics in a forest. They were then to get back the kingdom. Accompanied by poor Draupadî they set out for the Kâmyaka jungle on the banks of the Saraswatî.

This river was as holy to the early Aryas as the Ganges afterwards became to their descendants. Under instructions from the Brahmin Dhaumya Yudhishthira practises yoga under a tree. That of course was the meaning of the gambling and of the brothers becoming slaves. They had entered the mystic portal of the interior life. They sat under the tree where broods Garuda, the fire-dove. There is a fine hymn to this bird in the epic.

> " Of lofty race art thou,
> The first of wingèd things that cleave the sky;
>   Thou art the king of birds !
>   Thou art a god in heaven !
>   Agni thy name, and Wind,
>   And Brahm the lotus-born ;
>   Thou art the Holy Book,
>   Thou art the Priceless Food
> That touching mortal lips brings deathless being.
> Aloft upon thy shining wings outspread
> Thou bear'st the splendours of the universe.
>   Thou art the sisters twain,
>   That weave the double woof,
> Rapture and pang, bright deeds and infamy.
> Forth through the gleaming orbs that round us sail.
>   Forth through the spirit spheres,
> Impalpable to grosser mortal ken,
>   Thy fame is gloried near and far
> In all the mansions of the infinite.
>   The life that came and went,
>   The life that is to be,
>   O mystic bird art thou !
>   Thy name is Death.
>   Thou art the forky flame of smoke,
>   That with black wings that blot the sun,
> Amid amazement and great quiverings
> Will scorch the systems and burn out the life,
>   In the great day of Brahm.
>   Prostrate before thy feet,
> We beg protection from the King of Birds,
> Whose sheen makes dim the flashes of the storm,
>   Whose wings outroar the thunder.
> Thy flaming body fills us with affright,
>   We dread its hugeness.
>   Temper thy blinding rage,
>   Temper thy swelling form,
>   Prostrate we breathe our prayer,
>   Be good to us, sweet god,
>   And wing us peace."

I have said that the brothers and Draupadí eventually travesty themselves as servants. This is said to be done for fear of Duryodhana and his malice. I suspect they were

real slaves in the original story. The transformation gives
rise to some clever comedy. They repair to the court of
King Virâṭa at Matsya. Yudhishṭhira is master of the
ceremonies and head-dicer to the king. Bhîma is cook.
Nakula is groom. Sahadeva is herdsman. Arjuna puts on
a woman's dress, and conceals the scars of the twanging bow
Gâṇḍiva with many bracelets and trinkets. He is a eunuch
in the women's apartments. The magic arms are stowed
away in a hollow tree in a cemetery. On this a corpse is
swinging. This method of disposal of the dead seems to give
the poem great antiquity. At the time of the secession of
Zarathustra, corpses were thus left to be devoured by vultures
and dogs.

For two thousand years at least the "Mahâbhârata" has
been sung daily in all the Indian villages. For two thousand
years at least its incidents have been worked up into miracle
plays and acted at every great mystery and festival of the
people. The comedy of the disguised heroes has had its
share of popularity no doubt. It shows considerable knowledge of comedy intrigue. The heroes in their forest are
afraid of the malice of Duryodhana. They don their disguises as described. Draupadî goes to the palace as servant
to the queen. The favourite wife of King Virâṭa is called
Sudeshnâ, and she has a brother a mighty warrior, who is
the commander of all King Virâṭa's forces. This brother
is named Kîchaka. Brother and sister are soon consumed
with passion. One is madly jealous of the beauty of
Draupadî and fears her rivalry with King Virâṭa. The other
is madly in love with her. An infamous alliance is the consequence of these powerful incentives. Sudeshnâ plots with
Kîchaka to effect the ruin of Draupadî.

The bold commander-in-chief is not long in declaring his
passion—

"Thine eyes are very large, O woman of amazing beauty.
Thine eyebrows are like the petals of the lotus. Thy face
beams on mine eyes like the soft light of the moon.

"Art thou Lakshmî in person, or Modesty, or Fame, or
Beauty, or Auspicious Fortune?

" Hast thou robbed Love of his limbs ?

"The pupils of thy smiling eyes are veiled by their lashes as the moon by a fleecy cloud."

The honest warrior then proceeds to catalogue her beauties with an old-world literalness which shocks modern missionaries when they hear these songs droned out in the hush of a summer evening, accompanied by the rude music of an Indian bazaar ; but the general tone of the narrative is lofty, and the ethics unswerving. Kichaka offers to make all his wives her slaves, and give all his wealth to the beautiful stranger. Draupadi frames her answers with strong and evident desire to avoid extremes.

"My caste is abject. I am a servant. I dress the hair of my mistress.

"I am the wife of another. The wives of mortals are sacred. Remember thy duty. Five beings, superhuman, strong, terrible, watch over me. Thy craze to hold me in thine arms is like the delirium of the sick man in the presence of the tomb. The sinful mind that feeds on desire tastes infamy, perhaps death."

The bold warrior is not to be frightened. The plot develops rapidly, and so do the schemes of the impassioned brother and sister. She orders poor Draupadi to go to the house of Kichaka alone in the middle of the night. He possesses a delicious beverage. It is to be found in no other house ; and the queen is thirsty. Poor Draupadi remonstrates : "I cannot go to his house, O queen. He is immodest, without fear, without honour. Love puffs him out with an insensate pride."

The queen haughtily presents a golden vase to Draupadi, and orders her to go. She is called a voluntary servant in parts of the narrative ; but it is plain, from some of the warm sapphics of the general, that she was completely naked and in fact a slave.

But plot can be met with counterplot. Kichaka has the subtle Sudeshnâ as an ally. Draupadi confides her woe to Bhima. The catastrophe is tremendous. Kichaka, seeing a veiled female alone in a solitary bedroom, seizes her in his strong arms, and gets a return embrace which rather astonishes him. He is enlaced in the terrific hug of the Indian Hercules, and his life is literally squeezed out of him. This denouement acted before a rude audience in an Indian bazaar would be very effective. It may have been witnessed by Alexander the Great and Arthur, Duke of Wellington. According to some writers, chronology is no bar to Achilles having seen it. The travesty of the five brothers may have been seen by Buddha, Pythagoras, and Albert, Prince of Wales. Who can tell when this felicitous comedy was put on the stage and when it will be taken off?

Our drama develops. The bold soldier Kîchaka had one hundred brothers, which proves him to have been of the same mystic insect tribe as Scorpio. To avenge his death, they seize on Draupadî, and carry her off with his much mangled body to the graveyard. If she would not be his mistress on earth, she must go to his zenana in heaven. Her cries, as they are proceeding to burn her, attract the bold Bhima. He tears up a tree in the grave-yard, and makes sad havoc amongst the children of Rudra. Other complications soon occur. The brave Kichaka awed the neighbouring nations, and his death was the signal for much cattle-lifting and many raids. Duryodhana and the sons of Kuru took part in one of these expeditions. In another, Virâta was seized. Uttara, his son, to rescue him, hurried away with an army. Arjuna was his charioteer. The boy's heart failed him, and he jumped out and ran away. Arjuna forced him back, and recovering for the nonce the terrible bow Gândîva, the hero returned to the fight, the boy this time acting as the charioteer. The unrivalled archer soon dispersed his foes. And to keep up his disguise, he fathered all this prowess on the young boy. The donkey in the lion's skin is as old as the day of Arjuna, as old as the world.

Virâta, once more at liberty, holds a council of war. At it he is astonished to see his head dancing-master and dicer, his head eunuch, his cook, his cowherd, etc. Krishna is there likewise, for Duryodhana refuses to give back the kingdom now that the stipulated thirteen years are expired. Krishna

counsels peace, but though he is looked upon by both sides as
God Almighty on earth, no one pays any attention to him.
The reason of this is plain. At the time he was clumsily
added to the story, every man, woman and child in the
humblest bazaar knew every detail of the great battle of Kuru
Kshetra. He could not be made to take a prominent part in
it, for the prowess of Bhima and Arjuna had been sung by
countless wandering bards. A very lame explanation is
given that he could not take an active part in the contest
because the Kurus were his cousins as well as the five sons
of Pându. When all hope of peace has departed, he consents
to act as charioteer to Arjuna.

A scene of the Homeric pattern takes place at Hastinâpura
when the ambassador of the five sons of Pându arrives.
Karna, the Achilles of the army of the sons of Kuru, makes a
speech breathing defiance. Dhritarâshtra, the blind king, and
Bhishma counsel caution. Negotiations continue for some
time but without result.

Excepting when drilled by English or French drill-
sergeants, the barbaric hordes of India have always fought in
one way. A Bahador or doughty hero comes to the front
and inspires his followers and confounds his foes by a flood of
what he calls gali (heroic Billingsgate). He compares the
first to mighty elephants in the rutting season and Bengal
tigers. He compares his foes to pigs, to owls, and throws
serious doubts on the question of their birth in lawful wedlock.
It has been the fate of the present writer to witness an engage-
ment where this ancient Indian method of warfare was adopted.
The bow Gandiva twanged, and arrows fell thickly amongst
our sepoys. The drum of Rudra kept up a weird continuous
dull reverberation. Men as naked and almost as well limbed
as Bhima and the Râksha when they wrestled (and the fate of
Hidambâ was in the balance) flashed rude battle-axes and
swords aloft and shouted. These poor black men still
worshipped the serpent. They sacrificed a kid under the
holy Sal tree as our party came up, and we found the little
victim still warm. They were simple herdsmen and clearers
of jungle like the historical and early sons of Pându. They

slaughtered deer with their arrows. They were brave and truthful. Even before a court-martial they never attempted to conceal any acts of rebellion and breaches of the law. We came upon them in luxuriant bush amidst woody hillocks. The sun was setting, and I can see before me still the rude chief brandishing his sword and uttering his defiance to the bullets that were whistling near him. Mismanagement had driven these men (they were called Santals) into revolt. Their lair consisted of a few rude huts roofed with dried boughs.

I think this experience is of use to me in enabling me to understand the great battle of Kuru Kshetra. Axes and swords flashed ; the drum of Rudra rolled incessantly. It is called a "thunder" in more than one passage. We here get the root idea of that popular military instrument. Conch shells sounded. Even the five heroic sons of Pându condescended to intimidate their foes with loud blasts of that archaic music. From the paramount importance given to archery in all the Indian epics, I think the chief tactics on these occasions consisted in first trying to weaken portions of the enemy's line with a skilful use of the bow. We hear of terrible charges of "thousands" of elephants, and tens of thousands of war chariots ; but, if any such organized and combined attack had been made, the battle would have been ended in half an hour. The commander-in-chief of the Kuru army, Bhishma, was a wonderful bowman. Sweta, the rival commander-in-chief, was almost his equal. When commanders-in-chief are selected for their skill in archery, we may be sure that much of the battle will take place with the two forces not nearer than convenient bow-shot distance.

And this seems to have been what really occurred. "Heroes sounded hundreds of drums and sent up noble shouts of war."[1] "Torrents" of arrows passed between the armies ; and the click of the bow-string against the hand-leather dominated the bells of the elephants and the neighing of the horses. The rival commanders had to show themselves in the front of the battle, and the early descriptions are devoted chiefly to them.

[1] "Bhishma Parva," 1631.

" They described various circles, sweeping forward and back, so great was the skill of their coachmen. Each watched his opportunity for an attack." They sounded their conchs to outroar the din of battle. They emptied their quivers with terrible effect.

If an archaic Jomini had had to draw up the three great maxims of ancient battle, they must have been the following :—

1. Try with your arrows to make the rival commander-in-chief as much like a *poulet piqué au lard* as is practicable.

2. Try and kill the horse of his chariot.

3. Try and knock over his banner.

Of these maxims the last was evidently considered the most important. Archers were trained by Brahmins, and charms and incantations were deemed more potent than eye and muscle. From the pains taken to strike down a hero's banner it is plain that it was held to possess some weird influence. It was important to slay the horse, because when the warrior alighted he ran a great danger of being ridden over and trampled to death. The feat of transfixing his body with many arrows seemed to be held in less esteem. The commanders-in-chief, Bhishma and Śweta, in their great personal encounter, are stated to have been both stuck all over with shafts, without apparently arresting their ardour. And Dhrishtadyumna put "ninety sharp arrows" into Drona.[1]

Śweta lost his car and was killed eventually by Bhishma. The shafts of that terrible archer created something like a panic in the army of the sons of Pându.

Although much in his narrative is mystic, the poet gives us a real picture of an Indian battle in those ancient times. We have the flights of arrows, the single combats with dart and sabre, with breast-plate and shield. Duryodhana and Karna are conspicuous for their prowess in one part of the field. Arjuna and Bhima are terrible in another. The fight lasts several days, and soon the spectacle of the theatre of carnage is frightful to contemplate.

" The field of battle was covered with tall chiefs, sons of

---

[1] " Bhishma Parva," 2200.

kings dying or dead, wearing their earrings and armlets. There were chariots with broken wheels, and crushed elephants. Foot soldiers fled pell-mell amongst the horsemen. Fighting men in chariots fell in all directions. Overturned cars and torn flags, wheels and shafts, encumbered the ground.

"Bathed in the red blood of many horses and elephants and brave men, the battle-field shone out like a cloud of autumn.

"Dogs and crows, vultures and jackals, snarled and snapped and pecked over this rich prey. Quadrupeds and birds of the air became fierce foes.

"The winds moaned with the voice of the Râkshasas, the murky legions of hell." [1]

But Bhishma is still the great hero, and many kings visit the world of Yama. The ten points of heaven are darkened with his shafts.

"He stood bow in hand between the two armies, and no king could fix his eye upon him. None can stare at the blinding sun in the noontide of his career."

At length, on the tenth day of the fight, Arjuna drew near, with his ape banner fluttering in the breeze. The bow Gandiva was pitted against the powerful bow of Bhishma. Other heroes came up to assist the brave son of Pându. Shafts in thousands flew at the heroic Bhishma; his breastplate was beaten to pieces, and his body torn with darts and javelins and golden arrows, with clubs, with the weapon called "scorpion" (Śathagnî), with the mysterious Bhuśundi, which many scholars conceive to have been a pre-historic piece of artillery. At last his banner is lying in the bloody mud, the vexed hero is brought to the ground, and the fierce battle is hushed with the crash of his fall. Heroes of both armies crowd round him, and the bright forms of Vyâsa and other heavenly messengers are patent to his dying eyes. They tell him that the portals of Swarga, the shining refuge of the brave man who falls in battle, are already swinging wide open to receive him.

[1] "Bhishma Parva," vv. 5504-10.

The account of his death is very pathetic. His body is so transfixed with shafts that they actually prop him up on the bloody battle-field. He calls this heroic couch, a bed of arrows. Also he goes so far as to demand a grim boon from Arjuna, three new arrows to act as a pillow and prop up his head. Leeches draw near, and cunning arrow-extractors, but he beckons them away.

"The shafts of Arjuna are the messengers of Yama," he says. "They pierce through strong breast-plates, and like serpents full of venom they eat into my flesh. They are not like the puny missiles Śikhandi."

He lingers until the sun's cycle has reached "the northern point" (entered Sagittarius), and then the white swans of Swarga fly down and carry off his soul.

Plainly in the epic there are two Rudras—one the vulgar villain, with the poison of the scorpion. He is Duryodhana. But Bhishma in this canto is noble and majestic. The sun is in Scorpio, and the shapeless monolith worshipped during the month would represent to the Vedic worshipper the storm-cloud with its many shining arms. Its lightnings spread death and desolation, but still it is an aspect of the Eternal as much as the smiling flowers of May. It is to be remarked that the war arose from the capture of cattle by the sons of Kuru. The demon Vṛitra had carried them to his celebrated cavern. The last act of Bhishma is to request Arjuna to give him water. This is effected by an arrow which creates a spring in the ground. The thunderbolt of Indra calls forth the fertilizing moisture of the storm. The hero with his thousand adhering arrows is Scorpio again with his thousand arms, and the "pillow" the tridentine horns or crest. In case this somewhat overdone symbolism should still fail to impress initiates, King Yudhishthira before the battle takes off his breast-plate and tiara, and goes forward to kiss Bhishma's feet, humble and naked, like a slave.

The fall of Bhishma, in the old story, was probably the end of the campaign ; but ballad-makers like plenty of fighting. Drona succeeds Bhishma, but he is decapitated by Dhrishṭa-dyumna, the rival commander-in-chief. Bhima encounters Duhśâscna, who had dragged in Draupadî when she was won as a slave. As a retaliation, Bhîma cuts off his head and drinks his blood on the field of battle. The mighty Karṇa's head is also taken off by a weapon called an anjalika, launched by Arjuna. Duryodhana, by-and-by, is the only chief of note left alive. He escapes to a subaqueous cavern. There he is sheltered by his magic arts for a time ; but, stung by the taunts of his foes, he agrees to come out and fight Bhîma with a club. Bhîma slays him. Nearly all the forces, even of the sons of Pâṇḍu, were slain in the great fight. For victory Yudhishṭhira had a depeopled Indraprastha.

The termination of the epic is so beautiful that it has been often translated. The five sons of Pâṇḍu, tired even of a heaven in the Khandava wood, resolve to journey to the eternal city on the steeps of Mount Meru. They depart with the royal Draupadî. Behind them follows a dog. The king, Yudhishṭhira, is seventh in the procession. Townsmen and the women of the palace accompany them for a short way, but none say " Return ! " The citizens at last bid farewell to the pilgrims. Then the five sons of Pâṇḍu and the queen journey towards the east. They yearn for union with Brahm. All worldly thoughts are suffocated. They pass many a sea and river, and many weary lands. Yudhishṭhira walks in front, then Bhîma, then Arjuna ; The Twins follow. Then comes the Pearl of Wives—the woman with the lotus eyes. The dog walks last. On the shore of a mighty ocean Arjuna casts into the waves the celebrated bow Gaṇḍiva and the magic double quiver. Soon the tall steeps of Himavat glow above them. Beyond the Himalayas is a sea of sand. Across this the pilgrims footed wearily in the direction of the Hindoo Koosh, which probably contains the highest mountain peaks of the world. By-and-by—glad sight—the icy spires of the heavenly mount are seen glowing pink in the evening. But poor Draupadî can only see the promised land from afar. She falls with weariness. Arjuna and the Twins also perish. Stout Bhîma is astonished at this, and comes to the conclusion that they are all too gross for heaven.

This mysticism is a little intricate. We have seen from

the Aitareya Brahmaṇam that Prajâpati—the Divine Male—is the year.   He is Animisha, the Sleepless God, and starts at the end of February—a month whose symbol is quadruple. In all the old creeds this early god was quadruple.   Bhima and the Twins and Arjuna (the bow) die, or are passed in the zodiac before Yudhishṭhira, whose symbol is the Man with the vase of Ichor, dominates.   He stands alone with Yama's dog.   Madame Blavatsky gives seven stages of spiritual progress which mortals after thousands and thousands of re-births will successively reach.

1. The body (Rupa).
2. Vitality (Jiva).
3. Astral body (Liṇga śarira).
4. Animal soul (Kâma rupa).
5. Human soul (Manas).
6. Spiritual soul (Buddhi).
7. Spirit (Atma).

This, by many theosophists who have lost faith in the Russian lady, is still thought to be the esoteric doctrine of India, disclosed by Mr. Subba Row.   I must acquit that Hindoo of any such complicity.   These stages, if taken literally, and that we may take them literally Mr. Sinnett gives the Sanskrit words, are pure nonsense.   Body, vitality, animalism, soul, and spirit (five of the stages), must be acquired simultaneously with individuality.   But the hand of a Western is patent.   All Easterns know that the liṇga śarira is the envelope of the soul from the moment of its existence, and in a re-birth may have been in existence fifty thousand years before the body then assumed.[1]   The teachings of Madame Blavatsky were thus condensed in an article in the *Saturday Review*, which criticised my " Koot Hoomi Unveiled "—

1. There is no God.
2. The great secret of magic is to perform miracles with His " ineffable name."
3. Annihilation is the reward of the just.
4. Annihilation is the punishment of the wicked.

[1] Colebrooke's " Essays," vol. i. p. 245.

It is to be confessed that many graver teachers in India and the West have held some of these views ; but the original Mahâbhârata knew nothing of the modern misty doctrines of Moksha and Nirvâna. The hero goes to the eternal heaven of God, a heaven tenanted by the seven great legions of dead men made wise (vidyadharas). I will conclude with a fine hymn that shows this.

HYMN TO THE SUN.

Eye of the World art thou!
The soul of every mortal and the Womb
Of Being!
The huckster on the mart,
The calm philosopher removed from broils,
The yogi by his tree,
All turn to thee.
Natheless thou art the Way!
The Gate of Freedom !
Thou bear'st the burthen of the universe,
Lighting the gleaming worlds.
And glowing with thy beams
Our hearts grow pure ; and villainy
Lets fall his cloak.
Along the giddy pathway of the skies
Thy car sails on to sound of mortal hymns
And heavenly voices :
The sweet Gandharves, the minstrels of the stars,
The mighty Thirty-Three take up the sound.
Thee, with rich lore of mystic rites,
Adoring, to celestial eminence
Indra arrived.
And crowned with deathless flowers
Plucked from immortal steeps,
The Vidyadharas round thee stand
Celestial courtiers,
The seven great legions of dead men made wise.
In all the hemispheres that zone on zone
Climb up to Brahma's bliss, is none like thee !
Thou art the Light of Lights. Thy name is Power,
Thy name is Love,
Thy name is Truth.
Thee Viśvakarma, heavenly architect,
Gave the great wheel that girds the ambient skies :
Rise up each morn, sweet Light, or we are blind.

A myriad years, so say our oracles,
Make up that mighty cycle which we call
          A Day of Brahma ;
Of which thou art the Embryo and End,
          The First and Last !
And soon thy fires from out the womb of earth,
          Hungry and vast,
Midst many thunders pealing through the skies,
And silent serpents shining in the cloud,
A million worlds shall melt to nothingness
And lay a dead race by its slumbering brothers ;
          Men call thee many names :
The Twelve Adityas of the Zone of Heaven,
Indra, and Rudra, Vishnu, Soul and Fire !
Eternal Brahma, Vivasvat, Pushân,
          Eternal Lord ;
The Bird whose wings bring mortals skyey thought,
The Nurse, The Egg of Death, the Sire of Day.
The Mother of sweet Hours, the glittering God
With locks of sunbeams and untiring steeds ;
Thee I salute. Who trusts in thee
          Shall know no sorrow !

INDEX.

A LIST OF

KEGAN PAUL, TRENCH, & CO.'S
PUBLICATIONS.

11,86

A LIST OF

KEGAN PAUL, TRENCH, & CO.'S
PUBLICATIONS.

CONTENTS.

A. K. H. B.—FROM A QUIET PLACE. A New Volume of Sermons. Crown 8vo. 5s.

ALEXANDER (William, D.D., Bishop of Derry)—THE GREAT QUESTION, and other Sermons. Crown 8vo. 6s.

ALLEN (Rev. R.) M.A.—ABRAHAM ; HIS LIFE, TIMES, AND TRAVELS, 3,800 years ago. Second Edition. Post 8vo. 6s.

ALLIES (T. W.) M.A.—PER CRUCEM AD LUCEM. The Result of a Life. 2 vols. Demy 8vo. 25s.

A LIFE'S DECISION. Crown 8vo. 7s. 6d.

AMHERST (Rev. W. J.)—THE HISTORY OF CATHOLIC EMANCIPATION AND THE PROGRESS OF THE CATHOLIC CHURCH IN THE BRITISH ISLES (CHIEFLY IN ENGLAND) FROM 1771–1820. 2 vols. Demy 8vo. 24s.

AMOS (Prof. Sheldon)—THE HISTORY AND PRINCIPLES OF THE CIVIL LAW OF ROME. An aid to the study of Scientific and Comparative Jurisprudence. Demy 8vo. 16s.

ANCIENT and MODERN BRITONS : a Retrospect. 2 vols. demy 8vo. 24s.

ANDERDON (Rev. W. H.)—EVENINGS WITH THE SAINTS. Crown 8vo. 5s.

ANDERSON (David)—'SCENES' IN THE COMMONS. Crown 8vo. 5s.

ARISTOTLE—THE NICOMACHEAN ETHICS OF ARISTOTLE. Translated by F. H. PETERS, M.A. Second Edition. Crown 8vo. 6s.

ARMSTRONG (Richard A.) B.A. — LATTER-DAY TEACHERS. Six Lectures. Small crown 8vo. 2s. 6d.

AUBERTIN (J. J.)—A FLIGHT TO MEXICO. With 7 full-page Illustrations and a Railway Map of Mexico. Crown 8vo. 7s. 6d.

SIX MONTHS IN CAPE COLONY AND NATAL. With Illustrations and Map. Crown 8vo. 6s.

BADGER (George Percy) D.C.L.—AN ENGLISH-ARABIC LEXICON. In which the equivalents for English Words and Idiomatic Sentences are rendered into literary and colloquial Arabic. Royal 4to. 80s.

BAGEHOT (Walter)—THE ENGLISH CONSTITUTION. New and Revised Edition. Crown 8vo. 7s. 6d.

LOMBARD STREET. A Description of the Money Market. Eighth Edition. Crown 8vo. 7s. 6d.

ESSAYS ON PARLIAMENTARY REFORM. Crown 8vo. 5s.

SOME ARTICLES ON THE DEPRECIATION OF SILVER, AND TOPICS CONNECTED WITH IT. Demy 8vo. 5s.

BAGOT (Alan) C.E.—ACCIDENTS IN MINES : Their Causes and Prevention. Crown 8vo. 6s.

THE PRINCIPLES OF COLLIERY VENTILATION. Second Edition, greatly enlarged, crown 8vo. 5s.

THE PRINCIPLES OF CIVIL ENGINEERING IN ESTATE MANAGEMENT. Crown 8vo. 7s. 6d.

BAKER (Sir Sherston, Bart.)—THE LAWS RELATING TO QUARANTINE. Crown 8vo. 12s. 6d.

BAKER (Thomas)—A BATTLING LIFE; chiefly in the Civil Service. An Autobiography, with Fugitive Papers on Subjects of Public Importance. Crown 8vo. 7s. 6d.

BALDWIN (Capt. J. H.)—THE LARGE AND SMALL GAME OF BENGAL AND THE NORTH-WESTERN PROVINCES OF INDIA. Small 4to. With 20 Illustrations. New and Cheaper Edition. Small 4to. 10s. 6d.

BALLIN (Ada S. and F. L.)—A HEBREW GRAMMAR. With Exercises selected from the Bible. Crown 8vo. 7s. 6d.

BALL (John, F.R.S.)—NOTES OF A NATURALIST IN SOUTH AMERICA. Crown 8vo.

BARCLAY (Edgar) — MOUNTAIN LIFE IN ALGERIA. Crown 4to. With numerous Illustrations by Photogravure. 16s.

BARLOW (J. W.) M.A.—THE ULTIMATUM OF PESSIMISM. An Ethical Study. Demy 8vo. 6s.

SHORT HISTORY OF THE NORMANS IN SOUTH EUROPE. Demy 8vo. 7s. 6d.

BAUR (Ferdinand) Dr. Ph., Professor in Maulbronn.—A PHILOLOGICAL INTRODUCTION TO GREEK AND LATIN FOR STUDENTS. Translated and adapted from the German by C. KEGAN PAUL, M.A., and the Rev. E. D. STONE, M.A. Third Edition. Crown 8vo. 6s.

BAYLY (Capt. George)—SEA LIFE SIXTY YEARS AGO. A Record of Adventures which led up to the Discovery of the Relics of the long-missing Expedition commanded by the Comte de la Perouse. Crown 8vo. 3s. 6d.

BELLASIS (Edward)—THE MONEY JAR OF PLAUTUS AT THE ORATORY SCHOOL : An Account of the Recent Representation. With Appendix and 16 Illustrations. Small 4to. 2s.

THE NEW TERENCE AT EDGBASTON. Being Notices of the Performances in 1880 and 1881. With Preface, Notes, and Appendix. Third Issue. Small 4to. 1s. 6d.

BENN (Alfred W.)—THE GREEK PHILOSOPHERS. 2 vols. Demy 8vo. 28s.

BIBLE FOLK-LORE.—A STUDY IN COMPARATIVE MYTHOLOGY. Large crown 8vo. 10s. 6d.

BIRD (Charles) F.G.S.—Higher Education in Germany and England : Being a Brief Practical Account of the Organisation and Curriculum of the German Higher Schools. With Critical Remarks and Suggestions with reference to those of England. Small crown 8vo. 2s. 6d.

BLACKBURN (Mrs. Hugh)—Bible Beasts and Birds. A New Edition of 'Illustrations of Scripture by an Animal Painter.' With Twenty-two Plates, Photographed from the Originals, and Printed in Platinotype. 4to. cloth extra, gilt edges, 42s.

BLACKLEY (Rev. W. S.)—Essays on Pauperism. 16mo. sewed, 1s.

BLECKLY (Henry)—Socrates and the Athenians : an Apology. Crown 8vo. 2s. 6d.

BLOOMFIELD (The Lady)—Reminiscences of Court and Diplomatic Life. New and Cheaper Edition. With Frontispiece. Crown 8vo. 6s.

BLUNT (The Ven. Archdeacon)—The Divine Patriot, and other Sermons, Preached in Scarborough and in Cannes. New and Cheaper Edition. Crown 8vo. 4s. 6d.

BLUNT (Wilfrid S.)—The Future of Islam. Crown 8vo. 6s.

Ideas about India. Crown 8vo. cloth, 6s.

BODDY (Alexander A.)—To Kairwán the Holy. Scenes in Muhammedan Africa. With Route Map, and 8 Illustrations by A. F. Jacassey. Crown 8vo. 6s.

BOSANQUET (Bernard)—Knowledge and Reality. A Criticism of Mr. F. H. Bradley's 'Principles of Logic.' Crown 8vo. 9s.

BOUVERIE-PUSEY (S. E. B.)—Permanence and Evolution. An Inquiry into the supposed Mutability of Animal Types. Crown 8vo. 5s.

BOIVEN (H. C.) M.A.—Studies in English, for the use of Modern Schools. 7th Thousand. Small crown 8vo. 1s. 6d.

English Grammar for Beginners. Fcp. 8vo. 1s.

Simple English Poems. English Literature for Junior Classes. In Four Parts. Parts I., II., and III. 6d. each ; Part IV. 1s. ; complete, 3s.

BRADLEY (F. H.)—The Principles of Logic. Demy 8vo. 16s.

BRIDGETT (Rev. T. E.)—History of the Holy Eucharist in Great Britain. 2 vols. Demy 8vo. 18s.

BRODRICK (The Hon. G. C.)—Political Studies. Demy 8vo. 14s.

BROOKE (Rev. S. A.)—Life and Letters of the Late Rev. F. W. Robertson, M.A. Edited by.

I. Uniform with Robertson's Sermons. 2 vols. With Steel Portrait, 7s. 6d.
II. Library Edition. 8vo. With Portrait, 12s.
III. A Popular Edition. In 1 vol. 8vo. 6s.

The Fight of Faith. Sermons preached on various occasions. Fifth Edition. Crown 8vo. 7s. 6d.

The Spirit of the Christian Life. Third Edition. Crown 8vo. 5s.

Theology in the English Poets.—Cowper, Coleridge, Wordsworth, and Burns. Fifth Edition. Post 8vo. 5s.

Christ in Modern Life. Sixteenth Edition. Crown 8vo. 5s.

Sermons. First Series. Thirteenth Edition. Crown 8vo. 5s.

Sermons. Second Series. Sixth Edition. Crown 8vo. 5s.

BROWNE (*H. L.*)—REASON AND RELIGIOUS BELIEF. Crown 8vo.
3*s.* 6*d.*

BROWN (*Rev. J. Baldwin*) *B.A.*—THE HIGHER LIFE: its Reality,
Experience, and Destiny. Sixth Edition. Crown 8vo. 5*s.*

DOCTRINE OF ANNIHILATION IN THE LIGHT OF THE GOSPEL OF
LOVE. Five Discourses. Fourth Edition. Crown 8vo. 2*s.* 6*d.*

THE CHRISTIAN POLICY OF LIFE. A Book for Young Men of
Business. Third Edition. Crown 8vo. 3*s.* 6*d.*

BROWN (*Horatio F.*)—LIFE ON THE LAGOONS. With two Illustrations
and a Map. Crown 8vo. 6*s.*

BURDETT (*Henry C.*)—HELP IN SICKNESS : Where to Go and What
to Do. Crown 8vo. 1*s.* 6*d.*

HELPS TO HEALTH : The Habitation, The Nursery, The Schoolroom,
and The Person. With a Chapter on Pleasure and Health Resorts. Crown
8vo. 1*s.* 6*d.*

BURKE (*The late Very Rev. T. N.*)—HIS LIFE. By W. J. FITZPATRICK.
2 vols. With Portrait. Demy 8vo. 30*s.*

BURTON (*Mrs. Richard*)—THE INNER LIFE OF SYRIA, PALESTINE, AND
THE HOLY LAND. Post 8vo. 6*s.*

CAPES (*J. M.*)—THE CHURCH OF THE APOSTLES : an Historical Inquiry. Demy 8vo. 9*s.*

CARLYLE AND THE OPEN SECRET OF HIS LIFE. By HENRY LARKIN.
Demy 8vo. 14*s.*

CARPENTER (*W. B.*) *LL.D., M.D., F.R.S., &c.*—THE PRINCIPLES
OF MENTAL PHYSIOLOGY. With their Applications to the Training and
Discipline of the Mind, and the Study of its Morbid Conditions. Illustrated.
Sixth Edition. 8vo. 12*s.*

CATHOLIC DICTIONARY—Containing some account of the Doctrine,
Discipline, Rites, Ceremonies, Councils, and Religious Orders of the Catholic
Church. By WILLIAM E. ADDIS and THOMAS ARNOLD, M.A. Third
Edition, demy 8vo. 21*s.*

CHARLES (*Rev. R. H.*)—FORGIVENESS, and other Sermons. Crown 8vo.

CHEYNE (*Rev. Canon, M.A., D.D., Edin.*)—JOB AND SOLOMON ; or,
the Wisdom of the Old Testament. Demy 8vo.

THE PROPHECIES OF ISAIAH. Translated with Critical Notes and
Dissertations. 2 vols. Third Edition. Demy 8vo. 25*s.*

CIRCULATING CAPITAL. Being an Inquiry into the Fundamental Laws of
Money. An Essay by an East India Merchant. Small crown 8vo. 6*s.*

CLAIRAUT—ELEMENTS OF GEOMETRY. Translated by Dr. KAINES.
With 145 Figures. Crown 8vo. 4*s.* 6*d.*

CLAPPERTON (*Jane Hume*)—SCIENTIFIC MELIORISM AND THE EVO-
LUTION OF HAPPINESS. Large crown 8vo. 8*s.* 6*d.*

CLARKE (*Rev. Henry James*) *A.K.C.*—THE FUNDAMENTAL SCIENCE.
Demy 8vo. 10*s.* 6*d.*

CLAYDEN (*P. W.*)—SAMUEL SHARPE—EGYPTOLOGIST AND TRANSLA-
TOR OF THE BIBLE. Crown 8vo. 6*s.*

CLODD (*Edward*) *F.R.A.S.*—THE CHILDHOOD OF THE WORLD : a
Simple Account of Man in Early Times. Seventh Edition. Crown 8vo. 3*s.*
A Special Edition for Schools, 1*s.*

CLODD (*Edward*)—continued.

THE CHILDHOOD OF RELIGIONS. Including a Simple Account of the Birth and Growth of Myths and Legends. Eighth Thousand. Crown 8vo. 5*s.*
A Special Edition for Schools. 1*s.* 6*d.*

JESUS OF NAZARETH. With a brief sketch of Jewish History to the Time of His Birth. Small crown 8vo. 6*s.*

COGHLAN (*J. Cole*) *D.D.*—THE MODERN PHARISEE, AND OTHER SERMONS. Edited by the Very Rev. H. H. DICKINSON, D.D., Dean of Chapel Royal, Dublin. New and Cheaper Edition. Crown 8vo. 7*s.* 6*d.*

COLE (*George R. Fitz-Roy*)—THE PERUVIANS AT HOME. Crown 8vo. 6*s.*

COLERIDGE (*Sara*)—MEMOIR AND LETTERS OF SARA COLERIDGE. Edited by her Daughter. With Index. Cheap Edition. With one Portrait. 7*s.* 6*d.*

COLLECTS EXEMPLIFIED (*The*) — Being Illustrations from the Old and New Testaments of the Collects for the Sundays after Trinity. By the Author of 'A Commentary on the Epistles and Gospels.' Edited by the Rev. JOSEPH JACKSON. Crown 8vo. 5*s.*

CONNELL (*A. K.*)—DISCONTENT AND DANGER IN INDIA. Small crown 8vo. 3*s.* 6*d.*

THE ECONOMIC REVOLUTION OF INDIA. Crown 8vo. 4*s.* 6*d.*

COOK (*Keningale, LL.D.*)—THE FATHERS OF JESUS. A Study of the Lineage of the Christian Doctrine and Traditions. 2 vols. Demy 8vo. 28*s.*

CORR (*The late Rev. Thomas*)—ESSAYS, TALES, ALLEGORIES, AND POEMS. Crown 8vo.

CORY (*William*)—A GUIDE TO MODERN ENGLISH HISTORY. Part I.—MDCCCXV.-MDCCCXXX. Demy 8vo. 9*s.* Part II.—MDCCCXXX.-MDCCCXXXV. 15*s.*

COTTERILL (*H. B.*)—AN INTRODUCTION TO THE STUDY OF POETRY. Crown 8vo. 7*s.* 6*d.*

COTTON (*H. J. S.*)—NEW INDIA, OR INDIA IN TRANSITION. Third Edition. Crown 8vo. 4*s.* 6*d.* Popular Edition, paper covers, 1*s.*

COUTTS (*Francis Burdett Money*)—THE TRAINING OF THE INSTINCT OF LOVE. With a Preface by the Rev. EDWARD THRING, M.A. Small crown 8vo. 2*s.* 6*d.*

COX (*Rev. Sir George W.*) *M.A., Bart.*—THE MYTHOLOGY OF THE ARYAN NATIONS. New Edition. Demy 8vo. 16*s.*

TALES OF ANCIENT GREECE. New Edition. Small crown 8vo. 6*s.*

A MANUAL OF MYTHOLOGY IN THE FORM OF QUESTION AND ANSWER. New Edition. Fcp. 8vo. 3*s.*

AN INTRODUCTION TO THE SCIENCE OF COMPARATIVE MYTHOLOGY AND FOLK-LORE. Second Edition. Crown 8vo. 7*s.* 6*d.*

COX (*Rev. Sir G. W.*) *M.A., Bart., and JONES* (*Eustace Hinton*)—POPULAR ROMANCES OF THE MIDDLE AGES. Third Edition, in 1 vol. Crown 8vo. 6*s.*

COX (*Rev. Samuel*) *D.D.*—A COMMENTARY ON THE BOOK OF JOB. With a Translation. Demy 8vo. 15*s.*

SALVATOR MUNDI; or, Is Christ the Saviour of all Men? Tenth Edition. Crown 8vo. 5*s.*

COX (Rev. Samuel)—continued.

THE LARGER HOPE : a Sequel to 'SALVATOR MUNDI.' Second Edition. 16mo. 1s.

THE GENESIS OF EVIL, AND OTHER SERMONS, mainly expository. Third Edition. Crown 8vo. 6s.

BALAAM : An Exposition and a Study. Crown 8vo. 5s.

MIRACLES. An Argument and a Challenge. Crown 8vo. 2s. 6d.

CRAVEN (Mrs.)—A YEAR'S MEDITATIONS. Crown 8vo. 6s.

CRAWFURD (Oswald)—PORTUGAL, OLD AND NEW. With Illustrations and Maps. New and Cheaper Edition. Crown 8vo. 6s.

CROZIER (John Beattie) M.B.—THE RELIGION OF THE FUTURE. Crown 8vo. 6s.

CRUISE (F. R., M.D.)—THOMAS À KEMPIS. Notes of a Visit to the Scenes in which his Life was spent, with some Account of the Examination of his Relics. Demy 8vo. Illustrated.

CUNNINGHAM (W., B.D.)—POLITICS AND ECONOMICS : An Essay on the Nature of the Principles of Political Economy, together with a Survey of Recent Legislation. Crown 8vo. 5s.

DANIEL (Gerard)—MARY STUART : a Sketch and a Defence. Crown 8vo. 5s.

DANIELL (Clarmont)—THE GOLD TREASURE OF INDIA : An Inquiry into its Amount, the Cause of its Accumulation, and the Proper Means of Using it as Money. Crown 8vo. 5s.

DISCARDED SILVER : a Plan for its Use as Money. Small crown 8vo. 2s.

DARMESTETER (Arsène)—THE LIFE OF WORDS AS THE SYMBOLS OF IDEAS. Crown 8vo. 4s. 6d.

DAVIDSON (Rev. Samuel) D.D., LL.D.—CANON OF THE BIBLE : Its Formation, History, and Fluctuations. Third and revised Edition. Small crown 8vo. 5s.

THE DOCTRINE OF LAST THINGS, contained in the New Testament, compared with the Notions of the Jews and the Statements of Church Creeds. Small crown 8vo. 3s. 6d.

DAWSON (Geo.) M.A.—PRAYERS, WITH A DISCOURSE ON PRAYER. Edited by his Wife. First Series. New and Cheaper Edition. Crown 8vo. 3s. 6d.

PRAYERS, WITH A DISCOURSE ON PRAYER. Edited by GEORGE ST. CLAIR. Second Series. Crown 8vo. 6s.

SERMONS ON DISPUTED POINTS AND SPECIAL OCCASIONS. Edited by his Wife. Fourth Edition. Crown 8vo. 6s.

SERMONS ON DAILY LIFE AND DUTY. Edited by his Wife. Fourth Edition. Crown 8vo. 6s.

THE AUTHENTIC GOSPEL, and other Sermons. Edited by GEORGE ST. CLAIR. Third Edition. Crown 8vo. 6s.

BIOGRAPHICAL LECTURES. Edited by GEORGE ST. CLAIR, F.G.S. Large crown 8vo. 7s. 6d.

DE JONCOURT (*Madame Marie*)—WHOLESOME COOKERY. Third
 Edition. Crown 8vo. 3*s*. 6*d*.

DEMOCRACY IN THE OLD WORLD AND THE NEW. By the Author of 'The
 Suez Canal, the Eastern Question, and Abyssinia,' &c. Small crown 8vo. 2*s*. 6*d*.

DENT (*H. C.*)—A YEAR IN BRAZIL. With Notes on Religion, Meteorology, Natural History, &c. Maps and Illustrations. Demy 8vo. 18*s*.

DISCOURSE ON THE SHEDDING OF BLOOD, AND THE LAWS OF WAR.
 Demy 8vo. 2*s*. 6*d*.

DOUGLAS (*Rev. Herman*)—INTO THE DEEP ; or, The Wonders of the
 Lord's Person. Crown 8vo. 2*s*. 6*d*.

DOWDEN (*Edward*) *LL.D.*—SHAKSPERE : a Critical Study of his Mind
 and Art. Seventh Edition. Post 8vo. 12*s*.

    STUDIES IN LITERATURE, 1789–1877. Third Edition. Large post
 8vo. 6*s*.

DULCE DOMUM. Fcp. 8vo. 5*s*.

DU MONCEL (*Count*)—THE TELEPHONE, THE MICROPHONE, AND THE
 PHONOGRAPH. With 74 Illustrations. Second Edition. Small crown 8vo. 5*s*.

DURUY (*Victor*)—HISTORY OF ROME AND THE ROMAN PEOPLE.
 Edited by Professor MAHAFFY, with nearly 3,000 Illustrations. 4to. 6 Vols.
 in 12 Parts, 30*s*. each volume.

EDGEWORTH (*F. Y.*)—MATHEMATICAL PSYCHICS. An Essay on
 the Application of Mathematics to Social Science. Demy 8vo. 7*s*. 6*d*.

EDUCATIONAL CODE OF THE PRUSSIAN NATION, IN ITS PRESENT FORM.
 In accordance with the Decisions of the Common Provincial Law, and with
 those of Recent Legislation. Crown 8vo. 2*s*. 6*d*.

EDUCATION LIBRARY. Edited by Sir PHILIP MAGNUS :—

    AN INTRODUCTION TO THE HISTORY OF EDUCATIONAL THEORIES.
 By OSCAR BROWNING, M.A. Second Edition. 3*s*. 6*d*.

    OLD GREEK EDUCATION. By the Rev. Prof. MAHAFFY, M.A. Second
 Edition. 3*s*. 6*d*.

    SCHOOL MANAGEMENT ; including a General View of the Work of
 Education, Organization, and Discipline. By JOSEPH LANDON. Fifth
 Edition. Crown 8vo. 6*s*.

EDWARDES (*Major-General Sir Herbert B.*)—MEMORIALS OF HIS
 LIFE AND LETTERS. By his WIFE. With Portrait and Illustrations. 2 vols.
 Demy 8vo. 36*s*.

ELSDALE (*Henry*)—STUDIES IN TENNYSON'S IDYLLS. Crown 8vo. 5*s*.

EMERSON'S (*Ralph Waldo*) LIFE. By OLIVER WENDELL HOLMES.
 [English Copyright Edition.] With Portrait. Crown 8vo. 6*s*.

ENOCH, THE PROPHET. The Book of. Archbishop Laurence's Translation.
 With an Introduction by the Author of the 'Evolution of Christianity.'
 Crown 8vo. 5*s*.

ERANUS. A COLLECTION OF EXERCISES IN THE ALCAIC AND SAPPHIC
 METRES. Edited by F. W. CORNISH, Assistant Master at Eton. Second
 Edition. Crown 8vo. 2*s*.

EVANS (*Mark*)—THE STORY OF OUR FATHER'S LOVE, told to Children.
 Sixth and Cheaper Edition. With Four Illustrations. Fcp. 8vo. 1*s*. 6*d*.

FAITH OF THE UNLEARNED, THE. Authority, apart from the Sanction of Reason, an Insufficient Basis for It. By ' One Unlearned,' Crown 8vo. 6s.

'*FAN KWAE*' AT CANTON BEFORE TREATY DAYS, 1825–1844. By AN OLD RESIDENT. With Frontispiece. Crown 8vo. 5s.

FEIS (Jacob)—SHAKSPERE AND MONTAIGNE : An Endeavour to Explain the Tendency of Hamlet from Allusions in Contemporary Works. Crown 8vo. 5s.

FIVE O'CLOCK TEA. Containing Receipts for Cakes of every description, Savoury Sandwiches, Cooling Drinks, &c. By the Author of ' Breakfast Dishes ' and ' Savouries and Sweets.' Fcp. 8vo. 1s. 6d., or 1s. sewed.

FLOREDICE (W. H.)—A MONTH AMONG THE MERE IRISH. Small crown 8vo. 5s.

FRANK LEWARD. Edited by CHARLES BAMPTON. Crown 8vo. 7s. 6d.

FULLER (Rev. Morris)—THE LORD'S DAY ; or, Christian Sunday. Its Unity, History, Philosophy, and Perpetual Obligation. Sermons. Demy 8vo. 10s. 6d.

GARDINER (Samuel R.) and J. BASS MULLINGER, M.A.— INTRODUCTION TO THE STUDY OF ENGLISH HISTORY. Second Edition. Large crown 8vo. 9s.

GARDNER (Dorsey) — QUATRE BRAS, LIGNY, AND WATERLOO. A Narrative of the Campaign in Belgium, 1815. With Maps and Plans. Demy 8vo. 16s.

GELDART (E. M.)—ECHOES OF TRUTH. Sermons, with a Short Selection of Prayers and an Introductory Sketch, by the Rev. C. B. UPTON. Crown 8vo. 6s.

GEORGE (Henry)—PROGRESS AND POVERTY : an Inquiry into the Causes of Industrial Depressions, and of Increase of Want with Increase of Wealth. The Remedy. Fifth Library Edition. Post 8vo. 7s. 6d. Cabinet Edition, crown 8vo. 2s. 6d.

   *** Also a Cheap Edition, limp cloth, 1s. 6d.; paper covers, 1s.

SOCIAL PROBLEMS. Crown 8vo. 5s.

   *** Also a Cheap Edition, paper covers, 1s.

PROTECTION, OR FREE TRADE. An Examination of the Tariff Question, with especial regard to the Interests of Labour. Crown 8vo. 5s.

GLANVILL (Joseph)—SCEPSIS SCIENTIFICA ; or, Confest Ignorance, the Way to Science ; in an Essay of the Vanity of Dogmatising and Confident Opinion. Edited, with Introductory Essay, by JOHN OWEN. Elzevir 8vo. printed on hand-made paper, 6s.

GLOSSARY OF TERMS AND PHRASES. Edited by the Rev. H. PERCY SMITH and others. Medium 8vo. 7s. 6d.

GLOVER (F.) M.A.—EXEMPLA LATINA. A First Construing Book, with Short Notes, Lexicon, and an Introduction to the Analysis of Sentences. Second Edition. Fcp. 8vo. 2s.

GOLDSMID (Sir Francis Henry) Bart., Q.C., M.P.—MEMOIR OF. Second Edition, revised. Crown 8vo. 6s.

GOODENOUGH (Commodore J. G.)—MEMOIR OF, with Extracts from his Letters and Journals. Edited by his Widow. With Steel Engraved Portrait. Third Edition. Crown 8vo. 5s.

GORDON (*Major-Gen. C. G.*)—HIS JOURNALS AT KARTOUM. Printed from the Original MS. With Introduction and Notes by A. EGMONT HAKE. Portrait, 2 Maps, and 30 Illustrations. 2 vols. Demy 8vo. 21s. Also a Cheap Edition in 1 vol., 6s.

GORDON'S (GENERAL) LAST JOURNAL. A Facsimile of the last Journal received in England from General Gordon. Reproduced by Photo-lithography. Imperial 4to. £3. 3s.

EVENTS IN HIS LIFE. From the Day of his Birth to the Day of his Death. By Sir H. W. GORDON. With Maps and Illustrations. Demy 8vo. 18s.

GOSSE (*Edmund*) — SEVENTEENTH CENTURY STUDIES. A Contribution to the History of English Poetry. Demy 8vo. 10s. 6d.

GOULD (*Rev. S. Baring*) *M.A.*—GERMANY, PRESENT AND PAST. New and Cheaper Edition. Large crown 8vo. 7s. 6d.

THE VICAR OF MORWENSTOW : a Life of Robert Stephen Hawker, M.A. New and Cheaper Edition. Crown 8vo. 5s.

GOWAN (*Major Walter E.*) — A. IVANOFF'S RUSSIAN GRAMMAR. (16th Edition). Translated, enlarged, and arranged for use of Students of the Russian Language. Demy 8vo. 6s.

GOWER (*Lord Ronald*)—MY REMINISCENCES. Limp Parchment, Antique, with Etched Portrait, 10s. 6d.

LAST DAYS OF MARY ANTOINETTE. An Historical Sketch. With Portrait and Facsimiles. Fcp. 4to. 10s. 6d.

NOTES OF A TOUR FROM BRINDISI TO YOKOHAMA, 1883–1884. Fcp. 8vo. 2s. 6d.

GRAHAM (*William*) *M.A.*—THE CREED OF SCIENCE, Religious, Moral, and Social. Second Edition, revised. Crown 8vo. 6s.

THE SOCIAL PROBLEM IN ITS ECONOMIC, MORAL, AND POLITICAL ASPECTS. Demy 8vo. 14s.

GREY (*Rowland*).—IN SUNNY SWITZERLAND. A Tale of Six Weeks. Small crown 8vo. 5s.

LINDENBLUMEN, and other Stories. Small crown 8vo. 5s.

GRIMLEY (*Rev. H. N.*) *M.A.*—TREMADOC SERMONS, CHIEFLY ON THE SPIRITUAL BODY, THE UNSEEN WORLD, AND THE DIVINE HUMANITY. Fourth Edition. Crown 8vo. 6s.

THE TEMPLE OF HUMANITY, and other Sermons. Crown 8vo. 6s.

GUSTAFSON (*Axel*)—THE FOUNDATION OF DEATH. A Study of the Drink Question. Fourth Edition. Crown 8vo. 5s.

SOME THOUGHTS ON MODERATION. Reprinted from a Paper read at the Reeve Mission Room, Manchester Square, June 8, 1885. Crown 8vo. 1s.

HADDON (*Caroline*)—THE LARGER LIFE, STUDIES IN HINTON'S ETHICS. Crown 8vo. 5s.

HAECKEL (*Prof. Ernst*)—THE HISTORY OF CREATION. Translation revised by Professor E. RAY LANKESTER, M.A., F.R.S. With Coloured Plates and Genealogical Trees of the various groups of both plants and animals. 2 vols. Third Edition. Post 8vo. 32s.

THE HISTORY OF THE EVOLUTION OF MAN. With numerous Illustrations. 2 vols. Post 8vo. 32s.

A VISIT TO CEYLON. Post 8vo. 7s. 6d.

FREEDOM IN SCIENCE AND TEACHING. With a Prefatory Note by T. H. HUXLEY, F.R.S. Crown 8vo. 5s.

HALF-CROWN SERIES :—

A LOST LOVE. By ANNA C. OGLE (Ashford Owen).

SISTER DORA : a Biography. By MARGARET LONSDALE.

TRUE WORDS FOR BRAVE MEN : a Book for Soldiers and Sailors. By the late CHARLES KINGSLEY.

NOTES OF TRAVEL : being Extracts from the Journals of Count VON MOLTKE.

ENGLISH SONNETS. Collected and Arranged by J. DENNIS.

HOME SONGS FOR QUIET HOURS. By the Rev. Canon R. H. BAYNES.

HAMILTON, MEMOIRS OF ARTHUR, B.A., of Trinity College, Cambridge. Crown 8vo. 6s.

HARRIS (William)—THE HISTORY OF THE RADICAL PARTY IN PARLIAMENT. Demy 8vo. 15s.

HARROP (Robert)—BOLINGBROKE. A Political Study and Criticism. Demy 8vo. 14s.

HART (Rev. J. W. T.)—AUTOBIOGRAPHY OF JUDAS ISCARIOT. A Character-Study. Crown 8vo. 3s. 6d.

HAWEIS (Rev. H. R.) M.A.—CURRENT COIN. Materialism—The Devil — Crime — Drunkenness — Pauperism — Emotion — Recreation — The Sabbath. Fifth Edition. Crown 8vo. 5s.

ARROWS IN THE AIR. Fifth Edition. Crown 8vo. 5s.

SPEECH IN SEASON. Fifth Edition. Crown 8vo. 5s.

THOUGHTS FOR THE TIMES. Fourteenth Edition. Crown 8vo. 5s.

UNSECTARIAN FAMILY PRAYERS. New Edition. Fcp. 8vo. 1s. 6d.

HAWKINS (Edwards Comerford) — SPIRIT AND FORM. Sermons preached in the Parish Church of Leatherhead. Crown 8vo. 6s.

HAWTHORNE (Nathaniel)—WORKS. Complete in 12 vols. Large post 8vo. each vol. 7s. 6d.
  VOL. I. TWICE-TOLD TALES.
    II. MOSSES FROM AN OLD MANSE.
    III. THE HOUSE OF THE SEVEN GABLES, and THE SNOW IMAGE.
    IV. THE WONDER BOOK, TANGLEWOOD TALES, and GRANDFATHER'S CHAIR.
    V. THE SCARLET LETTER, and THE BLITHEDALE ROMANCE.
    VI. THE MARBLE FAUN. (Transformation.)
  VII. & VIII. OUR OLD HOME, and ENGLISH NOTE-BOOKS.
    IX. AMERICAN NOTE-BOOKS.
    X. FRENCH AND ITALIAN NOTE-BOOKS.
    XI. SEPTIMIUS FELTON, THE DOLLIVER ROMANCE, FANSHAWE, and, in an appendix, THE ANCESTRAL FOOTSTEP.
    XII. TALES AND ESSAYS, AND OTHER PAPERS, WITH A BIOGRAPHICAL SKETCH OF HAWTHORNE.

HEATH (Francis George)—AUTUMNAL LEAVES. Third and Cheaper Edition. Large crown 8vo. 6s.

SYLVAN WINTER. With 70 Illustrations. Large crown 8vo. 14s.

HEGEL—THE INTRODUCTION TO HEGEL'S PHILOSOPHY OF FINE ART. Translated from the German, with Notes and Prefatory Essay, by BERNARD BOSANQUET, M.A. Crown 8vo. 5s.

HENNESSY (Sir John Pope)—RALEGH IN IRELAND, WITH HIS LETTERS ON IRISH AFFAIRS AND SOME CONTEMPORARY DOCUMENTS. Large crown 8vo. printed on hand-made paper, parchment, 10s. 6d.

HENRY (Philip)—Diaries and Letters. Edited by Matthew Henry Lee, M.A. Large crown 8vo. 7s. 6d.

HINTON (J.)—The Mystery of Pain. New Edition. Fcp. 8vo. 1s.

Life and Letters. With an Introduction by Sir W. W. Gull, Bart., and Portrait engraved on Steel by C. H. Jeens. Fifth Edition. Crown 8vo. 8s. 6d.

Philosophy and Religion. Selections from the MSS. of the late James Hinton. Edited by Caroline Haddon. Second Edition. Crown 8vo. 5s.

The Law Breaker and The Coming of the Law. Edited by Margaret Hinton. Crown 8vo. 6s.

Hodson of Hodson's Horse; or, Twelve Years of a Soldier's Life in India. Being Extracts from the Letters of the late Major W. S. R. Hodson. With a vindication from the attack of Mr. Bosworth Smith. Edited by his brother, G. H. Hodson, M.A. Fourth Edition. Large crown 8vo. 5s.

HOLTHAM (E. G.)—Eight Years in Japan, 1873–1881. Work, Travel, and Recreation. With 3 Maps. Large crown 8vo. 9s.

Homology of Economic Justice: An Essay by an East India Merchant. Small crown 8vo. 5s.

HOOPER (Mary)—Little Dinners: How to Serve them with Elegance and Economy. Twentieth Edition. Crown 8vo. 2s. 6d.

Cookery for Invalids, Persons of Delicate Digestion, and Children. Fifth Edition. Crown 8vo. 2s. 6d.

Every-Day Meals. Being Economical and Wholesome Recipes for Breakfast, Luncheon, and Supper. Sixth Edition. Crown 8vo. 2s. 6d.

HOPKINS (Ellice)—Work amongst Working Men. Fifth Edition. Crown 8vo. 3s. 6d.

HORNADAY (W. T.)—Two Years in a Jungle. With Illustrations. Demy 8vo. 21s.

HOSPITALIER (E.)—The Modern Applications of Electricity. Translated and Enlarged by Julius Maier, Ph.D. 2 vols. Second Edition, revised, with many additions and numerous Illustrations. Demy 8vo. 12s. 6d. each volume.

Vol. I.—Electric Generators, Electric Light.
   II.—Telephone: Various Applications: Electrical Transmission of Energy.

HOWARD (Robert) M.A.—The Church of England and other Religious Communions. A Course of Lectures delivered in the Parish Church of Clapham. Crown 8vo. 7s. 6d.

HUMPHREY (Rev. William)—The Bible and Belief. A Letter to a Friend. Small crown 8vo. 2s. 6d.

HUNTER (William C.)—Bits of Old China. Small crown 8vo. 6s.

HUNTINGFORD (Rev. E.) D.C.L.—The Apocalypse. With a Commentary and Introductory Essay. Demy 8vo. 9s.

HUTCHINSON (H.)—Thought Symbolism and Grammatic Illusions: Being a Treatise on the Nature, Purpose, and Material of Speech. Crown 8vo. 2s. 6d.

HUTTON (Rev. Charles F.)—Unconscious Testimony; or, the Silent Witness of the Hebrew to the Truth of the Historical Scriptures. Crown 8vo. 2s. 6d.

HYNDMAN (H. M.)—The Historical Basis of Socialism in England. Large crown 8vo. 8s. 6d.

IDDESLEIGH (Earl of)—THE PLEASURES, DANGERS, AND USES OF DESULTORY READING. Fcp. 8vo. in Whatman paper cover, 1s.

IM THURN (Everard F.)—AMONG THE INDIANS OF GUIANA. Being Sketches, chiefly Anthropologic, from the Interior of British Guiana. With 53 Illustrations and a Map. Demy 8vo. 18s.

JACCOUD (Prof. S.)—THE CURABILITY AND TREATMENT OF PULMONARY PHTHISIS. Translated and Edited by MONTAGU LUBBOCK, M.D. Demy 8vo. 15s.

JAUNT IN A JUNK: A Ten Days' Cruise in Indian Seas. Large crown 8vo. 7s. 6d.

JENKINS (E.) and RAYMOND (J.)—THE ARCHITECT'S LEGAL HANDBOOK. Third Edition, Revised. Crown 8vo. 6s.

JENKINS (Rev. Canon R. C.)—HERALDRY: English and Foreign. With a Dictionary of Heraldic Terms and 156 Illustrations. Small crown 8vo. 3s. 6d.
STORY OF THE CARAFFA. Small crown 8vo. 3s. 6d.

JERVIS (Rev. W. Henley)—THE GALLICAN CHURCH AND THE REVOLUTION. A Sequel to the History of the Church of France, from the Concordat of Bologna to the Revolution. Demy 8vo. 18s.

JOEL (L.)—A CONSUL'S MANUAL AND SHIPOWNER'S AND SHIPMASTER'S PRACTICAL GUIDE IN THEIR TRANSACTIONS ABROAD. With Definitions of Nautical, Mercantile, and Legal Terms; a Glossary of Mercantile Terms in English, French, German, Italian, and Spanish; Tables of the Money, Weights, and Measures of the Principal Commercial Nations and their Equivalents in British Standards; and Forms of Consular and Notarial Acts. Demy 8vo. 12s.

JOYCE (P. W.) LL.D. &c.—OLD CELTIC ROMANCES. Translated from the Gaelic. Crown 8vo. 7s. 6d.

KAUFMANN (Rev. M.) B.A.—SOCIALISM: its Nature, its Dangers, and its Remedies considered. Crown 8vo. 7s. 6d.

UTOPIAS; or, Schemes of Social Improvement, from Sir Thomas More to Karl Marx. Crown 8vo. 5s.

KAY (David)—EDUCATION AND EDUCATORS. Crown 8vo. 7s. 6d.

KAY (Joseph)—FREE TRADE IN LAND. Edited by his Widow. With Preface by the Right Hon. JOHN BRIGHT, M.P. Seventh Edition. Crown 8vo. 5s.
  ₊ Also a cheaper edition, without the Appendix, but with a Review of Recent Changes in the Land Laws of England, by the Right Hon. G. OSBORNE MORGAN, Q.C., M.P. Cloth, 1s. 6d.; Paper covers, 1s.

KELKE (W. H. H.)—AN EPITOME OF ENGLISH GRAMMAR FOR THE USE OF STUDENTS. Adapted to the London Matriculation Course and Similar Examinations. Crown 8vo. 4s. 6d.

KEMPIS (Thomas à)—OF THE IMITATION OF CHRIST. Parchment Library Edition, parchment or cloth, 6s.; vellum, 7s. 6d. The Red Line Edition, fcp. 8vo. red edges, 2s. 6d. The Cabinet Edition, small 8vo. cloth limp, 1s.; or cloth boards, red edges, 1s. 6d. The Miniature Edition, 32mo. red edges, 1s.
  ₊ All the above Editions may be had in various extra bindings.

KETTLEWELL (Rev. S.) M.A.—THOMAS À KEMPIS AND THE BROTHERS OF COMMON LIFE. 2 vols. With Frontispieces. Demy 8vo. 30s.
  ₊ Also an Abridged Edition in 1 vol. With Portrait. Crown 8vo. 7s. 6d.

KIDD (Joseph) M.D.—THE LAWS OF THERAPEUTICS ; or, the Science and Art of Medicine. Second Edition. Crown 8vo. 6s.

KINGSFORD (Anna) M.D.—THE PERFECT WAY IN DIET. A Treatise advocating a Return to the Natural and Ancient Food of Race. Small crown 8vo. 2s.

KINGSLEY (Charles) M.A.—LETTERS AND MEMORIES OF HIS LIFE. Edited by his WIFE. With Two Steel Engraved Portraits and Vignettes. Fifteenth Cabinet Edition, in 2 vols. Crown 8vo. 12s.

** Also a People's Edition in 1 vol. With Portrait. Crown 8vo. 6s.

ALL SAINTS' DAY, and other Sermons. Edited by the Rev. W. HARRISON. Third Edition. Crown 8vo. 7s. 6d.

TRUE WORDS FOR BRAVE MEN. A Book for Soldiers' and Sailors' Libraries. Eleventh Edition. Crown 8vo. 2s. 6d.

KNOX (Alexander A.)—THE NEW PLAYGROUND ; or, Wanderings in Algeria. New and Cheaper Edition. Large crown 8vo. 6s.

LAND CONCENTRATION AND IRRESPONSIBILITY OF POLITICAL POWER, as causing the Anomaly of a Widespread State of Want by the Side of the Vast Supplies of Nature. Crown 8vo. 5s.

LANDON (Joseph)—SCHOOL MANAGEMENT ; including a General View of the Work of Education, Organisation, and Discipline. Fifth Edition. Crown 8vo. 6s.

LAURIE (S. S.)—LECTURES ON THE RISE AND EARLY CONSTITUTION OF UNIVERSITIES. With a Survey of Mediæval Education. Crown 8vo. 6s.

LEE (Rev. F. G.) D.C.L.—THE OTHER WORLD; or, Glimpses of the Supernatural. 2 vols. A New Edition. Crown 8vo. 15s.

LETTERS FROM AN UNKNOWN FRIEND. By the Author of 'Charles Lowder.' With a Preface by the Rev. W. H. Cleaver. Fcp. 8vo. 1s.

LEWARD (Frank)—Edited by CHAS. BAMPTON. Crown 8vo. 7s. 6d.

LEWIS (Edward Dillon)—A DRAFT CODE OF CRIMINAL LAW AND PROCEDURE. Demy 8vo. 21s.

LIFE OF A PRIG. By ONE. Third Edition. Fcp. 8vo. 3s. 6d.

LILLIE (Arthur) M.R.A.S.—THE POPULAR LIFE OF BUDDHA. Containing an Answer to the Hibbert Lectures of 1881. With Illustrations. Crown 8vo. 6s.

BUDDHISM IN CHRISTENDOM ; or, Jesus, the Essene. Demy 8vo. with numerous Illustrations.

LLOYD (Walter)—THE HOPE OF THE WORLD: An Essay on Universal Redemption. Crown 8vo. 5s.

LONGFELLOW (H. Wadsworth)—LIFE. By his Brother, SAMUEL LONGFELLOW. With Portraits and Illustrations. 2 vols. Demy 8vo. 28s.

LONSDALE (Margaret)—SISTER DORA: a Biography. With Portrait. Cheap Edition. Crown 8vo. 2s. 6d.

GEORGE ELIOT : Thoughts upon her Life, her Books, and Herself. Second Edition. Small crown 8vo. 1s. 6d.

LOUNSBURY (Thomas R.)—JAMES FENIMORE COOPER. With Portrait. Crown 8vo. 5s.

LOWDER (Charles)—A BIOGRAPHY. By the Author of 'St. Teresa.' New and Cheaper Edition. Crown 8vo. With Portrait. 3s. 6d.

LÜCKES (Eva C. E.)—LECTURES ON GENERAL NURSING, delivered to the Probationers of the London Hospital Training School for Nurses. Crown 8vo. 2s. 6d.

LYALL (William Rowe) D.D.—PROPÆDEIA PROPHETICA ; or, The Use and Design of the Old Testament Examined. New Edition, with Notices by GEORGE C. PEARSON, M.A., Hon. Canon of Canterbury. Demy 8vo. 10s. 6d.

LYTTON (Edward Bulwer, Lord)—LIFE, LETTERS, AND LITERARY REMAINS. By his Son the EARL OF LYTTON. With Portraits, Illustrations, and Facsimiles. Demy 8vo. cloth. Vols. I. and II. 32s.

MACAULAY (G. C.)—FRANCIS BEAUMONT : A Critical Study. Crown 8vo. 5s.

MACCALLUM (M. W.) — STUDIES IN LOW GERMAN AND HIGH GERMAN LITERATURE. Crown 8vo. 6s.

MACHIAVELLI (Niccolò)—HIS LIFE AND TIMES. By Prof. VILLARI. Translated by LINDA VILLARI. 4 vols. Large post 8vo. 48s.

DISCOURSES ON THE FIRST DECADE OF TITUS LIVIUS. Translated from the Italian by NINIAN HILL THOMSON, M.A. Large crown 8vo. 12s.

THE PRINCE. Translated from the Italian by N. H. T. Small crown 8vo. printed on hand-made paper, bevelled boards, 6s.

MACKENZIE (Alexander)—HOW INDIA IS GOVERNED. Being an Account of England's work in India. Small crown 8vo. 2s.

MAC RITCHIE (David)—ACCOUNTS OF THE GYPSIES OF INDIA. With Map and Illustrations. Crown 8vo. 3s. 6d.

MAGNUS (Lady)—ABOUT THE JEWS SINCE BIBLE TIMES. From the Babylonian Exile till the English Exodus. Small crown 8vo. 6s.

MAGUIRE (Thomas)—LECTURES ON PHILOSOPHY. Demy 8vo. 9s.

MAIR (R. S.) M.D., F.R.C.S.E.—THE MEDICAL GUIDE FOR ANGLO-INDIANS. Being a Compendium of Advice to Europeans in India, relating to the Preservation and Regulation of Health. With a Supplement on the Management of Children in India. Second Edition. Crown 8vo. 3s. 6d.

MALDEN (Henry Elliot)—VIENNA, 1683. The History and Consequences of the Defeat of the Turks before Vienna, September 12, 1683, by John Sobieski, King of Poland, and Charles Leopold, Duke of Lorraine. Crown 8vo. 4s. 6d.

MANY VOICES.—A Volume of Extracts from the Religious Writers of Christendom, from the First to the Sixteenth Century. With Biographical Sketches. Crown 8vo. cloth extra, red edges, 6s.

MARKHAM (Capt. Albert Hastings) R.N.—THE GREAT FROZEN SEA : a Personal Narrative of the Voyage of the *Alert* during the Arctic Expedition of 1875-6. With Six Full-page Illustrations, Two Maps, and Twenty-seven Woodcuts. Sixth and Cheaper Edition. Crown 8vo. 6s.

MARTINEAU (Gertrude)—OUTLINE LESSONS ON MORALS. Small crown 8vo. 3s. 6d.

MASON (Charlotte M.)—HOME EDUCATION. A Course of Lectures to Ladies, delivered in Bradford in the winter of 1885-1886. Crown 8vo. 3s. 6d.

MAUDSLEY (H.) M.D.—BODY AND WILL. Being an Essay Concerning Will, in its Metaphysical, Physiological, and Pathological Aspects. 8vo. 12s.

NATURAL CAUSES AND SUPERNATURAL SEEMINGS. Crown 8vo. 6s.

McGRATH (Terence)—PICTURES FROM IRELAND. New and Cheaper Edition. Crown 8vo. 2s.

MEREDITH (M. A.)—THEOTOKOS, THE EXAMPLE FOR WOMAN. Dedicated, by permission, to Lady AGNES WOOD. Revised by the Venerable Archdeacon DENISON. 32mo, 1s. 6d.

MILLER (Edward)—THE HISTORY AND DOCTRINES OF IRVINGISM; or, the so-called Catholic and Apostolic Church. 2 vols. Large post 8vo. 15s.

THE CHURCH IN RELATION TO THE STATE. Large crown 8vo. 4s.

MILLS (Herbert)—POVERTY AND THE STATE; or, Work for the Unemployed. An Enquiry into the Causes and Extent of Enforced Idleness, together with a statement of a remedy practicable here and now. Crown 8vo.

MITCHELL (Lucy M.)—A HISTORY OF ANCIENT SCULPTURE. With numerous Illustrations, including six Plates in Phototype. Super royal, 42s.

SELECTIONS FROM ANCIENT SCULPTURE. Being a Portfolio containing Reproductions in Phototype of 36 Masterpieces of Ancient Art, to illustrate Mrs. MITCHELL's 'History of Ancient Sculpture.' 18s.

MITFORD (Bertram)—THROUGH THE ZULU COUNTRY. Its Battlefields and its People. With five Illustrations. Demy 8vo. 14s.

MOCKLER (E.)—A GRAMMAR OF THE BALOOCHEE LANGUAGE, as it is spoken in Makran (Ancient Gedrosia), in the Persia-Arabic and Roman characters. Fcp. 8vo. 5s.

MOLESWORTH (W. Nassau)—HISTORY OF THE CHURCH OF ENGLAND FROM 1660. Large crown 8vo. 7s. 6d.

MORELL (J. R.)—EUCLID SIMPLIFIED IN METHOD AND LANGUAGE. Being a Manual of Geometry. Compiled from the most important French Works, approved by the University of Paris and the Minister of Public Instruction. Fcp. 8vo. 2s. 6d.

MORGAN (C. Lloyd)—THE SPRINGS OF CONDUCT. An Essay in Evolution. Large crown 8vo. cloth, 7s. 6d.

MORISON (James Cotter)—THE SERVICE OF MAN. An Essay towards the Religion of the Future. Demy 8vo.

MORRIS (George)—THE DUALITY OF ALL DIVINE TRUTH IN OUR LORD JESUS CHRIST: FOR GOD'S SELF-MANIFESTATION IN THE IMPARTATION OF THE DIVINE NATURE TO MAN. Large Crown 8vo. 7s. 6d.

MORSE (E. S.) Ph.D.—FIRST BOOK OF ZOOLOGY. With numerous Illustrations. New and Cheaper Edition. Crown 8vo. 2s. 6d.

NELSON (J. H.) M.A.—A PROSPECTUS OF THE SCIENTIFIC STUDY OF THE HINDÛ LAW. Demy 8vo. 9s.

INDIAN USAGE AND JUDGE-MADE LAW IN MADRAS. Demy 8vo.

NEWMAN (Cardinal)—CHARACTERISTICS FROM THE WRITINGS OF. Being Selections from his various Works. Arranged with the Author's personal Approval. Seventh Edition. With Portrait Crown 8vo. 6s.

*** A Portrait of Cardinal Newman, mounted for framing, can be had, 2s. 6d.

NEW SOCIAL TEACHINGS. By POLITICUS. Small crown 8vo. 5s.

NEWMAN (Francis William)—ESSAYS ON DIET. Small crown 8vo. 2s.

NEW TRUTH AND THE OLD FAITH : ARE THEY INCOMPATIBLE? By a Scientific Layman. Demy 8vo. 10s. 6d.

NICOLS (Arthur) F.G.S., F.R.G.S.—CHAPTERS FROM THE PHYSICAL HISTORY OF THE EARTH : an Introduction to Geology and Palæontology. With numerous Illustrations. Crown 8vo. 5s.

NOEL (The Hon. Roden)—ESSAYS ON POETRY AND POETS. Demy 8vo. 12s.

NOPS (Marianne)—CLASS LESSONS ON EUCLID. Part I. containing the First Two Books of the Elements. Crown 8vo. 2s. 6d.

NUCES : EXERCISES ON THE SYNTAX OF THE PUBLIC SCHOOL LATIN PRIMER. New Edition in Three Parts. Crown 8vo. each 1s.
*** The Three Parts can also be had bound together in cloth, 3s.

OATES (Frank) F.R.G.S.—MATABELE LAND AND THE VICTORIA FALLS. A Naturalist's Wanderings in the Interior of South Africa. Edited by C. G. OATES, B.A. With numerous Illustrations and 4 Maps. Demy 8vo. 21s.

O'CONNOR (T. P.) M.P.—THE PARNELL MOVEMENT. With a Sketch of Irish Parties from 1843. Large crown 8vo. 7s. 6d.

OGLE (W.) M.D., F.R.C.P.—ARISTOTLE ON THE PARTS OF ANIMALS. Translated, with Introduction and Notes. Royal 8vo. 12s. 6d.

O'HAGAN (Lord) K.P.— OCCASIONAL PAPERS AND ADDRESSES. Large crown 8vo. 7s. 6d.

O'MEARA (Kathleen)—FREDERIC OZANAM, Professor of the Sorbonne : his Life and Work. Second Edition. Crown 8vo. 7s. 6d.

HENRI PERREYVE AND HIS COUNSELS TO THE SICK. Small crown 8vo. 5s.

ONE AND A HALF IN NORWAY. A Chronicle of Small Beer. By Either and Both. Small crown 8vo. 3s. 6d.

O'NEIL (The late Rev. Lord).—SERMONS. With Memoir and Portrait. Crown 8vo. 6s.

ESSAYS AND ADDRESSES. Crown 8vo. 5s.

ONLY PASSPORT TO HEAVEN, THE. By One who has it. Small crown 8vo. 1s. 6d.

OSBORNE (Rev. W. A.)—THE REVISED VERSION OF THE NEW TESTAMENT. A Critical Commentary, with Notes upon the Text. Crown 8vo. 5s.

OTTLEY (Henry Bickersteth)—THE GREAT DILEMMA : Christ His own Witness or His own Accuser. Six Lectures. Second Edition. Crown 8vo. 3s. 6d.

OUR PUBLIC SCHOOLS—ETON, HARROW, WINCHESTER, RUGBY, WESTMINSTER, MARLBOROUGH, THE CHARTERHOUSE. Crown 8vo. 6s.

OWEN (F. M.)—JOHN KEATS : a Study. Crown 8vo. 6s.
ACROSS THE HILLS. Small crown 8vo. 1s. 6d.

OWEN (Rev. Robert) B.D.—SANCTORALE CATHOLICUM ; or, Book of Saints. With Notes, Critical, Exegetical, and Historical. Demy 8vo. 18s.

B

OXONIENSIS—ROMANISM, PROTESTANTISM, ANGLICANISM. Being a
Layman's View of some Questions of the Day. Together with Remarks on
Dr. Littledale's 'Plain Reasons against Joining the Church of Rome.' Small
crown 8vo. 3s. 6d.

PALMER (the late William)—NOTES OF A VISIT TO RUSSIA IN 1840-41.
Selected and arranged by JOHN H. CARDINAL NEWMAN. With Portrait. Crown
8vo. 8s. 6d.

EARLY CHRISTIAN SYMBOLISM. A series of Compositions from Fresco-
Paintings, Glasses, and Sculptured Sarcophagi. Edited by the Rev. PROVOST
NORTHCOTE, D.D., and the Rev. CANON BROWNLOW, M.A. With Coloured
Plates, folio, 42s. ; or with plain plates, folio, 25s.

PARCHMENT LIBRARY. Choicely printed on hand-made paper, limp parchment antique or cloth, 6s. ; vellum, 7s. 6d. each volume.

MILTON'S POETICAL WORKS. 2 vols.

CHAUCER'S CANTERBURY TALES. The Prologue ; The Knightes
Tale ; The Man of Lawes Tale ; The Prioresses Tale ; The Clerkes Tale
Edited by ALFRED W. POLLARD.

SELECTIONS FROM THE PROSE WRITINGS OF JONATHAN SWIFT. With
a Preface and Notes by STANLEY LANE-POOLE, and Portrait.

ENGLISH SACRED LYRICS.

SIR JOSHUA REYNOLDS' DISCOURSES. Edited by EDMUND GOSSE.

SELECTIONS FROM MILTON'S PROSE WRITINGS. Edited by ERNEST
MYERS.

THE BOOK OF PSALMS. Translated by the Rev. Canon CHEYNE, D.D.

THE VICAR OF WAKEFIELD. With Preface and Notes by AUSTIN
DOBSON.

ENGLISH COMIC DRAMATISTS. Edited by OSWALD CRAWFURD.

ENGLISH LYRICS.

THE SONNETS OF JOHN MILTON. Edited by MARK PATTISON.
With Portrait after Vertue.

FRENCH LYRICS. Selected and Annotated by GEORGE SAINTSBURY.
With miniature Frontispiece, designed and etched by H. G. Glindoni.

FABLES by MR. JOHN GAY. With Memoir by AUSTIN DOBSON,
and an etched Portrait from an unfinished Oil-sketch by Sir Godfrey Kneller.

SELECT LETTERS OF PERCY BYSSHE SHELLEY. Edited, with an Intro-
tion, by RICHARD GARNETT.

THE CHRISTIAN YEAR ; Thoughts in Verse for the Sundays and
Holy Days throughout the Year. With etched Portrait of the Rev. J. Keble,
after the Drawing by G. Richmond, R.A.

SHAKSPERE'S WORKS. Complete in Twelve Volumes.

EIGHTEENTH CENTURY ESSAYS. Selected and Edited by AUSTIN
DOBSON. With a Miniature Frontispiece by K. Caldecott.

Q. HORATI FLACCI OPERA. Edited by F. A. CORNISH, Assistant
Master at Eton. With a Frontispiece after a design by L. ALMA TADEMA.
Etched by LEOPOLD LOWENSTAM.

EDGAR ALLAN POE'S POEMS. With an Essay on his Poetry by
ANDREW LANG, and a Frontispiece by Linley Sambourne.

SHAKSPERE'S SONNETS. Edited by EDWARD DOWDEN. With a
Frontispiece etched by Leopold Lowenstam, after the Death Mask.

PARCHMENT LIBRARY—continued.

ENGLISH ODES. Selected by EDMUND GOSSE. With Frontispiece on India paper by Hamo Thornycroft, A.R.A.

OF THE IMITATION OF CHRIST. By THOMAS À KEMPIS. A revised Translation. With Frontispiece on India paper, from a Design by W. B. Richmond.

POEMS : Selected from PERCY BYSSHE SHELLEY. Dedicated to Lady Shelley. With Preface by RICHARD GARNETT and a Miniature Frontispiece.
*** The above Volumes may also be had in a variety of leather bindings.

THE POETICAL WORKS OF JOHN MILTON. 2 vols.

LETTERS AND JOURNALS OF JONATHAN SWIFT. Selected and edited, with a Commentary and Notes, by STANLEY LANE POOLE.

DE QUINCEY'S CONFESSIONS OF AN ENGLISH OPIUM EATER. Reprinted from the First Edition. Edited by RICHARD GARNETT.

THE GOSPEL ACCORDING TO MATTHEW, MARK, AND LUKE.

PARSLOE (Joseph) — OUR RAILWAYS. Sketches, Historical and Descriptive. With Practical Information as to Fares and Rates, &c., and a Chapter on Railway Reform. Crown 8vo. 6s.

PASCAL (Blaise)—THE THOUGHTS OF. Translated from the Text of AUGUSTE MOLINIER by C. KEGAN PAUL. Large crown 8vo. with Frontispiece, printed on hand-made paper, parchment antique, or cloth, 12s. ; vellum, 15s.

PAUL (C. Kegan)—BIOGRAPHICAL SKETCHES. Printed on hand-made paper, bound in buckram. Second Edition. Crown 8vo. 7s. 6d.

PAUL (Alexander)—SHORT PARLIAMENTS. A History of the National Demand for Frequent General Elections. Small crown 8vo. 3s. 6d.

PEARSON (Rev. S.)—WEEK-DAY LIVING. A Book for Young Men and Women. Second Edition. Crown 8vo. 5s.

PENRICE (Major J.)—ARABIC AND ENGLISH DICTIONARY OF THE KORAN. 4to. 21s.

PESCHEL (Dr. Oscar)—THE RACES OF MAN AND THEIR GEOGRAPHICAL DISTRIBUTION. Second Edition, large crown 8vo. 9s.

PETERS (F. H.)—THE NICOMACHEAN ETHICS OF ARISTOTLE. Translated by. Crown 8vo. 6s.

PHIPSON (E.)—THE ANIMAL LORE OF SHAKSPEARE'S TIME. Including Quadrupeds, Birds, Reptiles, Fish, and Insects. Large post 8vo. 9s.

PIDGEON (D.)—AN ENGINEER'S HOLIDAY ; or, Notes of a Round Trip from Long. 0° to 0°. New and Cheaper Edition. Large crown 8vo. 7s. 6d.

OLD WORLD QUESTIONS AND NEW WORLD ANSWERS. Large crown 8vo. 7s. 6d.

PLAIN THOUGHTS FOR MEN. Eight Lectures delivered at the Foresters' Hall, Clerkenwell, during the London Mission, 1884. Crown 8vo. 1s. 6d. ; paper covers, 1s.

POE (Edgar Allan)—WORKS OF. With an Introduction and a Memoir by RICHARD HENRY STODDARD. In 6 vols. with Frontispieces and Vignettes. Large crown 8vo. 6s. each vol.

B 2

PRICE (*Prof. Bonamy*)—CHAPTERS ON PRACTICAL POLITICAL ECONOMY. Being the Substance of Lectures delivered before the University of Oxford. New and Cheaper Edition. Large post 8vo. 5*s*.

PRIG'S BEDE: The Venerable Bede Expurgated, Expounded, and Exposed. By the PRIG, Author of 'The Life of a Prig.' Fcp. 8vo. 3*s*. 6*d*.

PULPIT COMMENTARY (THE). Old Testament Series. Edited by the Rev. J. S. EXELL and the Rev. Canon H. D. M. SPENCE.

GENESIS. By Rev. T. WHITELAW, M.A. With Homilies by the Very Rev. J. F. MONTGOMERY, D.D., Rev. Prof. R. A. REDFORD, M.A., LL.B., Rev. F. HASTINGS, Rev. W. ROBERTS, M.A.; an Introduction to the Study of the Old Testament by the Venerable Archdeacon FARRAR, D.D., F.R.S.; and Introductions to the Pentateuch by the Right Rev. H. COTTERILL, D.D., and Rev. T. WHITELAW, M.A. Eighth Edition. One vol. 15*s*.

EXODUS. By the Rev. Canon RAWLINSON. With Homilies by Rev. J. ORR, Rev. D. YOUNG, Rev. C. A. GOODHART, Rev. J. URQUHART, and Rev. H. T. ROBJOHNS. Fourth Edition. Two vols. 18*s*.

LEVITICUS. By the Rev. Prebendary MEYRICK, M.A. With Introductions by Rev. R. COLLINS, Rev. Professor A. CAVE, and Homilies by Rev. Prof. REDFORD, LL.B., Rev. J. A. MACDONALD, Rev. W. CLARKSON, Rev. S. R. ALDRIDGE, LL.B., and Rev. MCCHEYNE EDGAR. Fourth Edition. 15*s*.

NUMBERS. By the Rev R. WINTERBOTHAM, LL.B. With Homilies by the Rev. Professor W. BINNIE, D.D., Rev. E. S. PROUT, M.A., Rev. D. YOUNG, Rev. J. WAITE; and an Introduction by the Rev. THOMAS WHITELAW, M.A. Fifth Edition. 15*s*.

DEUTERONOMY. By Rev. W. L. ALEXANDER, D.D. With Homilies by Rev. D. DAVIES, M.A., Rev. C. CLEMANCE, D.D., Rev. J. ORR, B.D., and Rev. R. M. EDGAR, M.A. Third Edition. 15*s*.

JOSHUA. By Rev. J. J. LIAS, M.A. With Homilies by Rev. S. R. ALDRIDGE, LL.B., Rev. R. GLOVER, Rev. E. DE PRESSENSÉ, D.D., Rev. J. WAITE, B.A., Rev. F. W. ADENEY, M.A.; and an Introduction by the Rev. A. PLUMMER, M.A. Fifth Edition. 12*s*. 6*d*.

JUDGES AND RUTH. By the Bishop of Bath and Wells and Rev. J. MORISON, D.D. With Homilies by Rev. A. F. MUIR, M.A., Rev. F. W. ADENEY, M.A., Rev. W. M. STATHAM, and Rev. Professor J. THOMSON, M.A. Fourth Edition. 10*s*. 6*d*.

1 SAMUEL. By the Very Rev. R. P. SMITH, D.D. With Homilies by Rev. DONALD FRASER, D.D., Rev. Prof. CHAPMAN, and Rev. B. DALE. Sixth Edition. 15*s*.

1 KINGS. By the Rev. JOSEPH HAMMOND, LL.B. With Homilies by the Rev. E. DE PRESSENSÉ, D.D., Rev. J. WAITE, B.A., Rev. A. ROWLAND, LL.B., Rev. J. A. MACDONALD, and Rev. J. URQUHART. Fourth Edition. 15*s*.

1 CHRONICLES. By the Rev. Prof. P. C. BARKER, M.A., LL.B. With Homilies by Rev. Prof. J. R. THOMSON, M.A., Rev. R. TUCK, B.A., Rev. W. CLARKSON, B.A., Rev. F. WHITFIELD, M.A., and Rev. RICHARD GLOVER. 15*s*.

EZRA, NEHEMIAH, AND ESTHER. By Rev. Canon G. RAWLINSON, M.A. With Homilies by Rev. Prof. J. R. THOMSON, M.A., Rev. Prof. R. A. REDFORD, LL.B., M.A., Rev. W. S. LEWIS, M.A., Rev. J. A. MACDONALD, Rev. A. MACKENNAL, B.A., Rev. W. CLARKSON, B.A., Rev. F. HASTINGS, Rev. W. DINWIDDIE, LL.B., Rev. Prof. ROWLANDS, B.A., Rev. G. WOOD, B.A., Rev. Prof. P. C. BARKER, LL.B., M.A., and Rev. J. S. EXELL, M.A. Sixth Edition. One vol. 12*s*. 6*d*.

PULPIT COMMENTARY (THE).   Old Testament Series—continued.

JEREMIAH (Vol. I.). By the Rev. Canon CHEYNE, D.D. With Homilies by the Rev. F. W. ADENEY, M.A., Rev. A. F. MUIR, M.A., Rev. S. CONWAY, B.A., Rev. J. WAITE, B.A., and Rev. D. YOUNG, B.A. Second Edition. 15*s.*

JEREMIAH (Vol. II.), AND LAMENTATIONS. By the Rev. Canon CHEYNE, D.D. With Homilies by Rev. Prof. J. R. THOMSON, M.A., Rev. W. F. ADENEY, M.A., Rev. A. F. MUIR, M.A., Rev. S. CONWAY, B.A., Rev. D. YOUNG, B.A. 15*s.*

PULPIT COMMENTARY (THE).   New Testament Series.

ST. MARK.   By the Very Rev. E. BICKERSTETH, D.D., Dean of Lichfield. With Homilies by the Rev. Prof. THOMSON, M.A., Rev. Prof. GIVEN, M.A., Rev. Prof. JOHNSON, M.A., Rev. A. ROWLAND, LL.B., Rev. A. MUIR, M.A., and Rev. R. GREEN. Fourth Edition. 2 Vols. 21*s.*

THE ACTS OF THE APOSTLES.   By the Bishop of BATH AND WELLS. With Homilies by Rev. Prof. P. C. BARKER, M.A., Rev. Prof. E. JOHNSON, M.A., Rev. Prof. R. A. REDFORD, M.A., Rev. R. TUCK, B.A., Rev. W. CLARKSON, B.A. Second Edition. Two vols. 21*s.*

1 CORINTHIANS. By the Ven. Archdeacon FARRAR, D.D. With Homilies by Rev. Ex-Chancellor LIPSCOMB, LL.D., Rev. DAVID THOMAS, D.D., Rev. DONALD FRASER, D.D., Rev. Prof. J. R. THOMSON, M.A., Rev. R. TUCK, B.A., Rev. E. HURNDALL, M.A., Rev. J. WAITE, B.A., Rev. H. BREMNER, B.D. Second Edition. 15*s.*

II CORINTHIANS AND GALATIANS.   By the Ven. Archdeacon FARRAR, D.D., and Rev. Preb. E. HUXTABLE. With Homilies by Rev. Ex-Chancellor LIPSCOMB, LL.D., Rev. DAVID THOMAS, D.D., Rev. DONALD FRASER, D.D., Rev. R. TUCK, B.A., Rev. E. HURNDALL, M.A., Rev. Prof. J. R. THOMSON, M.A., Rev. R. FINLAYSON, B.A., Rev. W. F. ADENEY, M.A., Rev. R. M. EDGAR, M.A., and Rev. T. CROSKERRY, D.D. Price 21*s.*

EPHESIANS, PHILIPPIANS, AND COLOSSIANS.   By the Rev. Prof. W. G. BLAIKIE, D.D., Rev. B. C. CAFFIN, M.A., and Rev. G. G. FINDLAY, B.A. With Homilies by Rev. D. THOMAS, D.D., Rev. R. M. EDGAR, M.A., Rev. R. FINLAYSON, B.A., Rev. W. F. ADENEY, M.A., Rev. Prof. T. CROSKERRY, D.D., Rev. E. S. PROUT, M.A., Rev. Canon VERNON HUTTON, and Rev. U. R. THOMAS, D.D. Price 21*s.*

HEBREWS AND JAMES.   By the Rev. J. BARMBY, D.D., and Rev. Prebendary E. C. S. GIBSON, M.A. With Homiletics by the Rev. C. JERDAN, M.A., LL.B., and Rev. Prebendary E. C. S. GIBSON. And Homilies by the Rev. W. JONES, Rev. C. NEW, Rev. D. YOUNG, B.A., Rev. J. S. BRIGHT, Rev. T. F. LOCKYER, B.A., and Rev. C. JERDAN, M.A., LL.B. Price 15*s.*

PUNCHARD (E. G.) D.D.—CHRIST OF CONTENTION. Three Essays. Fcp. 8vo. 2*s.*

PUSEY (Dr.)—SERMONS FOR THE CHURCH'S SEASONS FROM ADVENT TO TRINITY. Selected from the published Sermons of the late EDWARD BOUVERIE PUSEY, D.D. Crown 8vo. 5*s.*

RADCLIFFE (Frank R. Y.)—THE NEW POLITICUS. Small crown 8vo. 2*s. 6d.*

RANKE (Leopold von)—UNIVERSAL HISTORY. The Oldest Historical Group of Nations and the Greeks. Edited by G. W. PROTHERO. Demy 8vo. 16*s.*

RENDELL (J. M.)—CONCISE HANDBOOK OF THE ISLAND OF MADEIRA. With Plan of Funchal and Map of the Island. Fcp. 8vo. 1*s. 6d.*

REYNOLDS (*Rev. J. W.*)—THE SUPERNATURAL IN NATURE. A Verification by Free Use of Science. Third Edition, revised and enlarged. Demy 8vo. 14s.

THE MYSTERY OF MIRACLES. Third and Enlarged Edition. Crown 8vo. 6s.

THE MYSTERY OF THE UNIVERSE : Our Common Faith. Demy 8vo. 14s.

RIBOT (*Prof. Th.*)—HEREDITY : a Psychological Study on its Phenomena, its Laws, its Causes, and its Consequences. Second Edition. Large crown 8vo. 9s.

ROBERTSON (*The late Rev. F. W.*) *M.A.*—LIFE AND LETTERS OF. Edited by the Rev. Stopford Brooke, M.A.

    I. Two vols., uniform with the Sermons. With Steel Portrait. Crown 8vo. 7s. 6d.

    II. Library Edition, in demy 8vo. with Portrait. 12s.

    III. A Popular Edition, in 1 vol. Crown 8vo. 6s.

SERMONS. Four Series. Small crown 8vo. 3s. 6d.

THE HUMAN RACE, and other Sermons. Preached at Cheltenham, Oxford, and Brighton. New and Cheaper Edition. Small crown 8vo. 3s. 6d.

NOTES ON GENESIS. New and Cheaper Edition. Small crown 8vo. 3s. 6d.

EXPOSITORY LECTURES ON ST. PAUL'S EPISTLES TO THE CORINTHIANS. A New Edition. Small crown 8vo. 5s.

LECTURES AND ADDRESSES, with other Literary Remains. A New Edition. Small crown 8vo. 5s.

AN ANALYSIS OF TENNYSON'S 'IN MEMORIAM.' (Dedicated by Permission to the Poet-Laureate.) Fcp. 8vo. 2s.

THE EDUCATION OF THE HUMAN RACE. Translated from the German of Gotthold Ephraim Lessing. Fcp. 8vo. 2s. 6d.

    The above Works can also be had bound in half-morocco.

    *** A Portrait of the late Rev. F. W. Robertson, mounted for framing, can be had, 2s. 6d.

ROMANES (*G. J.*)—MENTAL EVOLUTION IN ANIMALS. With a Posthumous Essay on Instinct, by CHARLES DARWIN, F.R.S. Demy 8vo. 12s.

ROSMINI SERBATI (*A.*) *Founder of the Institute of Charity*—LIFE. By FATHER LOCKHART. 2 vols. Crown 8vo. 12s.

ROSMINI'S ORIGIN OF IDEAS. Translated from the Fifth Italian Edition of the Nuovo Saggio. *Sull' origine delle idee.* 3 vols. Demy 8vo. 10s. 6d. each.

ROSMINI'S PSYCHOLOGY. 3 vols. Demy 8vo. [Vols. I. & II. now ready, 10s. 6d. each.

RULE (*Martin*) *M.A.*—THE LIFE AND TIMES OF ST. ANSELM, ARCHBISHOP OF CANTERBURY AND PRIMATE OF THE BRITAINS. 2 vols. Demy 8vo. 32s.

SAMUELL (*Richard*).—SEVEN, the Sacred Number. Its Use in Scripture and its Application to Biblical Criticism, with a Chapter on the Bible and Science. Crown 8vo.

SAMUEL (*Sydney M.*)—JEWISH LIFE IN THE EAST. Small crown 8vo. 3s. 6d.

SAYCE (*Rev. Archibald Henry*)—INTRODUCTION TO THE SCIENCE OF LANGUAGE. 2 vols. Second Edition. Large post 8vo. 21*s.*

SCOONES (*W. Baptiste*)—FOUR CENTURIES OF ENGLISH LETTERS : A Selection of 350 Letters by 150 Writers, from the Period of the Paston Letters to the Present Time. Third Edition. Large crown 8vo. 6*s.*

SÉE (*Prof. Germain*)—BACILLARY PHTHISIS OF THE LUNGS. Translated and Edited for English Practitioners, by WILLIAM HENRY WEDDELL, M.R.C.S. Demy 8vo. 10*s. 6d.*

SHAKSPEARE—WORKS. The Avon Edition, 12 vols. fcp. 8vo. cloth, 18*s.* : in cloth box, 21*s.* ; bound in 6 vols., cloth, 15*s.*

SHELLEY (*Percy Bysshe*).—LIFE. By EDWARD DOWDEN, LL.D. With Portraits and Illustrations, 2 vols., demy 8vo. 36*s.*

SHILLITO (*Rev. Joseph*)—WOMANHOOD : its Duties, Temptations, and Privileges. A Book for Young Women. Third Edition. Crown 8vo. 3*s. 6d.*

SIDNEY (*Algernon*)—A REVIEW. By GERTRUDE M. IRELAND BLACK-BURNE. Crown 8vo. 6*s.*

SISTER AUGUSTINE, Superior of the Sisters of Charity at the St. Johannis Hospital at Bonn. Authorised Translation by HANS THARAU, from the German 'Memorials of AMALIE VON LASAULX.' Cheap Edition. Large crown 8vo. 4*s. 6d.*

SKINNER (JAMES). A Memoir. By the Author of 'Charles Lowder.' With a Preface by the Rev. Canon CARTER, and Portrait. Large crown 8vo. 7*s. 6d.*

*** Also a Cheap Edition, with Portrait. Crown 8vo. 3*s. 6d.*

SMEATON (*Donald*).—THE KARENS OF BURMAH. Crown 8vo.

SMITH (*Edward*) *M.D., LL.B., F.R.S.*—TUBERCULAR CONSUMPTION IN ITS EARLY AND REMEDIABLE STAGES. Second Edition. Crown 8vo. 6*s.*

SMITH (*Sir W. Cusack, Bart.*)—OUR WAR SHIPS. A Naval Essay. Crown 8vo. 5*s.*

SPANISH MYSTICS. By the Editor of 'Many Voices.' Crown 8vo. 5*s.*

SPECIMENS OF ENGLISH PROSE STYLE FROM MALORY TO MACAULAY. Selected and Annotated, with an Introductory Essay, by GEORGE SAINTSBURY. Large crown 8vo., printed on hand-made paper, parchment antique, or cloth, 12*s.* ; vellum, 15*s.*

SPEDDING (*James*)—REVIEWS AND DISCUSSIONS, LITERARY, POLITICAL, AND HISTORICAL NOT RELATING TO BACON. Demy 8vo. 12*s. 6d.*

EVENINGS WITH A REVIEWER ; or, Bacon and Macaulay. With a Prefatory Notice by G. S. VENABLES, Q.C. 2 vols. Demy 8vo. 18*s.*

STAFFER (*Paul*)—SHAKSPEARE AND CLASSICAL ANTIQUITY : Greek and Latin Antiquity as presented in Shakspeare's Plays. Translated by EMILY J. CAREY. Large post 8vo. 12*s.*

STATHAM (*F. Reginald*)—FREE THOUGHT AND TRUE THOUGHT. A Contribution to an Existing Argument. Crown 8vo. 6*s.*

STRAY PAPERS ON EDUCATION AND SCENES FROM SCHOOL LIFE. By B. H. Second Edition. Small crown 8vo. 3*s. 6d.*

STREATFEILD (*Rev. G. S.*) *M.A.*—LINCOLNSHIRE AND THE DANES. Large crown 8vo. 7*s. 6d.*

STRECKER-WISLICENUS—ORGANIC CHEMISTRY. Translated and Edited, with Extensive Additions, by W. R. HODGKINSON, Ph.D., and A. J. GREENAWAY, F.I.C. Demy 8vo. 12s. 6d.

SUAKIN, 1885 ; being a Sketch of the Campaign of this Year. By an Officer who was there. Second Edition. Crown 8vo. 2s. 6d.

SULLY (James) M.A.—PESSIMISM : a History and a Criticism. Second Edition. Demy 8vo. 14s.

SUNSHINE AND SEA. A Yachting Visit to the Channel Islands and Coast of Brittany. With Frontispiece from a Photograph and 24 Illustrations. Crown 8vo. 6s.

SWEDENBORG (Eman.)—DE CULTU ET AMORE DEI, UBI AGITUR DE TELLURIS ORTU, PARADISO ET VIVARIO, TUM DE PRIMOGENITI SEU ADAMI NATIVITATE, INFANTIA, ET AMORE. Crown 8vo. 6s.

> ON THE WORSHIP AND LOVE OF GOD. Treating of the Birth of the Earth, Paradise, and the Abode of Living Creatures. Translated from the original Latin. Crown 8vo. 7s. 6d.

> PRODROMUS PHILOSOPHIÆ RATIOCINANTIS DE INFINITO, ET CAUSA FINALI CREATIONIS ; deque Mechanismo Operationis Animæ et Corporis. Edidit THOMAS MURRAY GORMAN, M.A. Crown 8vo. 7s. 6d.

TACITUS' AGRICOLA : A Translation. Small crown 8vo. 2s. 6d.

TARRING (Charles James) M.A.—A PRACTICAL ELEMENTARY TURKISH GRAMMAR. Crown 8vo. 6s.

TAYLOR (Rev. Isaac)—THE ALPHABET. An Account of the Origin and Development of Letters. With numerous Tables and Facsimiles. 2 vols. Demy 8vo. 36s.

TAYLOR (Jeremy)—THE MARRIAGE RING. With Preface, Notes, and Appendices. Edited by FRANCIS BURDETT MONEY COUTTS. Small crown 8vo. 2s. 6d.

TAYLOR (Sedley)—PROFIT SHARING BETWEEN CAPITAL AND LABOUR. To which is added a Memorandum on the Industrial Partnership at the Whitwood Collieries, by ARCHIBALD and HENRY BRIGGS, with Remarks by SEDLEY TAYLOR. Crown 8vo. 2s. 6d.

'THEY MIGHT HAVE BEEN TOGETHER TILL THE LAST.' An Essay on Marriage, and the Position of Women in England. Small crown 8vo. 2s.

THOM (John Hamilton)—LAWS OF LIFE AFTER THE MIND OF CHRIST. Two Series. Crown 8vo. 7s. 6d. each.

THOMPSON (Sir H.)—DIET IN RELATION TO AGE AND ACTIVITY. Fcp. 8vo. cloth, 1s. 6d. ; Paper covers, 1s.

TIDMAN (Paul F.)—GOLD AND SILVER MONEY. Part I.—A Plain Statement. Part II.—Objections Answered. Third Edition. Crown 8vo. 1s.

TIPPLE (Rev. S. A.)—SUNDAY MORNINGS AT NORWOOD. Prayers and Sermons. Crown 8vo. 6s.

TODHUNTER (Dr. J.)—A STUDY OF SHELLEY. Crown 8vo. 7s.

TOLSTOI (Count Leo)—CHRIST'S CHRISTIANITY. Translated from the Russian. Large crown 8vo. 7s. 6d.

TRANT (*William*)—TRADE UNIONS; Their Origin and Objects, Influence and Efficacy. Small crown 8vo. 1s. 6d.; paper covers, 1s.

TREMENHEERE (*H. Seymour*) *C.B.*—A MANUAL OF THE PRINCIPLES OF GOVERNMENT AS SET FORTH BY THE AUTHORITIES OF ANCIENT AND MODERN TIMES. New and enlarged Edition. Crown 8vo. 3s. 6d. Cheap Edition, 1s.

TRENCH (*The late R. C., Archbishop*)—SERMONS NEW AND OLD. Crown 8vo. 6s.

NOTES ON THE PARABLES OF OUR LORD. Fourteenth Edition. 8vo. 12s.; Popular Edition, crown 8vo. 7s. 6d.

NOTES ON THE MIRACLES OF OUR LORD. Twelfth Edition. 8vo. 12s.; Popular Edition, crown 8vo. 7s. 6d.

STUDIES IN THE GOSPELS. Fifth Edition, Revised. 8vo. 10s. 6d.

BRIEF THOUGHTS AND MEDITATIONS ON SOME PASSAGES IN HOLY Scripture. Third Edition. Crown 8vo. 3s. 6d.

SYNONYMS OF THE NEW TESTAMENT. Tenth Edition, Enlarged. 8vo. 12s.

ON THE AUTHORISED VERSION OF THE NEW TESTAMENT. Second Edition. 8vo. 7s.

COMMENTARY ON THE EPISTLE TO THE SEVEN CHURCHES IN ASIA. Fourth Edition, Revised. 8vo. 8s. 6d.

THE SERMON ON THE MOUNT. An Exposition drawn from the Writings of St. Augustine, with an Essay on his Merits as an Interpreter of Holy Scripture. Fourth Edition, Enlarged. 8vo. 10s. 6d.

SHIPWRECKS OF FAITH. Three Sermons preached before the University of Cambridge in May 1867. Fcp. 8vo. 2s. 6d.

LECTURES ON MEDIÆVAL CHURCH HISTORY. Being the Substance of Lectures delivered at Queen's College, London. Second Edition. 8vo. 12s.

ENGLISH, PAST AND PRESENT. Thirteenth Edition, Revised and Improved. Fcp. 8vo. 5s.

ON THE STUDY OF WORDS. Nineteenth Edition, Revised. Fcp. 8vo. 5s.

SELECT GLOSSARY OF ENGLISH WORDS USED FORMERLY IN SENSES DIFFERENT FROM THE PRESENT. Fifth Edition, Revised and Enlarged. Fcp. 8vo. 5s.

PROVERBS AND THEIR LESSONS. Seventh Edition, Enlarged. Fcp. 8vo. 4s.

POEMS. Collected and Arranged Anew. Ninth Edition. Fcp. 8vo. 7s. 6d.

POEMS. Library Edition. 2 vols. Small crown 8vo. 10s.

SACRED LATIN POETRY. Chiefly Lyrical, Selected and Arranged for Use. Third Edition, Corrected and Improved. Fcp. 8vo. 7s.

A HOUSEHOLD BOOK OF ENGLISH POETRY. Selected and Arranged, with Notes. Fourth Edition, Revised. Extra fcp. 8vo. 5s. 6d.

AN ESSAY ON THE LIFE AND GENIUS OF CALDERON. With Translations from his 'Life's a Dream' and 'Great Theatre of the World.' Second Edition, Revised and Improved. Extra fcp. 8vo. 5s. 6d.

TRENCH (The late R. C., Archbishop)—continued.

> GUSTAVUS ADOLPHUS IN GERMANY, AND OTHER LECTURES ON THE THIRTY YEARS' WAR. Second Edition, Enlarged. Fcp. 8vo. 4s.

> PLUTARCH: HIS LIFE, HIS LIVES, AND HIS MORALS. Second Edition, Enlarged. Fcap. 8vo. 3s. 6d.

> REMAINS OF THE LATE MRS. RICHARD TRENCH. Being Selections from her Journals, Letters, and other Papers. New and Cheaper Issue. With Portrait. 8vo. 6s.

TUKE (Daniel Hack) M.D.—CHAPTERS IN THE HISTORY OF THE INSANE IN THE BRITISH ISLES. With Four Illustrations. Large crown 8vo. 12s.

TWINING (Louisa)—WORKHOUSE VISITING AND MANAGEMENT DURING TWENTY-FIVE YEARS. Small crown 8vo. 2s.

TYLER (J.)—THE MYSTERY OF BEING; OR, WHAT DO WE KNOW? Small crown 8vo. 3s. 6d.

VAUGHAN (H. Halford)—NEW READINGS AND RENDERINGS OF SHAKESPEARE'S TRAGEDIES. 3 vols. Demy 8vo. 12s. 6d. each.

VILLARI (Professor)—NICCOLÒ MACHIAVELLI AND HIS TIMES. Translated by Linda Villari. 4 vols. Large crown 8vo. 48s.

VILLIERS (The Right Hon. C. P.)—FREE TRADE SPEECHES OF. With Political Memoir. Edited by a Member of the Cobden Club. 2 vols. With Portrait. Demy 8vo. 25s.
> *** Also a People's Edition, in 1 vol. crown 8vo. limp 2s. 6d.

VOGT (Lieut.-Col. Hermann)—THE EGYPTIAN WAR OF 1882. A Translation. With Map and Plans. Large crown 8vo. 6s.

VOLCKXSOM (E. W. v.)—CATECHISM OF ELEMENTARY MODERN CHEMISTRY. Small crown 8vo. 3s.

WALLER (Rev. C. B.)—THE APOCALYPSE, reviewed under the Light of the Doctrine of the Unfolding Ages, and the Restitution of All Things. Demy 8vo. 12s.

WALPOLE (Chas. George)—A SHORT HISTORY OF IRELAND FROM THE EARLIEST TIMES TO THE UNION WITH GREAT BRITAIN. With 5 Maps and Appendices. Second Edition. Crown 8vo. 6s.

WARD (William George) Ph.D.— ESSAYS ON THE PHILOSOPHY OF THEISM. Edited, with an Introduction, by WILFRID WARD. 2 vols. demy 8vo. 21s.

WARD (Wilfrid)—THE WISH TO BELIEVE: A Discussion concerning the Temper of Mind in which a reasonable Man should undertake Religious Inquiry. Small crown 8vo. 5s.

WARTER (J. W.)—AN OLD SHROPSHIRE OAK. 2 vols. demy 8vo. 28s.

WEDDERBURN (Sir David) Bart., M.P.—LIFE OF. Compiled from his Journals and Writings by his Sister, Mrs. E. H. PERCIVAL. With etched Portrait, and facsimiles of Pencil Sketches. Demy 8vo. 14s.

WEDMORE (Frederick)—THE MASTERS OF GENRE PAINTING. With Sixteen Illustrations. Post 8vo. 7s. 6d.

WHITE (H. C.)—REFORM OF THE CHURCH ESTABLISHMENT. The Nation's Rights and Needs. Crown 8vo.

WHITNEY (Prof. William Dwight)—ESSENTIALS OF ENGLISH GRAMMAR, for the Use of Schools. Second Edition, crown 8vo. 3s. 6d.

WHITWORTH (George Clifford)—AN ANGLO-INDIAN DICTIONARY : a Glossary of Indian Terms used in English, and of such English or other Non-Indian Terms as have obtained special meanings in India. Demy 8vo. cloth, 12s.

WILLIAMS (Rowland) D.D.—PSALMS, LITANIES, COUNSELS, AND COLLECTS FOR DEVOUT PERSONS. Edited by his Widow. New and Popular Edition. Crown 8vo. 3s. 6d.

STRAY THOUGHTS COLLECTED FROM THE WRITINGS OF THE LATE ROWLAND WILLIAMS, D.D. Edited by his Widow. Crown 8vo. 3s. 6d.

WILSON (Lieut.-Col. C. T.)—THE DUKE OF BERWICK, MARSHAL OF FRANCE, 1702-1734. Demy 8vo. 15s.

WILSON (Mrs. R. F.)—THE CHRISTIAN BROTHERS : THEIR ORIGIN AND WORK. With a Sketch of the Life of their Founder, the Ven. Jean Baptiste, de la Salle. Crown 8vo. 6s.

WOLTMANN (Dr. Alfred), and WOERMANN (Dr. Karl)—HISTORY OF PAINTING. Vol. I. Ancient, Early, Christian, and Mediæval Painting. With numerous Illustrations. Super-royal 8vo. 28s. ; bevelled boards, gilt leaves, 30s. Vol. II. The Painting of the Renascence. Cloth, 42s. ; cloth extra, bevelled boards, 45s.

YOUMANS (Eliza A.)—FIRST BOOK OF BOTANY. Designed to cultivate the Observing Powers of Children. With 300 Engravings. New and Cheaper Edition. Crown 8vo. 2s. 6d.

YOUMANS (Edward L.) M.D.—A CLASS BOOK OF CHEMISTRY, on the Basis of the New System. With 200 Illustrations. Crown 8vo. 5s.

Y. Z.—PAROCHIAL PARLEYS ON THE ATHANASIAN CREED, THE INSPIRATION OF THE BIBLE, SCIENTIFIC HERESIES, AND OTHER KINDRED SUBJECTS. Between the Rev. Hugh Hierous, M.A., M.C.U., and his Parishioner, Theophilos Truman. Edited by Y. Z. Crown 8vo. 6s.

THE INTERNATIONAL SCIENTIFIC SERIES.

I. FORMS OF WATER : a Familiar Exposition of the Origin and Phenomena of Glaciers. By J. Tyndall, LL.D., F.R.S. With 25 Illustrations. Ninth Edition. Crown 8vo. 5s.

II. PHYSICS AND POLITICS ; or, Thoughts on the Application of the Principles of 'Natural Selection' and 'Inheritance' to Political Society. By Walter Bagehot. Seventh Edition. Crown 8vo. 4s.

III. FOODS. By Edward Smith, M.D., LL.B., F.R.S. With numerous Illustrations. Ninth Edition. Crown 8vo. 5s.

IV. MIND AND BODY : the Theories of their Relation. By Alexander Bain, LL.D. With Four Illustrations. Seventh Edition. Crown 8vo. 4s.

V. THE STUDY OF SOCIOLOGY. By Herbert Spencer. Twelfth Edition. Crown 8vo. 5s.

VI. ON THE CONSERVATION OF ENERGY. By Balfour Stewart, M.A., LL.D., F.R.S. With 14 Illustrations. Sixth Edition. Crown 8vo. 5s.

VII. ANIMAL LOCOMOTION ; or, Walking, Swimming, and Flying. By J. B. Pettigrew, M.D., F.R.S., &c. With 130 Illustrations. Third Edition. Crown 8vo. 5s.

VIII. RESPONSIBILITY IN MENTAL DISEASE. By Henry Maudsley, M.D. Fourth Edition. Crown 8vo. 5s.

IX. THE NEW CHEMISTRY. By Professor J. P. Cooke. With 31 Illustrations. Eighth Edition, remodelled and enlarged. Crown 8vo. 5s.

X. THE SCIENCE OF LAW. By Professor Sheldon Amos. Sixth Edition. Crown 8vo. 5s.

XI. ANIMAL MECHANISM : a Treatise on Terrestrial and Aërial Locomotion. By Professor E. J. Marey. With 117 Illustrations. Third Edition. Crown 8vo. 5s.

XII. THE DOCTRINE OF DESCENT AND DARWINISM. By Professor Oscar Schmidt. With 26 Illustrations. Sixth Edition. Crown 8vo. 5s.

XIII. THE HISTORY OF THE CONFLICT BETWEEN RELIGION AND SCIENCE. By J. W. Draper, M.D., LL.D. Nineteenth Edition. Crown 8vo. 5s.

XIV. FUNGI: their Nature, Influences, Uses, &c. By M. C. Cooke, M.D., LL.D. Edited by the Rev. M. J. Berkeley, M.A., F.L.S. With numerous Illustrations. Third Edition. Crown 8vo. 5s.

XV. THE CHEMICAL EFFECTS OF LIGHT AND PHOTOGRAPHY. By Dr. Hermann Vogel. Translation thoroughly revised. With 100 Illustrations. Fourth Edition. Crown 8vo. 5s.

XVI. THE LIFE AND GROWTH OF LANGUAGE. By Professor William Dwight Whitney. Fifth Edition. Crown 8vo. 5s.

XVII. MONEY AND THE MECHANISM OF EXCHANGE. By W. Stanley Jevons, M.A., F.R.S. Seventh Edition. Crown 8vo. 5s.

XVIII. THE NATURE OF LIGHT. With a General Account of Physical Optics. By Dr. Eugene Lommel. With 188 Illustrations and a Table of Spectra in Chromo-lithography. Fourth Edit. Crown 8vo. 5s.

XIX. ANIMAL PARASITES AND MESSMATES. By P. J. Van Beneden. With 83 Illustrations. Third Edition. Crown 8vo. 5s.

XX. FERMENTATION. By Professor Schützenberger. With 28 Illustrations. Fourth Edition. Crown 8vo. 5s.

XXI. THE FIVE SENSES OF MAN. By Professor Bernstein. With 91 Illustrations. Fifth Edition. Crown 8vo. 5s.

XXII. THE THEORY OF SOUND IN ITS RELATION TO MUSIC. By Professor Pietro Blaserna. With numerous Illustrations. Third Edition. Crown 8vo. 5s.

XXIII. STUDIES IN SPECTRUM ANALYSIS. By J. Norman Lockyer, F.R.S. Fourth Edition. With six Photographic Illustrations of Spectra, and numerous Engravings on Wood. Crown 8vo. 6s. 6d.

XXIV. A HISTORY OF THE GROWTH OF THE STEAM ENGINE. By Professor R. H. Thurston. With numerous Illustrations. Third Edition. Crown 8vo. 6s. 6d.

XXV. EDUCATION AS A SCIENCE. By Alexander Bain, LL.D. Sixth Edition. Crown 8vo. 5s.

XXVI. THE HUMAN SPECIES. By Prof. A. De Quatrefages. Third Edition. Crown 8vo. 5s.

XXVII. MODERN CHROMATICS. With Applications to Art and Industry. By Ogden N. Rood. With 130 original Illustrations. Second Edition. Crown 8vo. 5s.

XXVIII. THE CRAYFISH: an Introduction to the Study of Zoology. By Professor T. H. Huxley. With 82 Illustrations. Fourth Edition. Crown 8vo. 5s.

XXIX. THE BRAIN AS AN ORGAN OF MIND. By H. Charlton Bastian, M.D. With numerous Illustrations. Third Edition. Crown 8vo. 5s.

XXX. THE ATOMIC THEORY. By Prof. Wurtz. Translated by G. Cleminshaw, F.C.S. Fourth Edition. Crown 8vo. 5s.

XXXI. THE NATURAL CONDITIONS OF EXISTENCE AS THEY AFFECT ANIMAL LIFE. By Karl Semper. With 2 Maps and 106 Woodcuts. Third Edition. Crown 8vo. 5s.

XXXII. GENERAL PHYSIOLOGY OF MUSCLES AND NERVES. By Prof. J. Rosenthal. Third Edition. With Illustrations. Crown 8vo. 5s.

XXXIII. SIGHT: an Exposition of the Principles of Monocular and Binocular Vision. By Joseph Le Conte, LL.D. Second Edition. With 132 Illustrations. Crown 8vo. 5s.

XXXIV. ILLUSIONS: a Psychological Study. By James Sully. Second Edition. Crown 8vo. 5s.

XXXV. VOLCANOES: WHAT THEY ARE AND WHAT THEY TEACH. By Professor J. W. Judd, F.R.S. With 92 Illustrations on Wood. Third Edition. Crown 8vo. 5s.

XXXVI. SUICIDE: an Essay on Comparative Moral Statistics. By Prof. H. Morselli. Second Edition. With Diagrams. Crown 8vo. 5s.

XXXVII. THE BRAIN AND ITS FUNCTIONS. By J. Luys. Second Edition. With Illustrations. Crown 8vo. 5s.

XXXVIII. MYTH AND SCIENCE: an Essay. By Tito Vignoli. Second Edition. Crown 8vo. 5s.

XXXIX. THE SUN. By Professor Young. With Illustrations. Second Edition. Crown 8vo. 5s.

XL. ANTS, BEES, AND WASPS: a Record of Observations on the Habits of the Social Hymenoptera. By Sir John Lubbock, Bart., M.P. With 5 Chromolithographic Illustrations. Eighth Edition. Crown 8vo. 5s.

XLI. ANIMAL INTELLIGENCE. By G. J. Romanes, LL.D., F.R.S. Fourth Edition. Crown 8vo. 5s.

XLII. THE CONCEPTS AND THEORIES OF MODERN PHYSICS. By J. B. Stallo. Third Edition. Crown 8vo. 5s.

XLIII. DISEASES OF MEMORY: an Essay in the Positive Psychology. By Prof. Th. Ribot. Third Edition. Crown 8vo. 5s.

XLIV. MAN BEFORE METALS. By N. Joly. Third Edition. Crown 8vo. 5s.

XLV. THE SCIENCE OF POLITICS. By Prof. Sheldon Amos. Third Edit. Crown. 8vo. 5s.

XLVI. ELEMENTARY METEOROLOGY. By Robert H. Scott. Third Edition. With numerous Illustrations. Crown 8vo. 5s.

XLVII. THE ORGANS OF SPEECH AND THEIR APPLICATION IN THE FORMATION OF ARTICULATE SOUNDS. By Georg Hermann von Meyer. With 47 Woodcuts. Crown 8vo. 5s.

XLVIII. FALLACIES: a View of Logic from the Practical Side. By Alfred Sidgwick. Second Edition. Crown 8vo. 5s.

XLIX. ORIGIN OF CULTIVATED PLANTS. By Alphonse de Candolle. Crown 8vo. 5s.

L. JELLY FISH, STAR FISH, AND SEA URCHINS. Being a Research on Primitive Nervous Systems. By G. J. Romanes. Crown 8vo. 5s.

LI. THE COMMON SENSE OF THE EXACT SCIENCES. By the late William Kingdon Clifford. Second Edition. With 100 Figures. 5s.

LII. PHYSICAL EXPRESSION : ITS MODES AND PRINCIPLES. By Francis Warner, M.D., F.R.C.P. With 50 Illustrations. 5*s*.

LIII. ANTHROPOID APES. By Robert Hartmann. With 63 Illustrations. 5*s*.

LIV. THE MAMMALIA IN THEIR RELATION TO PRIMEVAL TIMES. By Oscar Schmidt. With 51 Woodcuts. 5*s*.

LV. COMPARATIVE LITERATURE. By H. Macaulay Posnett, LL.D. 5*s*.

LVI. EARTHQUAKES AND OTHER EARTH MOVEMENTS. By Prof. JOHN MILNE. With 38 Figures. 5*s*.

LVII. MICROBES, FERMENTS, AND MOULDS. By E. L. TROUESSART. With 107 Illustrations. 5*s*.

MILITARY WORKS.

BARRINGTON (Capt. J. T.)—ENGLAND ON THE DEFENSIVE ; or, the Problem of Invasion Critically Examined. Large crown 8vo. with Map, 7*s*. 6*d*.

BRACKENBURY (Col. C. B.) R.A. —MILITARY HANDBOOKS FOR REGIMENTAL OFFICERS :

   I. MILITARY SKETCHING AND RECONNAISSANCE. By Colonel F. J. Hutchison and Major H. G. MacGregor. Fourth Edition. With 15 Plates. Small crown 8vo. 4*s*.

   II. THE ELEMENTS OF MODERN TACTICS PRACTICALLY APPLIED TO ENGLISH FORMATIONS. By Lieut.-Col. Wilkinson Shaw. Fifth Edit. With 25 Plates and Maps. Small crown 8vo. 9*s*.

   III. FIELD ARTILLERY : its Equipment, Organisation, and Tactics. By Major Sisson C. Pratt, R.A. With 12 Plates. Second Edition. Small crown 8vo. 6*s*.

   IV. THE ELEMENTS OF MILITARY ADMINISTRATION. First Part : Permanent System of Administration. By Major J. W. Buxton. Small crown 8vo. 7*s*. 6*d*.

   V. MILITARY LAW : its Procedure and Practice. By Major Sisson C. Pratt, R.A. Second Edition. Small crown 8vo. 4*s*. 6*d*.

   VI. CAVALRY IN MODERN WAR. By Col. F. Chenevix Trench. Small crown 8vo. 6*s*.

   VII. FIELD WORKS. Their Technical Construction and Tactical Application. By the Editor, Col. C. B. Brackenbury, R.A. Small crown 8vo.

BRENT (Brig.-Gen. J. L.)—MOBILIZABLE FORTIFICATIONS AND THEIR CONTROLLING INFLUENCE IN WAR. Crown 8vo. 5*s*.

BROOKE (Major C. K.)—A SYSTEM OF FIELD TRAINING. Small crown 8vo. 2*s*.

CLERY (C.) Lieut.-Col.—MINOR TACTICS. With 26 Maps and Plans. Sixth and cheaper Edition, revised. Crown 8vo. 9*s*.

COLVILE (Lieut.-Col. C. F.)—MILITARY TRIBUNALS. Sewed, 2*s*. 6*d*.

CRAUFURD (Capt. H. J.)—SUGGESTIONS FOR THE MILITARY TRAINING OF A COMPANY OF INFANTRY. Crown 8vo. 1*s*. 6*d*.

HAMILTON (Capt. Ian) A.D.C.—THE FIGHTING OF THE FUTURE. 1*s*.

HARRISON (Lieut.-Col. R.) — THE OFFICER'S MEMORANDUM BOOK FOR PEACE AND WAR. Third Edition. Oblong 32mo. roan, with pencil, 3*s*. 6*d*.

NOTES ON CAVALRY TACTICS, ORGANISATION, &c. By a Cavalry Officer. With Diagrams. Demy 8vo. 12*s*.

PARR (Capt. H. Hallam) C.M.G.—THE DRESS, HORSES, AND EQUIPMENT OF INFANTRY AND STAFF OFFICERS. Crown 8vo. 1*s*.

SCHAW (Col. H.)—THE DEFENCE AND ATTACK OF POSITIONS AND LOCALITIES. Third Edition, revised and corrected. Crown 8vo. 3*s*. 6*d*.

STONE (Capt. F. Gleadowe) R.A.—TACTICAL STUDIES FROM THE FRANCO-GERMAN WAR OF 1870-71. With 22 Lithographic Sketches and Maps. Demy 8vo. 30*s*.

THE CAMPAIGN OF FREDERICKSBURG, November to December, 1862 : a Study for Officers of Volunteers. By a Line Officer. Crown 8vo. With Five Maps and Plans.

WILKINSON (H. Spenser) Capt. 20th Lancashire R.V.—CITIZEN SOLDIERS. Essays towards the Improvement of the Volunteer Force. Crown 8vo. 2*s*. 6*d*.

POETRY.

ADAM OF ST. VICTOR—THE LITURGICAL POETRY OF ADAM OF ST. VICTOR. From the text of Gautier. With Translations into English in the Original Metres, and Short Explanatory Notes. By Digby S. Wrangham, M.A. 3 vols. Crown 8vo. printed on hand-made paper, boards, 21*s.*

AUCHMUTY (A. C.)—POEMS OF ENGLISH HEROISM : From Brunanburgh to Lucknow ; from Athelstan to Albert. Small crown 8vo. 1*s.* 6*d.*

BARNES (William)—POEMS OF RURAL LIFE, IN THE DORSET DIALECT. New Edition, complete in one vol. Crown 8vo. 8*s.* 6*d.*

BAYNES (Rev. Canon H. R.)—HOME SONGS FOR QUIET HOURS. Fourth and cheaper Edition. Fcp. 8vo. 2*s.* 6*d.*

BEVINGTON (L. S.)—KEY NOTES. Small crown 8vo. 5*s.*

BLUNT (Wilfrid Scawen)—THE WIND AND THE WHIRLWIND. Demy 8vo. 1*s.* 6*d.*

THE LOVE SONNETS OF PROTEUS. Fifth Edition. 18mo. cloth extra, gilt top, 5*s.*

BOWEN (H. C.) M.A.—SIMPLE ENGLISH POEMS. English Literature for Junior Classes. In Four Parts. Parts I. II. and III. 6*d.* each, and Part IV. 1*s.*, complete 3*s.*

BRYANT (W. C.) — POEMS. Cheap Edition, with Frontispiece. Small crown 8vo. 3*s.* 6*d.*

CALDERON'S DRAMAS : the Wonder-working Magician—Life is a Dream—the Purgatory of St. Patrick. Translated by Denis Florence MacCarthy. Post 8vo. 10*s.*

CAMOENS LUSIADS. Portuguese Text with English Translation, by J. J. AUBERTIN. Second Edition. 2 vols. Crown 8vo. 12*s.*

CAMPBELL (Lewis)—SOPHOCLES. The Seven Plays in English Verse. Crown 8vo. 7*s.* 6*d.*

CERVANTES.— JOURNEY TO PARNASSUS. Spanish Text, with Translation into English Tercets, Preface, and Illustrative Notes, by JAMES Y. GIBSON. Crown 8vo. 12*s.*

CERVANTES—continued.

NUMANTIA ; a Tragedy. Translated from the Spanish, with Introduction and Notes, by JAMES Y. GIBSON. Crown 8vo., printed on hand-made paper, 5*s.*

CHAVANNES (Mary Charlotte).—A Few TRANSLATIONS FROM VICTOR HUGO, AND OTHER POETS. Small crown 8vo. 2*s.* 6*d.*

CHRISTIE (A. J.)—THE END OF MAN. With 4 Autotype Illustrations. 4to. 10*s.* 6*d.*

CLARKE (Mary Cowden)—HONEY FROM THE WEED. Verses. Crown 8vo. 7*s.*

COCKLE (Mrs. Moss)—FANTASIAS. Small cr. 8vo. 2*s.* 6*d.*

COXHEAD (Ethel)—BIRDS AND BABIES. Imp. 16mo. With 33 Illustrations. 2*s.* 6*d.*

DANTE—THE DIVINA COMMEDIA OF DANTE ALIGHIERI. Translated, line for line, in the ' Terza Rima ' of the original, with Notes, by FREDERICK K. H. HASELFOOT, M.A. Demy 8vo.

DE BERANGER.—A SELECTION FROM HIS SONGS. In English Verse. By WILLIAM TOYNBEE. Small crown 8vo. 2*s.* 6*d.*

DENNIS (J.) — ENGLISH SONNETS. Collected and Arranged by. Small crown 8vo. 2*s.* 6*d.*

DENT (Mrs. William)—CEYLON : a Descriptive Poem, with Notes. Small crown 8vo. 1*s.* 6*d.*

DERRY and RAPHOE (William Alexander) Bishop of, D.D., D.C.L.—ST. AUGUSTINE'S HOLIDAY, and other Poems. Crown 8vo. 6*s.*

DE VERE (Aubrey)—POETICAL WORKS:

I. THE SEARCH AFTER PROSERPINE, &c. 6*s.*

II. THE LEGENDS OF ST. PATRICK, &c. 6*s.*

III. ALEXANDER THE GREAT, &c. 6*s.*

THE FORAY OF QUEEN MEAVE, and other Legends of Ireland's Heroic Age. Small crown 8vo. 5*s.*

DE VERE (*Aubrey*)—continued.
LEGENDS OF THE SAXON SAINTS. Small crown 8vo. 6s.

DILLON (*Arthur*)—RIVER SONGS and other Poems. With 13 Autotype Illustrations from designs by Margery May. Fcp. 4to. cloth extra, gilt leaves, 10s. 6d.

DOBSON (*Austin*) —OLD WORLD IDYLLS, and other Verses. Sixth Edition. 18mo. cloth extra, gilt tops, 6s.
AT THE SIGN OF THE LYRE. Fourth Edition. Elzevir 8vo., gilt top, 6s.

DOMETT (*Alfred*)—RANOLF AND AMOHIA : a Dream of Two Lives. New Edition revised. 2 vols. Crown 8vo. 12s.

DOROTHY : a Country Story in Elegiac Verse. With Preface. Demy 8vo. 5s.

DOWDEN (*Edward*) LL.D.—SHAKSPERE'S SONNETS. With Introduction and Notes. Large post 8vo. 7s. 6d.

DULCE COR : being the Poems of Ford Bereton. With Two Illustrations. Crown 8vo. 6s.

DUTT (*Toru*)—A SHEAF GLEANED IN FRENCH FIELDS. New Edition. Demy 8vo. 10s. 6d.

ANCIENT BALLADS AND LEGENDS OF HINDUSTAN. With an Introductory Memoir by EDMUND GOSSE. Second Edition. 18mo. Cloth extra, gilt top, 5s.

EDWARDS (*Miss Betham*) — POEMS. Small crown 8vo. 3s. 6d.

ELDRYTH (*Maud*)—MARGARET, and other Poems. Small crown 8vo. 3s. 6d.
ALL SOULS' EVE, ' No GOD,' and other Poems. Fcp. 8vo. 3s. 6d.

ELLIOTT (*Ebenezer*), The Corn Law Rhymer—POEMS. Edited by his Son, the Rev. Edwin Elliott, of St. John's, Antigua. 2 vols. crown 8vo. 18s.

ENGLISH VERSE. Edited by W. J. LINTON and R. H. STODDARD. In 5 vols. Crown 8vo. each 5s.
1. CHAUCER TO BURNS.
2. TRANSLATIONS.
3. LYRICS OF THE NINETEENTH CENTURY.
4. DRAMATIC SCENES AND CHARACTERS.
5. BALLADS AND ROMANCES.

EVANS (*Anne*)—POEMS AND MUSIC. With Memorial Preface by ANN THACKERAY RITCHIE. Large crown 8vo. 7s.

FOSKETT (*Edward*)—POEMS. Crown 8vo. 6s.

GOODCHILD (*John A.*) — SOMNIA MEDICI. Small crown 8vo. Two Series, 5s. each.

GOSSE (*Edmund W.*)—NEW POEMS. Crown 8vo. 7s. 6d.

FIRDAUSI IN EXILE, and other Poems. Elzevir 8vo. gilt top, 6s.

GRINDROD (*Charles*) — PLAYS FROM ENGLISH HISTORY. Crown 8vo. 7s. 6d.

THE STRANGER'S STORY and his Poem, THE LAMENT OF LOVE : An Episode of the Malvern Hills. Small crown 8vo. 2s. 6d.

GURNEY (*Rev. Alfred*)—THE VISION OF THE EUCHARIST, and other Poems. Crown 8vo. 5s.

A CHRISTMAS FAGGOT. Small crown 8vo. 5s.

HEYWOOD (*J.C.*) — HERODIAS. A Dramatic Poem. New Edition revised. Small crown 8vo. 5s.

ANTONIUS. A Dramatic Poem. New Edition, Revised. Small crown 8vo. 5s.

HICKEY (*E. H.*)—A SCULPTOR, and other Poems. Small crown 8vo. 5s.

HOLE (*W. G.*)—PROCRIS, and other Poems. Fcp. 8vo. 3s. 6d.

KEATS (*John*) — POETICAL WORKS. Edited by W. T. ARNOLD. Large crown 8vo. choicely printed on handmade paper, with Portrait in eau forte. Parchment, or cloth, 12s. ; vellum, 15s.

KING (*Mrs. Hamilton*)—THE DISCIPLES. Eighth Edition, with Portrait and Notes. Crown 8vo. 5s.

A BOOK OF DREAMS. Crown 8vo. 3s. 6d.

KNOX (*The Hon. Mrs. O. N.*)—FOUR PICTURES FROM A LIFE, and other Poems. Small crown 8vo. 3s. 6d.

KOSMOS : or, The Hope of the World. Small crown 8vo. 3s. 6d.

LANG (*A.*)—XXXII BALLADES IN BLUE CHINA. Elzevir 8vo. parchment, or cloth, 5*s.*

RHYMES À LA MODE. With Frontispiece by E. A. Abbey. Elzevir 8vo. cloth extra, gilt top, 5*s.*

LASCELLES (*John*)—GOLDEN FETTERS, and other Poems. Small crown 8vo. 3*s.* 6*d*

LAWSON (*Right Hon. Mr. Justice*)—HYMNI USITATI LATINE REDDITI, with other Verses. Small 8vo. parchment, 5*s.*

LESSING'S NATHAN THE WISE. Translated by Eustace K. Corbett. Crown 8vo. 6*s.*

LIVING ENGLISH POETS. MDCCCLXXXII. With Frontispiece by Walter Crane. Second Edition. Large crown 8vo. printed on hand-made paper. Parchment, or cloth, 12*s.* ; vellum, 15*s.*

LOCKER (*F.*)—LONDON LYRICS. New Edition, with Portrait. 18mo. cloth extra, gilt tops, 5*s.*

LOVE IN IDLENESS. A Volume of Poems. With an etching by W. B. Scott. Small crown 8vo. 5*s.*

LOVE SONNETS OF PROTEUS. With Frontispiece by the Author. Elzevir 8vo. 5*s.*

LUMSDEN (*Lieut.-Col. H. W.*)—BEOWULF: an Old English Poem. Translated into Modern Rhymes. Second and revised Edition. Small crown 8vo. 5*s.*

LYSAGHT (*Sidney Royse*).—A MODERN IDEAL. A Dramatic Poem. Small crown 8vo. 5*s.*

MAGNUSSON (*Eirikr*) *M.A.,* and *PALMER* (*E. H.*) *M.A.*—JOHAN LUDVIG RUNEBERG'S LYRICAL SONGS, IDYLLS, AND EPIGRAMS. Fcp. 8vo. 5*s.*

MAKCLOUD (*Even*).—BALLADS OF THE WESTERN HIGHLANDS AND ISLANDS OF SCOTLAND. Small crown 8vo. 3*s.* 6*d.*

MC'NAUGHTON (*J. H.*)—ONNALINDA. A Romance. Small crown 8vo. 7*s.* 6*d.*

M.D.C.—PASSAGES FROM SOME JOURNALS, and other Poems. Small crown 8vo. 3*s.* 6*d.*

M. D. C.— THREE LYRICAL DRAMAS : Sintram, The Friends of Syracuse, The Lady of Kynast. Small crown 8vo. 3*s.* 6*d.*

THE KALEEFEH AND THE WAG ; or, the Quintuple Deceit. An Extravaganza in Two Acts. Crown 8vo. 1*s.*

CHRONICLES OF CHRISTOPHER COLUMBUS : a Poem in Twelve Cantos. Crown 8vo. 7*s.* 6*d.*

MEREDITH (*Owen*) [*The Earl of Lytton*] LUCILE. New Edition With 32 Illustrations. 16mo. 3*s.* 6*d.* ; cloth extra, gilt edges, 4*s.* 6*d.*

MORRIS (*Lewis*) — POETICAL WORKS. New and Cheaper Editions, with Portrait, complete in 3 vols. 5*s.* each.
Vol. I. contains Songs of Two Worlds. Eleventh Edition.
Vol. II. contains The Epic of Hades. Twentieth Edition.
Vol. III. contains Gwen and the Ode of Life. Sixth Edition.

THE EPIC OF HADES. With 16 Autotype Illustrations after the drawings by the late George R. Chapman. 4to. cloth extra, gilt leaves, 21*s.*

THE EPIC OF HADES. Presentation Edition. 4to. cloth extra, gilt leaves, 10*s.* 6*d.*

SONGS UNSUNG. Fifth Edition. Fcp. 8vo. 5*s.*

GYCIA : a Tragedy in Five Acts. Fcp. 8vo. 5*s.*

THE LEWIS MORRIS BIRTHDAY BOOK. Edited by S. S. Copeman. With Frontispiece after a design by the late George R. Chapman. 32mo. cloth extra, gilt edges, 2*s.*; cloth limp, 1*s.* 6*d.*

MORSHEAD (*E. D. A.*)—THE HOUSE ATREUS. Being the Agamemnon, Libation-Bearers, and Furies of Æschylus. Translated into English Verse. Crown 8vo. 7*s.*

THE SUPPLIANT MAIDENS OF ÆSCHYLUS. Crown 8vo. 3*s.* 6*d.*

MOZLEY (*J. Rickards*).—THE ROMANCE OF DENNELL. A Poem in Five Cantos. Crown 8vo. 7*s.* 6*d.*

MULHOLLAND (*Rosa*). — VAGRANT VERSES. Small crown 8vo. 5*s.*

NOEL (*The Hon. Roden*)—A LITTLE CHILD'S MONUMENT. Third Edition. Small crown 8vo. 3*s.* 6*d.*

C

NOEL. (The Hon. Roden)—continued.
THE RED FLAG, and other Poems. New Edition. Small crown 8vo. 6s.
THE HOUSE OF RAVENSBURG. New Edition. Small crown 8vo. 6s.
SONGS OF THE HEIGHTS AND DEEPS. Crown 8vo. 6s.

OBBARD (Constance Mary).—BURLEY BELLS. Small crown 8vo. 3s. 6d.

O'HAGAN (John) — THE SONG OF ROLAND. Translated into English Verse. New and Cheaper Edition. Crown 8vo. 5s.

PFEIFFER (Emily)—THE RHYME OF THE LADY OF THE ROCK AND HOW IT GREW. Small crown 8vo. 3s. 6d.
GERARD'S MONUMENT, and other Poems. Second Edition. Crown 8vo. 6s.
UNDER THE ASPENS: Lyrical and Dramatic. With Portrait. Crown 8vo. 6s.

PIATT (J. J.)—IDYLS AND LYRICS OF THE OHIO VALLEY. Crown 8vo. 5s.

PIATT (Sarah M. B.)—A VOYAGE TO THE FORTUNATE ISLES, and other Poems. 1 vol. Small crown 8vo. gilt top, 5s.
IN PRIMROSE TIME. A New Irish Garland. Small crown 8vo. 2s. 6d.

PREVOST (Francis)—MELILOT. Small crown 8vo. 3s. 6d.

RARE POEMS OF THE 16TH AND 17TH CENTURIES. Edited by W. J. Linton. Crown 8vo. 5s.

RHOADES (James)—THE GEORGICS OF VIRGIL. Translated into English Verse. Small crown 8vo. 5s.

ROBINSON (A. Mary F.)—A HANDFUL OF HONEYSUCKLE. Fcp. 8vo. 3s. 6d.
THE CROWNED HIPPOLYTUS. Translated from Euripides. With New Poems. Small crown 8vo. cloth, 5s.

ROUS (Lieut.-Col.)—CONRADIN. Small crown 8vo. 2s.

SCHILLER (Friedrich)—WALLENSTEIN. A Drama. Done in English Verse, by J. A. W. HUNTER, M.A. Crown 8vo. 7s. 6d.

SCHWARTZ (J. M. W.) NIVALIS: a Tragedy in Five Acts. Crown 8vo. 5s.

SCOTT (E. J. L.)—THE ECLOGUES OF VIRGIL. Translated into English Verse. Small crown 8vo. 3s. 6d.

SCOTT (George F. E.)—THEODORA, and other Poems. Small crown 8vo. 3s.6d.

SEYMOUR (F. H. A.)—RIENZI. A Play in Five Acts. Small crown 8vo. 5s.

SHAKSPERE'S WORKS. The Avon Edition, 12 vols. fcp. 8vo. cloth, 18s.; and in box, 21s.; bound in 6 vols. cloth, 15s.

SHERBROOKE (Viscount)—POEMS OF A LIFE. Second Edition. Small crown 8vo. 2s. 6d.

SMITH (J. W. Gilbart)—THE LOVES OF VANDYCK: a Tale of Genoa. Small crown 8vo. 2s. 6d.
THE LOG O' THE 'NORSEMAN,' Small crown 8vo. 5s.
SONGS OF COMING DAY. Small crown 8vo. 3s. 6d.

SOPHOCLES: The Seven Plays in English Verse. Translated by Lewis Campbell. Crown 8vo. 7s. 6d.

SPICER (Henry)—HASKA: a Drama in Three Acts (as represented at the Theatre Royal, Drury Lane, March 10th, 1877). Third Edition, crown 8vo. 3s. 6d.
URIEL ACOSTA, in Three Acts. From the German of Gatzkow. Small crown 8vo. 2s. 6d.

SYMONDS (John Addington) — VAGABUNDULI LIBELLUS Crown 8vo. 6s.

TASSO'S JERUSALEM DELIVERED. Translated by Sir John Kingston James, Bart. 2 vols. printed on hand-made paper, parchment, bevelled boards, large crown 8vo. 21s.

TAYLOR (Sir H.)—Works Complete in Five Volumes. Crown 8vo. 30s.
PHILIP VAN ARTEVELDE. Fcp. 8vo. 3s. 6d.
THE VIRGIN WIDOW, &c. Fcp. 8vo. 3s. 6d.
THE STATESMAN. Fcp. 8vo. 3s. 6d.

TAYLOR (Augustus) — POEMS. Fcp. 8vo. 5s.

TODHUNTER (Dr. J.) — LAURELLA, and other Poems. Crown 8vo. 6s. 6d.
FOREST SONGS. Small crown 8vo. 3s.6d
THE TRUE TRAGEDY OF RIENZI: a Drama. Crown 8vo. 3s. 6d.
ALCESTIS: a Dramatic Poem. Extra fcp. 8vo. 5s.
HELENA IN TROAS. Small crown 8vo. 2s. 6d.

TYLER (*M. C.*) — ANNE BOLEYN : a Tragedy in Six Acts. Small crown 8vo. 2s. 6d.

TYNAN (*Katherine*)—LOUISE DE LA VALLIERE, and other Poems. Small crown 8vo. 3s. 6d.

WATTS (*Alaric Alfred and Emma Mary Howitt*) — AURORA : a Medley of Verse. Fcp. 8vo. cloth, bevelled boards, 5s.

WEBSTER (*Augusta*)—IN A DAY : a Drama. Small crown 8vo. 2s. 6d. DISGUISES : a Drama. Small crown 8vo. 5s.

WET DAYS. By a Farmer. Small crown 8vo. 6s.

WOOD (*Rev. F. H.*)—ECHOES OF THE NIGHT, and other Poems. Small crown 8vo. 3s. 6d.

WORDSWORTH BIRTHDAY BOOK, THE. Edited by ADELAIDE and VIOLET WORDSWORTH. 32mo. limp cloth, 1s. 6d.; cloth extra, 2s.

YOUNGMAN (*Thomas George*)—POEMS. Small crown 8vo. 5s.

YOUNGS (*Ella Sharpe*)—PAPHUS, and other Poems. Small crown 8vo. 3s. 6d.

A HEARTS LIFE, SARPEDON, and other Poems. Small crown 8vo. 3s. 6d.

WORKS OF FICTION.

'ALL BUT :' a Chronicle of Laxenford Life. By PEN OLIVER, F.R.C.S. With 20 Illustrations. Second Edit. Crown 8vo. 6s.

BANKS (*Mrs. G. L.*)—GOD'S PROVIDENCE HOUSE. New Edition. Crown 8vo. 3s. 6d.

CHICHELE (*Mary*)—DOING AND UNDOING : a Story. Crown 8vo. 4s. 6d.

DANISH PARSONAGE. By an Angler. Crown 8vo. 6s.

GRAY (*Maxwell*)—THE SILENCE OF DEAN MAITLAND. A Novel. 3 vols. Crown 8vo. 31s. 6d.

HUNTER (*Hay*)—CRIME OF CHRISTMAS DAY. A Tale of the Latin Quarter. By the Author of 'My Ducats and My Daughter.' 1s.

HUNTER (*Hay*) and *WHYTE* (*Walter*) MY DUCATS AND MY DAUGHTER. New and Cheaper Edition. With Frontispiece. Crown 8vo. 6s.

HURST AND HANGER. A History in Two Parts. 3 vols. 31s. 6d.

INGELOW (*Jean*)—OFF THE SKELLIGS. A Novel. With Frontispiece. Second Edition. Crown 8vo. 6s.

JENKINS (*Edward*)—A SECRET OF TWO LIVES. Crown 8vo. 2s. 6d.

KIELLAND (*Alexander L.*)—GARMAN AND WORSE. A Norwegian Novel. Authorised Translation by W. W. Kettlewell. Crown 8vo. 6s.

LANG (*Andrew*)—IN THE WRONG PARADISE, and other Stories. Crown 8vo. 6s.

MACDONALD (*G.*)—DONAL GRANT. A Novel. New and Cheap Edition, with Frontispiece. Crown 8vo. 6s.

CASTLE WARLOCK. A Novel. New and Cheaper Edition. Crown 8vo. 9s.

MALCOLM. With Portrait of the Author engraved on Steel. Sixth Edition. Crown 8vo. 6s.

THE MARQUIS OF LOSSIE. Fifth Edition. With Frontispiece. Crown 8vo. 6s.

ST. GEORGE AND ST. MICHAEL. Fourth Edition. With Frontispiece. Crown 8vo. 6s.

PAUL FABER, SURGEON. Crown 8vo. 6s.

THOMAS WINGFOLD, CURATE. Crown 8vo. 6s.

WHAT'S MINE'S MINE. Second Edition. With Frontispiece. Crown 8vo. 6s.

ANNALS OF A QUIET NEIGHBOURHOOD. Fifth Edition. With Frontispiece. Crown 8vo. 6s.

THE SEABOARD PARISH : a Sequel to 'Annals of a Quiet Neighbourhood.' Fourth Edition. With Frontispiece. Crown 8vo. 6s.

WILFRED CUMBERMEDE. An Autobiographical Story. Fourth Edition. With Frontispiece. Crown 8vo. 6s.

MALET (*Lucas*)—COLONEL ENDERBY'S WIFE. A Novel. New and Cheaper Edition. With Frontispiece. Crown 8vo. 6s.

MULHOLLAND (*Rosa*) — MARCELLA GRACE. An Irish Novel. Crown 8vo. 6s.

PALGRAVE (W. Gifford)—HERMANN AGHA: an Eastern Narrative. Third Edition. Crown 8vo. 6s.

SHAW (Flora L.)—CASTLE BLAIR; a Story of Youthful Days. New and Cheaper Edition. Crown 8vo. 3s. 6d

STRETTON (Hesba) — THROUGH A NEEDLE'S EYE. A Story. New and Cheaper Edition, with Frontispiece. Crown 8vo. 6s.

TAYLOR (Col. Meadows) C.S.I., M.R.I.A. SEETA. A Novel. New and Cheaper Edition. With Frontispiece. Crown 8vo. 6s.

TIPPOO SULTAUN: a Tale of the Mysore War. New Edition, with Frontispiece. Crown 8vo. 6s.

RALPH DARNELL. New and Cheaper Edition. With Frontispiece. Crown 8vo. 6s.

A NOBLE QUEEN. New and Cheaper Edition. With Frontispiece. Crown 8vo. 6s.

THE CONFESSIONS OF A THUG. Crown 8vo. 6s.

TARA: a Mahratta Tale. Crown 8vo. 6s.

WITHIN SOUND OF THE SEA. New and Cheaper Edition, with Frontispiece. Crown 8vo. 6s.

BOOKS FOR THE YOUNG.

BRAVE MEN'S FOOTSTEPS. A Book of Example and Anecdote for Young People. By the Editor of 'Men who have Risen.' With Four Illustrations by C. Doyle. Eighth Edition. Crown 8vo. 3s. 6d.

COXHEAD (Ethel)—BIRDS AND BABIES. With 33 Illustrations. Imp. 16mo. cloth gilt, 2s. 6d.

DAVIES (G. Christopher) — RAMBLES AND ADVENTURES OF OUR SCHOOL FIELD CLUB. With Four Illustrations. New and Cheaper Edition. Crown 8vo. 3s. 6d.

EDMONDS (Herbert) — WELL-SPENT LIVES: a Series of Modern Biographies. New and Cheaper Edition. Crown 8vo. 3s. 6d.

EVANS (Mark)—THE STORY OF OUR FATHER'S LOVE, told to Children. Sixth and Cheaper Edition of Theology for Children. With Four Illustrations. Fcp. 8vo. 1s. 6d.

MAC KENNA (S. J.)—PLUCKY FELLOWS. A Book for Boys. With Six Illustrations. Fifth Edition. Crown 8vo. 3s. 6d.

REANEY (Mrs. G. S.)—WAKING AND WORKING; or, From Girlhood to Womanhood. New and Cheaper Edition. With a Frontispiece. Cr. 8vo. 3s. 6d.

REANEY (Mrs. G. S.)—continued.

BLESSING AND BLESSED: a Sketch of Girl Life. New and Cheaper Edition. Crown 8vo. 3s. 6d.

ROSE GURNEY'S DISCOVERY. A Book for Girls. Dedicated to their Mothers. Crown 8vo. 3s. 6d.

ENGLISH GIRLS: Their Place and Power. With Preface by the Rev. R. W. Dale. Fourth Edition. Fcp. 8vo. 2s. 6d.

JUST ANYONE, and other Stories. Three Illustrations. Royal 16mo. 1s. 6d.

SUNBEAM WILLIE, and other Stories. Three Illustrations. Royal 16mo. 1s. 6d.

SUNSHINE JENNY, and other Stories. Three Illustrations. Royal 16mo. 1s. 6d.

STORR (Francis) and TURNER (Hawes). CANTERBURY CHIMES; or, Chaucer Tales Re-told to Children. With Six Illustrations from the Ellesmere MS. Third Edition. Fcp. 8vo. 3s. 6d.

STRETTON (Hesba)—DAVID LLOYD'S LAST WILL. With Four Illustrations. New Edition. Royal 16mo. 2s. 6d.

WHITAKER (Florence)—CHRISTY'S INHERITANCE: A London Story. Illustrated. Royal 16mo. 1s. 6d.

www.ingramcontent.com/pod-product-compliance
Lightning Source LLC
Chambersburg PA
CBHW032020110726
47901CB00004B/1145